T0285354

BEFORE
I FORGET

ADVANCE PRAISE FOR THE BOOK

'An honest and tumultuous journey of an accomplished artiste set in the background of an evolving post-Independence India. Well done, my friend'—Saeed Akhtar Mirza

'A human and heart-warming chronicle vibrant with passion, vision and real life, M.K. Raina's memoir tells us candidly about our times and the struggles of a dynamic career in theatre, cinema, cultural activism and social resistance. A Kashmiri by birth and lineage, Raina eloquently reaffirms the dictum: we should never forget but always forgive'—Ashok Vajpeyi

'Moving and objective. Burns with a deep lament about the fate of a land scarred by history, but also the author's deep love for his land and its people. There are many stories that are interwoven in this brilliant narrative. Some are harrowing but others are joyous, laced with humour and the spirit of coexistence'—Sudhir Mishra

BEFORE
I FORGET

a memoir

M.K.Raina

VINTAGE
An imprint of Penguin Random House

VINTAGE

Vintage is an imprint of the Penguin Random House group of companies
whose addresses can be found at global.penguinrandomhouse.com

Published by Penguin Random House India Pvt. Ltd
4th Floor, Capital Tower 1, MG Road,
Gurugram 122 002, Haryana, India

First published in Vintage by Penguin Random House India 2024

10 9 8 7 6 5 4 3 2 1

ISBN 9780670098811

Typeset in Adobe Caslon Pro by MAP Systems, Bengaluru, India
Printed at Thomson Press India Ltd, New Delhi

www.penguin.co.in

For
My beloved family
Anjali, Anant, Akila, Aditi and Filippo

Contents

Preface

In a lighter vein, I call myself the child of India's socialism. Had it not been for the opportunities that the young state of India provided to people like me with limited economic resources, I could not have even dreamed of doing the things that I did. I was privy to free education, scholarships, fellowships, travels and a safe and secure atmosphere to explore and experience life. All these allowed me to engage in the projects that questioned and even confronted the powers-that-be and offered me the opportunity of learning under experienced and committed teachers, whose compassion and empathy for the weak and the marginalized opened unknown worlds for me and engraved in me a sense of commitment for the ordinary.

Before I Forget contains the stories and experiences of my travels through the landscapes of this vast country—without many finances, shelter or support. Many unknown well-wishers opened their doors and supported me in my various endeavours and became friends and fellow travellers. The book has an underlying thematic thread, which keeps changing as the decades of India's tryst with destiny continued taking unknown directions.

While sharing my personal struggles, defeats, humiliation and triumphs along with some life-threatening instances, there is a great satisfaction within me that I did participate in the things that I believed in. While creating plays, films or cultural events, etc., one had to be aware, that India is living simultaneously in many centuries together, from the ages of primitive lifestyles to the highly digital space age.

Thus, I have faced the challenge of treading the present while creating contemporary Indian cultural experiences that are avant-garde and which have national and international outlooks.

Many years ago, I was on a teaching assignment at the theatre department of the Central University of Hyderabad. In the evenings, I would spend my time with the faculty members and during those hours, I would narrate some of my experiences about my work in theatre or films. One day, Anantha Krishna, then the head of the department, suddenly said, 'M.K., why don't you write about these multiple experiences?' I just brushed off his suggestions, but he insisted. 'You know, you have done so much work, in so many different regions, in different languages and cultures, but the problem with you is that you do not write. People should know what it is to work under the conditions you have been working in,' Krishna added. I just laughed and forgot all about it.

In 2000, I arrived in the Kashmir Valley—my journey here started with me secretly conducting a theatre workshop camp at a place hidden behind the Zabarwan mountains. This was like entering through a needle hole. Militancy was at its peak in that era. Kashmir was still in a frozen turbulence. After working for many years in the villages with traditional folk performers, one day I had a visitor from Stanford University's theatre school, Dr Jisha Menon. She stayed with us in a Kashmiri village for a few days and watched many folk theatre performances. During our free time, we would exchange notes, generally talk about my work during very tough times, particularly about the problems we faced off and on about unexpected difficulties.

One morning, she said, 'M.K. you must share these experiences, people should know what it is like working in the conflict zone.' I did not respond.

While these kinds of suggestions kept on coming from friends and well-wishers, India's socio-political situation kept on taking new strange and dangerous twists and turns, whether it was the murder of my friend Safdar Hashmi while performing a street play or the rise of the Hindu right and its politics, the nation seemed to be taking unusual historical turns culturally and politically. Losing my home in Kashmir was like a hidden wound which needed to be healed.

Many years later, Covid-19 put a full stop to my work and travels. I got stuck at home for the first time in my life. I did not know what to do, only hearing the stories of death and devastation of the ordinary public. I started feeling suffocated. One day out of frustration, I took out my car and along with two kids of my domestic help Ravi, Abhi and Kabhi, drove around Noida and Greater Noida for about an hour and a half and returned home feeling very empty—like those lonely, empty roads which I had travelled.

The next morning, I started writing whatever I remembered—particularly those incidents and experiences which had impacted me and had also shaped me as a person. This journey down memory lane took me back to places, regions and the people from many decades ago, with whom I had spent the best and crucial moments of my life. I had shared their angst and their joys or collaborated in creating some of the best cultural resistance events.

I want to thank my late parents, Babuji and Babi, who in their mundane simplicity instilled in me values of compassion and care from my early age, which I have been trying to preserve and practise. The only regret is, whenever I remember them,

I feel very sad for them for becoming homeless in their old age. It is like a dark and permanent mark left on my psyche.

My respects to my teachers from my school days, particularly to late Dina Nath Nadim, the iconic poet, for inculcating in me the values of Kashmiri culture and its legacy. My gratitude to the late Ebrahim Alkazi, the director at the National School of Drama—while trying to make me a professional theatre person, he gave me a talisman which I hold very essential in whatever I do; his words that I always remember when he said to me, 'You know, Raina, in our country, if you want to achieve anything, remember to lead yourself from the front, and don't wait for someone else to lead you.'

I want to thank my friends and mentors in Kashmir, who joined me in those days of death-like silences, who supported and helped me when I stepped into the Valley to see if I could be one of the catalysts for reclaiming those shared cultural spaces which were almost buried under the boots of militancy. Grateful thanks for their guidance goes to Saleem Beg, Nigat Shafi, Shafi Pandit, Nayeem Akther, Naseem Shafai, Rehman Rahi, Amin Kamil and many more.

My heartful thanks to Manzoor Ahmed Meer, Hakim Javed, Arshad Mustaq who joined hands with me from the very beginning of my work in the Valley. Many a time they risked their lives so that I could carry on my work without any tensions and now, they are carrying on their own the reclaiming of the cultural spaces in the Valley.

Before I Forget could not have been complete without the support of the ustads of the Bhand Pather community of Akingaam. The guidance and teaching lessons I received from the late Ali Mohamad Bhagat, Ghulam Rasool Bhagat, late Ghulam Ahmed Bhagat, Ghulam Mohad Bhagat, Ghulam Rasool Bhagat (Junior) and Gul Mohmad Bhagat.

Apart from being fantastic theatre performers, they opened my eyes to understanding the multilayered Rishi (Sufi) traditions of the Valley, where the Buddhist, Shaivite and Islamic confluences have created a unique sacred principal of living in harmony, popularly known as *Kashmiriyat*. I am indebted to them for adopting me as an integral part of their families, despite their poverty.

At SAHMAT (Safdar Hashmi Memorial Trust), for more than three-and-a-half decades of contesting and creating together with the best of the minds in the area of culture, I am grateful to Rajender Prasad, Sohail Hashmi, Ram Rehman, Parthiv Shah, Rajendra Arora, Shabnam Hashmi and Madan Gopal Singh and the solid support of Ashok, Banti and Naresh. It has been a dream team for creating the art of cultural resistance in the present contemporary times in India. I miss Vivan Sundaram at SAHMAT these days. He was one of the leading cultural forces who always drove and infused a fiery energy and ideas whenever the occasion or challenges for SAHMAT came up. We all miss you, Vivan, may you rest in peace.

The contribution of Rakesh Kumar Singh, Kriti V. Sharma and Aditee Biswas in most of my work over decades has to be acknowledged; these three have stood like a rock behind me, with their talent, and selfless friendship and commitment and I am still dependent on their contribution in my work.

I am grateful to Kanishka Gupta, who was the first person to read the complete draft of the book and convey his encouraging comments. He found me the publishers Penguin.

I am indebted to the entire team of Penguin Random House and particularly to Premanka Goswami, Rea Mukherjee, Gunjan Ahlawat and Yash Daiv. Their observations and comments gave much strength to my book. It has been a joy to work with them and made me believe that the book is being printed and published under their able talents. Huge thanks to you all.

I would also like to thank Alicia Wright for going through a very rough version of the book and trying to make sense of it.

And finally, my gratitude to my nuclear family, my better half Dr Anjali Raina, Anant Raina, Akila, Aditi and Filippo without whose enthusiasm, excitement and care I could never complete this book. My special thanks to Anjali and Anant who were correcting my drafts and my English.

1

Growing Up

The mohalla where I was born was called Sheetal Nath Sathu, where a 200-year-old temple by the name of Sheetal Nath stood. It was a very humble working-class neighbourhood with a mixed population of Kashmiri Pandits and Muslims. The Pandits were mostly educated and were doctors, teachers, engineers, clerks and court employees. The Muslims were *tangawallahs*, tailors, milkmen, small contractors and manual labourers. Many in the neighbourhood, both Pandit and Muslim, had not been able to go to school. It was a neighbourhood where many lived a hand-to-mouth existence, economically speaking, but still survived on their meagre earnings.

There was a school, the Hindu High School, open to all children of the mohalla to attend. This school, complete with a big playground, was located on the premises of the Sheetal Nath Temple. In fact, the school building, playground, temple and all other buildings on the premises belonged to the Sheetal Nath Sabha.

A building on the temple campus housed the office of a very important Urdu daily newspaper, *Martand*, named after the Martand Temple, famed for its stone architecture, located some eighty kilometres from Sheetal Nath Temple. *Martand* was the voice of the Kashmiri Pandits.

The playground of the school was also the epicentre of Kashmiri Pandit politics. During my growing-up years, from the 1950s onwards, I saw all the major Pandit leaders of that era, including Shiv Narayan Fotedar[1], Sham Lal Saraf[2] and Gopi Kishen[3]. The regular gossip among the community was that these leaders rarely agreed among themselves on issues faced by the community. The school was eventually rebuilt. The earlier building had a regular theatre hall where plays were

---

[1] Shiv Narayan Fotedar (1904–1976) Dedicated his life to the welfare of his Kashmiri Pandit community in the area of education and widow welfare. Was president of the Hindu Education Society and established seventeen schools in the valley. Maharaja Hari Singh nominated him as a member of Praja Parishad in 1935. President of Sanatan Dharam Yuvak Sabha. Joined the National Conference in 1947 and became a member of its governing council, later nominated as a member of the Parliament. In 1957, he was elected as a chairman of the Jammu and Kashmir legislative council.

[2] Sham Lal Saraf (1904–1983) A Gandhian and a freedom fighter worked for the welfare of the Kashmiri Pandit community, particularly for the equal rights of women. Was one of the leading lights of the Quit Kashmir movement against Maharaja Hari Singh. Worked closely with Sheikh. Muhammad Abdullah during the freedom movement. Became a very important cabinet minister from 1947 to 1957 under the prime ministership of Sheikh Muhammad Abdullah. Then again under prime minister Bakshi Ghulam Mohammad as a cabinet minister from 1953 to 1962.

[3] Gopi Kishen (1903–1984) A yogi, mystic, great social reformer and a writer. Worked relentlessly through his organization The Sudhar Samiti Kashmir for the welfare of the disadvantaged people of his community. Choose the path of Yoga and soon became a teacher of Kundalini Yoga and the salvation. The most well-known book is his autobiography *Kundalini: the Evolutionary Energy Man.* Other well-known works include *Search of Yoga.* After attaining the higher yogis knowledge travelled to many western countries giving discourses on the spiritual path of yoga.

performed from 1950 to 1958. These plays mostly focused on social issues or were themed around Hindu mythology. As a kid, I went to all these plays and watched them with great curiosity. These performances created many special effects using shadow theatre, which was of spectacular quality.

I recall one in particular, a play based on the 1947–48 war with Pakistan. Immediately after Kashmir acceded to India, a large force of armed raiders entered Muzaffarabad, then part of Kashmir supported by the Pakistan Army. They sacked Baramulla and were about to reach Srinagar airport. This war divided Kashmir into two—one part is occupied by Pakistan and the other is with India. The high point of the performance came when the Raiders entered the Valley, looting, killing and dishonouring the women. Then an aircraft would appear and bomb the enemy lines. All the people in the audience would wait, holding their breath till these scenes came to a close.

I was thrilled and fascinated by these scenes. I would watch these plays almost every day, begging my mother or grandmother to give me money for the tickets. Sometimes I would even plead with the gatekeeper to let me in for free. He would sometimes oblige me, but only when the rest of the audience had taken their seats.

I remember another play, *Akka Nandun*, based on a Kashmiri folk tale. In one scene, the Queen Mother must kill her only son, who had been given to her as a boon by a rishi on the condition that she return the child after thirteen years. When the rishi returns to take away the son, the Queen refuses to give him up and the Rishi threatens her with dire consequences. Finally, when the Queen relents and returns her thirteen-year-old son to the rishi, he orders her to kill him, cut off all his limbs and cook his body parts. She does this, going through the pathos and pain of losing her child.

This killing and cooking of the son by the Queen was the climax of the narrative. I used to watch people cry at the plight of the Queen Mother while she performed this sequence. The killing, dismembering and cooking were shown using shadow theatre techniques. My mouth would hang wide open during these scenes. To me, it was some strange magic happening before my eyes.

Then the rishi commands the Queen Mother to serve the cooked body parts of her son to her six daughters, the king, the rishi and to herself. Finally, he asks the Queen to place one more plate for her son, which she does through tears, wailing and in pain. Before they begin the meal, the rishi tells the Queen to call out for her son. When she does, her son enters the room and sits down at his plate to eat. The moral of the story was that the whole world is an illusion—*maya*.

This kind of theatre intrigued me greatly and I was hugely curious about the technique used to create these candle-lit shadow sequences. One day, when there was no one in the theatre, some of my friends and I quietly entered the backstage area through the back door. It was like entering into a mysterious den. There were animal masks, crowns, trees, costumes and painted scenery. In another room, we found human limbs and a skull, all made of cotton wool. When we touched them, we discovered the reality of the theatrical magic we had been witnessing. This kind of theatre may sound out of date now, but the purpose and intent of these performances still ignite my psyche.

It is ironic that almost three decades later, in the year 1992, when I was directing a contemporary Kashmiri play in Hindi by Moti Lal Kemmu with actors from the National School of Drama repertory company, this new play had the same sequence as *Akka Nandun*, of the Queen Mother killing her only son under the command of a rishi. Kemmu had incorporated this folk tale in the play, juxtaposing it against the present reality of terrorism in Kashmir, using the device of a play within a play and creating an interplay of myth and reality. Here the son Nunda is killed by the bullets of a terrorist. I was reminded of my childhood experience of discovering the secrets of the backstage at Sheetal Nath Theatre, where the killing of Nunda was done using the shadow theatre technique. As my tribute to *Akka Nandun*, I got this sequence executed using that very shadow technique, but in greater depth and using more sophisticated devices.

Sheetal Nath Mohalla and its temple grounds were not limited to the neighbouring community only. It was a hotbed of Kashmiri Pandit vernacular politics, an identity politics of a minority where, off and on, calls were given for agitations, processions and dharnas. As kids, these activities used to be fun. At that time, I couldn't understand much of what these community leaders were lecturing about. Years later, we were told that many national leaders and eminent state leaders had come there and addressed the community, some of the names being Mahatma Gandhi, Jawaharlal Nehru and Sheikh Abdullah. I was told that most of these speeches were about the liberation of India and Kashmir from the rule of the British and the Maharaja, respectively.

Any Pandit agitation that began in this temple ground would wind its way through the main arteries of Srinagar City in the form of a procession. However, it would often face opposition from the dissenting section of the Pandits at some crossings, which would erupt into big scuffles. I remember one such event that happened during the Janmashtami Shobha Yatra. Normally, the Shobha Yatra would start from the Sheetal Nath ground and pass through the main streets of the city. The Pandit women and men would shower flower petals on the main *rath* that carried little boys and girls dressed as Lord Krishna, Radha and gopis.

That particular year, I was dressed as little Lord Krishna. I still remember the scene. The moment the procession reached Chota Bazaar near Habba Kadal, located on the side of the River Jhelum, stones rained in from all directions, aimed at the procession and the rath carrying the dressed-up children. When the stones started hitting the rath, the police ordered a lathi charge on the stone-pelters. My father rescued me. He appeared from somewhere, lifted me off the rath and zipped through the narrow lanes until we reached home safely.

Primary School

As a child, I studied at the Lal Ded Primary School, an institution run by the Hindu Education Trust. This trust had a chain of schools and colleges in the city of Srinagar. It was a minority trust established by Kashmiri Pandits and located about two kilometres from my home in an old building owned by some rich man. Here the teachers were mostly from the Pandit community, but the students came from all communities. Although the building belonged to a rich man, it was not a rich school. All the kids came from modest households. There were regular classes throughout the week, and Saturday was meant for cultural activities, where the children would learn Kashmiri folk songs and enact little plays written and directed by our Hindi and Urdu teachers.

I remember my Urdu and Sanskrit teachers as being very tough. They always wanted us to learn by rote, which was very difficult for me. I was often punished by these teachers in very mean ways; they used a cane or sometimes placed a pencil between our fingers and squeezed our hands as we screamed in pain. Those were horrible punishments, so learning these languages was very difficult for me.

My teacher could not explain to me the difference between some of the letters of the alphabet. In Kashmiri, we do not have any letters for 'bha' or 'gha'. Kashmiris pronounce these sounds as 'ba' and 'ga'; the sound of 'h', the aspiration, is missing. Most of the time I would fail the test for these languages. Eventually, I lost interest in the Urdu language. It became boring and torturous for me. I abandoned Sanskrit too. It seemed impossible for me to improve my grades. But eventually, luck favoured me. Urdu books became available in the Devanagari script, besides the Nastaliq script. And I soon got higher marks in Urdu than all the other students, all of whom excelled at the Nastaliq script. Everyone in the school was surprised. I gave up Sanskrit because it was impossible to memorize the *gardhanas*.

I feel sad to think that if these teachers had inculcated in me some love for languages, I could have perhaps learned both Urdu and Sanskrit very well. Today, being a professional in theatre and film, I see this lacuna in my abilities; I am unable to read Urdu and Sanskrit texts in their original form. This vast ocean of knowledge is not available to me, and translations do not always give you the sounds and the textures of the original.

Notwithstanding these punishments meted out to us by our strict teachers, we were happy-go-lucky children. Some good teachers were like our grandparents, always encouraged us to learn more.

Near the time of the annual official school inspection, since our school was on the banks of the River Jhelum, locally known as the Veth, we were instructed to clean the school furniture in the water. We would float them on the river like some sort of raft for some distance, going with the flow of the water. The Jhelum (its ancient name is Vitasta) originates as the sacred spring of Verynaag in the south of Kashmir located at the foothills of the Peer Panjal mountain range. It flows down into the Valley, winding its way through fertile fields and many towns till it enters Srinagar. The city of Srinagar was founded by Ashoka the Great and has been the capital of many dynasties. The banks of this river are dotted with temples, mosques, *ziyarats*, ashrams and *khankhas*, as well as homes of Hindus and Muslims.

Earlier, this city had seven bridges connecting both the banks of the river.

Because of the growing population and the expansion of the city, two more bridges were built. The bridges were named after rulers, poets and generals. The Jhelum or Veth was (and still is) the lifeline of the city. It had been a witness to the rise and fall of many dynasties.

Now, coming back to school—for the inspection, we had to present our best to impress the visiting government officials.

On 8 August 1953, suddenly, the school closed, and all the children were asked to go back home. And we were told not to return to school. The children were very happy about this at first. When I left school for home every day, I would walk through lanes leading to the main road connecting to the Habba Kadal bridge. From that main road, I would go through more lanes to reach my house. Walking through those lanes that day, I sensed a strange silence everywhere. People were rushing, not talking to each other. Hardly anyone walked on the main road when I reached there. It was almost empty except for some army men stationed on the bridge every twenty feet with their guns mounted with bayonets. I saw a cyclist try to cross the bridge. He was caught and given a slap for not walking on foot as the city was under curfew. I was so frightened when I saw this that I started to cry. Someone from somewhere caught hold of my hand and helped me across the bridge. On the other side, he handed me over to another person and told him to help me reach my mohalla. This person, without even talking to me, held my hand and kept moving. When we turned into another lane, we saw a large number of young people running in all directions and pelting stones towards the main road where soldiers were on security duty. The sight was so scary I was in tears again, but this stranger reassured me that I would be safe. We kept moving until we entered the next lane. There he handed me to a third person. I remember that none of these people appeared to know each other. Nor did I know any of them.

Finally, this third man led me to my mohalla. Since I was in class two at the time, I had no idea what this was all about. Looking back now, I presume it must have been the dismissal and arrest of the prime minister of Jammu and Kashmir, Sheikh Mohammad Abdullah, on 8 August 1953. This was done by the Sadr-i-Riyasat, the constitutional head of the state of Jammu and Kashmir. Abdullah was imprisoned for eleven long years. A case was registered against him and twenty-two others, accusing them of conspiring against the state for allegedly espousing the cause of an independent Kashmir. It was called the Kashmir Conspiracy case.[4]

This agitation carried on for some time and we had many holidays from school. Stone-pelting, and people agitating and fighting with the security forces were part and parcel of my growing up. One gradually learned to cope during these disturbances and, during shutdowns, to keep the supply lines of essential items running. This exuberance of the Kashmiri people is age-old. It has served them for decades. The power of the olive-green uniform and what it means becomes clear from a very early age for every Kashmiri child.

When I joined middle school, I spent much of my time playing hockey, but I often got hurt and had bruises all over my legs. This worried my grandmother, Benjagari. She would

---

[4] P.N.K. Bamzai, *Cultural and Political History of Kashmir*, Volume 3, M.D. Publications, New Delhi, 1994; David Devadas, *The Story of Kashmir*, 2019; Sandeep Bamzai, *Bonfire of Kashmiriyat*, Rupa, New Delhi, 2006.

keep asking my father to make me stop playing hockey. Finally, my father tricked me into joining evening classes at a music school, Prem Sangeet Niketan, affiliated with the Gandharva Mahavidya Mandir in New Delhi. The head of this model school was a very versatile musician, Jagannath Shivpuri. Up to this time I had been some sort of bathroom singer with a very loud voice.

As a student at this music school, I learned classical Hindustani singing for five long years, from the time I was in class five, up to class ten. I regularly took practical and theory classes. Every year, Vinay Chandra Mudgal would come from Delhi as an examiner to conduct our practical exams. I passed the Sangeet Madhyama and was practising *bada khayal* with a dash of *dhrupad*, along with theory classes.

When I look back on those days of music learning, I realize that most of my training was simplistic and superficial, meant only to complete the syllabus. I was not improving, and I began to grow disinterested and bored with music at that age. I felt my teachers were not helping much. My voice had begun to crack too, and I started losing interest even faster. And when I chose the full sciences as my subject in school, there was no time for learning music. But interestingly, what remained with me from this experience of learning music for five years was the knowledge of ragas, taalas and the ability to recognize ragas.

Fortunately, these five years of music school did not go to waste. I realized this after many years when I went to the National School of Drama in 1968. What was interesting at Prem Sangeet Niketan were the music *mehfils* that took place after classes in the evening. The best musicians of Srinagar City would perform at these baithaks. I had the opportunity to listen to the best Hindustani classical music of those times, and the best Kashmiri Sufiyana by none other than the doyen of that form, Kalam Janab Tibet Bakaal. Music remained in my subconscious all these years.

Since my home was very near to the music school, I would stay there until nine in the evening. Many times, it so happened that I would fall asleep at the concert. When the mehfil ended, some teacher would drop me home on their bicycle. My grandmother Benjagari would stay up waiting for me and could be spotted at the first-floor window.

In the morning, she would give a dressing down to my mother and father for not stopping me from these 'bad activities'. My father would laugh and calm her down. She believed I was given a free hand to do what I liked and had no discipline. This would ruin her grandson. Even so, my grandmother shared a very secret bond with me, unlike her relationship with most of her other grandchildren. My aunts had some inkling about our closeness, and they seemed mildly jealous of it.

Home consisted of a clan of three elder uncles, each of whom had five children. At my father's we were three. We all lived in separate houses with a common lawn, and our grandmother served as the boss of the family. We formed our own cricket and hockey teams and would play against other family teams.

Each family had a kitchen garden where most of the vegetables we required would be grown. These small harvests were even distributed among the neighbours. My grandmother was a strong lady, highly regarded in the neighbourhood. She had many friends from both the Muslim and Pandit neighbourhoods, and many women often came to her for advice on herbal remedies or to discuss their family issues. In the evening, her four sons would spend an hour or so with her, discussing all kinds of subjects. We were a content clan with modest means. We were not affluent, and it was hard work that kept the families going.

Every year after the annual school examinations, some cousin or schoolmate would either pass or fail their board exams, an occasion for either celebration or despair. If anything happened to any member of the family, the entire clan came together and confronted the problem as one. This was our biggest strength. It was a clan of almost twenty living together, but still, each had his or her island of secrecy.

Often, there were many disagreements, hotly contested but resolved within the clan. If anyone had any problem involving an outside party or individual, then the clan would unite and face the consequences as a joint family. The mohalla had a great mechanism of interdependence and self-preservation. For example, if a girl from the mohalla was getting married, then all the community members would chip in to make the wedding a grand success. Crisis management had been woven into and among the communities by our ancestors.

During the autumn months, the entire population worked to store and stuff their houses with firewood, dried vegetables, pulses, kerosene and other supplies to endure the severe months of winter. Every house was a spectacle of multicoloured garlands of vegetables hanging from the windows, balconies and outer walls. The front lawns were covered with freshly harvested grains, red chillies, tomatoes and flowers for worship, spread on the ground like colourful carpets. It was when the houses were well stocked in the autumn months which is also when the wedding season started.

During one such wedding season, there was a fire in the top attic of our house where all the winter stuff was stored. All the members of the family were away at a neighbour's wedding. I was alone at home when I noticed these huge flames. All I could do was scream at the top of my voice and then run to call the firefighters from a phone in the nearby *Martand* newspaper office. It took me some minutes on the phone to get through to them, and when I rushed back home what I saw is still imprinted in my mind after so many years. The people of the mohalla were all over the place—on the rooftop, in the garden and the windows of the first and second floors. They had formed a chain, and hundreds of buckets were being transferred from one hand to the other. At one end of the line, water was being collected from the nearby water pond and being passed on up the chain leading up to the attic. By the time I had returned from the call, they had already extinguished the fire.

Ghani Chacha, our neighbour, guarded our main gate with a long pole so that no unknown person would try to enter and steal anything from the house in all that confusion. The youngsters of the mohalla had surrounded all the houses and kept a strict watch on them. Once the job was done, everyone came down from the house laughing, as if nothing had happened. Everyone started to tease me, asking me where I had disappeared after screaming. When I told them I had gone to make a phone call to the fire brigade, they laughed again and asked me, 'But, have they not arrived yet?'

Ghani Chacha intervened and told the mohallawallahs, 'You fools, it was his scream that stopped my heartbeat and made us all run to the rescue. If he had not screamed and alerted all of us, we would have been homeless by now. Don't forget, all our houses are made of wood, and all are well stocked for the winter months. We would have been ruined completely, but because of his screams, all is safe. So, from today all the mohallawallahs owe him two eggs every day so that his voice stays loud and strong.'

Around the Sheetal Nath Temple ground was a big water body. On the opposite side were vegetable and fruit gardens growing apples, pomegranates, carrots and more. When the fruits were ripe, these gardens tempted us children. We would plan out a full operation to enter these gardens without a sound so we would not be caught. We would steal fruits from under the very nose of the watchmen.

It was like guerrilla warfare for the children. We were all very serious and focused on our mission. First, we had to acquire a boat from the other side of the bank. We worked out silent hand gestures to communicate with each other while on our mission. In the final operation, one group of kids acquired a boat, and another quietly got into the boat and rowed it to the other part of the lake. Here, all the other group members joined and moved towards the gardens. Next, we anchored the boat on the edge of the garden and left two boys on board to enable a quick escape, in case we were discovered. Two other boys hid under some bushes nearby and kept a vigil to see if anyone was coming from the owner's side. Then the main group of around five boys proceeded with the main operation. They quietly moved towards the fruit trees, quickly climbed up in complete silence and started dropping the fruits, which were quickly collected by the boys waiting under the trees. No one was supposed to break branches or make any noise. In complete, silent coordination, we stole the fruits and quickly rushed back to the boat. Here the waiting crew were ready to push the boat into the water. Once the main group was in the boat with all the stolen fruits, within minutes the entire group gathered in the centre of the water body, giggling and enjoying the fruits of the adventure.

During winters, when the temperature dropped below zero, the pond froze. If the temperature went to -7 or –8 degree Celsius, the frozen water became so solid that one could walk over it and even play on it. In the harsh winters, this pond transformed into a stadium for playing proper cricket matches. Since schools were closed for the winter break, there was always enough time in the day to play. This heroic game of cricket on the frozen water was like ice skating. It was very exciting and enjoyable. For many of us, there was an element of 'herogiri', and we liked to show off to the people watching from the banks. Then there were our favourite girls, our imagined loves. For them, we would do anything to show off, but beyond that, no one had the courage or even the chance to talk to any of these girls. It was our fantasy, our silly, stupid and very innocent one-sided infatuation—'*majnugiri*'.

As evening descended, we would stop playing. Then our gossip sessions would start. It would go on for hours, right at the centre of the frozen pond. Sometimes a big gathering of around fifty boys would be chattering and laughing there, standing as if it was solid ground. One day, while everybody was busy chatting and having fun, there was a loud sound indicating a crack in the ice. Everybody screamed and ran for their lives towards the bank.

In the shock of that moment, I could not move. I just stayed there on the spot, fearing that if this chilled frozen surface broke open, we would all fall into the water. Luckily, nothing happened. From the banks, the other boys saw me and shouted for me to come back carefully, which I did. By morning, news of this incident had reached the neighbourhood and I saw the same Ghani Chacha enter my house to report all this to my father and my grandmother. Ghani Chacha was upset and warned my father and grandmother, 'This kid of yours will one day drown all the kids in the mohalla. For God's sake teach him some sense.' My grandmother started to yell at me, and my father was very angry and upset, but my mother was protective. I was worried that this story would reach my oldest uncle, who commanded a lot of respect among the members of the clan. God knows what kind of punishment he would have given me.

So, our winter ice-cricket games came to an end, along with our so-called one-sided romances and majnugiri.

Gagur (Rat)

After about two weeks of this incident, we were playing football in the dry, chilly weather at the Sheetal Nath ground. I saw a student on the opposite side of the frozen pond trying to cross carefully, step by step, with his school bag on his shoulder. This boy was quite a daredevil and never listened to anyone. To be honest, he was quite an arrogant nutcase. We called him by the nickname 'Gagur', which means rat. Watching him cross with hesitant steps, I yelled out to him warning him not to cross. It was risky; the frozen surface was fragile and could break at any time, and he would freeze in the ice-cold water. He shouted back, 'I am not a coward like you and your friends!' He continued to move over the lake, taking each step carefully.

We kept watching him and listening to the sound of his feet scratching the ice. As he reached the centre of the pond, the frozen surface of the water suddenly gave in and cracked. The Rat plunged into the chilly water, and only his head was visible now. His arms kept trying to grip the frozen surface, but the ice kept breaking as he tried to do that, struggling for his life. The ice of the pond was like a sharp razor, its edges cutting into his belly. We kids started screaming, asking him to put his school bag in front of his chest as a shield and to break the ice with it. Until he reached a dry patch of land in the middle of the pond, we kept screaming out instructions to him, also cheering him to keep his morale high. He inched forward, and as our screams reached the mohalla, a crowd gathered around the pond, shouting words of encouragement to him.

Suddenly the scene changed. Some men lugged in big logs of timber and huge tree branches, while other men from the electricity department were tying a thick rope around them, creating a floating contraption long enough to reach the dry patch of land. The men broke the icy surface of the pond at their end by getting into the sub-zero water themselves. It was an amazing technique to save a young boy's life. At one point, growing exhausted, the boy couldn't carry on further because of the cold of the water. His fingers looked red and almost frozen, but the words of encouragement from the onlookers seemed to propel him towards the dry patch of land. Once there, he was guided on to the contraption, which was then pulled with the help of the ropes back to the bank. The Rat was almost frozen, semi-conscious, and parts of his body had turned entirely pink.

I saw the same Ghani Chacha burst into the crowd surrounding the Rat. Ghani Chacha stripped the Rat naked, wrapped him in a woollen blanket and shoved lots of brandy into his mouth. He then lifted him on his shoulder and started running towards a nearby masjid. There they put him into the hot water of the masjid *hamam* for a few hours. The people who rescued him had already left to resume whatever work they had been doing, and it was now only the neighbourhood crowd waiting for the Rat to emerge from the masjid alive.

*

The principal of my school was Dinanath Nadim, a legendary name in Kashmiri literature. He was a poet and social activist who had been invited to visit China as a member of the Progressive Writers Association. In 1947, after Independence, there was a desire for the making of a '*Naya Kashmir*' (New Kashmir). It was felt then by the leadership that art and literature needed to be given great prominence, along with other aspects of development. This journey towards building a progressive cultural movement had already started in 1941. Some intellectuals, writers, poets and artists had already tried to create a socio–cultural patron in the form of the state unit of the Progressive Writers' Association. In order to streamline its functioning, the association had the following wings: the Progressive Writers' Association, the Progressive Painters' Association and the Progressive Performing Artists' Association. In today's context, it feels strange to know that Kashmir had a very strong progressive cultural movement where painters, poets, writers, playwrights and students were part of it. This movement was inspired by a larger pan-left political thought under the guidance of the Communist Party

of India. Progressive associations were formed in all the regional
languages of India, particularly, in the area of performing arts,
as the Indian Peoples Theatre Association (IPTA) and writers'
associations, known as Progressive Writers Association (PWA).
This movement inspired a huge number of people from the
cultural community of India. The central idea of this movement
was of very socialistic values and attracted great names from the
fields of music, painting, theatre, and literature across India. To
name a few like, Munshi Premchand Balraj Shani, Kafi Azmi,
Salil Chowdhary, Shambu Mitra, M.F. Hussain, Zohra Segal,
Dina Pathak and many more. This pan-Indian movement
also impacted the Kashmiri language poetry, theatre and other
cultural areas, contributing to the idea of Naya Kashmir, the
agenda of the new state government under Sheikh Muhammad
Abdullah, the prime minister.

However, the Government of India soon sacked this
Kashmiri state government and imprisoned Sheikh
Mohammad Abdullah for eleven long years.[5] Bakshi Ghulam
Mohammed replaced him, and he soon started a cultural event
with the first-ever Festival of Kashmir, called Jash-e-Kashmir,
held in 1956. This festival had to be celebrated by all sections
of the Kashmiri people, including the folk dancers, folk theatre
artistes, boatmen, police, agricultural department officials,
schools and colleges.

Our school produced a musical opera, *Neki Badi*, written
by Dinanath Nadim. It was a children's musical in which
most of the characters were birds and animals of the forest. It
featured two orphan children driven away from their homes

---

[5] P.K. Bamzai, *Culture and political History of Kashmir*, M.D. Publications, New
Delhi, 1994.

by their uncles. This brother and sister, in the midst of a dense forest among the friendly animal kingdom, find shelter and protection from all the inhabitants of the forest, who adopt them. This play became a landmark production at the Jashn-e-Kashmir festival.

For the final performance, we had to act before many VVIPs. It dawned on the organizers that at the main venue of the festival on the open stage specially made on the Hazoori Bagh grounds, we children were not visible from a distance. Tables were brought to raise the height of the stage so that the huge audience could see us small child actors. Today, at that very spot, stand the Bakshi Stadium, Srinagar Indoor Stadium and Tagore Hall. Later, the songs of the *Neki Badi* opera became famous folk songs in the Kashmiri language. The music for the opera was composed by Jagannath Shivpuri, my music school guru. Even today, many contemporary Kashmiri singers sing the poems of *Neki Badi* without knowing their origin. Dinanath Nadim, apart from being a versatile poet in Kashmir, brought in new trends in many forms of expression in the Kashmiri language.

*

My school was run by the Hindu Educational Trust. The trustees of the organization ran many schools in the downtown area, some meant for girls only. It was not a rich trust. Our monthly fee was never high as the school catered to the children of the working classes and was affordable for the working folk of both the Hindu and Muslim communities. It had some very fine teachers, some of whom were writers and intellectuals. This combination of features gave the school an added edge over the other schools in Kashmir in terms of quality of education.

For example, apart from the regular classes in different subjects, we had hobby classes in agriculture, scientific innovations, creative writing, drama, hygiene and more. All these activities were conducted after school hours.

The school had a rival, the Islamia High School. Whenever there was a state function or competition, the two would compete in all the categories and pick up all the trophies and awards. After the awards ceremony at the Srinagar Polo ground on Residency Road, students from both schools would march through the streets of the city to the accompaniment of their respective school bands playing folk melodies to the beat of drums, side drums and flutes, displaying our trophies to the public. The uniforms that we wore were specially laundered and stiff with starch, and ceremonious turbans in various colours were worn by the participating students of both schools. The drill masters of the two schools turned out to be good friends, a surprise to all the students because we were under the impression that they were sworn rivals too.

There was always a huge space for camaraderie between the people, which made communal attitudes irrelevant. Even those who may have had them were shy of displaying their prejudices openly. There was no room for or social sanction for it. Even so, there were strong elements of religiousness in every community, which reflected a certain degree of narrowness and orthodoxy in attitude. For school-going children, however, there were no strict restrictions.

The entire space belonged to us, whether it was the Shankaracharya Hill, Hari Parbat, Zabarwan or the Mahadev peaks. I was part of a group of children who would go up the hills, trek through the forests, and eat wild berries (*chanuch*) and wild grapes *(kav-dach)*. There would be the odd apple or apricot tree amid a thick forest, and like a group of wild monkeys, we would climb up those trees in no time. Usually, we would start our trek from Shankaracharya Hill and climb right to the top, where the tenth-century stone Shiva temple stood, majestically overlooking the valley of Kashmir. From here we would proceed towards Pari Mahal, a monument built by the Mughal prince Dara Shikoh, the son of Shah Jahan. In our childhood, it was a deserted, neglected place, the monument hidden by all kinds of wild bushes and shrubs. The view of the lake from this spot was breathtaking. Finally, we would come down to Chashme Shahi, drink cold, clear water from the spring, rest for some time in the gardens and then walk back home. We never had enough money to take the bus home. We always walked the boulevard route along the lake to reach home safely.

My group of friends called days like these our adventure days. We would repeat our walks and treks on these adventure routes on holidays. They took us one full day. Life was happy, relaxed and carefree then.

Once a year, our school arranged a hiking expedition to Zabarwan or the Mahadev mountains. Standing in front of Dal Lake, one could see those peaks standing tall and majestic. Today, I wouldn't call this a hiking event but rather a tough trek. We had to carry our blankets, mugs, plates some dried fruit or chana, and our food and shelter requirements. Climbing Zabarwan was quite tough, considering we were just school kids. On our way up to the peak, we would meet the Bakarwals, or shepherds, in their typical homes with their cattle. They would stay on these high mountains for months until autumn's end, letting their sheep, goats and cows graze in the meadows of these mountains. As autumn closed and the chill started to penetrate the air, the Bakarwals would begin their journey back through the mountain passes, walking for months until they reached the plains of India, where they would continue to rear their animals. The fact that they walked all year round from various places in India up into the mountains and then back into the plains again used to fascinate me. Their movement conjured for me images of ancient caravans, of the invaders from Central Asia, their soldiers walking like these shepherds to conquer distant lands. They too would have undertaken similar journeys via similar routes and passes. These Bakarwals have their own unique folk music, handicrafts and dress, very distinct from those of the people living in the Valley. Hence, they form a separate category of tribal people. Hiking in these mountains of Zabarwan and Mahadev gave us children the opportunity to interact with these people, sometimes even sharing their food and peeping into their tough lives in those harsh mountains.

Welcome to Kashmir

Suddenly one day, an announcement rang all over the city of Srinagar saying the riverfront of the Jhelum had to be cleaned up. In large numbers, government authorities descended on the population of Srinagar that resided on the banks the river and on the community of people who lived on the river itself in big boats, called *dongas* or *bahach*. All the dongas and bahaches had to be cleared, along with the people, to make them almost invisible. This meant either pulling the boats up the stream or letting them go down the river, beyond the seventh bridge and out of the municipal limits of the city. The banks on either side of the river had to be 'decorated' for a very big event—the official visit of top Soviet leaders Nikita Khrushchev and Nikolai Bulganin. This visit was happening at the height of the Cold War and against the background of Kashmir being one of the subjects of discussion at the UN.

The event was most probably organized to impress the Soviet leaders to gain their support on the question of Kashmir. The entire state machinery set to work to make this visit a memorable one. It had to be a historic one, with political impact, and which would reverberate internationally. The government left no stone unturned to make this event a big success. But it involved the displacement of thousands of people and it felt as if the army and civil administration together had taken over the town and its population. It was a big experience for me as a child. I watched all this activity happening from my school building right on the banks of the Jhelum near Kharyaar, which was between the first bridge and the second—the Amira Kadal and Habba Kadal, respectively.

Within a week or so, the riverbank from the first bridge, Amira Kadal, right up to the seventh bridge, Safa Kadal, had been done up. The buildings facing the riverfront were all decked with colourful shawls, creole textiles and buntings. Across the river, hundreds of welcome arches in different colours, draped in bright textiles and designs, hung on ropes across the river. Music, the chanting of slogans, traditional singing and police and school bands gave this event a unique and amazing significance for me as a school kid who participated in it and was a witness to the colourful pageant. All the children from the schools in Srinagar, both private and state-run, lined up along the banks of the Jhelum, donning smart, colourful uniforms and ceremonial headgear, waving both the Indian tricolour and the red Soviet flag they held in their hands. The general public, both men and women, wore their traditional *phirans*, or shalwar-kameez, and stood at the mohalla ghats singing the traditional 'Wanvun' to welcome the Soviet leaders. Most of the local police bands in their special ceremonial uniforms were stationed at vantage points along the route of the seven bridges playing their marching tune in honour of the visiting dignitaries. Almost the entire population of Srinagar, young and old, were lined up on both sides of the river. It created an unparalleled mood of festivity everywhere in the city.

Finally, when the Soviet guests came up the stream from
the seventh bridge, their long, colourful, heavily bedecked boat
pulled by almost 100 oarsmen wearing white uniforms and
starched red turbans, resembling a royal swan moving against
the currents. Years later, while recalling the movement of the
boat, I remembered a sequence from the Shakespeare play
Anthony and Cleopatra, where Cleopatra travels on a huge, fully
decorated royal boat to meet Caesar. The welcoming population
greeted the guests with the sounds of hundreds of *swarnais* and
dhols of the Bhands of Kashmir. Thousands of school children
waved Indian and Soviet flags and shouted slogans proclaiming
unity and '*Hindi-Russi Bhai-Bhai*', creating an ambience of an
India entering the gates of heaven.

This kind of show, with a large population shouting out
slogans that resounded in the air, was a rare and colourful
event for a school-going child. It was many years later that I
understood the geopolitical dimensions of this government-
sponsored mega-event. It was part of the Naya Kashmir project
initiated by the prime minister of Jammu and Kashmir, Bakshi
Ghulam Muhammad, who had rebelled against the first prime
minister of the state, Sheikh Mohammad Abdullah. It was
Sheikh Abdullah who had originally created the document for
development and change for the people of Jammu and Kashmir,
calling it 'Naya Kashmir', but fate had something else in store
for him. Bakshi was sworn in as the new prime minister after
Sheikh Abdullah's removal and imprisonment. Ironically, many
decades later, Sheikh Abdullah returned as the chief of the state
but passed away while in office. His body was wrapped in the
Indian tricolour when he was laid to rest.

My relaxed and carefree school days ended when I passed
my tenth class and joined college. At school, everybody
knew me, and I knew everybody. My name appeared on the
school honour board, but I was more a student of culture and
extracurricular activities than of academic studies. I passed all

the exams, but never with any outstanding results. I would consider myself an average student whose biggest horror was maths. I could only pass maths as I did well in geometry and trigonometry. I passed my class ten exams with high second-class marks. During this same period, I was awarded a gold-plated medal by the state government for participating in the Jashn-e-Kashmir festival in the iconic opera *Neki Badi*. My mother preserved this medal for years. She handed it over to me before Kashmir imploded in the 1990s. It was in the midst of the turmoil of those years that she passed away. I still cherish this medal like a treasure.

Throughout my school days, the atmosphere I grew up in was filled with people who had achieved some level of success in the creative fields. After the experience of Jashn-e-Kashmir, some of us school children were encouraged to develop our talents. We were enrolled in an organization called Young Writers Forum, where meetings were conducted by senior creative personalities who later became major figures on the cultural horizon of Kashmir. Some of them were Amin Kamil (poet, playwright and critic), Akhtar Mohiuddin (short story writer), Ali Mohamad Lone (playwright), Rehman Rahi (eminent poet) and Dinanath Nadim (legendry poet and opera writer)—all national or padma award winners. I hardly understood what this was all about. At the forum meetings, many youngsters would recite their poems or read out their short stories. Even I attempted to write. But I didn't pursue writing because I was too busy on the amateur theatre scene and was learning Indian classical music.

What was unique about the senior writers was that they seemed to want to inculcate a sense of seriousness among the people in their understanding of the arts and languages. In Srinagar, a small city then, these seniors participated in almost all the cultural happenings. This big group of welcoming elders was involved in building a very progressive movement in the arts. The most prominent names I became acquainted with were Bansi Parmoo (painter), Shamim Ahmed Shamim (journalist), Moti Lal Kemmu (playwright), Ghulam Rasool Santosh (painter), Triloki Kaul (painter), Radha Krishan Braroo (theatre), Pran Kishore (radio and theatre) and Ali Mohamad Lone (playwright). They inspired us and gave us opportunities for our cultural advancement. It surprised us to be treated as equals by them as they guided us in our artistic or cultural pursuits.

It was because of my association with these stalwarts of Kashmiri culture that I, as a schoolboy, could witness performances by artistes from other parts of the country. My family used to be surprised when I received invites to major state events featuring musicians or performers like Begum Akhtar, Birju Maharaj or Mohammad Rafi.

I still remember a concert by Muhammad Rafi Sahab at Bakshi Stadium. The entire stadium was packed. Rafi Sahab, without any orchestra, gave a stellar performance to the accompaniment of just a harmonium, which he played himself, and one tabla, played by a local musician. People were enraptured when he opened his concert with his super-hit song 'Yahoo' from the film *Junglee*. He performed for almost two hours, and the crowds lapped up every bit of his singing.

It was during my school and college days that I got a glimpse of many a Bombay film star—like Shammi Kapoor, Sharmila Tagore, Nanda, Shashi Kapoor and Pradeep Kumar. One felt safe being out during those days, even when one returned home late in the night alone. Though it was safe, returning from these events was a difficult exercise, especially when I was a schoolboy. There were hardly any streetlights, and I would have to take a longer route to reach home to avoid the barking street dogs that were at large late in the night.

In short, growing up in Kashmir was full of simple cultural opportunities, which left a deep impression on me from an early age, and which have remained with me after all these years.

Today, when I move around in Kashmir and interact with school children or with college and university students, I realize what they are missing. I see only anger, distrust and fear in their eyes. It appears from my conversations with them that they are conscious that they've been told only half-truths, not the whole truth. So many of them keep asking me questions, which I feel is a sign of hope. I was surprised when a girl at the Centre for Kashmiri Studies at Kashmir University asked me a question during my introductory lecture to them: 'What happened in 1990? What was the reason that Kashmiri Pandits, who were a part and parcel of Kashmiri life, left this place of their ancestors?' For a moment I was unnerved and didn't know how to reply to this young mind. I was conscious of the fact that I should not mix untruth with the truth. She had put her question with absolute sincerity, and I had to be truthful. When I related my eyewitness version of the 1990s, I did not interpret the events at all. I only reported what I had gone through. While telling my story, I looked at the innocent faces in front of me and realized that these young university students had never even seen any Kashmiri Pandits. By the time they grew up, Kashmiri Pandits had already left the state. My lecture was their first experience of meeting and interacting with a Kashmiri Pandit.

There was a long, long silence. I said, 'Yes, when they ran away from the Valley, it was accompanied by a lot of violence.' The girl who had asked me the question said, 'We are suffering because of the sins of our elders.' At this, most of the students in the room turned to look at her. I did not respond to her statement, but I did ponder on the question of who would tell them the truth. Is it possible to come together as Kashmiris and share our truths?

College Days

I joined Shri Pratap College in Srinagar, popularly known as SP College. It was a college with many separate buildings, each dedicated to a special faculty. Here, for the first time in my life, no one would keep an eye on me or catch me if I did anything wrong. Here I was on my own, with no insistence on attending classes. The college had a strong tradition of sports. Our college teams in hockey, cricket and football were strong in all the tournaments that the state organized throughout the year. For us students there was no uniform; one could wear anything. There was no one to question us when it came to what we chose to do. Style and fashion were most important for students to show off.

My college was situated hardly a mile from my home; it was practically in my neighbourhood. Even before we joined college, as children we would regularly visit the campus from our mohalla in the late afternoon to play or watch an inter-college or inter-university national sports tournament or even state competitions in hockey and football. All the major tournaments were held here, and the general public from the city too came to watch the matches. Football has always been a favourite game with Kashmiris. Tennis and cricket were elite games played by the well-off students who had come from English-medium schools.

In my first year of college, I almost got lost in its free ambience. I belonged to no team or organization in the college. I drifted, bunking classes to watch movies in the cinema halls near the campus. For months I didn't attend my botany classes, but I had a very obedient friend who proxied my attendance—the teachers in charge never knew that I was absent. There were three cinema halls in the city near our college, and it was a passion for my group of friends to watch films on the opening day and, more particularly, the very first show of that day. I remember watching the first opening shows of *Dharamputra*, *Jis Desh Mein Ganga Behti hai*, *Ramayana*, *Junglee*, *Jab Jab Phool Khile* and many others. It was a matter of prestige for us to show off to the rest of our friends in the college that we had seen the first screening of a film on the first day of its release in the city theatres.

Our gang of friends from the college was notorious for managing tickets. Since we used to have a limited amount of money, we had to purchase what we all could afford, which was always third-class tickets. If we didn't have sufficient money for all our friends, we fought our way to get to the ticket counter to get more tickets. This fight was really an adventure. There was never a disciplined queue, just chaos created by unruly crowds and some black marketers. For us, the principle we applied to reach the ticket window was 'might is right'. When we got a few tickets, we would sell them to someone who desperately wanted them but could not fight his way to the counter. Once we made some additional money from selling these tickets in black, we would fight our way again to the ticket counter to purchase more tickets so the entire gang could get tickets and watch the film together.

I remember the time I couldn't get tickets to watch a super-hit film, *Insaaniyat*, starring Dev Anand, Dilip Kumar and Zippy the Monkey. I was so determined to watch this film that I waited until the Indian news documentary began to be screened. The general chaos in the theatre had settled down. I went into the 'box class' area from where the elite of the city watched films. It was calm and quiet because there was no one in the foyer. I stood there and peeped through a keyhole at the screen and watched the whole movie that way.

Adjacent to our college and beyond its boundary wall was the famous College for Women. Imaginary romances happened across the wall, and they were legendary. Most of the time one not only did not know the name of the girl one was supposedly attracted to but also had never even seen her. It was all fantasy based on the sounds one heard from the other side of the wall. This comedy developed further one day when some of my friends who regularly met next to the wall made all kinds of sounds and remarks to the girls across. Strangely, we could hear responses from the girls' side too. We followed this up with cheap filmy songs from our side and the girls on the other side responded with suitable lines from some other song. This singing across the dividing wall developed into a game and continued for an hour at least.

After some time, the game advanced when one of our gang members developed a new device to enhance our agenda in this new relationship. One day he made a paper airplane, wrote 'Captain Bashir' on it, as if it were his name, and launched it across the wall. Our group waited for some response, but there was none. The next day, more paper airplanes were made and flown across the wall. After about fifteen minutes of this, there appeared an airplane bearing the words 'Air Hostess Shamim'. There was dumb silence on our side. We just stared at the plane. Who was this Shamim? No one knew. 'This could be a false name, 'someone said, but no, we liked to believe it was a real name and kept sending paper planes in large numbers across the wall. Soon this became a regular game for us, and it went on for weeks. It was like Air Force dog fights, this carrying of names and messages across the boundary wall. The fun of this game continued for almost a month. It was always in the afternoon, when this so-called dog fight of love began, and a large number of paper planes carrying messages of love, promises and the possibility of meetings would fly across in both directions.

One day, this lovely and innocent game of love suddenly stopped. Neither planes flew from across from the other side and nor exchange of songs took place. We waited, but nothing happened. We lost many planes because they never made their way back. We felt quite lost and couldn't comprehend what could have caused the sudden silence. Nobody had sent across any bad or vulgar messages. Finally, after a few days, our group lost interest and the boys each went their own way. A strange ceasefire had come into place.

After a gap of a few weeks, the women's college had its annual day function, for which the chief minister was the chief guest. When the function was in full swing and we could hear music on the loudspeakers, one of our seniors threw a big firecracker over the wall into the girls' college function grounds. When the cracker landed it made a big bang, sounding as if a bomb had exploded. There was commotion in the women's college. Suddenly we saw cops appearing on top of the boundary wall, looking for the culprits. By then all the boys had disappeared from the ground. Some of us were watching from the nearby botanical garden through the green bushes. What we saw next was strange and worrisome. The principal of our college ascended to the top of the wall, looking for the culprits who had set off the firecracker. We all quietly dispersed and went home.

The next day, our group was summoned to the principal's office. We wanted to drop dead when we realized that they had somehow zeroed in on our group. When we entered the office of our principal, we saw on the table most of our paper airplanes in a big heap. We didn't know where to look. Our names were on those papers. The principal's gaze scanned the lot of us. We didn't know what to do. The principal picked up a few paper planes and read out loud, 'Captain Bashir, Air Hostess Shamim, Flight Pilot Raina, Air Hostess . . .' he read out the words from at least ten more planes. He gave us a solid dressing-down. He

wanted to call our parents, but that would have meant the end
for all of us. Sheepishly we begged for mercy and forgiveness.
Suddenly, a smile spread across his face. He said, 'You should have
at least some respect for me as your principal. You know, I had
to face the chief minister!' We immediately offered more profuse
apologies and promised that we would never make him face
such embarrassment on our behalf again. He made us sign an
undertaking and warned us that if any of us committed the same
offence again, he would bar us from appearing in our final exams.

The college had always something happening, besides
classes. I attended many inter-state and inter-university football
tournaments alongside thousands of fans. As the games would
heat up, people would hoot and shout for their favourite teams.
The Jabalpur University team had a talented African player
who soon won the hearts of all the spectators in Kashmir. From
our university, we had our hero, the brilliant scorer Farouk, and
all eyes used to be focused on him. When he scored a goal, the
entire crowd would erupt, many rushing onto the field to hug
him and wish him well. Chaos would ensue for some time until
the spectators were forced out of the field so the match could
resume. When our own SP College played, the entire student
community would surround the grounds on all sides to support
our team. This would be the day when the college had to win at
any cost. A loss was considered a big disaster for all of us, and
we would be upset for days.

The arch-rivals in the intra-state tournament were the state
police department. They had some of the best players on their
team because the police higher-ups hunted for and recruited
the best talent by giving them employment. Whenever the
police team played against our college, it was like an Indo–Pak
war for us students. There was this belief in all the students'
minds that the police were our enemy. And there was a reason
for this. There were these Romeo-type guys in the college who
would fashion themselves after all kinds of famous stars. They

dressed like them and trailed behind the girls, trying to impress them. In the morning, one could see hundreds of them chasing girls. This behaviour was not socially acceptable, so the police had to take action. They would nab these guys and hit them. If the boys resisted, they were taken to the police station and their parents were called to confront their wards. It could turn into a remand of the boys for a few days.

The tradition of rivalry between the boys of our college and the city police had been legendary for generations. Therefore, it was supposed to be the duty of every college boy to uphold and continue this tradition.

Looking back on those peaceful days, the energy and camaraderie between the communities of Kashmir was immense. Imagine football or hockey events featuring matches between army teams, food and supplies department teams, state police teams, khalasa blues team; or national tournaments featuring college and university teams from many parts of India, all playing each other in the best spirit of the game and watched by thousands of ordinary people at the football grounds of SP College, Srinagar. Today it really seems like a dream. For decades now, those huge sports events have been things of the past and faded into history.

Kashmir Kala Kendra

I had been acting in school plays from my primary-school days up to high school, and I was sort of a known and dependable child actor. Whenever amateur theatre needed a child actor, I was the one sought after, of course with my father's permission. He was surprised but quite impressed by my activities, so I didn't have many restrictions placed on me.

Those days, the city of Srinagar had dozens of theatre organizations, each with its own offices and rehearsal spaces where plays were rehearsed. A majority of these theatre groups were located near a place called Kral Khud near Habba Kadal, close to my house. These amateur theatre groups were very active during the summer months and were closed in the severe winters. I remember several occasions when people watched these rehearsals from the pavement or standing in the narrow lanes close by. They found great entertainment in these plays, enjoying themselves even before a performance went public. Every evening this sight of peeping audiences was common in the Kral Khud area.

The biggest problem for these groups was finding female actors. There were women eager to act, but strong orthodoxy and strange taboos that dictated principles of morality made it difficult for them to participate in theatre. Very gradually and quietly, however, theatre people fought this hypocrisy, and female actors started appearing in amateur productions.

The most important group during my time as a young actor was the Kala Kendra. This group had senior and veteran actors, painters, singers, broadcasters and writers as members. I was polished into a competent amateur actor by this group. It was like a family with a large number of uncles and teachers. It was on the advice of one of Kala Kendra's major talents, Suraj Ticku, a painter, experienced actor and a fine set designer, that my father let me join the National School of Drama. By then Ticku had joined the song and drama division, the Government of India, under the Ministry of Information and Broadcasting in New Delhi as a set designer. He had visited the National School of Drama many times. Perhaps he recognized my growth as an actor. He also knew that our state cultural academy had scholarships for young people who wanted to pursue drama, music or dance training at nationally recognized institutions. With the permission and well-wishes of my senior, I was selected to join the National School of Drama, supported by the state of Jammu and Kashmir.

I always say that I am a product of Indian socialism because had there not been state support for art institutions in different parts of India that imparted training, it would not have been possible for many young people to pursue their passion for art, painting, sculpture, theatre, dance and music. They would not have been able to make their place in their respective fields. None of us from the Valley had the capacity to support ourselves financially. India was a poor nation, but one heard story after story of young people getting grants or scholarships from their state governments and becoming engineers, doctors and artists. Perhaps it was the only way to develop the human capital of the Jammu and Kashmir state as part of its Naya Kashmir project. Let us not forget that this was the first state in the Union of India to give land to the tiller in one stroke and where education from primary school to university level was made entirely free.

2

Moi—Muqadas (the Holy Relic)

It was one of the harshest winter months of *Chalai Kalan* (severe cold months) in the Valley when all the education institutions closed for the winter break. On the morning of 27 December 1963, I went to open my father's clinic at Habba Kadal. My father was a dentist, and during the winter holidays, I assisted him in various odd jobs, like making plaster-of-paris denture models for his patients. I loved doing this job because it involved some craft in creating an exact model. I was encouraged to assist my father because there was a possibility that I would take up dentistry as my profession and join some medical college.

That day, when I was about to open the main shutters of the clinic, the place seemed pervaded by a strange air of tension. I noticed some shopkeepers hadn't opened their shutters, as if waiting for some signal. Small groups of Muslim men had started to belt out slogans like '*Nara-e takbeer Allah Hu Akbar* [Allah is the greatest]'. One man waved a black flag on a long pole. The group stationed itself at the crossing on the road, sending people back to their residences. Nobody seemed to actually know what had happened or what was going on.

I saw Abdul Gani, who was like an uncle to me, and asked him what all the tension was about. He looked at me with his intense eyes as he locked his shop and told me to just keep quiet. My father arrived and told me to close the clinic. I did so quickly. On the road it was all tense—people were talking in whispers and locking the shutters on their shops. Then they sat down in front of their shops. My father told me to go home, saying he would follow me soon.

As I started walking home, a well-built man galloped by on a tonga drawn by horses. At one of the crossings, he halted and shouted, '*Hoshiyar, khabardar* [Be watchful, be attentive]!' He announced the orders as to what had to be done. He said there had to be a shutdown, a complete hartal, in the Valley. Anybody flouting this order would be dealt a strong hand by the 'Action Committee' that had come into power from that day. '*Hoshiyar, khabardar*,' he shouted again and moved on.

Within minutes the situation had changed. Small groups of people began marching on the road shouting Islamic slogans. As the gathering gained momentum, many more small processions followed, marching from one direction to another. Within hours it swelled into a larger procession led by unknown people. All appeared to be awaiting orders from the volunteers who sprouted from these very processions. Throughout the day, the atmosphere remained surcharged in most of the localities in Srinagar. There were street discussions amongst the people, all angry and agitated and planning further agitations. At the time of namaz, all the masjids of the city were packed with people, and the congregations were in large numbers. People started occupying streets, lanes and roads, offering namaz. In the area where we lived, there were around a dozen mosques, all filled beyond capacity. After the namaz ended, the religious sermons and recitation of the *Durudkhani* (Quranic recitations) began.

Once that was over, people again marched towards the historic Lal Chowk in large numbers. My father asked me to go home. On the way, I saw more and more processions converging from different directions, all moving towards Lal Chowk and Pratap Park near Residency Road.

Once I reached home, all I could hear were slogans coming from Pratap Park and a commotion as if some confrontation was taking place. Soon a huge column of black smoke started rising in the sky. And as evening descended, one could see the orange glow of the distant fires. Burnt black paper started flying through the air, like flocks of parachutes. Some of these burnt papers landed in our garden, creating tense moments for the family. A stranger who was returning home told us that the Regal and Amrish cinema halls had been set on fire by the protesting mobs.

Someone reported that the brother of the prime minister of Jammu and Kashmir had come to control the mobs at Residency Road. This made the situation at home worrisome, actually scary.

There seemed the possibility of a communal riot. The minorities were concerned about a situation where some elements could be exploited to turn the mobs against them. There was a radio announcement saying that the holy relic of Prophet Muhammad had been stolen from the Hazratbal shrine. This was a big shock. There was silence for quite some time in my home. The radio was switched off and my grandmother, looking at the sky awash with flying burnt black paper, said, 'What has happened is not good. Something terrible is going to take place.' The distant noises of the mobs were still audible, and nobody knew what was going to happen.

The next day, all kinds of rumours spread—that the Holy Relic had already reached Pakistan; that some local politician had managed to steal it in order to overthrow the present Jammu and Kashmir government; and that it was a conspiracy to start a communal riot in the Valley, which would then spread all over India and create a chaotic situation in the subcontinent.

Some said that the relic had been taken by some influential person with the intention of showing it to some very eminent person before he passed away, as a blessing to him. All kinds of rumours circulated, and no one had any clue as to who had planted them all.

The situation deteriorated further, and curfew was imposed in certain parts of Srinagar. The shutdown continued for many days, and daily amenities grew scarce. People started hoarding articles for their day-to-day needs. The civil administration had completely collapsed, and people had taken administration into their own hands. Every morning, young volunteers from the Action Committee rode around on open tongas, stopping at various crossings to shout '*Hoshiyar, khabardar*' and announce the rates of each item, like sugar, salt, rice and oil. These rates were binding on every citizen and every shopkeeper. Anyone who did not comply with these orders would have to face the punishment of the Action Committee, which had come up suddenly due to public reaction. This body was formed, headed and led by well-known religious personalities. These kinds of announcements would happen many times during the day. Sometimes they were sprinkled with instructions to the general public to behave like brothers with each other. If anyone needed anything, the people of the area were to rise to the occasion and cooperate and support that individual. There were clear instructions to the people to maintain communal harmony and brotherhood with those of other faiths. Kashmir became a shining example of communal amity during these days of grief.

Within a few days, the peasantry from the countryside descended into the city of Srinagar, coming in thousands from all parts of the Valley, to mourn the theft of the Holy Relic. All roads and lanes were filled with ordinary village folk. The landscape of Srinagar City changed. There were community kitchens organized on all the main roads of the city.

Called *susras* and supported by different localities, these kitchens were part of an old tradition in Kashmir that brings the Kashmiri brotherhood to the fore. Most of the time, susras provide yellow rice, an auspicious grain for all Kashmiris, and with it, warm water for the people in the winter.

Every day, lakhs of people marched in planned processions from one end of the city to another, simultaneously with other processions in other parts of the Valley. These processions carried black flags and green flags as marks of mourning, sacrilege and fury. Apart from normal Islamic slogans, there would be slogans about Hindu, Muslim and Sikh unity. All through the night, mosques recited Quranic verses for the thousands of people from the countryside who had come and camped in the city. The mosques became shelters for these visitors by night, as it was a chilly winter and had snowed a few days back.

I used to move freely within the city those days and see those thousands of village folks occupying nearly the whole city. The scenes were like those one sees in Russian documentaries showing the days of the Bolshevik Revolution when the peasantry marched into the city of Moscow to see for themselves the change after the czars' rule.

Hushed conversations speculated on how events could suddenly take a turn and bring violence against minorities. There were rumours about communal riots and killings in Dhaka, then a part of East Pakistan, as a response to the happenings in Kashmir. However, even when this news reached Kashmir, there was no adverse response among the public.

The Kashmiri Pandit community responded to this loss of the holy relic by organizing a procession in solidarity with the Muslims. The march began from my mohalla at the Sheetal Nath grounds, the epicentre of Kashmiri Pandit politics. Some of us young teenagers were tasked with leading the procession and shouting slogans. I loved doing this. A couple of thousand

Pandits joined this important procession as a mark of solidarity with our Kashmiri Muslim brothers. This procession moved slowly with a few black flags and a solitary saffron flag in the lead. When we crossed into the Muslim localities there was a surprise, even disbelief. We were shouting slogans like *'Marenge ek saath, jiyenge ek saath* [We will die together, we will live together]'; *'Moye-Muqaddas Pak ko wapas karo aye zalimon* [Return Moye-Muqaddas to us, O tormentors]'; and *'Hindu Muslim ittehad, zindabad, zindabad* [Long live union of Hindus and Muslims]'. The moment we reached Habba Kadal, we saw that a community kitchen had already sprung up on the roadside. There the Muslim volunteers, moved upon seeing us, came with warm water and yellow rice to feed us. Some of the elders blessed us. I remember some men with moist eyes hugging us. After a small break, the procession moved on towards the downtown area where we were very encouraged by the response. People came from the mosques to watch our procession and lined up along the road. At one point, as we raised slogans, all the people on the roadside joined in.

On reaching Khanaka-i-Moulla, near the Shah Hamdaan Shrine, I saw women watching us from their windows with their hands raised in prayer to the Almighty. One could see that this procession had glued the two communities closer in their mutual sharing of pain. A little further on, an elderly Muslim gentleman got so emotional and excited when he saw our procession that he screamed *'Naara-e-Takbeer!'* Our whole procession responded, *'Allah-hu-Akbar!'* The poor man couldn't believe his ears and did not know how to respond, but he kept walking with us until some point near Navid Kadal, where he left us.

We moved on and entered the area of Mirwaiz. Pandits used to call this area Pakistan, but I don't know why. For Pandits, entering this area was like walking into enemy territory, probably because of unfounded suspicions formed over the years. This time our procession had no fear. Here again, we were stopped by people and offered warm water as the chill in the air had grown very bitter. Thousands of Muslims from all walks of life watched us in silence, but in their eyes, one could see the message: 'We appreciate and respect this gesture of yours.'

In the late evening, when I reached home, I saw my grandmother, who had worried about me all day. All her four sons and their families had reached home, except me. When I entered the home, all were waiting for me. There was a long silence, and I felt the weight of it. Finally, my grandmother asked me, 'What did you do all day?' When I started narrating my story, she cut me short and asked my mother to give me some food as I must be hungry and tired. After finishing my dinner, I bid goodnight to my grandmother, and she blessed me.

We Kashmiri kids always studied during the winter months and then appeared for our external examination around spring. Before blessing me, my grandmother had asked me, 'When are you going to start your studies for the coming examination? These processions have disturbed your routine. You better get serious now since there are only three months left for your final exam.' She used to wake me up at four in the morning by banging her walking stick against the ceiling of her room on the ground floor. My bedroom was right upstairs. I had to reply with bangs on the floor back, confirming that I had woken up to study. Immediately after waking up, I would make tea for her and myself. I would come down with her cup of tea, and only then would she be satisfied that I was really up. After that, I had to rush and get pure milk from the traditional milkman. Grandma had an ulcer, which used to give her acute pain, and the doctor had advised her to take a lot of cold milk for it. And I, as a good grandson, took on the responsibility of getting up very early in the morning to fetch the milk for her. It was after all this that I would finally settle in at about five in the darkness of the winter months to study.

That day, when I took leave of her, she said, 'From tomorrow, you will start your serious studies, and if you follow what I ask you to do, then I will give you five rupees to watch a talkie.' This deal had been on offer by my grandma for a long time. But her money was to be used to watch English movies only. That night I told her, 'Okay, I will study from tomorrow.' Bidding her goodnight, I asked her to wake me up with her stick in the morning. She turned, gave me a long look and smiled. I left. All night there were Quranic recitations going on in the mosque nearby.

Early the next morning, I heard the bang of my grandmother's stick from the ground floor. I woke up, made tea and asked her if she would like to have hers. She turned to the other side of the bed in her sleep and mumbled, 'What will I do now with the tea?' So, I left to get her milk, and when I returned I started my studies. At about seven, when it was still very dark because it was winter, I suddenly heard my father scream, 'Lightning has fallen!' He screamed again, 'She's gone!' The family members, now alerted, were all at her bedside. Yes, Benjagari, my grandmother, had left us forever.

It had snowed that night. A thin film of white snow covered the landscape. As the head of the clan, Benjagari had to be given a grand funeral, but because of the hartals the question of how came up. Where could one arrange for a shroud and other items for her funeral? All the shops and markets were closed. Who would give us what was needed for the funeral? My cousin and I were dispatched to inform all the relatives living in far-off areas in the city about her passing. We had to walk for hours, visiting one locality after another to convey the message. When we returned in the afternoon, my grandmother had been given a bath and was now fully prepared for her final journey. Her four sons carried her on their shoulders. They were followed by her grandchildren, many community members and some relatives. There is a saying in Kashmiri Pandit homes that from birth to death the participation of Muslims in our lives has been a custom for us for centuries. But the Muslim population was in mourning for weeks now. Still, there were a few Muslim neighbours also present to bid her a final farewell.

As we moved towards the main road where people were gathered in the thousands in agitation against the disappearance of the holy relic, everyone gave way to our procession and stood quietly on either side of the road, as a mark of respect for the departed. I even heard someone say, '*Ya Allah, raham kar* [Allah, have mercy].' Late afternoon, after the cremation, the family members sat together for a simple meal. In Kashmiri Pandit households, as a custom we do not douse the kitchen fire; it has to go on. A simple meal is prepared and shared together. While at the meal, I quietly asked my father, 'How did all that funeral *samagri* get organized?' He smiled and answered, 'As an age-old practice when someone leaves this world, all help comes naturally. All the shops opened for a while, and all of them wanted to be a part of our grief and wanted to do a good deed and share our loss.'

The interdependence in Kashmir between the two communities, despite their differences, has been a connecting thread which never really broke. The folklore of Kashmir is filled with stories of conflict between them, some real and some imagined. Each community's interpretation of historical events is based on its own perspective, and each carries a different narrative of the same event. And yet life continues in Kashmir, like the flow of the River Jhelum. It is true that the temples on the banks of the Jhelum have been silent for decades now, but they still stand, even without worshippers.

The holy relic agitation had built itself into a sort of mass uprising, all directed by the leadership of the Action Committee.

The reverberations of the uprising could be felt in other lands of the world. Internationally, it was a hot issue that needed very careful handling. To douse the flames of this uprising, the prime minister of India, Jawaharlal Nehru, made an address on All India Radio appealing to the people of Kashmir for calm and peace. He promised that the holy relic would be found at any cost soon and that the culprits would be punished appropriately. He dispatched Lal Bahadur Shastri to Kashmir and appointed some prominent civil servants to assist him in this mission.

The communal amity during this period set an example for the whole world. Kashmir became once again a symbol of peace and brotherhood after the Partition. Many Hindu delegations from Jammu visited Kashmir in a show of solidarity, to stand with their Muslim brethren. And despite the anger and pain everywhere, Kashmiris again held up the principle of communal harmony, something Mahatma Gandhi had noted during the communal massacre when India was partitioned.

Shastri was a simple, honest and noble soul who had to borrow a woollen overcoat from Nehru for the severe winter of Kashmir. His team worked hard, and soon news spread to all corners of the Valley that the holy relic had been recovered. There was general jubilation and relief all over the Valley, followed by celebrations. The final identification of the relic was the responsibility of Syed Meerak Shah Kashani, a very old spiritual figure who was highly respected by the Kashmiri population. The identification *deedar* was done on 14 February 1964, the anniversary of the martyrdom of the fourth Khalifa of Islam, Hazrat Ali.

However, to this day no one knows who took the relic and how it was recovered. The entire story of this colossal theft and recovery remains a mystery, like many mysteries of Kashmir Valley.

3

Return of Sheikh Abdullah

It was 8 April 1964. There was a buzz in the air about some big event, but what it was I had no idea. I only witnessed the cleaning of the city roads as they were decorated with arch gates. On most of them was written 'Welcome Sher-e-Kashmir'. Small groups of people led small processions in the city, shouting slogans like '*Sher-e-Kashmir Zindabad* [Long Live Lion of Kashmir]', '*Nara-e-Takbeer Allahu Akbar* [Slogan of Allah is the greatest]', '*Nara-e-Risala, Ya Muhammed Rasoolillah*', '*Yeh mulq hamara hai* [This nation is ours]', '*Iska Faisla Hum Kareinge* [We will decide about this]' and '*Sher-e-Kashmir ka Kya Irshaad, Hindu Muslim Sikh Ittehad* [What is the command of Lion of Kashmir? The unity among Hindus, Muslims and Sikhs]'. Soon it was announced that Sheikh Mohammad Abdullah had been released from prison after eleven years. Upon reaching Jammu, he was honoured with a huge reception by the citizens of Jammu District. Now he was travelling by road to Srinagar, and the entire city waited to welcome the 'Lion of Kashmir' back after so many years of imprisonment. Shiekh Abdullah had been released from Kodaikanal jail, in the south of India where he had been imprisoned for years.

It was a day of festivity and happiness. The route from Qasi Gund to downtown Srinagar had a festive look, with colourful flags and paper buntings everywhere. Thousands of Kashmiris stood on both sides of the road for hours to greet their leader. Time passed and the people became impatient. An occasional announcement reported that Sheikh Sahab would arrive any minute. From time to time a commotion stirred as if he had arrived, but then soon the public would realize that it was a false alarm and burst into laughter.

Suddenly I saw an open jeep coming up the road at full speed, and standing in that jeep was a tall man in a double-breasted suit with a necktie and a fur cap. Before I could take a thorough look at this tall man, the jeep zipped past me, and before I even realized who he was it had gone. Following him was a river of humanity. The human stream was so long that for hours I could not cross the road. This procession did not stop for almost three hours and continued to flow, appearing to have no possibility of even slowing down. This river of running people is still imprinted in my mind like a documentary clip from the Indian freedom moment when Gandhi visited rural Bihar—proof of Sheikh Abdullah's popularity among the people.

When the procession reached downtown, Sheikh Sahab delivered a fiery speech about self-determination for Kashmir and the Kashmiri people. After this event, there was a series of lectures at various venues across the Valley. Sheikh Sahab visited many districts of Kashmir State, delivering speech after speech. The crux of his speeches asserted that the fate of the Kashmiris would be decided by the Kashmiris themselves and by nobody else.

His presence in the state over a few months polarized the political atmosphere in the Valley between the pro-Indian Prime Minister Bakshi Ghulam Mohammed and him. This was despite Bakshi having been one of Abdullah's comrades-in-arms during their political struggles against the Maharaja of Kashmir and during the Quit Kashmir movement. However, now they had fallen apart on the question of accession of Jammu and Kashmir to India.

Every week, Sheikh Abdullah would deliver provocative speeches against the Central government for being unjust to him and to the state. Through these regular speeches, he reconnected with people from all regions of the state. He travelled from one part of the state to another, galvanizing the public and increasing his own popularity.

After a couple of months of this, on Republic Day, 26 January 1958, it was Bakshi's turn to show his hold on the politics of Kashmir. His party organized a procession of people to celebrate the Republic of India. This time the procession marched from the northern part of Srinagar City towards the south. It continued for four hours, with an almost equal number of people as at Abdullah's processions, carrying their party flags for the National Conference. It was snowing that day, but the procession was huge, a kind of rebuttal to Sheikh Abdullah's earlier procession. Here the slogans were 'Azad Hindustan Zindabad' and 'Khald-e-Kashmir Zindabad'. Since the show of strength was very impressive, there were street discussions among the people as to whose procession was bigger and who had more support among the Kashmiri masses.

I had watched both processions from the same spot at Badeyaar (near the famous Ganpathyaar Temple), and the memories of both come back to me whenever I am at that spot. Now, to me, the difference between the processions was very obvious. In Sheikh Abdullah's procession, the emotional state of the masses was one of energy and excitement. Imagine the masses running after their leader with joy, just to get a glimpse of him. In Bakshi's procession, people were just walking without any energy and showed little excitement.

4

Delhi Fulcrum

Years ago, in early 2000, the Film and Television Institute of India Pune, restarted a training course in acting decades after it had discontinued it. I was a member of the committee tasked with conceptualizing the course, along with Jaya Bachchan, Shabana Azmi, Naseeruddin Shah and many other well-known names from the field of theatre and cinema. The acting course had been discontinued years back when Girish Karnard was the director of the film institute. The deliberations continued for two or three days, revolving around the kind of courses needed now, given the changing nature of cinema. The committee made some path-breaking recommendations in terms of the faculty it believed was needed to lead this new training course. Many names came up, but somehow no one satisfied all the members' expectations. Out of the blue, Shabana asked me, 'Why don't you take up this position as the head of the acting programme?' I laughed and replied to the committee, 'No thanks. I've never in my life done a job, and I am not the right person for it.' Shabana insisted, saying, 'Now you can have a job and shape this course according to your own vision, and Pune is a nice place to work.' Again, I laughed and told Shabana, 'You know, I'm a Kashmiri. I can only compromise up to the trees and monuments of Delhi after leaving the gardens and chinars of Kashmir.'

After Kashmir, Delhi is the best city in India. I love it and have made my home here since I came here as a young lad in 1967 to study at the National School of Drama. However, the pain of losing my permanent home address at Sheetal Nath Sathu in Srinagar bothers me quite often. When you come from a small place to a big metropolis like Delhi, you're lost for some time. I did not know a soul in Delhi. I came here with a small tin trunk, a few pairs of clothing and one bedroll. I got my admission at the country's premier drama school where the doyen of Indian theatre, E. Alkazi, was at the helm of affairs.

In the beginning, I stayed for a few months with a relative of mine at the R.K. Puram government quarters. Then I shared a room in the Railway Quarters at Bengali market, then at Kasturba Gandhi Marg, earlier known as Curzon Road. Nearby, a Mr Nair from Kerala ran a South Indian mess known as Nair's Mess. It had a few rooms and great South Indian food. Many members of Parliament would come to eat there. Even the great musician Subbulakshmi, along with many other luminaries of south Indian culture, visited and ate there.

After passing out of drama school, I stayed in Lodhi Colony in Nizamuddin East and in Defence Colony. After two and a half decades in Delhi, my wife Anjali and I built a small home outside Delhi in Noida, because I could not afford to stay on in Delhi as the cost of living there was soaring. But at home, we say we live in Delhi and just sleep in Noida.

In these five decades of living in Delhi, I have received offers for many positions outside Delhi, but from the beginning, I had decided that I would remain a freelancer all my life. The city of Delhi has been the fulcrum of my scale, and the two balancing pans have continuously shifted up and down. Still, my fulcrum has been managed quite well.

The city of Delhi, from the days of the Mahabharata to this day, has survived a long and epic saga, making histories, getting razed to the ground, reappearing vandalized and looted, but emerging again and again. This piece of land has been the home of nine cities and their dynasties. The lineages of great poets like Souda, Mir, Dard, Ghalib Momin, Zafar Zouq and many more, have chiselled through the centuries with their words their pains and their love for this great city. It holds something poetic and mysterious, and I love to sense that when I crisscross my way through the lanes and by lanes of Delhi every day.

The third floor of Rabindra Bhavan housed the tiny National School of Drama, where students from many parts of India came to study theatre. Most of us came from little places and lesser-known cultures. In the beginning, nothing made much sense. One was thrown into the big ocean of world cultures, like Greek, Sanskrit, Asian and modern Indian drama. They were all too distant to understand. Often the students wanted to run back to their familiar regions. Since most of us students were not from literature or arts backgrounds, it was tough to comprehend what was being taught. The library meant nothing to us. We did not know which books to read or how to get one issued.

One day, the students were asked to come down and assemble on the Rabindra Bhavan lawns. We were then ordered to perform actual manual labour. We had to carry big baskets of earth and dump them at a certain spot, then carry baskets of bricks on our heads. This continued for two weeks and made all of us new students very angry. We started to quietly raise questions. We had almost started protesting this forced manual labour and complaining that we had come to school to become actors and directors of theatre when, to our shock, we saw our director, Alkazi, working alongside us, and his senior student carrying big baskets of bricks on his head. This levelled

our small-town egos. We couldn't believe that the head of our
institution was performing manual labour with students like us.

That was our first lesson on the dignity of labour. As time
passed, all that manual labour bore an open-air theatre, now
known as Meghdoot Theatre. Soon we learned that the school
didn't have enough funds to complete the project, but with
our labour and with Alkazi's vision it now had a nice open-air
performance space. At the centre of the stage stood a big babul
tree, giving the Meghdoot a distinct personality and character.
We learned to polish the wooden floors of our studio theatre with
our own hands before performing. This place of performance
was our sacred space and was treated like our temple.

Meghdoot Theatre has been where a major part of
contemporary Indian theatre history has happened, as the best
of world drama, from Sanskrit to Western classics and major
contemporary works of Indian and foreign playwrights, has been
presented here. Some of these productions became milestones
of contemporary Indian theatre history. This was the stage
where Om Shivpuri, Uttara Baokar, Surekha Sikri, Manohar
Singh Pankaj Kapoor, Seema Biswas, K.K. Raina, Naseeruddin
Shah, Om Puri, Anupam Kher, I and many others trained to
become seasoned actors and directors of Indian theatre.

The National School of Drama under Alkazi always dreamed
of major theatrical breakthroughs. The school had become a
flag-bearer of experimentation and innovation in Indian theatre.
Theatre personalities and experts from various parts of the world
frequently worked with and interacted with the students here
to produce major works of theatrical experience. They came
from the West and from the East. Similarly, great exponents
of traditional theatre worked with the students to teach them
the elements of Bharata's Natyashastra in the existing folk and
traditional performing arts of India. The drama school was
an open house where all kinds of performances, theories and
practices were studied and celebrated.

Personalities like Shivram Karanth, K. V. Subbanna, Kovalam Narayan Panniker, Giriraj Kishore, Master Fida Hussein, Bala Saraswati—the great gurus of the Indian performing streams—laid in us the foundations for understanding and decoding the multiple plural traditions that are India's cultural treasures and infusing in students the desire to build modern Indian theatre in all its many regions. The National School of Drama opened their eyes to the challenges that lay ahead in making the evolution of Indian theatre their professional endeavour.

Here I also met some of the best Western theatre teachers and directors, who worked with the students to give them first-hand experience of the various Western theatre forms and processes. Directors and writers like Carl Weber, Fritz Bennewitz, Richard Sechner, Harold Clurman, Jerome Lawrence, Allen Stewart, John Arden and his wife Shozo Sato and Joan Littlewood are some of the names I remember. They came from Europe, the US, the Soviet Union, Australia, the UK and Japan. Once out of drama school, life as a freelancer opened many areas for me as an actor and director, but I had to create my own opportunities and build my own work for survival.

I left the drama school in 1971 after three and a half years of training. This was a fervent time of great ideas and change, the period of the Vietnam War and the Bangladesh Liberation struggle. There was enough openness to express one's social and political views. In theatre, you could hardly escape participation in the innumerable protests happening in the city. I joined these protests, along with many well-known poets, painters, musicians and theatre people.

The first thing I did as a freelancer was to go to the Old Delhi Pahadganj market. I bought a military backpack and a second-hand sleeping bag from a hippie. Those were the days of hippies, anti-war activists, peace movements, anti-war rock and pop music, and poetry—the years of anti-establishment ideas, the student revolution in Paris, and the anti-Vietnam

War demonstrations in the US and other parts of the world. There was an atmosphere of anti-imperialism all around, and a desire to change the world order. Many works, like the poems of Allen Ginsberg and the path-breaking books by Frantz Fanon, Bertold Brecht, Meyerhold, Pablo Neruda, Paulo Freire, Jone Bied, Heiner Muller and Goerge Jackson fed us youngsters. It was a time of new idealism inspiring every young man to bring about change.

This urge for change was sharpened by the post-colonial discourses contained in the works of a large number of intellectuals, writers, poets, playwrights and painters from many regions of South Asia. Some of them were Faiz Ahmed Faiz, Makdoom, Subhash Mukhopadhyay, Nazarul, Muktibodh, Sahir Ludhianvi, Sarveshar Dayal Saxena, Raghuvir Sahai, Srikant Verma, M.F. Hussain, K.G. Subramanyan, S. Swaminathan, Salil Chowdhury, Vanraj Bhatia, Mohan Upreti and Pachanand Pathak.

When the genocide of Bengalis in East Pakistan by the Pakistani army happened, we put up many street performances to support the people of Bangladesh. We had with us a Baul singers' group. When the US threatened to bring its Fifth Fleet into the Bay of Bengal, we staged short improvisational street plays framed around the poetry of Faiz Ahmed Faiz at the US library building at Bahawalpur House. During these demonstrations, one met many strangers who came to join hands for a common cause.

From the street play came a unique act of protest performance. We bandaged a man (Shyam Kamath) from head to toe and stood with him at the entrance of the US embassy; Shanta Gandhi, Rajeev Sethi, the Bauls and I sang. The US Embassy staff didn't know why this bandaged man stood at their doorstep. Some believed he was a wounded Bangladeshi. Soon a huge contingent of police arrived but were surprised to see that it was hardly a huge protest at all that was happening. The police requested us to take away the bandaged man from the premises of the embassy.

In those times we could do these protests inside the premises of foreign embassies. Today we would be shot dead immediately if we even ventured into the US Embassy, let alone protested. When Bangladesh was finally liberated, a huge procession of young people from central Delhi walked up to the newly established Bangladesh embassy at Greater Kailash to celebrate the occasion by singing and dancing on the lawns of the new embassy for hours. They were joined by the new Bangladeshi diplomats.

Within a few years of these events, we witnessed the declaration of the state of Emergency in India, which froze all fundamental rights for its citizens. Even a person like me, just starting his career, felt the effects of the Emergency. Soon I became a persona non grata. My play, Bertolt Brecht's *Chalk Circle*, was banned. I received a letter from the chief metropolitan councillor, Radha Raman, who was now like a chief minister, asking me to see him at his office. Luckily, the letter was delivered to the National School of Drama address, which I had left long back. I did not understand the significance of the letter and showed it to the poet and journalist, Sarveshwar Dayal Saxena. He understood its hidden meaning. He said, 'So, it may be better for you to quietly leave Delhi for some time.' So, I did exactly that. Sometimes I feel I have been cursed to protest even if I do not want to, but the circumstances around me ensure that I join protests.

Since I was alone and without any support, I had to make sure I earned my living without any problems and yet keep my sense of protest alive in me and my work. It was my idea in 1972 to conduct short-term theatre courses for people who could not join the long-term programmes. In collaboration with Yatrik, a leading theatre group in Delhi, and under the veteran theatre director Joy Michael, I conducted two-month-long theatre workshops. Through this, I established myself in theatre as an actor, director and teacher.

From here, my long, tough roller-coaster ride started. It took me to various parts of the country to work with local theatre people, usually for at least six weeks at a time. I would move from region to region, planting new seeds of south Asian theatre— from Delhi to Punjab, Madhya Pradesh, Haryana, Jammu and Kashmir, Ladakh, Kolkata, Manipur, Kerala, Andhra Pradesh, Rajasthan Lahore, Dhaka, Kathmandu . . . I ploughed new and barren lands of theatre, irrigating them and waiting for fresh crops of theatre activity to germinate.

Soon, other friends of my generation, like Bansi Kaul, Ravi Basvani, Bhanu Bharati, Prassana and Ranjeet Kapur all freelancers joined in this spontaneous endeavour, and a time came when a great theatre movement was celebrated all over the country. All of us worked in the remote corners of the country. We worked with urban and rural traditional performers in small mufassil towns, cities and villages, thus creating post-independent India's new contemporary theatre movement in all its diverse forms and colours.

Unfortunately, this movement was gradually appropriated by the officially appointed bureaucracy of state and central academies of theatre, called Sangeet Natak Academies, who soon with their myopic vision, reduced all this pan-Indian happening into a typical Sarkari programme, where it became a project of transport and allowances bills.

The original creative and aesthetic idea, which came to life thanks to efforts of the individual creative theatre people independently got highjacked and became merely an officially money-sucking exercise.

My friends and I formed a theatre group, Prayog, and our inaugural play was Badal Sircar's *Juloos*, which was performed at

Turkman Gate. Here, during the Emergency, houses had been
demolished under heavy police oppression. We performed this
play as our tribute to the victims of the demolition. From that
day onwards, Prayog became one of the major experimental
theatre organizations in Delhi. We travelled all over the country
performing a wide range of plays. To date, we continue our out-
of-the-box performances woven around strong socio-political
themes. Our recent work featured documentary plays based
on Mahatma Gandhi's life to commemorate his 150th birth
anniversary. Prayog has never accepted any grants from official
or unofficial sources. We believe in the principle of 'earn and
burn'—that is, we earn individually from our professional work
and then burn our earnings on Prayog to create new theatre
performances.

Thus, Delhi has been my fulcrum for all these years, with
Prayog and many other organizations being the catalysts for
the kind of work I wanted to pursue. When Prayog wasn't in
production, I would accept various assignments that took me
to various places in the country and even to other South Asian
countries. Working in many languages of the subcontinent has
been a joyful exercise of learning and imbibing humanity in
all its colours and textures, and this has kept my boat sailing
through all kinds of personal and social storms.

Delhi became the epicentre of a new Hindi theatre
movement, avant-garde and path-breaking in terms of new
playwriting and styles of presentation. Along with this, the new
parallel cinema from the 1970s brought a new energy to the
Indian film space. I was cast by the late Avtar Kaul to act as the
main lead in his film *27 Down*. This started my involvement
with the parallel cinema movement as an actor and as a strong
supporter of this new and avant-garde cinema movement. This
movement was not about money or glamour. The films were
made on shoestring budgets but had strong content, mostly
drawn from contemporary literature in many Indian languages.

It was a real fusion of literature, cinema and performance, created with the support of the best technical people. This movement in India earned a very significant place in most of the international film festivals, winning prestigious international and national awards.

For me, it was an extension of my experimental theatre work. It was a period of creative changes. I felt very much a part of this new cinema and this new theatre. I got to work with some of the leading film-makers of this movement, like Mani Kaul, Avtar Kaul, Kumar Shahani, Buddhadev Bhattacharya, T.S. Ranga, Mrinal Sen, Govind Nihalani, Romesh Sharma, Ketan Mehta, Basu Chatterjee and Basu Bhattacharya. Unfortunately, this movement gradually lost its bearings when it began to cast commercially successful film stars. This gradually eroded the principal codes established by the filmmakers themselves. It was a kind of compromise that unfortunately didn't succeed for Hindi parallel cinema. However, the parallel cinema movement continued in Malayalam and Kannada, and to some extent Bengali too.

I continued my film and theatre journeys. Delhi has remained my base, from where I take off to various destinations, be it for films or some social movement close to my heart. Delhi exposed me to various social and political ideas. It gave me opportunities to engage with people from diverse positions in diverse fields. It gave me many experiences, which had historical echoes. One day I was invited by Nadira Zaheer Babbar, now a senior theatre director and playwright, and a friend and a fellow student at NSD, to a musical evening where the famous Anil Biswas sang Faiz Ahmed Faiz. The event was conducted by Sajjad Zaheer, Nadira's father, who was fondly known as Bane Bhai, the famous communist intellectual and founder of the Progressive Writers Association. It was a rare evening because it did not consist of mere listening to Faiz's poetry set to music but included a special element. Faiz and

Sajjad Zaheer had been imprisoned together in Lahore for years, and Sajjad Zaheer narrated the stories and incidents that had provoked and inspired Faiz to write each poem that was featured and explained the circumstances and contexts in which each was born. Sajjad Zaheer's narration itself was poetic and inspiring.

When Sajjad Zaheer passed away, a memorial meeting was held in Delhi where his wife, Razia Sajjad Zaheer, a renowned Urdu short-story writer herself, read aloud a letter Sajjad Zaheer had written to her from that Lahore prison where he had been jailed with Faiz Ahmed Faiz for years for their underground work as the members of the Communist Party of Pakistan. In fact, it was the Communist Party of India who had sent Sajjad Zaheed as an underground worker in Pakistan to establish the Communist Party of Pakistan. Finally, when both were arrested and tried for treason against the State of Pakistan in what was called the Rawalpindi Conspiracy case. In my memory, the letter went roughly like this:

Dear Razia,

My cell is next to the cells of condemned prisoners who are being hanged regularly. Their cries and prayers one hears all day and night. From the window of my cell, I can see the gallows. In my cell, there is no pen, or paper, only the Quran Sharif kept deliberately knowing very well that I'm a communist but hoping that my willpower will give in someday and I may open the pages of the Quran. But they do not know the fact that the cell I am in was the cell of Bhagat Singh, who went to the gallows smiling. That memory is my strength.

My love,

Sajjad Zaheer

Meetings and mehfils like these and the performances, protests and lectures of many inspiring people in Delhi have been my food all these years. They have always been, and still remain, my strength, keeping me on my journey.

Delhi is one of those cities in the world where past and present co-exist in harmony. And yet the city expands, grows and accommodates the new people and new ideas that arrive. Many centuries live simultaneously in Delhi next to each other, and the city yet keeps changing and building new futures. It is a place of Sanskrit, Persian, English, Urdu, Hindi, Punjabi and Sindhi—and now Bihari, Pahadi and Bangla. It is a true syncretic, modern and promising multi-religious, and multi-linguistic city. It has many painful surprises and challenges; it also has its dark and conflicting enclaves, simmering all the time. Hence Delhi is a place of adventure for me, which I cannot leave or live without—Delhi has made me what I am.

5

1984—Assassination of Indira Gandhi

We stayed in an area called Defence Colony in New Delhi after Anjali and I got married. Our son Anant was born in 1982, and our daughter Aditi in 1983.

My freelancing would always take me away from home for months, and I missed my family and home immensely during those days. Our two lovely kids would narrate many a story and incident to me on my return home after these long gaps. It was fun with them because they had so much to tell me, and I had so much to explain to them. Our family routine was a constantly action-packed programme.

In the early morning, Anant and Aditi would join me for a walk at a nearby park which had many silver oak trees. I would show them the peacocks, parakeets, doves and sparrows there. During April and May, I would help them climb the mulberry trees there to collect the fruit which we would bring home, clean and eat contentedly.

Anjali, a medical practitioner, had to go to the hospital for work but would return in time for the evening sessions of reading out Western short stories for the children. Come late evening and it would be my turn to tell them stories until they went to sleep. My stories were taken from Indian folk tales and mythology. When I finished my stock of short stories, I would move on to stories from Sanskrit drama or those that I remembered from *Katha Sarit Sagar*, the ocean of ancient tales, like the stories from the *Arabian Nights*. The story that was the biggest hit with them was that of Ghatotkach, the son of Bheem and Hidimba, from a play by Bhaas called *MadhyamVyayog*, based on one of the episodes in the Mahabharata. The children were thrilled with my narration of the tussle between the child Ghatotkach and the mighty Bheem, whom Ghatotkach did not know was his father. I can't remember the number of times I have repeated that story on their demand.

My exposure to children's literature in English came through my wife. She had studied in an English-medium school, while I had attended a vernacular school. I was familiar with a little English, a little Hindi, a little Urdu and lots of spoken Kashmiri.

Every weekend we took the children for swimming lessons at the Lodhi Hotel swimming pool. It was a small pool but very close to our home. At the pool, the main attraction was to order finger chips, along with peanuts, because that was all we could afford at the hotel. To get them out of the pool was a big task; they loved the water like ducklings.

When Anjali finished her registrar-ship after her master's in paediatrics, she started to work. In the beginning, she applied for jobs at government hospitals. After several rejections, the chairperson of the selection committee sweetly told her, 'You know, Anjali, with your gold medals, certificates and your personality, you should go for private practice. That would be the best for you.'

That was it. She was told to her face that she had no chance there, so she decided to start her private practice and searched for a clinic where she could begin. Finally, she found a medical chamber in D Block in Defence Colony, belonging to a physician, Dr Mahajan. On 31 October 1984, at around eleven in the morning, Anjali and I went to set her things at the clinic. When we arrived, the senior doctors present there gave us a very cold welcome. We did not know any of them. After a few minutes, a doctor came in and quietly said that Prime Minister Indira Gandhi had been shot. She had been taken to Safdarjung Hospital, but no one knew what her condition was. There was silence all around. We stayed at the clinic for some time, and then everyone left. We made our way back home through deserted streets. There were very few vehicles on the roads. That was Anjali's first day of private practice as a doctor.

As the day progressed, something strange was unfolding. Small groups of people had gathered at various spots in my area in Defence Colony and nearby places like Kotla and Lajpat Nagar and were speaking agitatedly. In the afternoon, I took a bicycle and rode up to South Extension, where I found a traffic diversion. Delhi Transport Corporation (DTC) buses were being diverted from All India Institute of Medical Sciences on to this road, slowing traffic and creating a jam of buses, autorickshaws and cars, now all on the same narrow road. I re-routed myself and cycled around the area behind South Extension, adjacent to Lodhi Colony on the road next to the nala there.

I stopped for some time and saw a lone Sikh inside a DTC bus being manhandled by the people. He was arguing with them. The people harassing him were not aiming to head back home; they meant trouble. The bus moved on. I don't know what fate that lone Sikh passenger met. I circled around to Safdarjung Hospital. The area was filled with people gathering in large numbers. The bullet-ridden body of Indira Gandhi was still at AIIMS, and still, there was no official announcement of her death. I decided to go back home.

The area was now deserted, but people were moving on foot trying to reach their homes. My entire neighbourhood was glued to the television, listening to various announcements and news bulletins. In the late afternoon, it was announced that Indira Gandhi, the prime minister of India, was dead, shot by her own Sikh security guards.

I did not know how to react to this news or what needed to be done. Sitting at home, I heard distant noises and slogans coming from the direction of AIIMS. Some neighbours said Indira Gandhi's body was being taken to her residence, and that was why there was so much noise. As evening descended, the noise got louder and louder. My wife and I had plans to go to a friend's house for dinner. It was in another block in Defence Colony, along the main road facing the Kotla Mubarakpur and Seva Nagar areas. As we reached the main crossing of Defence Colony on the Seva Nagar side, it was a now different scene. We saw a mob with rods, sticks and burning tyres. A black-and-yellow tax and an autorickshaw were on fire. The mob was checking every vehicle in search of Sikhs. It was a warning call. We reversed our car and rushed home. I immediately took out my bicycle and rode to the nearby taxi stands, mostly run by Sikhs. I asked them to move their taxis into the lanes of the colony so that the rioters wouldn't burn their vehicles. By this time, it was dark, and it had become clear that the mobs were burning Sikhs, their homes and anything that might belong to them.

As the night progressed, panic seeped into our block. The security guards were put on alert and a small committee was formed to keep a night vigil. The rented house I lived in belonged to a Sikh gentleman. I started worrying about the house. I went to the rooftop and looked at the skyline. What I saw worried me even more. In the dark of the night, an orange colour permeated the sky, and as I turned my head, I saw a Delhi that was burning in all directions. It reminded me of my maternal grandmother, who had told me about a similar situation when she was caught in Rawalpindi during Partition.

As I stood on my rooftop, a shiver ran down my spine at the very thought that they were killing people at the sites where I could see the orange flames.

As Indira Gandhi's body lay at her official residence, riots happened all around the city. A flashback of meeting Indira Gandhi crossed my mind.

I had received an invitation from the prime minister's office to have tea with her, along with my wife. I was rather surprised because I had no connection with any political person. Why this invitation? Even my wife was curious. I imagined this must be one of those get-togethers where hundreds of people belonging to the arts community were invited to share a cup of tea with the prime minister.

Anjali asked me, 'Are you going?' I said, 'Are you crazy? I'm not going to a tea party with a huge crowd of people from the arts circle. Because I have heard that normally at these parties a huge number of artists get invited, and then there is a long queue to meet the VVIP for a few seconds or to have a picture taken with that person, with some asking for some petty favours. It will all look like a comic parade of artists, who finally have a cup of tea and snacks and leave. There is no possibility of any serious dialogue.' So, we both decided to ignore the invitation. But to my surprise, the next day a telephone call came from the prime minister's office asking for confirmation of our acceptance of the invitation. I did not know what to say, so I said yes, we would be there.

On the day of the meeting at 1 Safdarjung Road, my wife and I lost our way and barely made it on time. We arrived just as Indira Gandhi made her entry. I still remember that the security guard who let us in was one of the Sikh bodyguards whose picture I later saw in the newspaper was one of her assassins. The meeting, which I thought would be a big gathering, turned out to be a small collection of people. There was Mursheel-ul-Hassan and his wife Zoya Hassan, both academic scholars. There were Bruta and Vasundhara, his wife, both well-known painters; the journalist Shamim Ahmed; the principal of Gargi College, and the two of us. While we sat with Mrs Gandhi, I wondered why we had been invited. The meeting went on for several hours, and many times we guests even told the prime minister that we had to take leave of her. But she replied, 'No, I have no appointments this evening.' So, we had tea and pakoras. Out of politeness and, admittedly, some nervousness, I picked up only two small pakoras. Mrs Gandhi caught me at it and asked, 'Why are you taking only two pakoras? They are really delicious. Have some more.'

I remember that we talked about education, health, arts, politics, the Punjab crisis, Bhindranwale and his terror politics. Mushir-ul-Hasan asked her, 'How is the Punjab situation going on?' She said, 'Whom do we talk to? There you talk to one group of politicians and then another group appears. 'She even mentioned Kashmir, talking about Sheikh Abdullah and his decision to convert the beautiful meadows of the sacred Hari Parbat area in Srinagar into a housing colony, which had encroached on the paths of the sacred sites of both Kashmiri Pandits and Muslims, where they used to worship and meditate under the huge chinar trees. A great site of composite culture had changed . . . I was very surprised, and appreciative, to know that she had accurate knowledge about the situation.

We spent almost two-and-a-half hours with her. Even today I do not understand the purpose of that meeting. She listened to us most of the time and wanted to talk more. But for what purpose? We did not know. Finally, when we rose to leave, she asked me out of the blue, 'I heard that you have done a play on Kabir. Why don't you come to perform it here on our lawns? I would like to see it. You just call my office, and they will do the rest.' I never intended to perform at her house, so I never called her office.

*

The noise of the riots continued all night on the day of her assassination, and I could not sleep. I rose very early the next morning and went for a walk to check what had happened all night. I went to a friend's house in another block in Defence Colony. We drove in her car to take a round of South Delhi. We drove from Defence Colony to R.K. Puram, and then around Ashram, Lajpat Nagar, Nizamuddin, Bhogal and other areas. We saw burnt buses, charred cars and taxis, many autorickshaws and truck tyres. The violence that had happened was very visible, and it was scary. The silence spoke of the horror that had transpired. We didn't know what would follow in the day. There were no police anywhere, only a few individuals walking along the roads. After returning home, I heard about the violence against the Sikhs from concerned friends calling to talk about the attacks on them. I noticed that the nameplates on Sikh homes in my neighbourhood had been removed or broken by the residents because the mobs were trying to identify and attack Sikh homes.

I did not know what to do. Around midday, I received a call from Jaya Jaitly, who later emerged for a few years as a political leader of the Janata Dal Party asking if I would gather my theatre group members that afternoon for a peaceful march. I called each member, and they all agreed to come.

At about two in the afternoon, we all met at the Moolchand Hospital crossing. Socialist leaders like George Fernandes and Chandra Shekhar awaited our arrival. There were around 150 people there, ready to march. Eminent people like Swami Agnivesh, Lolly Ramdas, Ravi Nair, Madhu Dandavate, Sumanto Bannerjee, Jaya Jaitly, Dinesh Mohan, Chandra Shekar, George Fernandes and Chiman Bhai Patel were part of the procession.

The march proceeded through Lajpat Nagar, Bhogal and Ashram and drew up at the office of the 'Servants of India

Society', a pre-Partition organization that had worked in 1947 against communal violence.

When this small procession entered the interior lanes of Lajpat Nagar, a group of about twenty youngsters with lathis and trishuls confronted us. They wanted us to go back, but we persisted despite their verbal threats. We were not a very large group, but the opposing group was even smaller. Since we stayed there without provoking them in any way, they retreated, and we moved on. When we reached Jangpura Extension next to Eros Cinema, there was a big taxi stand with a few Sikh drivers huddled together. When they saw a small procession, they started to withdraw into an adjacent lane out of fear, but we stopped them and assured them of our support. One very tall and handsome taxi driver burst into loud sobs, 'I have been scared to death all night.' I could not recall ever seeing a Sikh with so much fear in his eyes. From our childhood, we were made to believe that Sikhs were very courageous people. I could not believe that a community that was so much a part of mainstream India had been made to feel so marginalized, helpless and lonely.

Our procession moved towards Ashram after crossing Bhogal. The scene there was very grim. There were some tough-looking men standing by the side of the road giving us hateful looks and refusing to talk to us. We heard a command from the gathered thugs, 'Keep moving. Do not stop here. Move on. Next time you will come to us for votes.' None of us wanted to argue with them because the atmosphere was tense, and the consequences could be dire. By the time we reached Lajpat Bhawan, all of us felt that a peace march did not do much for a city still seething with hatred for the Sikhs. We needed to do something more constructive.

News trickled in from various parts of Delhi that Sikhs were abandoning their homes and moving to gurudwaras or setting up camps in schools and college buildings. There had been large-scale looting of their homes and other properties. The most shocking stories were of the brutal killings. Sikhs had been burnt alive, their hands tied with wire and a tyre dropped around their necks, poured petrol on them and then set alight. This news shook me completely. I felt sick to my stomach.

These were barbaric acts being committed by the citizens of Delhi on their own people. I had read the stories of Nadir Shah and Taimur's invasions of Delhi, of their killing and looting of its citizens, but these were not medieval times. Here the killers and the killed were both from the same country, from the same city. In 1857, when the British army captured Delhi from the Indian freedom fighters, the British government ordered the killing of every Indian male in the city. In 1984, it was Indians killing Indians.

The next morning, a small meeting of concerned citizens was called at Lajpat Bhawan to form a steering committee. I joined as one of the committee members. The people present at the meeting were from all walks of life, all there because of their concern about the plight of the Sikhs. The core group consisted of social activists, bureaucrats, journalists, photographers, college professors, filmmakers, students and everyday people. We hardly knew each other and had never worked together, but everyone there shared a united purpose— to help the Sikh community of Delhi in their time of need. The Servants of India Society, headed by Balak Ram, had its offices at Lajpat Bhawan and owned larger premises with a big lawn, a large hall and some rooms. Balak Ram was very kind and offered the entire space of Lajpat Bhawan to house our operation, an outreach programme for Sikhs in the camps in the trans-Yamuna areas and places in west Delhi.

Responsibilities were divided between two groups: one tasked to find out about the needs of the people in terms of food, clothing and shelter; and the other to work on a report on this entire tragedy. Ravi Nair, an old friend, came up with a name for this: Nagrik Ekta Manch.

The day the Sikh population was under attack, no authorities were visible in the city. Indira Gandhi's funeral was to take place on the third day after her assassination, so the officials and the bureaucracy were busy with arrangements for the funeral and for VIPs arriving from around the world.

Those days of November were surreal times; the streets of Delhi were deserted, devoid of any security personnel. News of killing and looting came from various colonies across the Yamuna River as All India Radio simultaneously broadcast commentary about the funeral preparations.

There were no leaders to help the citizens, and the Opposition was almost invisible. We wanted to reach out to someone, any known face, to ask for security to reach the areas of Kalyanpuri and Challa Gaon in East Delhi. We worried about the violence that had happened in those areas the previous night. Someone reported that a group of Opposition leaders was meeting in the bungalow of a member of Parliament near Prithvi Raj Road. We rushed there immediately and barged into the meeting. The leaders there were caught unawares and visibly displeased.

Present at the meeting were, among others, Chandra Shekhar, Chiman Bhai Patel, Madhu Dandavate and George Fernandes. We asked them for help in getting military units to Kalyanpuri and Chilla Gaon. Chandra Shekar's immediate reaction was, 'No, we do not want to be accused of disturbing the funeral of the prime minister.' I said, 'Oh! I'm sorry that we have disturbed your meeting.' It turned into a small showdown between the leaders and us. As we were about to leave, Madhu Dandavate suddenly got up, picked up his small notebook from the table and said, 'Wait! I am coming with you.'

With him in one of our cars, we drove straight to 1 Safdarjung Road, the official residence of Indira Gandhi, the very place where she was assassinated. It was surrounded by security, guarding an empty house. We stopped at the gate, not knowing whom to ask to meet. To our surprise, Arun Nehru, the minister for internal security, emerged with a Nehru cap in hand, heading for Teen Murti Bhawan for the final funeral procession of Indira Gandhi, which was shortly to begin. When he saw us, he stopped. Noticing Madhu Dandavate, he asked why we were there. Before Dandavate could answer, Nandita Haksar replied, 'I am Nandita Haksar. We know that there have been killings and looting in Kalyanpuri and Challa Gaon. We want you to order some military to that area.' Arun Nehru said he would immediately send out an order and rushed off for the funeral. Nandita shouted back, 'We are taking you on your word!' Within an hour we heard on the radio that the military had been ordered to reach the two areas.

As winter approached and the cold set in, an appeal was made to the people of Delhi to donate clothes, blankets and food for the displaced Sikh population. Lajpat Bhawan was converted into a full-fledged social service centre. It was heartening to see the people of Delhi rise to the occasion in response to our call. Initially, donations only trickled in, but soon the quantities snowballed. Lajpat Bhawan was filled with all kinds of materials. As the donations came in bulk, a big store was created to house all the goods. The Nagrik Ekta Manch was active in many areas of operation, so eventually multiple groups were created to handle different responsibilities: food and clothing, transport, medical support, documentation, press and publicity, for example. A big notice board was erected listing what articles were required, with the contact telephone numbers of the people handling donations below. There were no cell phones then, so only the residential numbers of the steering committee could be supplied. We opened an emergency bank account to deal with the cash donations that were pouring in.

A large group of volunteers would fan out in the morning to the various camps across the city and return in the evening to Lajpat Bhawan for the debriefing session. Each group would report on what work had been done, what they had seen and what was needed in each camp. The preparations for the next day would be planned based on these discussions before everyone dispersed for the night.

As the work continued, fresh problems cropped up needing immediate handling. An improvised fully functional organization emerged organically, and the Nagrik Ekta Manch began working round the clock. More and more people from the city joined in to help. It was hard to believe that the same city which had been brutalizing its own citizens so recently was now showing great compassion in helping those affected by the violence.

From the stories that emerged about the violence, fingers were pointed at the Congress (I) for its role in the violence in East Delhi and West Delhi. At one of the evening meetings, one of the volunteers, a young research scholar, reported a story from Challa Gaon in East Delhi where, allegedly, a list of Sikh residents was obtained from the ration shops.

As our workload increased, I was put in charge of transport. This meant that it was my job to make sure that the supplies reached the camps every morning in time. We were running short of vehicles to manage our operations, but a novel solution to address the shortage emerged. Many office-going people offered us their vehicles during work hours. We would pick up their cars, use them during the day and return them by 5.30 p.m. The logistics were complicated because we needed licensed drivers, and sadly I was not one. Many people also offered the services of their chauffeurs along with their cars, and on weekends many car owners drove themselves.

Many people came to our office to check whether we were actually doing the work we claimed to do. We could understand why. There were many stories of people collecting donations on false promises. We encouraged people to come and participate in the work so they could see the magnitude of the tragedy for themselves.

Being in charge of transport, I was stuck at the base camp. However, I desired to visit the camps myself to witness the reality of the situation first-hand. So, one day I went in one of the vans carrying relief materials to the Farsh Bazaar camp in a faraway part of East Delhi. The Farsh Bazaar camp was located in a newly constructed police residential quarter. It was sheer wisdom on the part of the police officer in charge of this thana to permit the fleeing Sikhs to take shelter in the empty police quarter. This compassionate police officer had instructed his men to aid the helpless women, children and old people who poured in for shelter.

To my utter shock, when I reached the camp in my open travel tempo carrying supplies of food, towels and soaps, a crowd of Sikh refugees ran behind the open vehicle and looted everything from it in a matter of a few minutes. They fought with each other, pulled and pushed and cursed at one another, and the tempo was emptied right before my eyes in no time at all. For a moment I was very upset and angry, but I did not say a word. I realized that these people had nothing, and perhaps for days had not even eaten or had a bath. That the peaceful and brave community of Sikhs has been reduced to this disturbed me very much. I could not bear it. I came to know that this kind of incident had happened before too. I stood alone, not knowing what to do next. One elderly Sardarji who had watched the entire episode, was looking at me. He came forward and apologized for this unruly behaviour on the part of the others, and in a very dignified way said to me, 'Please try to understand this tragedy. All these Sikhs you see are poor but used to earn their living by doing petty jobs like making beds (manjas), carpentry, and painting houses. We are not educated. So, son, try to understand. We had to run to save the lives of our women, children and the honour of our women. We have lost our way.' He advised me to create a storeroom, which some of his friends would help to organize so that there was proper order in the camp. There was already one Lalaji who was feeding the camp people on his own with a simple meal of puri and sabzi. This was a great voluntary gesture on the part of a man who had no axe to grind with the Sikh community.

The principle of seva is a great tradition in the gurudwaras from the days of their gurus. Everyone visiting the gurudwara is fed; each person doing seva performs community service in various capacities. Here at this camp, the same principle was applied, and within two days all the supplies we brought were stored in a room and responsible members of the camp would distribute them to the needy. The initial anger, helplessness and sense of loss were temporarily contained. But the psychological trauma of the pogrom ate them from the inside. Their loss of faith and trust in others was apparent in every conversation one could manage to have with them. Providing the necessary things to help them survive as possible, and easy, but healing their deep psychological wounds was not. Hate and humiliation at the hands of their own countrymen baffled them. One had to be very careful when any conversation about the riots took place with them.

One day, it happened that my wife Anjali, being a paediatrician, went as part of a medical team to some of the camps. Some BBC crew members were also visiting the camps. While the doctors examined and treated the patients, Anjali was asked by the anchor person of the BBC crew what kind of diseases she was mostly treating. As she was about to reply, a young Sikh man pounced on her suddenly from nowhere, yelling, 'You are lying. No medicines are being given here.' He accused her, on camera, of not supplying medicines and then switched to the subject of the violence that had taken place. 'All those who are coming here to the camp are all government agents, and no help is being provided,' he yelled. This young man's outburst upset the entire team of doctors, and they wanted to discontinue their work. They did not appreciate working in this hostile atmosphere. It took a lot of convincing for these medical volunteers from various Delhi hospitals to continue their work.

As the work increased, we had a huge number of volunteers contributing their services in various areas. Some worked as drivers; some were busy at the base camp, collecting all kinds of articles from donors; and some were making parcels of essential items for distribution the next day at the camps. The Nagrik Ekta Manch had by now turned into a centre for collection, distribution and dissemination of information about the real conditions in the camps. We started making regular briefings to presspersons who wanted to get more stories about the tragedy from the people who were actually working in the camps. I kept going to the camps whenever I could get time from my work at the base camp.

One evening, during a debriefing, we realized that people donated clothes that the habitants of the camps didn't feel comfortable wearing. Sikh ladies needed kurtas and shalwars, not trousers. That day, I had seen a very elderly Sikh at the Farsh Bazaar camp with his head covered in a child's underwear instead of a proper turban. I asked this old man in broken Punjabi, '*Ae Paji, ay ki hai, pug nahi hai. Ye ki paa leya tuse?*' Whatever had he covered his head with? The old man in his helplessness replied, '*Kaka ki kariye. Ejeet haigena. Pug nahin hai par sar to dhakna haina?* It was a matter of honour for him to keep the head covered, using whatever he could find. I understood his pain. Among many communities in India, a turban symbolizes an individual's honour and respect. Here this

old man meant that both his honour and respect had been taken
away. To see him sitting in the corner with a child's underwear
on his head upset me very much. I recalled all my elder uncles in
Kashmir wearing graceful turbans on their heads. I understood
this old man's suffering. In the evening meeting, I narrated the
story to all, and it was decided to issue an urgent appeal for
turbans, kurtis, shalwars, dupattas and *tambis*. As a practice, the
appeal was put on the notice board with some of our telephone
numbers, should anyone want to get in touch with us or needed
any clarifications.

After two days, late in the night, I got a call from someone
saying, in a solid Punjabi accent, 'Sir, are you Raina sahab?
I have come with a truck of turbans, kurtas, shalwars and
dupattas. My sahib gave me your telephone number, and I have
to report to you.' I asked him, 'Where are you with your truck?'
He was near the All-India Institute of Medical Sciences, on the
main road. I asked him to wait for me there, and I would meet
him within twenty minutes to take him to the base camp. Since
my house was in Defence Colony, not very far from AIIMS,
I rushed to meet him. I asked him to follow my car to Lajpat
Bhawan. Upon reaching there, I asked if he had had dinner.
He said, 'Sir, you do not have to worry about me. I am going to
be with you as long as you need me and my truck. You do not
have to worry about my food, stay or fuel. I will manage all that
myself.' I asked him who had sent him and from which part of
Punjab he had come. He replied that his sahib had told him not
to reveal his name or his whereabouts. He was here to work for
us, and that was what was important.

For a moment I could not comprehend what he was saying,
and I just could not believe my eyes. I looked at the truck. It
was a large truck carrying everything we had asked for. It was
such a relief to see such a huge quantity of the stuff we had been
asking for the camps. The truck driver worked with us for many

weeks, delivering all kinds of things to the camps across the city. This truck was a boon, but to this day I do not know who sent him. Whenever I remember him, I ask myself, 'Is this what *seva* in the Sikh religion is all about? Is this what is called *guptdaan*, secret donation?'

The November cold had settled in. Now we needed blankets and razais for the camps. Again, we put up notices on our board. We had calculated exactly the number of blankets that would be needed at each camp. By now the volunteers at each camp, along with the elder advisors, had organized things so well that there was none of the strife among the inhabitants that we had seen in the initial days of the riots.

A very real problem lay before us—how to ensure at least one blanket for each inmate of each camp? We could take a smaller number of blankets or razais and distribute them to some and wait for more to arrive, but this step would invite trouble and anger among the camp people, and that could lead to violence and distrust between the community and the volunteers of the Nagrik Ekta Manch. We had collected 100 blankets, but this was not sufficient to distribute in even one of the camps, so they sat at our base camp at Lajpat Bhawan as we waited and prayed for more blankets to come.

One morning, a large van rolled in with a large number of lovely-looking imported blankets. With it came a very imposing, elite-looking lady who met me and introduced herself as a senior executive from some European embassy. She wanted to donate these blankets but was not ready to part with them without a foolproof assurance that the blankets would be distributed to the really needy. She went to the extent of telling me, 'What is the assurance that you guys will not take these fine blankets for your personal use? After all, they are imported blankets.' I controlled my anger and responded, 'You can come with us and distribute them yourself.' She didn't want to do that.

I finally told her that she had to trust us, but she would not accept that either. Finally, we told her that we could not accept her contribution and that she would have to take her stuff back as we needed to attend to more urgent work. She left with all the blankets, and our frustration grew worse.

We needed 800 blankets and we had only 400. In total, we needed 1200 blankets for the Farsh Bazaar camp. Those days, disappointment and helplessness had become our companions. Surprisingly, that same day, just an hour or so after the European lady had left, an elderly man walked into our office and asked how he could help. In my utter frustration I told him, 'Can you give us 800 blankets?' The gentleman asked, 'Where can I get 800 blankets?' 'The Khadi Bhandar, Delhi, has got them,' I replied. To my surprise, he said that his assistant, who was standing next to him, would accompany us to the Khadi Bhandar store and pay for the 800 blankets we required to distribute at the camps. I almost froze. I could not believe what he had said. I offered him a seat, which he politely refused, but inquired further as to what else we needed. I explained to him our major problem with transport, as we were using borrowed vehicles. He immediately offered us two Ambassador taxis. All we had to do was to sign the vouchers at the end of the day and the rest he would take care of. I could not believe that this simple-looking gentleman just walked into our small office and resolved all our issues within minutes. As he was leaving, I thanked him. All he said was, 'You're all doing good work. Keep it up. You will be rewarded in the future.' He said he had been a refugee after Partition and had possessed nothing at the time. But with God's grace and his own determination, he had made enough wealth for himself. He felt and understood the pain of being in a refugee camp. Then he left. He did not reveal his name or his business, but I saw him leaving in a very luxurious car.

My friend, actor and famous painter Manjeet Bawa, who happened to be a Sikh, had cut his hair long before. He visited often during those days of crisis as he could not be identified as a Sikh and so could move freely in the city. He met me in the office to inquire about what things were needed. Since the problem of supplying the Farsh Bazaar camp with blankets had been solved, we were now concentrating on collecting blankets for the other camps. Manjeet Bawa came with the message that Ajit Kaur, the well-known Punjabi short-story writer and her daughter Arpana, an eminent painter, had purchased razais and were bringing two tempos full of them to distribute in the camps. But again, the same problem as with the European lady cropped up. Bawa said the Kaurs were not sure that these contributions would reach the people they were intended for. It was difficult to find out who was fake and who was genuine. Many groups had sprung up all over Delhi, all claiming to work for the Sikhs.

Ajit and Arpana Kaur did arrive with two tempos packed with razais. It was a huge relief to see so many. Ajit Kaur, in her typically blunt fashion, asked me, 'Raina, how are you sure that these razais will reach the right people?' These questions were saddening and frustrating for me to hear, but then again, human nature being what it is, she was demanding some kind of surety from me, which was fair. For a moment I did not have any answer, but I wanted these two tempos of razais. I suggested to her that she and her daughter go with the tempos to one of the camps and supervise the distribution themselves. She replied to me, 'Do not think I doubt your integrity.' My immediate response was, 'No, it is not only about me, but also about our group. We are trying to do our best, and please believe me, it would be good for you also to see the conditions in these camps. You are a writer, and who knows what may come out of your pen. I think you need to visit and witness with your own eyes the scale of the tragedy.' Finally, she agreed and left our base camp, accompanied by one of our volunteers and followed by two tempos of razais. I was relieved that the razais were finally going to reach the camp.

I went again to the Farsh Bazaar camp in a jeep carrying regular supplies. As the supplies were unloaded, one young woman, almost dehydrated, with froth coming out of her mouth, came running towards me, begging for help. At first, I could not understand what she was saying, as she was speaking a dialect of Punjabi different from what I was familiar with. A relative of hers explained that she had heard that someone in another camp had spotted her children, and she wanted me to help her rescue them and bring them to this camp. I asked her how she knew that her children were in another camp. She said that a person had come from that camp and let her know. She asked one of her kinsmen to go with me in the jeep and fetch her little ones from there. She had been separated from her children for almost a week since the riots had started. She was very weak, perhaps had not eaten for days, and in her agitation collapsed. After reviving her, I gave my jeep to her kinsman and asked him to go and bring her children back. I stayed with the woman. We got some food for her, but she refused to eat until she could meet her kids. She kept calling me 'Veera [brother]'.

While we waited, she told me the story of the day her clan was attacked and how all the members of this large family had to run away to save their lives. In the confusion, she could not find her own children and landed here in this camp with other members of her baradari.

We waited for a considerable period of time for the jeep to return, and fear started to grip my mind. Suppose her children were not found, what would this poor woman do? Waiting with my fingers crossed for almost two hours, I finally saw in the distance the silhouette of a jeep coming towards the camp. She rose like a hungry tigress with renewed hope, reciting verses from the Gurbani, eyes fixed on the jeep. As the vehicle came closer to us, I listened to her recitation, worried. But I also hoped that this Jeep was indeed bringing her children back and this young woman would be reunited with them. Finally, we saw some young people alight from the Jeep. Many young boys, adults and some middle-aged men, nearly eighteen in all, popped out of the small Jeep. The young mother recognized her three children and ran towards the Jeep, embracing them in great joy. The reunion felt like a celebration, even though in reality they had arrived in another refugee camp. Who knew how long or how much more they would have to suffer?

In their joy, they forgot about me. I watched them for a few minutes and then headed back to the base camp.

On another day, I got a chance to go to the Sham Lal College camp in East Delhi. The condition of the camp was filthy, and I had with me UNESCO experts to advise us about mass sanitization methods and hygiene-related issues. As I walked across the lawns of the college, I spotted under a tree a woman named Baby, who used to be in charge of costumes at the National School of Drama, sitting with her family as refugees in the camp. This ever-smiling young girl had always been a delight to work with at NSD. Here she was, thrown into an open-air shelter, not knowing how long she would be there. Before I could ask her how she had landed there, I saw another friend of mine, Bedi, from the National School of Drama administration. To my shock, he had chopped off his long hair to save his life. Bedi revealed that the mobs had come to his house intending to kill him, but before that, in panic and fear, he had cut his hair. That had saved his life. I could not say anything and was silent for some time. All I could say was if they needed anything they should ask for it, but they didn't ask for anything.

That night, at home, Bedi's face appeared in front of me, his shabbily chopped-off hair like a mask of death staring at me. I could not sleep. What must he have gone through that dreadful night of 31 October? How many Sikhs must have cut their hair in hopelessness? What did that signify? My phone rang, and as I picked it up a theatre friend from the trans-Yamuna area informed me that Bhag Singh had been killed, burnt alive. I went numb. Bhag Singh was just a carpenter, working at Delhi Doordarshan in the department of sets and art direction—a hard-working, tough, confident Sardar who did not care about anything except his work and his wages. He made sets for our plays and did this service for many theatre groups for minimal remuneration. With his relaxed attitude, he was an asset to the amateur theatre movement in Delhi. All the theatre people loved him and depended on him. Even if they could not pay him, he would not let them down.

He was killed because of his overconfidence and trust, which he had cultivated over the years through hard work. Perhaps he believed that nothing would happen to him, so when the thugs came into his gali, he had come out, fearlessly scolding the attackers. But they caught him, beat him, tied his hands with a metal wire behind his back, put a tyre around his neck, poured petrol on his body and burned him alive. I dropped the phone without saying a word to the caller.

The goons had played the dance of death at the gates of Delhi with impunity.

My friend Madan Gopal Singh, now a renowned Sufi singer, linguist and film scholar, was stuck in his *barsati* flat in the Delhi University area. All his friends could do was to call him every hour to find out how he was and how they could help him. One day, when I was on the phone talking to him, he asked me to find out about his parents who lived in Mansarover Gardens in West Delhi. I didn't know this area, so he gave me the address and directions to the house. The next morning, I rode a couple of buses and finally reached their home. His father, Shree Harbhajan Singh, was an eminent Punjabi poet and scholar of Punjabi literature under whom many Punjabi scholars had done their doctoral theses. No nameplate hung on the main gate of the newly constructed house, perhaps removed for obvious reasons. There weren't many neighbours around the house because it was a new housing colony. I met Madan's parents. Their body language was stiff, but fortunately, they were safe. After an hour or so, I left the house and rang Madan to tell him that his parents were well. I asked him when he could leave his area, but he was not sure. There it was very tense, and coming out safely didn't seem possible. He wanted to stay back. After two or three days, Manjeet Bawa went to Madan's flat in his jeep, picked him up and brought him to the Lajpat Bhawan base camp.

I remember Madan's face that day. It had a different landscape painted over it. I cannot describe what I read on his face and in his eyes. When we sat together, we hardly talked. He spent the next two nights at our house in Defence Colony. All he asked for was a book to read at night. He picked up a book but didn't sleep all night. We only talked about superficial things. The expression on his face bothered me. I didn't know what he was thinking. From those days of the riots, Madan's face and the look in his eyes changed forever. It isn't the face I knew before 31 October 1984, though he remains a warm and affectionate friend.

Madan and I met during the performances of some of my plays around Mandi House. We would have brief conversations about theatre happenings in Delhi. During the shooting of *Satah se Uthtaaadmi*, a film by Mani Kaul based on the works of Muktibodh, we grew close. He had joined the film unit at Bhopal for some days and immediately became part of the unit. After a long day of shooting, Mani would take out his *tanpura* and start his *dhrupad riyaaz*. In his typical way, he would persuade everyone to follow his improvisations. Since those days my friendship with Madan had grown into a deep bond.

Recollecting the Madan of 1984 and now, it seems he has swum across many oceans and many cultures, and this change perhaps came to him from the experiences of 1984 when Sikhs were singled out for crimes they did not commit.

As the days passed, fresh problems emerged in the camps. The inhabitants of these camps were ordinary Sikhs, many of them very poor. They wanted to communicate with their relatives in Punjab and other distant places. They wanted at least one message to reach their loved ones to say they were alive had survived the horrors of the communal violence and were now in the refugee camps.

At our debriefing in the evening, the problem of sending these messages was discussed. We realized that their families and relatives would have no clue whether their Delhi relatives were alive or dead. Unfortunately, no one in the camps could write in Gurmukhi. A call was sent to the people of Delhi for those who could write Punjabi in the Gurmukhi script to come forward to help the inmates. The letter writing began after a couple of days when the atmosphere in the city had cooled a bit.

Soon a large number of young students, girls and boys and many adults, arrived at our base camp, ready to go to the camps to write postcards and letters dictated by the victims of the riots. The general mood in the camps shifted. This activity helped in many ways. First, the victims poured out their pain while dictating their stories. The stories gave goosebumps to the listeners. There were tearful eyes on both sides. It turned into a sort of catharsis for the victims, the depth and magnitude of this tragedy now felt by them in totality. The letter-writing exercise was like an epic being unfolded and narrated by a huge number of eyewitnesses. It was a violent and bloodthirsty act of oppression by the majority and reminded me of the Greek tragedy, *The Trojan Women*. It reminded me of my grandmother, who had told me stories of people during the days of Partition when she had witnessed the riots in Rawalpindi.

Though the violence continued for almost a week, gradually the city limped back to some degree of normality. The transport vehicles started plying on the roads and people returned to work. The camps continued to function, but the government was sending signals for the camps to be closed. They wanted the Sikhs to go back to their homes but didn't realize that they didn't feel safe to do so. The idea of sending them back was an absurd attempt by the government to save face politically.

We continued our work in the camps as usual. Rumours swelled that a large number of Sikhs would strike back in Delhi and would attack with guns and swords. One night I came home quite late. My neighbours on duty that night stopped me at the main gate of our block. At first, they questioned me about why I was there. When it finally dawned on them that I lived only four houses away from the picket as a tenant, they let me into the colony. I was surprised at this new development—of people guarding their homes. When I asked them what it was all about, they gave me the same story about the Sikhs coming and avenging the attacks on them by killing Hindus in the city. I laughed at their ignorance and at the disinformation they were acting on. I told them that the entire Sikh population of the country was in shock and mourning. 'Do you people have any idea what has happened to them?' I asked. Silence lingered in the air, for they had believed all the rumours but had never ventured to come out and see for themselves the plight of the Sikh community. While it was true that the Sikhs living in my colony had been rescued by their neighbours, it was also true that many people were whispering that they deserved this because they were killing Hindus in Punjab and that could not be overlooked. While taking leave of them, I said to them on a lighter note, 'Please go home and relax. No one is going to come and attack us. And finally, do not believe these motivated and false reports.'

In the morning, when Anjali and I were about to leave, my son Anant, now about two years old, did not respond to my goodbye. He sat in a corner in silence. We had a domestic help, Nana, who took care of the children during the day. When I asked him why he wouldn't talk to me, his replay was straightforward: 'I do not see you both. And I'm not talking to you.' This little child was missing his parents, and we were hardly spending any time with him these days. Anjali would leave for the medical camps to see patients there, and I either went to the base camp or the refugee camps. Feeling guilty, Anju and I discussed this problem with Nana. It was decided that I would take Anant with me to the base camp while Aditi could stay in the care of Nana. Anju would leave later for medical work at the camps.

So tiny Anant Raina became the youngest volunteer at the base camp, spending his days among a large number of uncles and aunts. He ran all over the lawns of Lajpat Bhawan, where supplies and clothing were laid out for sorting and parcelling into packages for the camps. Anant enjoyed being amongst the volunteers, who indulged him a lot. He would play with them while they worked to make food and other packages. Sometimes he would lie on the piles of stuff on the lawn; sometimes he would pick up a cloth and hand it to some auntie who would give him a kiss or a hug and bless him. Anant's tense body language changed here. He relaxed, finding confidence and enjoying his day with the people in the camp. Many a time, I would find him in the lap of some lady or man I didn't even know. At some point in the afternoon after his lunch, I would spot him sleeping on a heap of clothing. Anju and I were relieved of the guilt of neglecting our kids. For Aditi, Anju returned home early to be with her and take care of her until she went to sleep.

At some time during all these days of working at the camp, my friend, the late Ashok Jaitley, a civil servant from the Jammu and Kashmir cadre who had served in Kashmir in various senior positions, such as chief secretary and even advisor to the Governor of Jammu and Kashmir during the height of terrorism in the state, asked me to make a play on this tragedy. I replied to him to say that I did not see any play performance in this tragedy. I saw it as a shame for my nation. And, honestly, I felt better serving and helping the victims rather than making a theatrical event out of their plight. This was hardly the time to do all that when one could not be objective enough when one was so involved with the tragedy. Plays could happen later when one gained some objectivity.

As time passed, many significant political events occurred post the Indira Gandhi times. Her son Rajiv Gandhi, as the prime minister of India, released many political prisoners in Punjab who had been imprisoned in the post-Operation Blue Star era under the shadow of the Bhindranwale phenomenon. Punjabi political aspirations had grown mired between several factions. Nothing was resolved. One day, I got a call from a Nagrik Ekta Manch volunteer asking me to come to Dashmesh Colony, next to Pamposh Colony in South Delhi, to the house of a Sikh gentleman who had worked with us. The purpose of this meeting was to meet Sant Longowal, the Sikh saint leader, who had also been released from prison with Barnala. They had come to Delhi to thank the people who had helped and taken care of Sikhs during the riots. Most of the Nagrik Ekta Manch committee members had reached in time for the meeting. The drawing room was packed with people. Sant Longowal was seated with his eyes closed, as if in meditation. He looked quite impressive in the lotus posture of the Buddha. Barnala sat next to him. I was told by some committee members that I would have to deliver the vote of thanks.

When the meeting started, the owner of the house, a Sikh and an ex-Air Force officer, welcomed Santji and Barnala. He talked about our work during the riots in the camp. After this,

Barnala addressed us. He talked about the injustice inflicted on the Sikhs for years and about the present situation in Punjab. All this time, Sant Longowal sat in his Buddha posture with his eyes shut. Finally, Barnala asked him to speak a few words.

Sant Longowal opened his eyes, ran his gaze over the place and the people present and spoke. He thanked us all for saving and helping the Sikhs at a time when no one in the world was there for their aid. He elaborated on the injustices perpetrated on his *qaum* over the centuries, and the justice needed to heal the wounds of the Sikhs. Again, he closed his eyes and went back into meditation. Now, it was my turn to give the vote of thanks. I had never done anything like this before and was quite tense. I addressed Sant Longowal directly, saying, 'Santji, I think you should not thank us for anything. What we, the people of Delhi, did was nothing except what we would do for our brothers and sisters. What we did is what is expected of every citizen to do when another citizen is in danger and needs support and security. That is the tradition we have learned from our freedom movement, where all faiths fought together for the liberation of this country. So, it was our duty, and we did not think about doing this so that someone would come and thank us as if we were different from them. This, us and them, is not relevant, we were working for ourselves.

'Therefore, may I humbly request and remind you that now that you're out of prison and picking up the pieces of the Punjab tragic landscape, you have a big responsibility. For God's sake, do not play politics with the Sikh faith. When you go to the bhog ceremonies of the militants these days, it gives a dangerous communal colour to the entire problem, and then it becomes hard for people like us to work beyond faith and caste. God forbid if again this fire is lit, let me tell you, people like us will be the first victims, and the road will be cleared for a new massacre to happen. So, Santji, with folded hands I beg you to tread your path carefully for all of us.'

Santji opened his eyes and looked at me but did not say a word, and the meeting came to an end. Before leaving, Barnala tried to explain to me the purpose of their attending the bhog ceremonies, but I did not say anything to him because I did not agree with him on this.

We continued working for about three months helping the displaced Sikhs of Delhi until things settled down. Before finally leaving Nagrik Ekta Manch, I realized that our group had people who professed different political beliefs. Soon these schisms began unfolding, and often in our discussions I could see the differences cropping up very clearly. One thing that I must admit is that all the members worked with honesty and compassion despite their political differences.

Looking back, I think I was politically naive and, in the beginning, could not see the political contours of this big group. One day, when the discussion felt very charged, I couldn't take it anymore. I said to the group, 'I do not think the public would have donated so freely to us to do our work or would have trusted us if they had known that we have so many political differences between us. We did our immediate job to help and support. Turning this hard work into a political outfit will be a dishonest decision.'

The Nagrik Ekta Manch gradually melted away. We donated the many remaining items we had to the victims of a riot in Gujarat. Most of the group members remained friends and met occasionally. After some time, we all grew busy with our own personal and professional work and moved on. For me, this experience changed me and my outlook towards life. I had never seen a communal riot like this in my entire life.

After the Sikh Riots

In 1976, during the Emergency, I worked on a play, an adaptation of Bertolt Brecht's *Caucasian Chalk Circle*, with the newly founded Punjab Drama Repertory, which was the first state repertory in the country. We had drafted a written manifesto of ambitious theatre projects for the state of Punjab. This initiative could lead to a model for other states keen to set up their own repertory companies for theatre projects in their own vernacular languages.

Once this play was performed, it gathered its own momentum and became highly successful. We toured all over Punjab and many parts of India. The play had a powerful musical score, which was a hit and remained so across generations. The musical score was developed after thorough research and documentation of folk music and other ritual traditions in the interiors of Punjab. I helped in the selection of actors and other technical people. We had to pick the best and most promising young talent from rural Punjab to form the main body of the repertory. Punjab State Drama Repertory's very first production of *Parai Kukh* (Caucasian Chalk Circle) became a milestone in the history of Punjabi theatre. Thousands of people watched this young repertory's performances, and people loved the play. Regular invitations poured in from various organizations inviting us to perform. In Kolkata, I remember performing at a maidan on the eve of Baisakhi. The entire Punjabi population of Kolkata was present at the massive maidan, and the performance was a big, big success.

But it was also the time of Indira Gandhi's Emergency. Being young and having just started my career, I did not understand the undercurrents or the political intrigues doing the rounds. I was too immersed in the success of my Parai Kukh production and had no clue about the things that were happening behind the scenes politically.

Unfortunately, after twenty-six performances to packed audiences, the government of Punjab banned the play, even though it had itself produced it. I was made 'persona non grata'. I didn't know what that meant but was very curious to know and wanted to fight it out with the government of Punjab. Some of my mentors explained to me that since it was Emergency in India and since people had no fundamental rights, it wouldn't bring any good to me to do so. I still didn't understand all this, so I took a bus to Chandigarh the same night and met the principal secretary of the Punjab government in his office in the morning. I made my protest known to him. I even told him that there was a joke making the rounds in Delhi that the Punjab government had issued an arrest warrant against German playwright Bertolt Brecht. The officer smiled but did not say much. Then he asked me, 'When did you arrive in Chandigarh?'

'This morning,' I replied.

He continued, 'Did you go anywhere, or to any other place besides my office?'

I replied, 'No, I did not.'

Then he looked straight at me and said, 'You know, you're like my son. And may I advise you not to go anywhere in Punjab, otherwise I will have to arrest you. Take a bus back to Delhi. You are persona non grata, which means I have orders to arrest you.'

I remained silent as he continued, 'I've seen your play and enjoyed it. It is an important theatrical production. But unfortunately, your own well-known theatre friends, just out of jealousy and meanness, have complained to the chief minister about your play.'

He pulled open a drawer in his office table and showed me a handwritten script of the play filled with foul language and swear words. I could not believe my eyes. I said, 'But there are no such words in the play.'

He replied, 'I know, in fact I told your director of culture affairs to throw some biscuits at these dogs before they damage this project. Today even my chief minister does not trust me. So, my advice to you, son, is to just quietly leave for Delhi, without anyone noticing.'

I was stunned. I asked him, 'Can you tell me who these people are?'

He said, 'You know them. Some of them are your seniors, and also some are eminent theatre personalities. You're very young, and you do not understand the cultural politics of theatre in Punjab. Be careful and don't move around here in Chandigarh.'

This made me realize that the state of Emergency checked even people like me just starting their careers. The banning of the play got me lots of sympathy from many people and from my mentors and teachers. Alkazi, director of the National School of Drama, was most understanding. We met in his office, and I explained everything to him. He even volunteered to take my case to Mrs Gandhi and said he would ask her to remove all the restrictions on the play and on me. That never happened as the screws of the Emergency tightened further and deeper.

Many years later, at the lawns of the India International Centre in New Delhi, someone called me by my name and said, 'Why, Raina sahab, don't you remember me?'

I replied, 'Of course, sir, I remember you.'

He said, 'No, you do not. Remember many decades back, you met me in my office in Chandigarh at the Punjab Government Secretariat when you had done a play which had been banned.'

I said, 'Yes, I do remember that meeting.'

He laughed and said, 'That officer who advised you to get out of Punjab before you were arrested was me.'

I exclaimed, 'No! Was that you, sir?' He laughed as he walked away. This fine bureaucrat and human being was N.N. Vohra. He had recently demitted office as Governor of Jammu and Kashmir. As the governor of that state, he had become very popular and had earned a lot of respect from the people of the state.

After a year or so of this, one day film-maker Saeed Mirza came to Delhi and announced that he was making a documentary on post-Blue Star Punjab and needed support. With my hands-on experience in Punjab and its people and my familiarity with its culture, I joined his unit as a volunteer. So did Madan Gopal Singh. The filming unit consisted of about ten people, including cameramen, sound recordists and other technicians. Suresh Jindal, who had produced films like Basu Bhattacharya's *Rajnigandha* and Satyajit Ray's *Shatranj Ke Khiladi*, was the producer of this film.

In 1985 June, we as a ten-member film team started travelling inside Punjab in a hired bus. It was a limited-budget project, which meant making sure we managed our meal breaks near some gurudwaras, where we could eat our lunch. For tea breaks, we would stop at some street stalls. During the shooting, we spent many nights in gurudwaras or even on the roadside. The only saving grace and luxury was an air-conditioned bus where we could relax during the very hot month of June. We drove all over Punjab, from village to village, talking to people on all sorts of topics, from agriculture to terrorism. At one point the unit decided to make me an interviewer. In the evenings, Madan, Suresh, Saeed and I would have very heated discussions that ended in sharply different stances on Punjab terror and the cult of Bhindranwale. Sometimes these discussions turned ugly, leading to angry exchanges between us, but the next morning, like good professionals, everything would be back to normal.

The film unit's first stop was Patiala. We had to shoot with the students in the evening in their hostel dining hall. There were Hindu and Sikh students waiting for us, around eighty of them, cracking jokes with each other while we set up our cameras. Once the cameras were positioned, there was a sudden silence. Saeed Mirza initiated a normal kind of discussion around the present situation in Punjab after Operation Blue Star. He posed another question to the students about their take on the assassination of Indira Gandhi and the anti-Sikh riots in Delhi.

Again, a long silence, longer than the earlier one. One could sense tension and anger among the Sikh students. Then one Sikh student stood up and started to talk about how Sikhs were brutally killed in Delhi and other places, and how there had been injustice against the Sikhs for a very long time. He blamed the Congress party for their ills. At that point, many Sikh boys joined in support of what this boy was saying, and gradually their responses zeroed in on us, a team of Hindu filmmakers pouring salt on their wounds.

At that point, the Hindu students began to respond. They complained about the Sikh boys' attitude towards them before Indira Gandhi's killing. They expressed resentment at the provocation and the taunts thrown at them by the Sikh boys every day in the refrain, 'What is the score today?' This slyly referred to the number of Hindus killed every day in Punjab.

When news of the anti-Sikh riots arrived from Delhi, the game reversed. The same refrain was thrown back at the Sikh students. 'What is the score today?' It was bizarre watching them discuss this game of scores. They were neither angry nor accusatory towards each other. At this point they were talking with great humour; it sounded strange and abnormal and unnerved the team.

The meeting grew tense as these young minds continued to express their helplessness. I thought I should intervene to tell them a few things that could perhaps help to heal their disillusionment. I addressed these students and said, 'It is not true that citizens of Delhi did not help or rescue Sikhs. In fact, enormous volunteer support came from the Hindus of Delhi, in cash and kind. There were large numbers of voluntary groups and organizations that worked relentlessly to save people when the Dance of Death happened in Delhi.'

At that point, a Sikh student got up to hug me and kiss my hands. I was surprised. He said, 'I've heard the name of this organization and about their work.' He revealed that he was caught with his parents in the Delhi riots. That experience had changed him completely. He said, 'I became a cut Surd.' He opened his turban and showed his hair, which was short and said, 'After that experience, I stopped cutting my hair, and now with the grace of Wahe Guru, it is growing back. I want to assert my identity as a Sikh in my own country.'

Now a strange silence and calmness pervaded the dining hall. It was quite late in the night, so in silence, we packed our cameras, and the boys began to go back to their hostel rooms. When I was about to exit the room, this Sikh boy came close to me and said, 'Sir, I really want to give you a hug and want to thank you for what you people did.' I was moved by his words. I felt I had received the biggest gift of my life from this young boy, and I gave him a very tight hug. We left together.

The next morning, Saeed wanted to interview some hard-core Khalistanis. But they were difficult to find. Madan Gopal Singh, through his family contacts, helped us through a lot of this difficulty. We were directed to meet a contact who would guide us to a certain location, and if the Khalistani agreed to talk we could possibly get an interview.

So, at the scheduled time, we arrived at the place, a mohalla, after negotiating our way through really narrow lanes. There a Sardar waited for us. He led us on his scooter, and after travelling through many more narrow and zigzagging lanes, we reached an ordinary brick house in the old city of Patiala. Here we had to wait for another fifty minutes, and we were still not sure whether the man we were to interview would show up or not. While waiting, we learned that this fellow could not move freely in the city as he was wanted by the police.

After a long wait, a young Sikh in an orange turban arrived, riding a pillion on a scooter. He was in a hurry and was tense, and upon meeting us, immediately started ordering us around. We had already fixed our camera, so he sat down facing it. Suddenly he got very upset and shouted, 'I'm not facing the camera. I will not show my face to the people. I will only show my back to the camera.' Finally, it was I, as his interviewer, who faced the camera.

As I started with the questions, he flatly refused to enter into any kind of question–answer conversation or any discussion. He rudely warned me, 'Ah, you, listen to me. Do not interrupt when I'm talking. You Hindu, you better listen to me.' Unnerved by his hostility, I kept quiet, and Saeed signalled to me to continue. For almost an hour, I sat silently facing the camera as his monologue continued. It was crazy and bizarre. I did not know how to respond to him, so I did not, whatever he said, but I also did not give a damn until he stopped his solo performance.

What he talked about in his monologue was what we already knew about Bhindranwale and his ideology. He was angry with the Arya Samaj people. He called them gaddars. His sense of history was convoluted. There was no chronology or consistency in his monologue. The funny thing was that our cameraman could not switch off his camera even to change tapes, so the camera stayed in recording mode even when it was not recording. Since the atmosphere around us was so overcharged, our cameraman on his own had quietly switched off the camera until the man stopped talking. It really ended up being a comic interlude which takes place in between the main scenes of a theatre performance.

After finishing his solo performance, the man left immediately. We all looked at each other. We did not know whether to laugh or to cry. We had recorded a full tape of his so-called interview, though the video had been switched off—it was his interpretation of the crisis and the demands of the Khalistanis. His presentation was filled with hatred and contempt for the state of India, but yes, one got an idea of and a small peek into the thinking of the Khalistanis from his monologue.

The next day, our bus started for Rode, the village Bhindranwale came from. We wanted to meet his family and see for ourselves what sort of upbringing he might have had. He was a person who had become an icon for Sikhs all over the world, a daredevil who waged an armed war against the state of India, and whose young men killed their opponents with impunity. The movement he unleashed had culminated in a nightmarish scenario of violence, killing, disappearances and tragedies.

While approaching Rode, we passed through many villages of mud houses, which was in stark contrast to the other villages in Punjab we had seen, where their affluence was on display. Here the peasantry had harvested their crops. In the morning, when we boarded the bus, I noticed a different driver at the wheel. I asked someone, 'Where is our driver, the one who was with us from Delhi? How did we manage another driver overnight?' He looked surprised and laughed, 'What? It is the same driver except that he has put on a turban today.' I retorted, 'But he was not Sikh.' Again he laughed and said, 'He's a cut Surd, and from now onwards, it is safer to be a Sikh and that is the reason why he has put on his turban to make it easier for him to drive in the interiors of Punjab.'

We reached Rode, a small village of mud houses surrounded on all sides by paddy fields, typical of rural Punjab. When we reached the Bhindranwale family home, a big group welcomed us—his uncles, his mother and his brother, who looked exactly like him. They served us cold water followed by tea. All the time I observed Bhindranwale's mother, who was like any Punjabi mother, very hospitable, kind and warm. I did not see any trace of anger or strain in her. She was going through her usual household routine while keeping an eye on us guests to see that we were properly looked after. I met one of his uncles, his *phoopha*, a farmer who had returned from harvesting his crops. There was a husk sticking to his body. He looked, in Neruda's words, like 'The Earth'. He was more communicative than the other family members. He told me that he had studied till FA (done after class ten for two years even called intermediate, before one qualifies for graduation in the old education system) in 1948, but when he could not get a job, he decided to work on his land.

Bhindranwale's real brother, whom I wanted to interview, declined politely, saying, 'I am a school teacher and these are all political issues, about which you should talk to my Babaji (his father, Sardar Joginder Singh), who is at the Golden Temple at Amritsar.' He showed me a small mud hut in their family compound that belonged to his brother, Bhindranwale. The hut was locked and could not be opened. While we talked, a summer dust storm stirred and within no time we were surrounded by a huge cloud of dust. We had to hide our camera and other equipment on the bus. We could not shoot anything here except on Saeed's instructions. Our cameraman took several shots of the village, the fields, the people and the dust storm. As we were leaving, one of the relatives attributed this dust storm to the phenomenon of Santji, which is Bhindranwale. No one used the past tense when they spoke about him. It was never 'he was' but always 'he is', meaning he was still alive for them. And they believed he would always be alive.

There was a conscious attempt to build a myth around the name of Bhindranwale as a person who never dies. They always addressed him as '*Santji jade sun*'.

Once the dust storm settled, we bid farewell to the Bhindranwale family that was living a simple village life even after one of their sons had created history by becoming part of the international debate on terrorism.

6

Amritsar

Our next destination was Amritsar, the epicentre of the Sikh
religion and Sikh politics. Here we had the major job of
acquiring a set of audio tapes of Bhindranwale's speeches. These
speeches had been banned from circulation but were secretly
sold recorded in cassettes. Another important job was to meet
with his father, Sardar Joginder Singh, who stayed at Golden
Temple premises and had emerged as one of the protagonists
of Sikh politics after Blue Star. In a way, with the statements he
had made, he had taken on the mantle of his son. In the media,
he had been touted as one of the major minds among the Sikh
leadership. His pictures appeared in all the media. He created
an impression of being a strong, intelligent and formidable
leader of the Bhindranwale faction of Sikh politics.

At the Golden Temple, we found Sardar Joginder Singh
in one of the rooms. All kinds of media people from various
places speaking a range of languages were there to talk to
him. He was an emerging star of Sikh politics. One of our
local contacts had arranged for us to meet him, but we had to
wait for hours outside his room in the summer heat of June.
I somehow managed to sneak in before our camera could be
brought in. There were many press persons in there, asking
him all kinds of questions. Singh was directly answering the

questions addressed to him in Punjabi, but the journalists who spoke only Hindi or English had to pose their questions to a Sardarji, Khanna, who seemed to be Joginder Singh's junior and was fluent in English.

I watched the journalist Ajay Bose, now a very senior media man, then representing *Sunday* or *India Today* as he interviewed Singh. He fired question after question at this Khanna in English, which were then translated for Sardar Joginder Singh into Punjabi. Singh was replying to Khanna in Punjabi, which Khanna would then translate into English for Ajay Bose. This exchange was hilarious and at one point I began to laugh. Ajay looked at me and asked, 'Why are you laughing?' I said, 'It is funny. What you asked in English was twisted and changed in Punjabi by Mr Khanna, and the replies Joginder Singh gave you get further changed when Khanna replies to you in English. It is all incongruous because neither your questions are reaching Joginder Singh, nor his replies accurately are reaching you. It is Khanna's question-answer session with you and not yours with Joginder Singh.' I do not know what Ajay did with that interview.

Finally, when our camera arrived in the room with the rest of the unit, the comedy continued. The moment Joginder Singh saw the tripod and camera, he perked up and, like any other actor, started arranging his Nishan Saheb badges on his blue cross-belt, which carried his kirpan, and straightened his posture, as if getting ready for a film shot. I had a cassette tape recorder with me to record our conversation. The moment the camera focused on him, I asked my first question, 'So, where are you going to take this movement of Bhindranwale's?' I asked this in my manageable Punjabi. Luckily, Khanna was not my intermediary to pose my question to him.

Sardar Joginder Singh took a long pause, and after deep thought, he replied in Punjabi, '*Je sada qaum haiga* [This must be my people].'

Then he suddenly stopped for a second and asked me, 'Do you agree that Sikhs are a qaum?'

I replied, 'You say whatever you have to say, don't ask me questions.'

He insisted, '*Tu manda hai ki nai manda, asi alag qaum hai?*'

Again, I insisted that my answer did not matter and that he should say whatever he had to say, but he would not budge from his stubborn insistence on getting his question answered.

Again, he asked the same question, this time insisting like a child, '*Manda hai ki nai. Bol, manda hai ki nai* [Do you agree? Tell me, do you agree]?'

I said, 'How does it matter.'

He repeated, '*Manda hai ki nai manda, bol, bol* [Do you agree or not, tell, tell]!'

Amused at his childlike insistence and in a light mode, I said, '*Nahi, Daji, nai manda* [No Daji, I do not agree].'

And that was it. He immediately switched off my cassette recorder and said, '*Ta main interview nai dena* [Then, I do not want to give the interview].'

That was the end of my interview with Bhindranwale's father. A large number of people present there could not stop laughing at our conversation. He brooded a bit and did not want to talk to anyone. This whole episode ended like a short comic sequence, and everyone was having fun and enjoying the childishness of this old man. Strangely, he was not upset or even angry but took vicarious pleasure in ending our conversation. Even I was amused and having fun with him, as one would with one's own grandfather or an elderly person, and he was enjoying his attempts to fix me with his rural wit.

My impression of Sardar Joginder Singh was as elderly, warm-hearted 'Tau' in a village who wanted to be taken seriously. A very innocent and honest man, purely rural, he did not have much understanding of the complexities of contemporary politics.

Preet Nagar

Next, we had to visit Preet Nagar, about thirty-five kilometres from Amritsar. Preet Nagar is a place beyond the second line of defence, very close to the Wagah border, and also quite close to Lahore in Pakistan. In fact, at the time of Partition, Preet Nagar was considered as belonging to Pakistan for about seven days until it switched to being part of India.

It was Sardar Gurbaksh Singh, an agricultural engineer who had studied in California, who established Preet Nagar in 1935 at a place which was in between Amritsar (the holy city) and Lahore (the cultural capital of undivided pre-partitioned Punjab). A unique man, he bought a huge piece of barren land where nothing was cultivated. In fact, locals believed it was a cursed land where ghosts and wild beasts lived. Harbouring a dream project for this land, he named it Preet Nagar (which literally means Love Town). It was still the time of undivided India. Singh created a village of art, culture, literature and craft. Preet Nagar soon became a great home for people like Balraj Sahni, Faiz Ahmed Faiz, Rajinder Singh Bedi, Achala Sachdev, Madanjeet Singh and Mulk Raj Anand. It is difficult to name a writer, theatre person or poet of those times who did not stay or visit here. They all contributed their creativity to build a contemporary, progressive North Indian Cultural Renaissance centre in undivided India.

The Punjabi magazine *Preet Lari* was launched here. This magazine became the favourite journal among the new, young authors who wrote in Punjabi. Along with the magazine, many craft workshops were also launched, making this place somewhat of a Shanti Niketan of north India. Rabindranath Tagore sent the vice-chancellor of Vishwa Bharati to visit Preet Nagar to get a first-hand report of the work happening there. Unfortunately, with Partition, this dream project of Preet

Nagar and *Preet Lari* started to crumble, as if its soul had been taken away.

I had visited this place before, in 1976, on my travels for the shows of *Parai Kukh*. At that time, I had met Sardar Gurbaksh Singh through his grandson Sumeet, a sweet and sensitive short-story writer. Sumeet was helping his father, Navtej Singh, an eminent Punjabi short-story writer, run *Preet Lari*. The entire family lived in a large house, together with Uma-ji, the unmarried daughter of Gurbaksh Singh.

When we reached Preet Nagar in the morning with our unit, we had an unexpected guest among us—M.J. Akbar, the well-known editor of *Sunday* magazine. Saeed Mirza and Suresh Jindal had told us that he might join the unit at some point, revealing that he was in some way part of the film, as a co-producer perhaps. Madan and I had never met him but were glad to know he would join us. I had read his book *The Siege Within* and had liked it. The book had grown quite popular, stirring chatter because its theme dealt with the enemy within the country which was tearing it apart internally.

I was visiting Preet Nagar after many years. Things had changed. The large family of Gurbaksh Singh had lost some of its lead intellectuals. Terrorism had impacted this house in such a way that a strange loneliness had descended on the place. Sardar Gurbaksh Singh had passed away. His son Navtej had died after a long battle with cancer. Sumeet, my friend, had been gunned down by Khalistani terrorists. In the family house now lived Sumeet's mother Pavel, the eldest son, who had returned from the USSR after many long years of study there, and his Russian wife. Sumeet had married Poonam, who had left her studies at the National School of Drama immediately after his killing. She now lived in Chandigarh, publishing *Preet Lari* with the help of Sumeet's younger brother.

When I entered the house, Sumeet's mother broke down and asked me, 'Where were you? You had said that I am like your son years back.' I had no answer.

After filming all around Preet Nagar, we finally interviewed Sumeet's mother. Her interview was very moving and upsetting. She talked about the great days at the Nagar when writers and artists came from far-off places and lived there for weeks. She had arrived here as a young bride and had joined the intellectual world of undivided Punjab, but gradually she saw that dream crumble. The first blow came with Partition, which broke links and contact with Lahore. Its impact affected Preet Nagar's activities. Then even our own state governments or the Central government did not have the time or the inclination to support this cultural space of great value it further deteriorated. The final blow came from the terror attacks, which took away her son and many other sons of Punjab, many writers, trade union leaders, poets and journalists. Anyone who did not agree with the Khalistanis was eliminated. Punjab was a sad place today, she lamented—artistically and intellectually a desert. Preet Nagar had paid a heavy price for its dreams, which now could never be revived. However, Sumeet's uncle, Hriday Pal Singh, had tried hard to keep things going.

Looking at her, I remembered Sumeet, who had taken me to the Wagah border. That day, when we reached Wagah, we had walked on the black tarmac of G.T. Road up to the gate, the last point on Indian territory. After that began the land of Pakistan. Between these two gates lay a few feet of road, called 'no man's land'. Sumeet pointed towards the city of Lahore, where his parents and his grandparents had lived. After a long pause, I said to him, 'Sumeet, one day we will cross this border and drive on your motorbike into the city of Lahore, and after having a good meal there we will come back to Preet Nagar again.' Many years later I did cross the border, with the actors of my Punjabi play *Buhe Bariyan*. I stopped at the same spot before the no man's land and remembered Sumeet.

After interviewing his mother, we talked to Sumeet's younger brother, who had been riding pillion on Sumeet's motorbike on the day of his killing. They were on their way to Amritsar when the Khalistani terrorists stopped them and shot Sumeet. They were just a mile or so away from the village. Sumeet's brother had run into the fields in panic. He saw Sumeet gunned down to the ground. The terrorists shot another round into Sumeet's neck, and he was gone. Sumeet seemed to have upset the Khalistanis with his writings in *Preet Lari* magazine.

Having spent the whole day with the family, the unit departed. It was hard to leave. My legs wouldn't allow me to move. I looked at Sumeet's mother, who perhaps understood my predicament. She came forward and quietly gave me a hug, saying, '*Jinda rahe puttar. Pher aana. Der na karna* [Stay alive, son. Come again. Soon].' Both of us had moist eyes. I could not say a word; my throat was completely choked.

We checked into a hotel to rest in an air-conditioned room, a relief after working and travelling long days and spending nights in all kinds of places. We had travelled right through the day in temperatures averaging 46 degrees Celsius, and the heat had exhausted us. After some rest at the hotel, we moved out in the early evening to visit one more family that we needed to interview. This family seemed to have some more information about the events that had taken place in Amritsar. At the interview were our crew of four—Saeed Mirza, Madan Gopal Singh, Suresh Jindal and I—with M.J. Akbar joining in.

We were received by the family with all the courtesy of a Punjabi household. This was a family of three: a husband, wife and their son. The husband worked as a doctor, the lady of the house was a professor of history at Guru Nanak Dev University, and the son was a student. After we had all settled down in the drawing room, the lady, realizing the purpose of our visit, started recollecting the days before Operation Blue Star and then the days after the operations. In her words, one could sense the hurt sentiments of the Sikhs for being singled out for the deeds committed by a few people who believed in violence and killing the people of other communities, first by the Indian state and then by the majoritarian Hindu nation. Her husband joined in. He said that even after such a tragedy, the Khalistanis had not succeeded in dividing the Sikhs and the Hindus of Punjab against each other for a very simple reason—they were blood relations. From the day of the Sikh Gurus, there was a tradition in most of the Hindu families that one son would always be raised as a Sikh while the others remained Hindu. In addition to being blood relations, both respected, revered and worshipped the Guru Granth Sahib, and the sacred text of the Sikhs, and treasured every gurudwara. On all auspicious occasions, both communities prayed at gurudwaras, particularly at the Harminder Sahib, the Golden Temple, the highest place of Sikh worship.

The family were critical of the violent operation of Blue Star. They felt it was sacrilege of the divine place of worship. The conversation that evening was filled with their accounts of those days. At one point, the history professor suddenly got up and left the room. We could not understand the reason for her sudden exit but kept the conversation going with her husband and son. She soon came back with a saffron cloth which had something wrapped in it. She unfolded the cloth, revealing a heap of dark black ashes, which were from the site of Operation Blue Star. She said they were the ashes of burnt articles like clothes, shoes and turbans picked up during and after the Blue Star operation. With a very serious look in her eye, she said, 'I am a historian, and I have kept this safely as evidence of that nightmare and of that aggression against our faith.' We all looked at the ashes, speechless, and the family stared at us. I looked at Madan, who appeared very perturbed by the ashes. He himself had endured a life-threatening experience during the Delhi Sikh riots. I thought about the ramifications of this pain on the Sikhs.

Later in the night, we assembled for dinner in Suresh Jindal's room. The hangover of our visit to this family still lingered. When we settled for quick drinks, an agitated discussion started among us as to the reasons for the problems in Punjab. These reasons generally fell on terrorism, Khalistan and the Indian state. Soon the arguments turned politically heated, each man giving his opinion, no one seeming to agree with the other. The arguments were turning a little hostile. I listened carefully to Saeed, Suresh, Akbar and Madan.

As the discussion in the room gained momentum alongside the effects of the liquor, I decided to have dinner, hoping to retire to my room because I was tired and frankly did not like the line of their arguments. So, I had my dinner, bid goodnight to all and headed for my room.

At around 2 a.m., I heard a banging on my door. I opened the door to see Madan standing there looking very tense. I asked him what had happened. He looked not only disturbed but in pain and very upset. He said, 'You know, Akbar has been shouting at me as if I was the representative of Sikh politics.'

This made me furious. I told him to come with me. 'What is his room number?' I asked him. But Madan, being Madan, calmed me down and said, 'There is no point in fighting . . . We will see him in the morning.' We left it at that for the night but decided we would give him a piece of our mind in the morning.

In the morning, when we were ready to confront Akbar, he was nowhere to be seen. He had left for Delhi in the early hours of the day. When we met with the other unit members, there was an air of uneasiness. But again, to Madan's credit, he defused the tension in a very quiet, gentle way. We felt used and taken advantage of for our good knowledge of Punjab. Initially, it bothered both of us and made us feel silly. We believed that this film was being made for a cause and had offered our services as volunteers. Now we didn't know the intent of this project. Yet, knowing Saeed as a filmmaker, he was not a person who would take part in a hidden political agenda. It confused us.

We had heard that audio cassettes of Bhindranwale's speeches existed and were sold all over Punjab. After Operation Blue Star, all these recorded tapes were said to have been banned. In fact, they had gone underground. It was left to Madan and me to acquire them. There would be explosive material for the film. Out of our own bravado, we decided that if any tapes were being sold in the open market in Amritsar, then we could surely go and get them.

After breakfast, the team decided that Madan and I would go on a hunt for the cassettes while the rest of the team, with Saeed and Suresh, would wait for us at the highway until we returned. Madan and I went to the Golden Temple market. There a relative of Madan's owned a shop selling kirpans and other Sikh religious articles. When we asked him about the existence of the tapes containing Bhindranwale's seditious speeches, he got very serious and said, 'Yes, they used to be sold openly when Bhindranwale was alive. But now, possessing them is very dangerous and one can be arrested for it.' When we explained to him why we wanted the tapes, he thought for a moment and called over one of the boys working in the shop. He asked him to take us to the electronic gadgets shop nearby those who sold tapes, cassette players and other such stuff. At the shop too the manager wanted to know the purpose for which we wanted the tapes. He then paused and said, 'If I find those tapes, you have to promise that you will return them because that is the last lot of these speeches. So, after you copy them do return them.' We promised to return them, and he sent a young boy someplace to fetch the box of cassettes. While the boy was gone, he entertained us with anecdotes about Santji. He offered us large glasses of lassi from the adjacent shop. He said, 'You know, whatever Santji said, he did. Officer Atwal was shot dead while visiting the Durbar Sahib. He did what he promised.' The shop owner burst into laughter. He was showing off his proximity to Santji to us. I asked him, 'How come you're so close to him when you are a Hindu?' He again gave a big laugh. 'I was always recording his speeches. In fact, he used to joke about me too. Santji once said to his disciples that all Hindus are not evil. Look at this man. He is an okay Hindu.' He had fond memories of Bhindranwale and had great admiration for him.

After a long wait, the boy returned with a bag containing a box of cassettes. Very quickly we paid for it, promising to return the tapes. The shop owner gave me an envelope containing a few pictures of the Golden Temple on the day of Operation Blue Star. They showed dead bodies lined up in the open courtyard of the Golden Temple—a horrific sight. He warned us to be careful of informers and police in the area, lest they should catch us with the banned items we were carrying. We rushed away, walked around for a while and soon got into an autorickshaw. The Bhindranwale cassettes were in a polythene bag and the pictures were hidden in the cap I was wearing. We wanted to reach our bus quickly.

Our scooter had travelled about a kilometre when a Punjab police officer signalled our vehicle to stop. We brought it to a stop and our hearts sank with fear. The policeman squeezed in next to the driver and the auto took off again. Madan and I looked at each other but could not say a word. Then we looked at the bag with the cassettes. At that moment, I even thought of throwing out the bag and jumping out of the moving vehicle. The policeman and the scooter driver were chatting continuously with each other, but about what we could not understand. Madan and I kept glancing at each other, sweating from the tension and the heat. Every minute that passed felt like a full day. We had no clue as to whether we were taking the right road either. I suspected that we were being driven straight to some police station. The tense ride continued for almost twenty minutes. Looking at Madan's eyes gripped with fear, I thought to myself—if we were arrested, no one would even know. I started cursing myself. How could I be so stupid as to undertake such a dangerous job as a volunteer?

Saeed and Suresh and the other members of the team were waiting. They had no idea of our plight. Suddenly I became conscious of my cap. We had hidden the photographs of the dead bodies of people killed during Operation Blue Star in it. I was almost fainting with anxiety and fear now. The scooter suddenly stopped. Madan gave me a look of resignation; we both believed this was the end for us and we would be arrested. There would be very solid proof of our crime—the banned articles in our hands and the pictures in my hat.

But something unexpected happened. The policeman got off and said goodbye to all of us matter-of-factly, and the scooter driver moved on to the highway. Madan looked at me and we both smiled at each other without uttering a single word. Madan asked the driver in Punjabi how long it was going to take. The driver replied, 'We would have reached earlier but because of the policeman I had to make a bit of a detour. One cannot refuse these cops. They are the lords of the city.' After some time, we saw our bus parked on the highway.

When I opened the door of the bus, the entire unit, which was comfortably sleeping in the cool air-conditioned vehicle, was roused by our arrival. I shouted, 'Come on, get up, you fellows, we have got the material we wanted.' Looking at the box of cassettes, Saeed was delighted. I again shouted, 'Give us some cold water. Both of us almost died from fear of being caught by the police.'

Saeed shouted out to the driver to start the bus and directed him to stop at the next refreshments shop. 'I want to treat them to a good, chilled Coke,' he said. I looked at Madan, and he gave me a smile and closed his eyes. The bus moved on.

Our next stop was the city of Jalandhar, a regular target of the militants for quite some years. All the leading Punjab newspapers had their headquarters here. It was here that pro-India, pro-Akali or pro-Khalistan movements were manufactured and manipulated with the use of dramatic headlines. We had to meet the owners and some of the journalists of the *Punjab Kesari* group of newspapers.

Many years back, on 9 September 1981 the founder of the group, Lala Jagat Narain, had been killed by Khalistani terrorists on a Punjab highway. Lalaji's killing had created national outrage; it was wake-up call as to what was happening in Punjab. After this murder in broad daylight, killings of both Hindus and Sikhs in the state became a regular affair. This time on 12 May 1984 another tragedy had taken place with the same *Punjab Kesari* group—the killing of Ramesh Kumar, son of the late Lala Jagat Narain, who had taken over the newspaper group after his father's death.

When we entered the lane where the *Punjab Kesari* offices were located, we were checked by a group of Punjab police. They frisked us thoroughly before lowering the barbed wire barricade to let us move in.

At the very entrance of the office building was parked a Fiat car, empty but with bullet marks on all sides, like the face of a smallpox survivor. The car reminded me of a sequence from the Hollywood film *The Godfather*, where the son of the godfather, Sonny, is killed when his car is fired on indiscriminately from all sides. The very sight of the car showed the intensity of the ruthless violence that had eaten into the marrow of the state of Punjab.

When we climbed up the steps to reach the first floor, a Sikh private security guard stared at us with a loaded gun aimed in our direction. From this point on, *Punjab Kesari* security frisked each one of us. Finally, having cleared this strict security checking we entered the main office floor where many journalists worked and went about their business. I looked around, and my eyes caught the sight of a few young men with small pistols in the back pockets of their jeans. It was a strange ambience, like from some Western cowboy movie where all the characters roam around with guns.

We were told to meet a young man who was sitting behind a table in a cabin. We introduced ourselves and explained to him the purpose of our visit. We wanted to talk to the members of the family that had suffered two horrible killings. Initially, he was very wary, but realizing that we had been given an appointment to meet the family, he asked us to wait for some time as the new boss of the group was about to arrive. We eventually understood that this was his father. He ordered tea for us, and as he lifted his right hand off the table, we saw a small, pretty pistol that had been concealed under his hand. It was a shock to all of us. Looking at our faces, he smiled and said, 'What can we do? I was prepared for any eventuality. Who knows, you could have turned out to be killers in the guise of film-makers. In that situation, I would have opened fire and shot you.' I could not believe him and was a bit unnerved. I requested him to please turn the barrel of his pistol in another direction. He laughed, picked up his firearm, opened its magazine and removed all the bullets from it.

After tea, we took in the general atmosphere of the newsroom, realizing that it was not easy to bring out a newspaper in an atmosphere of fear, violence and killings. The family had paid a heavy price to keep it going.

We soon entered the cabin of Vijay Kumar Chopra, the youngest son of Lala Jagat Narain. He now headed the *Kesari* group and served as the editor of the newspaper. Of short height, he wore the usual white dhoti–kurta. His cabin had glass partitions on all sides so he could have a clear view, almost 360 degrees, of the entire floor. He too brought out his personal revolver when we began our conversation. It had been tucked into his waist under his dhoti. He placed it on the table.

I remarked, 'It's very scary here. Everyone is carrying a firearm here at work.' He replied, very matter-of-factly, 'What is the choice? My father killed . . . my brother killed. If we have to run this newspaper, we have to be prepared. Just turn around and see for yourself how many eyes are watching you. They're all with loaded arms—and keeping an eye in case something untoward happens.' We looked around and saw at least eight men with their eyes fixed on us.

Then I asked him, 'Why don't you leave this city?' He immediately responded, 'And go where? They can come for us anywhere. Was Indira Gandhi safe in her prime minister's residence? We have no escape, and if we migrate from here the entire Hindu population will also leave Punjab. And that is what the Khalistanis want. We have a responsibility beyond our newspaper, a newspaper founded before Partition. We represent a principle. Even after so many tragedies in our family, we have created a widow's fund. We donate for the welfare of the people who have suffered at the hands of terrorists. This is for both Hindus and Sikhs. Every month we hold open public camps where we distribute all kinds of things, both cash and in kind. I know it is tough to live, work and survive here. Every morning, all the members of our family go for weapons training. Even our women have learned to use the carbine. We sleep with our weapons next to our beds.

'When my father, Lala Jagat Narain, was killed, all of Punjab was shaken. Thousands came to pay condolences. But one person who should have come did not turn up. My father had campaigned for him during the elections. In one of the public rallies, my father had appealed to the Hindus to vote for his party because Guru Gobind Singh had taken it upon himself to save the honour of the Hindus, and the least we could do was to make this person win the election with our Hindu votes.'

As we exited the well-fortified offices of the *Kesari*, I looked at the residences opposite the press building. On its rooftop bunkers of security, cops on duty sat, their guns aimed for any eventuality. I looked at the Fiat car with bullet marks all over its body. It occurred to me that this car represented the present state of Punjab, the land of five rivers of Heer Ranjha, of the Sufis and the Gurus.

The drive from Jalandhar to Delhi took several hours. When we reached Delhi, we were stopped at the police checkpost. A policeman asked us to get down from the bus so they could check us individually. Once we alighted from the bus and stood on the highway, one cop singled out Madan and said, 'Sardarji, you come on this side, away from them all.' His tone was rude and insulting, and he was profiling people based on their appearance and whether they were wearing turbans. This was too much for me. I could not control myself and could not bear this humiliation of Madan. I began an argument with the policeman. A solid shouting match followed between me and the policeman. I insisted on standing next to Madan, and so did the other members of the team. Finally, the cops gave in and asked us to go back onto our bus and move on.

Returning to Delhi after fifteen days, we got off the bus one by one, saying goodbye to each other. Back in my home I pondered over the entire experience and asked myself whether my nation and my people had any idea about what was really happening in the land of Punjab and its people. The film for which Madan and I had risked our lives was never made. Nothing was heard of it. Where did all that rare footage shot for the film go? Who funded the project? No one revealed anything to us. It was as if our work in Punjab had not happened at all. Everything was forgotten, and Madan and I, as the helping volunteers, felt used and foolish.

But as a creative person, the work I did for the film transformed me into a cultural activist of sorts. I continue to be involved in tackling injustice and anti-people situations. In my theatre and my teaching, there have always been traces of this experience. I realized that in consciously avoiding participation in social causes that had a direct or even indirect bearing on your personal life, you come dangerously close to living in a cocoon. On the contrary, your fears subside when you join or share in the struggles of the people. Your understanding widens and deepens. This opens new gates of knowledge when it comes to interpreting your work, and your creativity matures with time and becomes layered with the multi-dimensional perspectives you have gathered.

7

1989—The Killing of Safdar Hashmi

On 1 January 1989, I had gone with my wife to a friend's house for lunch. After a nice lunch accompanied by some Bloody Mary, we left for home. I felt very relaxed, ready for a nice winter nap. However, one of my theatre friends, Bansi Kaul, dropped by to see me. So instead of a nap, we indulged in our usual theatre gossip.

After about half an hour, I got a call from Rahul Varma, a common friend, saying, 'Safdar has been attacked while performing his latest street play *Halla Bol* at Sahibabad.' He had patchy information about the attack, but he said Safdar had been badly injured and was in the Irwin Hospital emergency ward. Shocked, I asked him where the other team members were and where Mala, Safdar's wife, was. He replied, 'Nobody knows. Safdar has been brought to the hospital by Brijesh, one of the members of the theatre group and a medical doctor.'

Anju, Bansi and I immediately rushed to Irwin Hospital in Anju's old Ambassador car. As we entered the emergency ward, Safdar was lying unconscious on a stretcher, blood all over his body and on his face, nose and lips. Anju, as a doctor, started asking the junior doctor in charge about his treatment. These doctors insisted that we take Safdar to Ram Manohar Lohia Hospital because he needed a CAT scan immediately and Irwin

116

Hospital did not have these facilities. Safdar was a member of the CPI(M), and I expected his fellow party members to be at the hospital. But only one comrade from his party, Ved Prakash, a faculty member from a Delhi college, was there.

I asked one of the junior doctors, 'How do we take him to the Lohia Hospital?' He said, 'We can arrange an ambulance.' Two junior doctors volunteered to come with us up to the Ram Manohar Lohia Hospital. The hospital doctors carried an Ambu bag and a mask in case Safdar had difficulty breathing.

At this point, Ved Prakash, a member of the Delhi CPI(M), informed us that most of the members and leaders of the party were in Kerala for the party congress. Even Safdar's brother Sohail was in Kerala. My thoughts went to Mala and the group members and the memory of the massacre of Maliana, where the bodies of the victims were found later floating in the water canals, brought up a chill of fear in me. I hoped they were safe, wherever they were. While still at Irwin Hospital sorting out the details as to how Safdar could be shifted, we met Brijesh. He looked exhausted, and all over his face was written a sense of loss. I asked him what had happened. He narrated his story of the attack.

He said, 'When the goons attacked, we all ran for our lives. Jhandapur, the spot of the performance, was like a scene of a riot conducted by professional thugs who had come prepared to attack us with their iron rods and lathis. They had come with the clear intention of not allowing our performance to take place.' Bansi, or maybe Anju, asked, 'Brijesh, how did you manage to get Safdar here to this hospital?' He said he lifted Safdar with some help onto a cycle-rickshaw and then took him to Mohan Nagar Hospital. It took him some time because he had to change his route as the goons who had attacked them were still roaming in the area. For safety's sake, he had changed routes several times to get to Mohan Nagar Hospital, but that hospital was of no help. He finally managed an autorickshaw to bring Safdar to Irwin Hospital.

As all the doctors insisted that we shift Safdar to Ram Manohar Lohia Hospital, I saw Mala, with great courage, taking stock of the situation to try to understand Safdar's condition. Finally, Brijesh and I, along with two junior doctors, took Safdar to Ram Manohar Lohia Hospital. Mala and Bansi followed with Anjali in her car.

In the Ram Manohar Lohia Hospital casualty ward, Safdar's body was placed on a very unclean bed. He started convulsing, unconsciously tossing his limbs all over the bed. He looked like a wounded soldier who had fallen after a great battle with injuries all over his body. The accompanying junior doctors from Irwin Hospital introduced us to the junior doctors of Lohia Hospital. These young doctors tried their best to help and to do whatever was possible. Soon, Safdar was taken on a wheeled stretcher to another block in the ICU for his CAT scan.

By this time, people who knew Safdar had started pouring into the hospital lawns. Safdar's mother, Ammaji, arrived. She went straight into the ICU ward to see Safdar. Mala stayed near the ICU. Then I saw most of the actors of the group arrive and felt relieved that they were all safe. Each one of them narrated their version of what had happened.

As evening descended, the junior doctors told us to get in touch with a Dr S.P. Agarwal, the most experienced doctor in the hospital to treat Safdar's kind of injuries. They told us that he should examine Safdar as he may need an operation, but they told us that he was on leave for a wedding in his family. They explained that Dr Jain was the only hope for Safdar and urged us to ask him to examine Safdar. Hesitantly, I asked them to give me his number. These young doctors took me to the duty room so I could use the hospital phone. I dialled the number and Dr Agarwal was on the line.

I was unsure how to put my request to him. I introduced myself to him and told him about the case. I nearly begged him. I said, 'Sir, everybody here in this hospital is telling me that you are the doctor who can save his life.' Dr Agarwal replied, 'Look, I am on leave, and I am already dressed up to attend the family wedding. I'm very sorry. It is very difficult for me at this hour to come.' I persisted, 'Sir, I am nobody. I have no authority. But, sir, tomorrow you will come to know who this man is. Every doctor here in your hospital is referring only your name to me. I can only plead with you. Please, please, I beg you.' He cut me short and said, 'Okay. I am coming.' The junior doctors and Bansi, listening to me plead with Dr Agarwal, felt relieved.

By this time Safdar's CAT scan had been completed and he was brought back to the ICU for observation. No one was allowed to enter. When, finally, Dr Agarwal arrived, he went straight into the ICU ward, and after some time he came out and asked, 'Who had called me?'

'It was I,' I replied.

'How are you related to him?'

'I am his friend.'

'No. Is there any relative of his here?'

'I am his wife,' Mala, standing next to me, said.

Dr S.P. Agarwal, who later became the director-general of health services Government of India and retired as a director-general with the Red Cross, explained to Mala and the many friends surrounding him, 'Only a miracle can save him. We cannot open him up for surgery in this condition. It is never done. His skull has been cracked I three places, his brain is swollen, and the brain fluid is leaking from his ears. This is a very difficult situation, and under these circumstances, we cannot operate on him. Only pray for him.' All were silent. Nobody knew how to respond. I thanked him for coming. Dr Jain, a gentleman, said, 'I wish I could do something, just pray.'

By now the hospital lawns were filled with people. Some I knew and some I had never met. Anger simmered all around. Mala went back to the ward, but I didn't go inside. I really did not know what to do next. Old members of the Jan Natya Manch—Manish, Tyagi, Asif, Manoj, Gulati—all had arrived, all of them at a loss to know what to say or do. Manish even said they had faced many tense, difficult and hostile situations, but had managed them and still performed. 'This attack, I do not understand how this horrible attack could happen,' he said.

Sudhanva Deshpande, who was acting in the play when the attack happened, stood next to us, narrating his eyewitness account. 'While we were performing the play—and only around five minutes were left to complete the performance—a local procession came from one side of the crossing where we were performing. Since our performance had closed the movement of people and also vehicles on the road, the procession needed to wait, but they were not prepared to do so. They wanted us to stop the performance. We were requesting them to hold their procession for just five minutes and the performance would be over. They refused to wait and started to argue with us, and this argument turned hostile. All of a sudden, we saw some people coming towards us with rods and lathis, and they started attacking everybody who was watching the play as well as the people who were performing. In the confusion, Safdar, who was not performing but was standing with the crowds, intervened with the processionists. The group started beating up the actors and the public, and in this chaos, while Safdar was still trying to pacify them, he was attacked with rods and lathis on his head. While the other group members ran to save their lives, Safdar fell on the ground where his play *Halla Bol* had been cut short by these goons. One of the attackers also fired bullets from his revolver, and one factory worker, Ram Lal, was killed. He was simply a spectator who was watching the play.'

All of us were hoping and waiting for a miracle to happen. More people were now on the lawns of the hospital, and they stayed on till late into the night. Some theatre people decided to have a public meeting on the Rabindra Bhavan lawns, where all the National Academies of art, literature and performing art are located.

The next morning, at 11 a.m., a large number of people met to protest against the attack. Somebody mentioned that the attacker was a person named Mukesh Sharma, a small-time political worker who was rumoured to be very close to a political leader in Delhi. Mukesh Sharma was arrested, but after some time released on bail and later completely set free because of a lack of evidence against him. After this meeting, it was decided to assemble again at 5 p.m. to work out the next course of action.

On the afternoon of 2 January, I returned to the hospital. By now the leaders and workers of the CPI(M) party had come to the hospital. Mala's mother and father, along with Safdar's mother, were met by a crowd of people expressing their solidarity with the family. Anju informed me that there was no improvement in Safdar's condition. As a doctor, Anju was allowed inside the ICU to see Safdar, who was kept on a ventilator now.

After some time, I rushed back to Rabindra Bhavan for the evening meeting. A large number of theatre people and many cultural and social activists had come. I saw many teachers from the NSD: Habib Tanveer, E. Alkazi, Manohar Singh, Krishen Khanna, Balwant Gargi, Manjeet Bawa, Anand Patwardhan, Madan Gopal Singh, Aparna Caur and students from NSD, Jawaharlal Nehru University, Delhi University and Jamia Millia Islamia. This big crowd of concerned citizens and members of the cultural community gave a strong voice to this protest against the attack. Most of the senior personalities spoke, expressing their anguish at the incident.

Suddenly, somebody brought the news that Safdar had passed away. There was pin-drop silence, but before we could react another message came that he was alive. I couldn't bear the confusion, so I rushed back to the hospital. To my relief, Safdar was alive but struggling for his life and in a very critical condition.

The newspapers carried lead stories about the attack and the press wrote many editorials. There was an uproar all over the country over his attack. The theatre community across the nation held protest meetings to condemn the attack on their people. At the hospital, all we could do was to continue to wait, talking in groups. Most of us were waiting for the arrival of Sohail Hashmi, Safdar's brother, who was still away at the CPI(M) annual congress in Kerala. When he finally arrived, he rushed into the ICU ward where the entire family waited, hoping for a miracle. I remember that during the day, when Anju went into the ICU to see Safdar, Ammaji, his mother, who sat all the time outside the ICU, had asked her, 'What do you think?' Anju replied, 'I have faith in Safdar, and I am waiting for him to perform that miracle.' Ammaji said, 'I can see the hope in your eyes, and it gives me faith.'

Everybody—all of Safdar's family members, his friends and well-wishers—waited in the corridors and other parts of the hospital in the hope of that miracle. Many quietly struggled to come to terms with the reality of what had happened.

After some time, Sohail came out of the hospital and met all of us. It was dark by now and he told me to go home as I had been there throughout the day. He asked me to come back early in the morning. With great reluctance I agreed to go, but my legs refused to move. After a while, however, Manish Minocha (actor and founding member of Jan Natya Manch) and I decided to go home and return early the next morning. I dropped Manish at Sheikh Sarai. As I entered my flat in Defence Colony, the phone rang. It was Kavya Kumar, an actor from my theatre group, Prayog. 'Rush back,' he said, 'Safdar has passed away.' A dark silence descended on me. Anju understood what the phone call meant. I called Manish. 'We have lost Safdar. I am coming to pick you up.' Both of us rushed back to the hospital.

The news of Safdar's death spread like wildfire. People from the party, from theatre, press reporters and a huge mob of others were now at the hospital. Many CPI(M) leaders had arrived from Kerala. Most of them were agitated and angry. Some were very emotional and raised slogans like, '*Comrade Safdar Hashmi lal salaam lal salaam, Comrade Safdar Hashmi amar rahey [Red salute to comrade Safdar Hashmi, long live comrade Safdar Hashmi].*' There was fervour in their voice and tears in their eyes; they couldn't control their emotions and their helplessness.

Mala told us that Safdar had said some time back that if anything ever happened to him his organs should be donated. This wish of Safdar's had to be honoured—his family was quite firm on this. Strangely, the hospital discouraged it, and the behaviour of those in charge was silly. The arguments were stupid and meaningless—like, 'Why do you want to disfigure his body?' In this way, a lot of time was wasted. Finally, his brother Sohail contacted the AIIMS authorities, but only his eyes could be donated in time.

While all this was happening, I observed the courage of the family and how they conducted themselves. Mala was like a mine of fortitude; Ammaji, calm, deep in her thoughts, responding to every moment with the utmost dignity; Mala's parents mourning, but quietly observing and imbibing everything with grace. Sohail took control of the situation, constantly consulting Mala for her consent and guidance. It was then that I saw what these revolutionary families are made of.

Safdar's funeral was the next morning. His body was brought to the Delhi party office at VP House at Rafi Marg,

New Delhi, wrapped in his party's red flag. It had now become a party affair. One by one, party workers stood before Safdar's body and saluted with their traditional tight-fist gesture. I stood in a corner of the room watching these customs. Ammaji stood next to Mala near the body of Safdar. Each party comrade would stand in front of them to express their condolences. A young lady stood behind Ammaji and Mala, constantly wiping her tears. Her sight moved me, and I wanted to know who she was. Someone whispered to me, 'She is Shabnam, the younger sister of Safdar.' There was also Safdar's aunt, visiting them from America. I was lost in a different world when suddenly it dawned on me that I had lost a very, very dear friend. My eyes watered, but Sohail whispered in my ear, 'No tears. Ammaji is there in front of you.' I realized the gravity of the moment and quietly stepped out of the room. Outside on the lawns of VP House under a tent, people from various organizations of the CPI(M) waited. Ordinary citizens of Delhi had come to pay their last respects; people from various civil societies, organizations, offices, theatre people, painters, film-makers, writers, poets, journalists . . . People brought flowers, garlands and wreaths to show their respect for and solidarity with Safdar. Many national leaders came to pay homage to Safdar: Atal Bihari Vajpayee, V.P. Singh and several senior leaders of the CPI(M) stood in front of Safdar's body and saluted the departed soul with raised fists.

As the crowds swelled, it became a mass of people from all walks of life. Looking around, I realized that most of these people did not know Safdar and may not have even seen his plays or heard his poetry or known of his social and political activism.

Before the funeral started, Rajendra Sharma, who was then the general secretary of the Delhi unit of the CPI(M), gave a long speech. The lecture went on and on, unnecessarily repeating the same content over and over again. It felt as if he considered it his own historic moment as the general secretary of the part. Many of his party workers standing nearby commented, '*Arre, yeh kya kar raha hai? Bahut ho gaya* [What is he doing? This is too much].'

Finally, at around 1 p.m., the body of Safdar, covered in the party's red flag, appeared from the tent where people were paying their respects. They shouted loud slogans of '*Comrade Safdar Hashmi ko lal salam* [Red salute to Comrade Safdar Hashmi]' and '*Comrade Safdar amar rahe* [Long live Comrade Safdar]'. It built up to a highly charged emotional climax all around the lawns of VP House. First, his friends and the actors of his group appeared, all holding wreaths raised high above their heads. Next came the pallbearers of the party with their red flags, walking slowly in a ceremonial march. Then, very slowly, Safdar's body was placed on a carriage decorated with flowers, and his final journey commenced. At some point, someone from the party asked me to climb on to the carriage, and I did so. In the carriage sat Sohail Hashmi, Mala Hashmi, Prakash Karat, general secretary of the CPI(M), Bhisham Sahni, the eminent Hindi writer and a teacher of Safdar's, and I. I think I was the only one not from the CPI(M) asked to be on the carriage carrying Safdar's body.

As the funeral march proceeded, emotions ran high, and no one obeyed police instructions. Nobody followed the approved route that the police had given us to follow. The funeral procession wound its way from VP House through Connaught Place, Barakhamba Road, Mandi House, ITO, Delhi Gate, Daryaganj, Kashmiri Gate, and finally to Nigambodh Ghat. The funeral procession was almost two-kilometres long; normally such a long procession was only seen at the funerals of departed national leaders. During this journey, I felt quite guilty to be on the carriage as most of my friends and theatre people were on foot.

On reaching the cremation ground, again, Rajendra Sharma began to deliver another lecture, going on and on about the Safdar's sacrifice and speaking against the Indian government. When it felt too long, I saw Harkishen Singh Surjit, the tall leader of the party, signal to him to close his speech and let the cremation take place. Rajinder Sharma finally concluded his speech. People laid flowers on Safdar's remains as a final salute, and Safdar was cremated in an electric crematorium, according to his wishes.

Very gradually but hesitantly, people moved away from the site. I remember seeing and meeting people who had nothing in common with Safdar or his work. I saw many bureaucrats, their wives, professors, schoolteachers, UNESCO workers and officers. Many people who had come from different parts of the country to the city for their personal work had joined the procession as a mark of protest. When most of the people had left, Anju and I looked back at the cremation site. In our minds, we both bid farewell to Safdar quietly.

Buta Singh, House Protest

The cultural community of Delhi decided to march to the house of the home minister, Buta Singh, near Patel Chowk. On the very day, 2 January 1989, Safdar died. It was a spontaneous decision, and we all marched together. It was to register the anger of the people and the protest of the cultural community to the killing of Safdar Hashmi. We hadn't taken police permission, and emotions were running very high. When we reached the home minister's house, we were confronted by a strong contingent of armed police. We demanded to meet the home minister, but the police refused to let us proceed towards the main gate of his residence. A confrontation started to brew between us and the police. They tried to push us back.

The crowd shouted slogans and a minor scuffle ensued. Things took an ugly turn when the police shoved Habib Tanveer, Keshav Kothari and Manohar Singh. This enraged the artists, and the situation looked as if it could turn nasty. Habib Tanveer and Manohar Singh started to shout at the police for not allowing us to meet the home minister. Manohar Singh, whom I knew as a cool and reserved person, had lost his patience and was now shouting at the police for their incompetence when Safdar was attacked. He provoked the police, daring them to arrest him. Habib joined in, and within no time all of us protesters started shouting, 'Arrest us, arrest us, arrest us.' The situation was on the verge of veering out of control when a senior police officer intervened. He politely requested us to submit a protest letter to him and promised that he would forward it to the home minister, who was either hiding in his house or didn't have the courage to face us.

Two kinds of protests were taking place over Safdar's killing—one organized by the creative community of Delhi and the other organized by Safdar's party, the CPI(M). I was mostly involved with the creative community and had little to do with the CPI(M) except to join some of their protests. The creative community in Delhi, meaning its theatre people, musicians, dancers, painters, photographers, filmmakers and civil society members, met and planned a big national protest through a memorial meeting. We called for ideas and looked at the possibilities and scale the meeting could take on.

Within a few days of Safdar's death on 4 January 1989, there were spontaneous suggestions from several quarters that the play *Halla Bol* should be staged to its finish at the very spot where Safdar fell. This demand came from theatre people and also from CPI(M) party workers and their leaders to reassert the democratic rights and the freedom of speech and the right to perform of the people. It was also generally felt that the fundamental rights of the people had been violated by the killing of Safdar. Hence that space had to be reclaimed. It must have been a tough decision for Mala to agree to act, as she was the lead actor in the play. On the morning 4 January 1989, a huge number of people from the left parties and the creative community of Delhi headed together for Jhandapur from Rabindra Bhavan, where all the national academies of art, dance, theatre and literature are located. Rabindra Bhavan became the ground zero for all the meetings and protests. The protests assumed deeper meaning as the place itself was founded in the name of a great icon of the Indian arts and aesthetics. When we all reached Jhandapur near Sahibabad on the outskirts of East Delhi where Safdar was attacked, thousands of industrial workers from the nearby factories joined us in the long procession. The procession wound around the industrial town of Sahibabad and culminated at the Jhandapur crossing, the very spot where the play *Halla Bol* was attacked and Safdar was brutally wounded in the head. This huge march around the living quarters of the workers was also meant to remove the fear created among them by the goons after their killing of Safdar. After some opening lectures by the leaders of the left explaining the importance of returning to perform *Halla Bol* at the very spot where Safdar had lost his life, along with the labourer Ram Bahadur who was in the audience that day, it was time for the play to be performed.

The atmosphere was surcharged and there was pin-drop silence. The thousands of people in the audience were tense as they waited for the play to begin. A strange feeling seemed to pass through the audience and the actors, who had lost their comrade just four days back at the same place. They all seemed completely possessed with the intent of the performance. There may hardly be another example in the world of theatre where a performance took place to reclaim the same space where a theatre group had lost its director, actor and organizer. The performance of *Halla Bol* was a high point in India's theatre history, a new chapter written. It was a historic moment for Indian protest theatre.

Watching *Halla Bol* that day without Safdar made me feel empty, and I moved away from the performance and sat quietly pondering his loss. I realized that the real killers of Safdar weren't those goons who hit him with iron rods that day but rather the hidden villains who didn't value democratic dissent on the chessboard of Indian politics. These enemies aren't mentioned in the footnotes of Indian history, but their actions change its course. After all, the 1984 anti-Sikh riots had already unfolded the devastation of Indian politics by violence, criminal intent and majoritarianism.

The protests kept up their pace even on 5 January, with another march organized from Shivaji Park to the home minister's residence. I could not join it, as I was busy with other artists organizing the national protest. On 9 January, on the lawns of Rabindra Bhavan, we had a long meeting at the Sangeet Natak Academy. It was attended by Ebrahim Alkazi, who had regularly attended the protest meetings at the place. At this meeting, he took a lead role and wanted to know all the minute details about the participants and the design of the venue. As his students, Bansi Kaul and I were tasked with getting the details required to arrange the space on the lawns of Rabindra Bhavan. Alkazi even said, 'Raina, your neck is on the chopper. You'd better remember that.' I replied, 'Sir, we are now grown-up theatre people, please trust us as such.' He shot back, 'We must have a dignified and solemn memorial for Safdar.'

Once we finalized the programme, we had to think about its execution. There were many artists who contributed, even spending their own money to see the memorial happen. Some of them were Manjeet Bawa, Bansi Kaul, Ram Rahman, Parthiv

Shah, Sashi Kumar, Dadi Pudumjee, Anand Patwardhan, Sohail Hashmi and Rajendra Prasad (Rajan). Safdar's death had bound us all together.

Sitting at the Mandi House circle between the fountain and the tea corner, a group of us decided to design a badge for the memorial meeting. Anand Patwardhan, the famous documentary filmmaker, coined the line 'Stop the murder of culture.' So, the final badge had this line, along with Safdar's picture in black and white. That became the first badge of the protest. On 9 January, national protests simultaneously took place in many parts of the country. In Delhi, it started at around 5.30 p.m. with a torch-light procession from the Supreme Court of India. It proceeded through Bhagwan Dass Road to reach the Rabindra Bhavan lawns. It was a silent march demanding justice for the murder of Safdar Hashmi.

At Rabindra Bhavan, as it started getting dark, the torchbearers fixed their torches in a large circle. A big cloth banner with Safdar's portrait was hung from a tree softly lit by the many torches from above and light glowing from below. The space inside the torch circle had four stages, equidistant from each other. On each stage stood actors from four different theatre groups—Jana Natya Manch, Prayog, Nishant and Parcham—in black casuals. Each group sang a song as a theatrical tribute to Safdar, after which several senior and eminent theatre artists—Zora Sehgal, E. Alkazi, Habib Tanvir, Bhisham Sahni and Moloyashree (Mala) Hashmi—spoke for a few minutes each, underlining the significance of the event. Their words were warm, touching and moving.

The crowd that stood all around the torch circle and in between the stage spaces created a humbling, unique ambience. None of us had ever witnessed such a moving memorial meeting.

Lalita Ramdas, a social activist and wife of Admiral Ramdas, whom I had worked with during the anti-Sikh riots in 1984, sent me an inland letter from Kerala saying she had attended the memorial meeting, which had reminded her of Spanish memorial meetings. During this national memorial meeting, a demand was made to rename the College Road around Mandi House as Safdar Hashmi Marg.

When the meeting was over, many people who knew Safdar or did not know him came with tears in their eyes and thanked all the participants by either giving them a gentle hug or shaking hands with them. It was perhaps for the first time in Delhi that people shared this loss and had come spontaneously to show their solidarity with the members of the theatre group JANAM with Mala and with other members of his family. They even talked about the ways how to keep his sacrifice alive. The atmosphere that evening after the memorial meeting was so surcharged that nobody wanted to leave the venue. I met some people for the first time who were offering any kind of support to keep the essence of Safdar's sacrifice alive. I met a bearded gentleman who was wearing a Kashmiri shawl, who quietly offered a scholarship in Safdar's name. I took his name and phone number, and over the years he's become a close friend and a great supporter of the Safdar Hashmi Memorial Trust. His name was Anil Chandra.

International Film Festival of India

On 12 January 1989, India celebrated its twelfth International Film Festival at Siri Fort Auditorium. The opening function was to start at around 6 p.m. Many international film-makers had been invited to the festival, and some of us had snuck into the Siri Fort lawn area with some placards against the current regime and a few thousand handbills of protest printed by Safdar's friends hidden in our bags. We had no invitation cards to enter the main auditorium where the gala was set up for a galaxy of film-makers from India and abroad. Still, we wanted to protest inside the venue before the international community of artists to appraise them of the actual state of affairs of the arts in India. Since we could not enter the main venue, we stayed outside the entry gate as a mark of protest, holding up our posters, placards and flyers. The stand-in protest made news, and many foreign television crews started covering our protest. Many celebrities, as they entered the function, stood with us for a few minutes as a mark of solidarity. Some even made statements about the attack on Safdar and condemned the Indian state for its intolerance towards the arts in general. This created quite a bit of tension between us and the security guards and government officials. It also embarrassed the organizers of the festival. Since many VIPs were slated to attend, the police wanted to remove us, but we stood our ground. They did not use force against us because that would have created a law-and-order problem. We protesters were determined to stay.

A little later, we saw Shabana Azmi, accompanied by director John Schlesinger, enter the venue. Their film *Madame Sousatzka* was scheduled to be screened at the festival. Both stood with us for some minutes and made comments about the protest to the media there. Gautam Ghosh and M.S. Sathyu joined them. I carried a leather bag with the protest handbills, and I quietly requested Shabana to carry some of them into the auditorium. Gautam Ghosh commented, 'Can't you come in and distribute them yourselves to the audience?' I replied that none of us had entry passes, so Shabana and Sathyu suggested that some of us join their group and act as if we had all come together. Three from among us followed these four celebrities as if we were part of their crowd, and we succeeded in entering the main venue.

The official inauguration was to happen any moment now, so Shabana, Sathyu and Gautam Ghosh left us to take their respective seats in the front rows. I quietly opened the grip of my bag in the darkness of the hall and took out the handbills. I gave one bundle to my colleagues and kept the other for myself. The function started with Kabir Bedi, as the master of ceremonies, reciting all the adjectives he knew in praise of the Ministry of Information and Broadcasting. We quietly distributed our protest handbills among the audience. Some people who were already seated also helped us pass along the handbills to other guests. Then Kabir Bedi invited Shabana Azmi on stage with actor Victor Bannerjee to make individual statements about the festival, to praise the Government of India and to talk about Indian cinema.

By this time, we had nearly covered the entire auditorium with our black-and-white handbills, so almost all the guests had one each in their hands. When Shabana was asked by Kabir Bedi to speak, she took out the protest handbill and waved it in front of the audience as she spoke, 'I am sure you have this paper in your hands, and I am reading the same from the stage to register the artists' protest against the brutal killing of Safdar Hashmi.' She continued, reading the bill, 'With the murder of Safdar Hashmi, freedom of expression in the year 1989 has begun on an ominous note. The barbaric murder of our fellow artist and writer has come as a stunning blow to artists and intellectuals all over the country. It has come as a tragic and grim reminder of the extreme dangers to which we are exposed in living by our vocation and beliefs. Incidents of assaults on artists have occurred in the past, but their frequency has now increased alarmingly. With the tragic death of Safdar Hashmi, the time has come for us to organize ourselves against these near-fascist forces of disruption so that we are no longer brittle, vulnerable and alone.'[6]

---

[6] SAHMAT Archives.

The minute she finished speaking, there was an uproar in the auditorium. The solemnity of the function had entirely gone. People were shouting, and all this commotion was captured live by the television cameras and witnessed by millions across the country. We saw in the confusion a fuming, black-spectacled H.K.L. Bhagat then the minster of Information and Broadcasting of Congress government headed by Rajeev Gandhi rush onto the stage to mumble a rebuttal to all the allegations and try to defend himself and his government. But with the protest by Shabana and the people in the auditorium, the opening function of the festival was over.

The next day the national and vernacular media were filled with stories of the last evening, garnished with comments from national and international film personalities. It was a big embarrassment for the Indian state. The festival opening was perhaps the climax of that phase of protests by the creative community.

8

Safdar Hashmi Memorial Trust—SAHMAT

The making of SAHMAT started with many meetings and discussions about who the members of the trust would be and what kind of work the trust would do. In the first meeting, I sensed that some friends who were full-time members of the CPI(M) wanted it weighed towards their party. Frankly, I had no objection to this. Safdar was a card-holding member of the CPI(M) party who had sacrificed his life at the altar of the performance space while staging a very fine piece of street theatre. This play, apart from being an experimental attempt to show a love story in a street play, was also a story concerning working-class struggles, hence very openly a pro-CITU (Centre of Indian Trade Unions) play. Janam plays had always been pro-working class, upholding the rights of workers and highlighting their struggles to secure them better wages and better living conditions. To have trust in the name of Safdar with members of his party was a natural thing.

But Safdar was also a creative writer, a poet, a playwright, a film man, an actor and so much more. He had personal relationships with people not connected with his party and had made friends over his several years as a senior officer in the West Bengal Information Centre in New Delhi. His office at Baba Kharak Singh Marg at Connaught Place was an open adda for all kinds of creative people who would drop by to spend time with him, and discuss the latest films, books, plays and paintings. Safdar's warm personality and open heartedness made it easy for people to relate to him and create long-lasting creative synergies with him. He was not a narrow-minded ideologue or an orthodox political Brahmin; his strength lay in the intellectual grit with which he used to apply Marxism as a scientific tool to understand life as it existed in its various manifestations. A trust which had only people from his political party did not satisfy me. I felt it would be missing something, and I articulated my thoughts with utmost honesty. I said in the meeting that having me, or another person like me, on the trust would not give it any prestige. It would be an average organization since we were all young and could at best be volunteers to work and execute Safdar's ideas. We really needed trustees known for their contributions in their fields and who could bring honour to the trust.

This intervention of mine led to a long silence among the participants. I presumed they had thought it would be a smooth meeting, but it did not go that way. After I had spoken, some others did, but we could not reach any consensus on the names of those who would sit on the board of the trust. I wanted the names of internationally known seniors, whose inclusion would lend some weight to this new organization. Our protests had raised new hope all over the country, so the trust had to be one that people would look up to nationally.

I came out from the meeting accompanied by Madan Gopal Singh. He put his arm around my shoulders and took me aside, very quietly saying, '*Sir, aap ne to bomb gira diya* [Sir, you dropped a bomb].' I could not understand what he meant. I could not comprehend his analysis of the sub-text of this meeting. I laughed, 'Madan, I really believe that the names put forward in the meeting for the trust were not all heavyweights.' Now he started to laugh and said, 'Raina sahab, you are too innocent, and you did not understand the political undercurrents of the meeting.' I replied, 'Madan, I did not need to. We both lost our friend, and if any organization at all has to be created in his name, then you and I should be inspired to work for it and not to become its office-bearers.'

After a few days, another meeting was called, and many more names were suggested. Everyone present at the meeting gave their consent and objections. Those names that fetched maximum approval were finally put on the trust: Bhisham Sahni, Vivaan Sundaram, Moloyshri Hashmi, Suhail Hashmi, Govind Deshpande, E. Alkazi, Utpal Dutt; my name was also on the trust. I was more than happy with the names. They gave me confidence that this trust would last.

Finally, in February 1989, the Safdar Hashmi Memorial Trust, or SAHMAT, was formed. Its office was the closed veranda of a Vithal Bhai Patel flat, Number Four. The trust had no major financial contributions from anywhere. But SAHMAT has continued for thirty-one years as a major cultural resistance front that is firm in its basic mission of standing up for creative freedom and for the democratic rights of the cultural community of India. The strength of SAHMAT has always been its vast fraternity of artistes across the country and abroad. Its major ideas always come from the creative community. There is a phrase I have coined: 'SAHMAT happened to him.' This means that once you're caught by the fragrance of SAHMAT, it never leaves you. You always remain in it, and you always want SAHMAT. When SAHMAT needs you, you're always there.

SAHMAT is a unique ensemble of minds who work on very political, explosive ideas, which when presented or performed grow into a most refined avant-garde cultural construct. Often, it is like a university or a laboratory where political and cultural dynamics give birth to an out-of-the-box presentation. Disagreement between individuals has been SAHMAT's inherent strength, as it shapes and improves based on these points of difference. The results are fruitful and miles away from what the initial differences might have indicated.

In India, after the Indian People's Theatre Association (IPTA), SAHMAT has been the most important development in the left democratic cultural space. Whatever SAHMAT did or achieved, it always created a contested socio-political debate amongst the common people and the state authorities. Never before in India had the political class been forced to take up a position vis-a-vis artistic freedom, freedom of expression and democratic rights. Many hypocrisies of the political class were exposed during the major artistic challenges thrown up by the cultural and creative endeavours of the SAHMAT collective. SAHMAT has also had its share of confrontations with the state, all recorded in various publications in the form of books and exhibitions, paintings, films and some mega cultural sit-in programmes. These publications and activities have themselves set new standards and trends in the world of contemporary art and cultural resistance in India. In achieving these goals set thirty-one years back by the establishment of SAHMAT, there have been innumerable, dramatic behind-the-scenes stories and incidents. These are the stories of crises, confrontations, loneliness and achievements. We at SAHMAT sometimes laugh at ourselves when we recall those times and ask ourselves, 'Was that us?'

Safdar's Dreams and Ideas

When Safdar was alive he used to share his ideas with me, as he did with many other like-minded friends. He would discuss the possibilities of having a Jan Utsav, a real people's festival of India, for factory workers, agricultural workers and the office-going public—meaning, simply a festival for the downtrodden people of India. We talked about this against the background of the massive Apna Utsav organized by the Congress government in various parts of the country, funded by huge amounts of money.

Safdar had written a large number of film scripts for UNICEF on the theme of literacy and other social topics. He expected substantial remuneration from this assignment, using which he wanted to fulfil one of his pet dreams—to create a travelling street theatre group. For that he wanted to buy a van, designed and converted into a performance stage, and another vehicle to ferry his theatre group around.

One morning he showed up unannounced at my house. He took out a long white paper from his bag and said, 'I want your response to this poem that I have written for the ongoing literacy campaign in the country.' When he finished reciting it, I smiled, 'Safdar, you have become a poet.' He laughed, 'Yaar, you know, I cannot compete with Bertolt Brecht's poem in his play *Mother*.' This play was an adaptation of the novel *Mother* by Gorky.

Long back, when I had produced the play *Mother*, the song on adult literacy in the play was written by a famous German poet and playwright Bertold Brecht which had become very popular. But when this new poem of Safdar was composed it was an instant hit. It became an anthem song for the literacy campaign in India, played at all literacy-related functions at the state and national levels. The then minister of education of the Government of India had also liked Safdar's song, but unfortunately, he wanted to replace a few words in the poem, which we found silly.

The original lines were:

Padhna likhna sikho o mehnat karne walon,
Padhna likhna seekho o bhook se ladne walon.

The great minister's objection was to the words in the second line. He wanted to remove the word *bhook*, hunger. Instead, he suggested that the second line say:

Padhna likhna seekho o desh mein rehne walon.

['Learn to read and write, you who are fighting hunger' was changed to 'Learn to read and write, you residents of this nation'].

When we heard the song with this change, we both laughed at the minister's stupidity and showered him with some sweet four-letter curses. The minister objected to the word 'hunger', but it has not been removed to date.

My last meeting with Safdar was when he came to watch my new theatre production *Veergati*, written by Asghar Wajahat. I remember waiting for him and his group in the foyer of Shri Ram Centre. He was late by almost ten minutes. When I saw him coming, I shouted at him, 'Why are you so late?' He replied, 'Yaar, I had gone to Jama Masjid to buy laal rotis for Ammaji.' I grabbed the packet of rotis, took one and began to eat it. Safdar laughed, took out another and began to eat it. Some friends standing nearby picked up the rest of the rotis. It was all quite comical, all of us laughing and eating. Then we all immediately rushed in for the performance. After the show, he said, 'We will discuss this play later, but come to the Central Secretariat Park for the performance of my new play *Halla Bol*. I have tried for the first time to do a love story in a street play.' Sadly, I never saw him alive after that eating of laal roti and laughing in the foyer of Shri Ram Centre. He was murdered three days later for performing *Halla Bol*.

The Making of SAHMAT

When SAHMAT began, we started with the Safdar Samaroh event. A call went out across the country for the celebration of

12 April, Safdar's birthday, as National Street Theatre Day. On this day, street theatre groups all over India would perform street plays in many different Indian languages. SAHMAT designed a poster simply saying, 'Street Theatre Day'. The rest of the poster was blank, leaving space for the street theatre groups to fill it in with matters in their respective languages. We sent these posters to theatre groups all over the country in large numbers, requiring that one copy of the poster, with the local information added, be sent back by each group to SAHMAT with all the details of the programmes put up by the respective group.

On 12 April 1989, 3000 performances happened all over the country in various vernacular languages. This was a first in the history of Indian theatre, and the overwhelming response from theatre people all over the country established a great network of theatre activists countrywide.

The next day, there was a huge protest march to the residence of the home minister. Nothing had happened to the culprits who had murdered Safdar. Not even the court case had moved. That same day, late in the afternoon, the first published series of children's books written by Safdar, with illustrations by eminent artists like Mickey Patel, Mona Ray, Bindiya Thapar, Arpita Singh, B.V. Suresh and Vasudevan Akkitam, was released. Also, that evening, *Mote Ram*, a play directed by Habib Tanveer and previously produced by Janam with Safdar and Zohra Sehgal in the lead roles, was presented by Jan Natya Manch.

The following day, 14 April, Astad Deboo and Dadi Pudumjee performed a dance-and-puppet performance, a fine piece of theatre. The same day there was a seminar on street theatre, which was attended by a large number of theatre people.

Shubha Mudgal, a Hindustani classical singer, and Pandit Durga Lal, an eminent Kathak dancer, performed too. An 'Artists Alert' exhibition of works by hundreds of artists from all parts of the country opened on the first day of the Safdar Samaroh and was on display until the last day of the festival.

On 16 April, an auction of these artworks raised the seed money to keep SAHMAT going. The Safdar Samaroh concluded on the evening of 16 April with the screening of a film by Shashi Kumar on Safdar.

From here began the long journey of SAHMAT, working for and in defence of cultural freedom through cultural action programmes. In the thirty-one years of its existence, it has had its highs and lows as it confronted the distortions and deviations attempted against the programme and against the syncretic culture of India. Let us not forget that in 1989, sectarian forces were on a dangerous path, using majoritarianism as a weapon against the age-old values of communal harmony in the country.

SAHMAT employed all forms of art, both traditional and contemporary, to celebrate cultural resistance in India and position the arts politically in the growing atmosphere of intolerance. It fought much opposition while holding on to its values. Some of this opposition came from the state, and some from organizations that believed in the politics of hate, violence and intolerance. All the work that SAHMAT has achieved rides on the backbone of the artists of India, who not only contribute to the nation by means of their art but also through their donations. Artists look to SAHMAT as a safety valve to express their protest against the injustices that were happening.

Personally, SAHMAT has been a great engine for my growth in understanding the mechanics of the system that operates behind the scenes. It has given me great opportunities to understand many individual artists and the world of contradictions and compromises. It has given me the chance to closely witness many political figures make dangerous somersaults that have had a major bearing on the future of the nation. It also made me learn how to work in an organization where your own personal ideas are not the only ones that will move forward. It has taught me how to respond to, respect and honour the ideas of others.

SAHMAT has been a laboratory attracting divergent ideas and resources that churn out multiple realities from multi-disciplinary perspectives. The eminent historian Zoya Hassan once described SAHMAT as the '*Gharib Nawaz ki degh*', or vessel of the poor, in that it provides sufficient food for everyone's ideas to be nurtured. Over the years it has evolved many strategies to effectively combat the wrongs that displace the truth socially or politically. This way, its strategy never weakens but rather sharpens and strengthens. This idea was important. When the general elections of 1998 took place after the BJP's *rath yatra* of Lal Krishna Advani, the communal rhetoric of the BJP peaked, and major communal riots broke out in the country. SAHMAT wanted to prick the bubble of the BJP and challenge the onslaught. Many ideas were proposed, but they needed big resources, which SAHMAT did not have. Finally, we zeroed in on one idea—to issue a single sheet or Fax or email to the secular leaders and several regional newspapers containing factual rebuttals of the BJP's propaganda. The leaders could use the information in their election campaigns, and the regional media, which had meagre resources, could publish the details for their readers. All this could dent the BJP's vicious communal campaign. SAHMAT collected around 300 fax numbers or email Ids of leaders, parties and media organizations. That meant more than 300 emails or fax sheets were sent out every day. The new counter-discourse of facts would make it difficult for the communal elements to oppose.

SAHMAT started receiving requests from the offices of other political leaders and publication houses for more information. We numbered these fact sheets, which were titled 'Communalism Alert [#]'. Complaints started to arrive if Communalism Alert had not reached, with messages requesting us to please send it soon. It became an exciting project for SAHMAT. One day, a man from Rajesh Pilot's office arrived at the SAHMAT office to collect a few editions of the fact sheets they had misplaced. A similar request came from Sunil Dutt's office saying, 'Your Communalism Alert sheets are very useful for Sunil Dutt's election campaign.'

The Communalism Alert sheets were written by scholars, journalists and others after great in-depth research. All this was voluntary work on their part. It took an exciting turn when SAHMAT began receiving material from unknown sources in villages and towns across India about the excesses committed by the BJP and the RSS. They requested that the information be included in the Communalism Alert sheets.

This single-sheet campaign was effective because of its uniqueness and cost-effectiveness. It led to the regional news media carrying our stories, with more facts of their own. It became a legal, inexpensive counter-narrative against the BJP, which that party found difficult to defend.

As the temperatures in national politics ran high, we at SAHMAT worked on developing our responses to the ongoing communal BJP election campaigns. Madan Gopal Singh, Sohail Hashmi, Ram Rehman, Rajan and I thought of organizing a cultural event to bring together Indian traditional music in all its forms and manifestations. For quite some time we toyed with the idea of holding a 'Sufi Rock' concert, but what that would entail we had no concrete idea about. It was just an abstract notion in our minds. We kept talking about it but couldn't imagine how we would do it. The fusion of Sufi and rock music was unheard of until then in India, but we persisted with this idea.

Sometimes political developments act as catalysts for your brewing abstract notions and concepts to germinate. Suddenly, the form and content of what you have been dreaming out sprouts and flowers before your own eyes. This is exactly what happened at SAHMAT. As religious majoritarianism in politics gained momentum, it helped us unfold our ideas for a Sufi rock concert. The communal riots happening all around triggered the sounds of pain and anguish in us, and we could see now a need for a counter-sound to play out loud during these troubled times. Culture is a pillar of support and comfort that needs to be foregrounded during dark times of crises.

India, a crucible of many cultures and languages, has a great tradition—one of the most significant legacies from its medieval times. During the fourteenth and fifteenth centuries, with the political situation in great turmoil and India facing many conflicts and challenges, a unique voice of love and brotherhood emerged from all corners of South Asia. These voices were from the downtrodden, the lower castes and the Untouchables. These voices spoke about the universality of the human race. They stood against organized, ritualistic religions, challenging their hierarchies of caste, colour and race. They questioned the orthodoxy of faiths on what salvation was. They said salvation did not need the medium of any high-caste Brahmin. They were the voices of the weakest, the voices of fusion and love among all human beings. They were the voices of the Sufis and the Bhakti poets, steeped deep in the landscape of South Asia, singing in innumerable languages and dialects.

Attempting to reclaim this legacy of secular India, SAHMAT finally arrived at a structure for a musical concert on a mega scale, where the message of Sufi and Bhakti poets would be invoked by traditional performers from different regions of India. We decided that the concert poster would include all the names of the artists, intellectuals, academicians, singers, poets, and sportspersons attending, and carry an appeal by them to uphold the values of the secular traditions of India.

The concert was the first Artists Against Communalism cultural sit-in by SAHMAT in India, and it was much easier said than done. We had to convince musicians and other artistes to perform on the SAHMAT platform. Each artiste was to give a short concert, performing for fifteen minutes. Before the concert, the artiste could speak for two or three minutes to explain why he or she was performing that day. In addition to this, at some point during the day, each artiste would serve as a compère, introducing and welcoming another artiste.

We had the support of two great friends of ours, one of them the late Sabina Sehgal Saikia, whom we lost in the 26/11 terrorist attack on the Taj Mahal Hotel in Mumbai in 2008; and the other, Kalidas Swaminathan. Both were connoisseurs of Indian music and very well-known journalists who knew most of the Indian musicians personally. Since it was not a typical music concert but rather a protest-cum-appeal for peace, it was meant to express the worry and disgust of the art fraternity over the communal divide taking place in India. We thought it would take some convincing to get artistes to join in such a cultural sit-in spanning at least eighteen hours with a large number of participants. To our surprise, hardly any invited artiste, dancer, poet, painter, or filmmaker refused to participate.

The concert was held on 1 January 1990, on Safdar's second death anniversary. The response of the public was overwhelming. The programme started at 9 a.m. at Safdar Hashmi Marg near Mandi House roundabout in New Delhi.

When you have no funds but big dreams, sometimes the impossible happens. It was a sit-in of the who's who of the Indian cultural community. All who came, spoke and performed raised one voice that spoke about our nation and its age-old syncretic cultural history, which was in need of preservation.

I remember going to the Asiad Village to meet the Dagar brothers and Asadullah Khan Sahab, the great Rudra veena player. The Dagar brothers confirmed immediately, and Asadullah Khan Sahab was so excited by the whole concept that he volunteered to open the concert with raga Des on his veena, the oldest musical instrument in India. His plan was then to go home but return in the afternoon to be the compère for another performing artist, which he did so with great flair.

There were many fun incidents when we approached the artistes to convince them to participate. Much of this job was accomplished by Sabina and Kalidas, as both knew most of the musicians personally. Sometimes they asked me to approach those whom they did not feel as comfortable with. For me it was a new world, but I had no choice but to accept this responsibility.

When I called one of the sarod maestros, he was quite cold in the beginning but was curious to know about SAHMAT was and who was behind the concert. When I explained to him the idea of the event, he said he would let me know about his participation the next day. When I called the following day, he again had more questions to ask: 'Who are the other artistes? Had Ashok Bajpai anything to do with the performance?' When I said no, the next question was, 'Who is funding the programme?' I explained we had very limited funds and that no one would receive any payment for performing as we just had enough money to pay for the expenses of the event. He replied, 'Oh, is that so? You are doing a great job, which it is very much needed.' I cut him short and straightaway asked him, 'So, Ustadji, are you coming and participating?' After a long pause, he assured me that he would call the next day, as he had another programme in Madras that day.

I did not know what to do. I reported my conversations to Sabina and Kalidas and begged them to talk to him since they knew him very well. Both laughed and one of them said, 'No way. You do it. You are also good at it.'

It was late afternoon the next day and there was still no call from Ustadji. In the evening when I arrived home, Anant, then eight years old, told me that some Ustadji had called and asked that I return the call. I was hesitant to call him. I dreaded his questioning, but I did call because I wanted him to come. He again started with questions about which politicians were involved with the programme, what my involvement was and why we were so keen to have him come. That was more than enough for me to launch into small talk. Everyone knew my relationship with Safdar and with SAHMAT in Delhi, but I politely explained to him that Safdar was my old and personal friend, murdered by political goons. I became a little sentimental also.

The least we could do for him as artistes would be to uphold his values and his sacrifice. 'That is why,' I said to him, 'I think a master like you should come and be there in solidarity with us.' After a pause, he asked, 'But was not Safdar part of a political party?' That was the last straw for me. I said, 'Ustadji, you know what has been happening in the country. They have been killing people, and we are doing this event in response to the atmosphere of hatred and want to appeal for peace. 'Then I thought I should recite some lines from Pastor Martin Niemoller about the silence of German intellectuals and the clergy on Nazism, including his own in his confession speech at a church in Frankfurt on 6 January 1946. The engraving of the confession in poetic form can be seen at the New England Holocaust Memorial in Boston, Massachusetts.

> *They came first for a communists*
> *And I did not speak up because I wasn't a communist*
> *Then they came for the Jew*
> *And I didn't speak up because I wasn't a Jew*
> *Then they came for the trade unionists*
> *And I did'nt speak up because I wasn't a trade unionist*
> *Then they came for me and by that time no one was left to speak up*

But I thought it would not be appropriate to recite those lines as he had every right to refuse us. Before I could complete what, I was saying, he said, 'Okay, I will let you know.' I felt very sad but could not say anything. I realized he would not come. He definitely had some reservations about the event, and he was free to make his own decisions. But still, I wanted him to participate because I loved the sarod, and he was one of the finest players of that instrument in the country.

I was helpless and did not know how to convince him to perform for us. I told myself, 'He has every right to refuse. After all, I am not any big or rich person.' But I was disappointed about my failure to convince him to perform. The next day I again got a call from my son Anant at the SAHMAT office. 'Baba,' he said, 'Ustadji said he is coming and to tell you immediately.' I was surprised, not totally convinced. I asked Anant, 'What did he tell you? Are you sure?' Anant replied, 'He made me write on a paper for you. He said phone your Baba now. He even asked me my name.'

He came for the event directly from Madras. He did not play but spoke about India being a bouquet of many flowers of different colours and fragrances. He said this bouquet belonged to us all and it was our duty to preserve its fragrance. I thanked him profusely for coming and exchanged smiles with him— which said quite a lot.

Most of the performers had been given fixed timings for their performances, but still it was not possible to keep to the schedule. Birju Maharaj was given his preferred time in the early evening, but from the afternoon itself a disciple of his began to ask me, 'At what time is Maharajji supposed to appear?' I would tell him the time, and he would acknowledge it and disappear. After some time, he would ask me the same question again and peep into the auditorium to confirm how big the audience was. When he repeated his question yet again after some time, I asked him, 'Where is Maharajji? Why has he not yet arrived?' The disciple replied, 'Don't worry. He is

waiting at the Kathak Kendra in Bahawalpur House and will
be here any moment.'

As there were many artistes performing, we had not
scheduled any break. I had no choice but to move on and ask
the other artistes to perform, presuming that Maharajji would
be there at any moment. But he still hadn't come. To my surprise
and shock, I saw the same disciple standing before me with the
same message from Maharajji a little later.

Suddenly, Hari Prasad Chaurasia arrived backstage. He was
in a hurry and wanted to get on the stage immediately. He came
to me and said he wanted to go up next. Very politely, I replied
to him, 'But Hariji, after this next performance is Uma Sharma,
the Kathak dancer.' He cut me short, 'No, you have to put me
on now. I am hungry.' I offered him a quick meal, 'I will get
some fruits for you, sir, right now.' He said, 'No Baba, I fast on
the day I am performing. I have just now finished my concert
at the FICCI auditorium, and from there I had rushed here to
honour my commitment to you. Only after performing here
can, I break my fast.'

In the meantime, Uma Sharma stood ready, waiting in the
wings to go on stage with her musicians. Suddenly, before I
could come on stage to introduce Umaji, Hari Prasadji ran onto
the stage with his bansuri bag and a tabla in his hands and
occupied it, followed by his tabla player. After sitting down and
taking out his flute, he gave me a smiling look. I couldn't stop
laughing. He didn't even wait for me to introduce him. He did
all that himself and even cracked a couple of jokes, and said,
'Umaji, *maafi*. I am starving, so please bear with me.' Umaji
smiled too, and then Hariji commenced his short but sweet
performance.

A few days before this event, I had been asked by my group
at SAHMAT to contact the renowned poet Rahi Masoom
Raza, renowned poet and dialogue writer of most famous

television serial Mahabharat of B.R. Chopra, and invite him to our event. I had never met him, but I had his telephone number, and with all my courage dialled his number. When I asked for Rahi Sahab, the voice on the other side replied, '*Haan, boliye. Main Rahi bol raha hoon* [Yes, speak. I am Rahi speaking].' I introduced myself and explained what SAHMAT was all about and described the event Artists Against Communalism. Before I could go on, he had invited himself, saying, '*Hum zaroor aayenge aur apni nazm bhi padhenge* [I will certainly come and also read my nazm].'

I was delighted with his encouraging words. I asked him what time would suit him. He said, 'I'll come around 11 a.m. and spend some time with you all, meet some people, and whenever you feel I should recite my nazm, I will do that. Do not worry, it is a very noble cause that SAHMAT has undertaken and please convey my congratulations to all. *Bahut nek kaam aap kar rahe hain* [You are doing a very good deed].'

Rahi sahab came and spent hours with the people who were painting on the roads outside the venue. He met many of his old friends and, in fact, enjoyed the ambience of the place. He went through the exhibition of paintings, posters and books. It was a delightful and relaxing time for him. When Sohail Hashmi announced his name, there was a huge applause. With that, he took the stage. In his beautiful Urdu, he talked about the centuries-old traditions of brotherhood in the lives of the Indian people. He talked about how, for hundreds of years, people of all faiths had fought the freedom struggle together and why it was necessary to preserve that legacy in this era of tragedy and pain. Finally, he recited his famous poem to the spellbound audience.

Masjid to Allah ki thri,
Mandir Ram ka nikla,

Lekinmera yeh awaaradil,
Bolo kiskaam ka nikla,
Banda kiskaam ka nikla.

The Artists Against Communalism cultural sit-in fetched a
very positive response from the general public and the media.
The media coverage was large and there were editorials and
write-ups in it. An idea that had been nursed for years by
Madan Gopal Singh, Sohail Hashmi, Ram Rehman, Vivaan
Sundaram, Shabnam Hashmi, Ashok Kumari, Parthiv Shah,
Kalidas Swaminathan, Rajendra Prasad and I had had its
first exposure.

9

Anhad Garje

In December 1992, *karsevak* of the Hindu right demolished the Babri Masjid at Ayodhya during a mass rally led by BJP leaders Lal Krishna Advani, Murli Manohar Joshi and Uma Bharti. Great anger exploded all around against the vandalism. The Indian National Congress government under Prime Minister Narasimha Rao had let down the nation, and was now a suspect in the deed, alongside the right-wing parivar. Some Congress leaders displayed strong reactions against their own government while condemning this act of vandalization before the tense nation. No one knew what was to come.

We at SAHMAT did not know what to do. At a meeting, various members threw up various ideas, but there was no agreement on any of them. One idea was to create and send out a poster as a mark of protest. But nobody was clear about what kind of poster it would be. I suggested that we go beyond political lines and put in an appeal to the conscience of the nation.

I coined the slogan, '*Ab koi naara na hoga, bas desh bachana hoga* [Now there will be no sloganeering, it will only be about saving the nation].'

A long silence followed. Some liked the idea, and others opposed it (particularly Vivaan Sundaram, who did not like it at all and argued against it). I pushed for the slogan to be printed and released on a poster. As we debated it, Madan Gopal Singh noted at one point that the slogan didn't say what the nation would have to be saved from. That wasn't clear from the slogan, and I conceded that. Then it suddenly came in a flash to me— we could print that slogan along with a poem by Kabir that I had used in my play *Kabira Khada Bazaar Mein*:

Sadhu dekhoyeh jag baurana,
Hindu kahat hain Ram hamara, Musalman Rehmana,
Aaapas mein dou lade marathain
Maram koi najana.

These lines would add a call for unity to the poster, and finally the group at SAHMAT agreed on it. Rajendra Prasad suggested that we print the poster on cheap paper and distribute it with the morning newspapers. Overnight, thousands of posters were printed and given to newspaper vendors in Delhi who volunteered to insert them in the newspapers. In the morning, Delhi residents received their morning newspapers with the headline announcing that Babri Masjid had been brought to the ground, and with them, our poster tucked in among the pages. The poster spread all over India as its photograph was displayed by many regional newspapers through their own sources. I saw on the front page of the *Times of India* a picture of a little boy carrying the poster in his hands.

On 7 December, the day after the Babri Masjid demolition, SAHMAT asked for a meeting with the president. No one was sure when the appointment would be granted, but surprisingly, we received a response that same day, confirming a meeting at 11 a.m. with the President of India, Shankar Dayal Sharma. Led by Vivaan Sundaram, the SAHMAT team comprising Rajendra Prasad, Indu Chandra Shekar, Suhail Hashmi, Anil Chandra Madan Gopal Singh and I went over in a delegation.

The president met us in a big colonial room at Rashtrapati Bhavan. Vivaan expressed his anguish over the demolition, then gave the president a memorandum signed by many intellectuals, artistes and academicians. The president read its contents and for quite some time remained silent. Then he asked, 'Who else have you met?'

Vivaan replied, 'No one, only you, sir.'

After a pause, he suggested that we meet the prime minister and tell him that we had met him, the president. Again, he sat silent, a little longer this time. I sensed his helplessness. He stared down at the carpet as he said, 'Nobody told me about the demolition. I saw it on BBC News. No one in the government has met me yet.'

He glanced around at the walls and the ceiling, and with watery eyes he continued, 'We had not abandoned our education when Bapu (Mahatma Gandhi) had asked us to join the freedom struggle—and now to witness this.' His eyes still moist and his voice almost cracking, he asked us to have tea with him. The ambience in the room was one of gloom. Vivaan requested him to excuse us. Shanker Dayalji insisted, 'Since you have come in this cold and are the first delegation, please stay for a cup of tea.'

We had our tea in almost complete silence, as if in a session of mourning. After tea, he stood with folded hands and thanked us each, one by one. We left Rashtrapati Bhavan. The political mechanics behind the act of the demolition became so apparent . . . even the commander-in-chief of the nation was not officially intimated about this major happening in the country. Someone said that with the demolition of the masjid, one of the pillars of Indian democracy had been razed to the ground. Who knows when the other pillars—the Judiciary, the Parliament and the Executive—will fall?

The aftermath of the Babri Masjid demolition was horrible. There were repeats of communal riots and the blood of Indians

was spilt across the length and breadth of the country. During
violent times in most parts of the world, the weapons of the
cultural community come through the spirit of the arts. Artistes
aren't politicians, police or thugs on the streets. The message
they convey is one of peace, brotherhood and harmony. They
won't be street fighters, but they will occupy the streets with
their songs of love and unity. They hold up a torch to show
people the light of their real heritage. They glue and bind people
of all colours and faiths together.

SAHMAT decided to go out and reclaim the peace in the
streets of Mumbai, Ahmedabad, Lucknow, Pune, Hyderabad
and many more places where there had been clashes and killings
between communities. Many innovative cultural programmes
were designed to travel across India, spreading the message of
unity. In the planning discussions, Madan Gopal Singh coined
the term *Anhad Garje*, the words from a poem by Kabir and
which figure in the verses of Sufi poets, as a clarion call to the
nation to unite and spread the message of love.

Anhad Garje grew into a mega-cultural sit-in, but it began
in Delhi on 19 January, very soon after the Babri Masjid
demolition. The Delhi programme featured musicians from
Afghanistan, Pakistan and Bangladesh, all of whom participated
along with performers from various parts of India representing
diverse languages and traditions, from the classical to the folk.
Anhad Garje travelled to the major Indian metropolises.

Many touching moments dotted the journey of Anhad
Garje. The cooperation it fetched was overwhelming. At every
venue where Anhad Garje was held, most of the local regional
talents joined in as part of the event, not only participating but
also volunteering to help.

In Delhi, Allan Fakir of Pakistan invited all the musicians of
Bangladesh, West Bengal, Rajasthan and beyond onto the stage.
He improvised, and they all performed together as if the borders

of their nations were being melted away. None of the performers understood each other's language, but the magic of the arts and hearts joined them together, creating a musical space invoking peace for the subcontinent. It was not only folk performers who participated. We saw the contemporary painter, Manjeet Bawa, in his colourful *faqeer chogha*, Madan Gopal Singh, Kajal Ghosh, Deepak Castellino and many others join in. The audience experienced the vibrational essence of Anhad Garje.

In Mumbai, Pandit Jasraj, before opening his concert, spoke to the audience: 'I have come to tell you something I believe in. This nation has many religions, each believing in that unknown in its own way. But remember, your faith is with you always but display it within the confines of your home. Outside we are one as a nation and let not our faiths divide us.'

After the concert, as Jasraj was leaving, I reluctantly handed over an envelope to him towards the travel expenses of his musicians. It was an embarrassingly small amount, I felt. He sensed my embarrassment, and he leaned out of his car and whispered in my ear, 'Keep that amount. You need it. You people are doing pious work. And yes, I will also come and perform in Ahmedabad, but keep my programme timing in the morning, as I will have to catch my flight for Madras immediately. I have a concert there in the late evening.' I didn't know what to say. I folded my hands. He looked at me, blessed me and left.

When Anhad Garje happened in Lucknow, someone amongst us asked a local friend how far Ayodhya was by car. He replied that it was two-and-a-half hours from Lucknow. Vivaan grew excited and wanted to visit Ayodhya. Ram Rehman joined in the excitement, and it was decided that they would make a trip to Ayodhya. While this was being arranged, the others in SAHMAT—Rajan, Madan, Suhail, Sabina and I—started considering the possibility of organizing a cultural sit-in in Ayodhya.

All of us recognized that it would be a challenge, not at all an easy effort, but all agreed to think about the possibility of this concert. Obtaining permission would be very difficult, given the attitude of the Narasimha Rao government. He would not like anything to happen at Ayodhya, not even a peaceful cultural event. He was under fire from the people in his own party and from millions of people in the country.

Ram and Vivaan went to Ayodhya and returned. Ram brought back pictures of the ghats on the river Saryu. The beautiful photos showed the long line of ancient buildings—temples, mosques, dharamshalas, homes, and more—from all schools of architecture standing next to each other in harmony. The river site lay far from the conflict site, where once the Babri Masjid stood. The riverbed area looked serene and poetic.

After much deliberation, SAHMAT finally decided to take Anhad Garje to Ayodhya. This was a very serious decision, which could have political ramifications. We held innumerable meetings with intellectuals, artists, historians, musicians, academicians, and many well-wishers of SAHMAT. On the advice and information gathered at these sessions, we chalked out a rough programme, including a major exhibition on Ayodhya under the guidance of and in collaboration with major historians. We decided on a night-long cultural event, from midnight to sunrise on 15 August, Independence Day. The Ayodhya exhibition, titled *Hum Sab Ayodhya,* would open on 12 August, Quit India Day. It would unfold the long history of the place up to the present times and would contain all the layers of historical events in Ayodhya, from ancient times to 1993. It would foreground the multiple versions of the Ram Katha, from Valmiki's *Ramayana* to the vernacular variations of the Ramayan. This project was ambitious and handled by the eminent historians Romila Thapar, Suvidha Jaiswal, Irfan Habib and Dr Shrimali.

For the night performances, we gave a general call to people working in the performing arts to participate in the event and register their protest by performing one of their relevant pieces. We received an overwhelming response. About 3000 artists from different fields confirmed their participation. They would arrive on 14 August and leave on the evening of 15 August. Contingents of artists would come from South India, and East India, as well as many from the Hindi-speaking states. Some big stars planned to come too: Girish Karnad, Shahji Karun, Unniyal Paran Shivram, Sitara Devi, Habib Tanveer, Suhag Sen, Girija Devi and many others. Sabina Sehgal Saikia and Kalidas Swaminathan put in all their talent, contacts, might and goodwill to find the best artistes to perform at the Ayodhya all-night sit-in.

Getting the permission from the Uttar Pradesh government was a project all by itself. Now under Governor's Rule, with senior Congress leader Motilal Vora as the governor of the state, we knew we had to exercise caution in acquiring permissions. We made our plans known through the media, and all kinds of stories started appearing about SAHMAT's plan. Leaders of all political parties began to give their opinions, some in favour of SAHMAT and some against it.

The reverberations of our efforts echoed in Parliament. Right-wing parties led by the BJP opposed the programme tooth and nail, while a section of the Congress party openly supported it. Arjun Singh of the Congress party, who was a union minister, gave his open support. He even went to the extent of saying he would personally attend the event, and if he were arrested so be it.

Meanwhile, in Lucknow, we awaited the local government's go-ahead. Shabnam followed up with the bureaucracy daily, but the Uttar Pradesh government showed no sign of responding. The political classes had taken their positions on the issue, and

pressure mounted on the UP government to permit this to
event happen.

SAHMAT, all through this suspense, continued organizing
the event at every level. Ram Rehman designed an iconic poster,
unusual in its design and content, captioned '*Hum Sab Ayodhya*'.
All involved with SAHMAT were brimming with excitement,
waiting for the permissions to come. Time was running short;
the dates for the event loomed near. With excitement and
suspense lingering on, SAHMAT decided that the exhibition
'Hum Sab Ayodhya' would be readied and on Quit India Day
would open simultaneously in seventeen cities across India.

We titled the all-night concert, on Madan Gopal Singh's
suggestion, *Mukta Naad*, slated to begin at the stroke of
midnight on 15 August on the banks of the river Saryu. Never
before in independent India had politics faced such a challenge
from the cultural community as it had now. During the period
leading up to Mukta Naad, every day there were warnings and
even threats from the people who were against it and did not
want it to happen.

One day, out of the blue, a call came from the office of
the governor of Uttar Pradesh requesting a meeting with the
representatives of SAHMAT in Lucknow. Shabnam Hashmi
and Rajendra Prasad left for Lucknow to meet the Governor.
The Uttar Pradesh government had offered them tickets to
come to Lucknow, which they refused. The next morning,
Shabnam and Rajan were escorted by UP officials to the Raj
Bhavan to meet the governor, Moti Lal Vohra.

The meeting, as reported by Shabnam and Rajan, revealed
subtle shades of differences of opinion within the ruling party.
They could sense a pro-BJP tilt within a section of the Congress
party and felt that Motilal Vohra tried to discourage SAHMAT
from proceeding with the 'Hum Sab Ayodhya' exhibition and
the Mukta Naad concert.

Vohra requested Shabnam and Rajan to shift the event to Lucknow, and he would render all help for the event. When he finally realized that SAHMAT wouldn't change its decision on the venue, he asked Joshi, one of his senior bureaucrats to accompany them to Ayodhya to see for themselves how difficult it would be to hold the event there.

Joshi kept a state helicopter ready to take Shabnam and Rajan to Ayodhya. Shabnam refused to fly in a government helicopter and told Joshi that she and Rajan would reach there on their own. Joshi, with his wife and daughter, flew to Ayodhya in the official helicopter. There the first thing Joshi did was to visit the disputed site where a makeshift Ram temple had been erected. He paid his respects there, along with his family members.

All this drama of the Raj Bhavan meeting, the helicopter ride and the visit to the makeshift temple was to make it clear that the government of UP was pro-BJP and not interested in our event. After this visit, when Shabnam and Rajan met the senior bureaucrat, all he said to them was that they would be informed about the government's decision. He took off in the same helicopter for Lucknow. Nothing came out of the visit, which turned out to be a waste of time for our two SAHMAT members.

Since SAHMAT stood its ground and huge social and political support was building, the government finally relented and granted it permission to hold the event in Ayodhya. But that didn't end their efforts to thwart it. There were many screws in the wheels of the UP administration. Those unhappy with this development were bound to create more hurdles and problems for us as we proceeded further.

After receiving the green signal, SAHMAT went into full and final preparation. Sohail Hashmi and Shabnam Hashmi left for Ayodhya to establish a base camp office there, and the rest of us stayed busy with the opening of the 'Hum Sab Ayodhya' exhibition. Copies of the exhibition had to reach seventeen centres in the country to open simultaneously in seventeen cities on Quit India Day. All was going according to plan.

The exhibition opened. Rajan and I left Delhi to reach Faizabad, where SAHMAT had booked rooms at the Faizabad Awadh Lodge. It was a very hot and humid day. Upon reaching the lodge, Sohail met us and immediately took us aside. He warned us not to speak to anyone present in the lobby of the lodge. The exhibition had been attacked and vandalized. We would hold a press conference around 4 p.m. and address the issue.

A hostile local press stood waiting, and when Suhail made his opening statement about the vandalization of the exhibition, one reporter asked, 'What are you going to do now?' Sohail replied, 'Nothing. We have so many printed copies of the exhibition that there will be no problem in mounting another exhibition. We have nothing to say to the attackers. The authorities will take action according to the law.' Another reporter, asked very angrily, 'Are you going to do your proposed concert on 15 August, and do you really believe you can do that now after this attack?' To this, I answered, 'Yes, we will do our work for which we have got official permission, and it is the duty of the authorities to make sure that we complete our programme.' Another question was thrown at us, 'Have you been to the disputed site?' Shabnam replied, 'We have come here to do a programme, and we have no intention of visiting the disputed place.' To this Rajan further added, 'The people of Ayodhya have welcomed us, and large numbers of them are helping us in every possible way. And for that, we are grateful to all of them.'

Once the conference concluded, we got calls from all sorts of people inquiring about our welfare. 'Has anyone been hurt?' Our only reply to everyone was that all was going as scheduled and that Mukta Naad would happen. When all the people dispersed, we went to our rooms to bathe and freshen up. When I had finished, I stepped out of my room but was surprised to see a policeman with his gun guarding my room. I looked down the corridor, where other gunmen stood guard outside my friends' rooms. I asked the policeman who he was and why he was there. He answered, 'Sir, I'm your security guard and I will be with you always, wherever you go.' I burst out laughing. I couldn't believe that suddenly it seemed we had to be protected. To top it all, we had two cops guarding the main gate of the Awadh Lodge. When we all met, we could not help laughing. We had not asked for security, but it was thrust upon us, and this was baffling. Later in the evening, we concluded that these were typical tactics to mount psychological pressure on us, to discourage us from doing this programme.

There were rumours that some local leaders who were against our Mukta Naad had issued warnings that they would enact a '*singha naad*'. What they meant by that one had no idea. We presumed it would be difficult for us to book rooms in the dharamshalas for the artists to stay. I remember Rajan, Sohail and Shabam advising me to keep cool in the face of provocation. They would relish a confrontation, which would give them enough reason to cancel our permission and we as a team had to avoid one at all costs.

The next morning, when we ventured to book rooms in the various dharamshalas in the area, the cops accompanied us. We looked ridiculous going around with them. People welcomed us everywhere and opened every dharamshala for us, a surprising and heartening sign. When we went to meet the Maharaja of Ayodhya, he did not greet us personally but offered his palace rooms for our senior and renowned artists. He even opened his Peacock Room, intricately decorated with elaborate mirrorwork all over the walls. We felt relieved and happy with the way people received us everywhere.

There were large local volunteer groups that helped and guided us and made sure everything went according to plan. In fact, this group of volunteers became the real backbone of Mukta Naad. They took over most of the work of looking after the artistes, receiving them and taking care of them until they departed Ayodhya after the event. In the meantime, the four of us concentrated on the actual programme and its details. The support of Sheetalji, the owner of the local newspaper *Lok Lahar*, and his office was amazing. He opened it for us to treat it like our own office. At some point, I asked myself, 'If the people of Ayodhya are so open, welcoming and not at all averse to our programme, then why is Ayodhya projected as some kind of hostile town?' From the rickshaw puller to the tea shop owner, no one had a problem with our presence.

We were informed by an officer that the collector sahib wanted to have a meeting with us. This sounded like a red alert. I reacted before anyone else could reply to the officer, 'Just now we are very busy, and it is too late. We are also tired now. Maybe we'll come tomorrow.' He left, but we suspected some mischief was afoot and needed to stay on guard.

It felt strange that in Ayodhya, SAHMAT consisted of just the four of us making arrangements and making decisions on everything, though of course with the support of many volunteers from Faizabad and Ayodhya who guided us and gave us advice at every step since they knew and understood the local political ways better. But the number of calls and inquiries we were receiving from all sorts of places in India gave people the impression that we had a very big establishment run by a large number of people with a secretarial office. The fact was that Shabnam was the main engine of the SAHMAT Trust, and she was managing with her desktop computer and one telephone. Rajan had a sharp mind that understood the various perspectives from which a problem could be viewed and would offer in-depth critiques with clarity.

The next day, 13 August, was very hot and humid, but lots of work had to be accomplished. We all tuned to the same frequency and wavelength, reacting and analysing together the developments as they unfolded at Faizabad and Ayodhya. It was fantastic to experience the synchronicity we had fallen into . . . almost able to guess each other's thoughts and next moves. We considered why the collector would want to meet us now. The collector knew quite well that hardly any time remained before the final programme. We got a little concerned and were curious about this sudden request for a meeting. We had to be prepared, so we delayed the meeting to gain more time for the teams of artistes to board their trains from all parts of the country to arrive at Ayodhya, either on the night of 14 August or the morning of 15 August. If anything happened to us four, all 3000 members of the creative community of India coming to gather in Ayodhya would court arrest together in the presence of hordes of national and international media.

Wearing my shorts and veiled with a gamchha, I walked with Sohail through the local bazaar of Faizabad. One of my chappals broke, so Sohail and I popped into a shop to buy a new pair. As we sat on the bench, the shopkeeper showing us some chappals, he casually remarked to me, 'You people don't seem to be from Faizabad.' I replied, 'Yes, you are right, but how did you guess?' He answered, 'From your speech. Where are you from?' When I said we had come from Delhi, he said, 'You are SAHMATwalas. You have done a wrong thing.' Shocked, I retorted, 'What wrong?' He described the exhibition, vandalized the day before in Faizabad, remarking, 'You have displayed a poster showing Rama and Sita as brother and sister.'

I looked at Sohail, who asked the shopkeeper, 'Who told you that?'

'It was all over the local papers,' he answered.

I immediately asked, 'Are you going to beat us now?'

He shot back, 'No, but why did you do that, sir? It is wrong.'

We explained to him that no poster of this kind was part of the exhibition. On the contrary, the exhibition showed Ayodhya over the centuries, the many Ram Kathas from many sources in various Indian languages, even from Southeast Asia. All these variations, these Ram Kathas, do exist, and one of them, written centuries back, was not even authored by an Indian but sat in the libraries of India.

When you do an exhibition on Ayodhya, you cannot delete any of these versions. Plus, many eminent historians had worked on the exhibit. We assured him that there was no poster such as what he had described. We realized that a deliberate lie had been propagated by the people who didn't want anyone to attend the exhibition and consider the story of Ayodhya.

The shopkeeper said, 'Even if it is in the old shastras, then the shastra is wrong.'

Still, he was enjoying our discussion and called for tea and samosas. When we declined, he insisted, 'Sahab, you have to drink tea. This is Ayodhya, and you are our guests. Differences apart, you must.'

We accepted his hospitality, over which he curiously asked, 'Did you have a darshan of the temple?'

I replied, 'No. We are here for peace, and that place is where the conflict is going on. We love the Saryu River, and our programme is for peace and harmony.'

He wanted to know what we had planned for the next night, and we invited him to come. 'When you come, do meet us,' we insisted. We paid for the chappals, and he agreed he would come to see what we were going to do.

While returning to our lodge, Sohail and I considered this exchange. 'There seems to be quite a simmering rumour deliberately spread about a poster which does not exist,' Sohail said. 'This is a typical technique of spreading lies and then to keep repeating them till people believe it them to be true.'

Back in the lodge, the messenger from the collectorate arrived again, requesting that we come to a meeting with a collector. We looked at each other, quietly calculating the timing of the departure of the trains from various destinations and their times of arrival in Ayodhya. We delayed the meeting further, and I asked the manager where the meeting would be held. 'Sir, at the collector's office,' he answered. Shabnam immediately shot back, 'No, we are not going to any office, and if that is the condition then we do not want to meet the collector.'

It became a war of nerves now. Many local friends had warned us about the dubious relationship between the dismissed BJP leaders and many civil servants.

The messenger returned and informed us that the meeting had been relocated to the Circuit House, next door to our lodge. The timing was fixed for after lunch, at around 3 p.m. We suspected that this meeting might have been called either to arrest us or to cancel our permissions to ensure that our event did not take place. We worked out a strategy before leaving the lodge for the meeting. Shabnam would act aggressively while Rajan would maintain neutrality, staying very reasonable. They would keep up this tactic all through the meeting.

When it was time to go to the Circuit House, a comic situation arose. Neither of the parties wanted to reach first and have to wait for the other. Finally, the cars bearing each party arrived simultaneously. The Circuit House had a very large hall with all types of colonial furniture. Since no one knew each other, formal introductions took place—Collector Bhagwati Sharan Varma and Superintendent of Police Satyendra Kumar Garg. Then we all settled in our respective places.

There was a long pause. No one intended to speak first. Finally, the collector signalled to Garg to begin. Garg's voice took on a harsh and offensive tone as he said, 'You know what

the CID reports are. I'm going to let you know the contents.'
He took out a sheet of paper and prepared to read it out to us.

I cut him short, 'We do not want to know your CID reports.
We have got the necessary permissions, and we are going ahead
with our preparations.'

Garg did not like my interruption and raised his voice, 'Who
do you think you are? You are just artistes only. We have to take
care of law and order. It is our responsibility to see nothing
untoward happens.'

I too raised my voice and said, 'Exactly. Your responsibility is
law and order, not ours. We are free citizens. We are not bound
to wear uniforms, but you are. So, you do your duty while we do
our work.'

At that point, I told them to remember that if anything
happened the next day there would be 3000 artists, musicians
and poets from all parts of the country that they would have to
face. We would court arrest, so the authorities had better keep
that in mind before they thought of creating more mischief.

Garg shouted back at the top of his voice, 'I am in charge
of security'; to which Shabnam retorted, 'You are in charge of
insecurity. We can see that.'

At that point, Rajan intervened and appealed to all of us to
calm down and find a solution since the function had to take
place at any cost. We sat in silence for some moments. Finally,
the collector unfolded his second plan and said, 'The venue that
you have decided for your function is on the banks of the Saryu
River, and we want you to change it to some other spot.'

Since his first plan of scaring and threatening us had not
worked, his new idea was to change the venue. Unfortunately
for him, all of us rejected it and told him that was out of the
question. The venue had been chosen after due consideration,
for both convenience and aesthetic reasons, as there was a large
park where people could sit without any problems. Here the
superintendent of police raised another objection: 'Suppose

there is some sort of riot-like situation, or some disturbances take place. People could be running into the water for safety. They could drown.'

Shabnam categorically refused to change our venue. We had hardly any time; people had been working at the site for almost three days, and now it was neither possible nor practical to change the site. But she conceded, 'If there are some minor changes or adjustments which will not create problems for the final performances, we will accept them. Please understand that very eminent creative personalities in the field of music, dance, fine arts and theatre are coming to perform here. We cannot have a shabby stage. The stage will remain floating in the waters of the river and the city of Ayodhya will be the backdrop for the performance.'

Since they had spent a lot of time on these fireworks, the collector asked us, 'Why not go to the site itself and see what can be done?' We agreed and got up to leave, but then he said, 'We are not going with you, but the magistrate of Ayodhya is waiting outside and will accompany you to the site.'

Another surprise. Since Faizabad and Ayodhya are twin cities about twenty kilometres apart, the post of magistrate of Ayodhya falls under a separate office. The government had posted a separate magistrate for Ayodhya, who was not part of the meeting between us and the collector and the police. This seemed very strange to us. When we came out of the Circuit House, we met a young officer by the name of Sudhakar Abdi in whose Jeep I rode to the venue, followed by Rajan and Shabnam Sohail in our taxi. In the magistrate's car, I mumbled to myself, 'Why did they waste so much of our time? They could have said right in the beginning that we have to deal with the administration of Ayodhya. Just a colossal waste of time.'

The magistrate, driving his official Jeep himself, did not respond, only smiled and gave me a look. After driving the twenty kilometres we reached the venue. It was a beautiful sight with a huge park in front of the sacred river and red sandstone steps and ghats leading down to the level of the water. On the other side of the river, pilgrims had come to bathe and to pray. Also, on the opposite side stood beautiful red sandstone buildings of various styles of architecture, including Mughal, Rajasthani, Gothic, Baroque and Elizabethan. Many of these old buildings held ancient temples where pilgrims offered puja. In the evening, at sunset, this long grand line of ghats looked timeless. Ayodhya, Ayujjha, Saketa, Vinita, Vishakha, Kosala, Mahakosala, Ishvakabhoomi, Ram Janmabhoomi—whatever name you want to call it by—all these names mark this place.

We waited for almost one hour at the site with the magistrate of Ayodhya for some police officers to arrive. I asked the magistrate to call the officer concerned on his walkie-talkie command him to come soon as the humidity that evening was draining our strength. After the magistrate talked to someone, he asked me over to his jeep.

He pulled out two books of poems in Hindi from the glove compartment of the jeep. Written on them was 'To Raina Sahab'. He handed them to me as a gift. I asked him if they were his poems, and he said yes.

'I am Sudhakar Abdi,' he continued. 'My family is originally from Kashmir. You may have heard of an actor Abdi in the film industry. He was my uncle.'

I said, 'Oh, that is remarkable.'

He replied, 'Now you know you can trust and understand where my sentiments lie, and you can believe me. I'm going to show you.' He took out a small yellow handbill from his trouser pocket and showed it to me. On the handbill was printed: '*TURKI PARTY MASJID BANANE AA RAHI HAI* [Turki Party is coming to build a mosque].'

Looking seriously at me, he warned me, 'You know they have spread a rumour about you people that there are artistes who are coming here who will drink liquor, eat chicken and dishonour the sacred place of Ayodhya. The administration has banned the sale of bricks, cement and sand. So, my request to all of you is not to give them any chance to create a situation where it will be counterproductive and may even create violence.'

I was alarmed and told him, 'Please do not allow any eatable sellers around this area. Please ban their presence. They can be asked to go to the main road site and not be allowed in this area at all.' I thanked him for providing us with this most important information. He smiled, 'Don't worry. Nothing will happen.'

The security officer in charge had still not arrived, so Sudhakar again called him on the walkie-talkie. In the meantime, Sohail brought over some peanuts and, seeing the books I had been gifted, asked me quietly, 'What is going on?' I replied, 'Later. Let us first get through with these officers.'

An olive-green Gypsy arrived and a very young, handsome police officer alighted from the jeep, greeting us all. He asked Abdi what this meet-up was about, and Abdi explained to him the programme for the next day. He took a long look around and simply said, 'Okay, it is all right.' He wanted to know more details about the programme, and he began to understand the whole event.

He asked us, 'Are you from Delhi?' and when we confirmed this, he replied, 'I was in Delhi, too, at JNU, where I prepared for the IPS.'

I immediately said, 'Please wait,' and called Sohail over. 'Do you by any chance know him?' I asked.

The officer responded, 'He is Sohail Hashmi, the general secretary of Students' Federation of India (SFI) at JNU.' They shook hands, and then he turned to Abdi and said, 'All is fine. No problem.'

When we asked him about the rumours floating around, he laughed and assured us, 'Don't worry. We know what we have to do, and you do your bit.' He laughed but looked unsurprised

when we told him about the meeting with the collector. He
smiled and took our leave, as did Abdi.

*

14 August 1993 was a historic day for SAHMAT. From the
morning people began arriving from all corners of the country.
Our local volunteers had made all the necessary arrangements
for the performers in the many dharamshalas around the city of
Ayodhya. Most of the SAHMAT members had already arrived,
so there were not just the four of us but also a large group of
team members and well-wishers. SAHMAT was now focused
on the arrangements for the musicians. Most of them would
travel by road from Lucknow and Banaras. Some would fly to
Lucknow and had to be received at the airport and brought to
Ayodhya by road. It was a massive operation—to take care of
all the performers and make sure they were comfortable during
the day and would be in good shape to perform in the night.
Local artistes were involved in the final performance. We
heard rumours that in the evening some people would hold a
demonstration to try to make sure the performances would not
take place.

It was after many days of planning and work that we had
all came together, and morale was high. By early evening, all
arrangements at the main venue were complete. On the other side
of the river, Ram Rehman had organized for the entire facade of
the ghats and buildings to be dimly lit with the help of electric
generators. The entire riverfront would be the backdrop for the
floating stage on which the performances would take place.

At the stroke of midnight on 15 August 1993, the
programme opened with 3000 artistes from various parts of the
country standing at the ghats of the Saryu, holding lit candles
which they floated in the waters of the river while the speech
of the first prime minister of India, Pandit Jawaharlal Nehru,

played on a soundtrack. 'At the stroke of midnight when the entire world sleeps, India will awake to freedom and liberty,' he said. It was a symbolic recall of 15 August 1947, a reminder of what the nation had pledged then and where we had reached.

The prologue to the event went smoothly. I served as the first anchor of the night, appearing on stage to open the evening with the first concert featuring veteran musician Umayalpuram Shivraman, master of the mridangam in the Carnatic music style, and Pagal Das, the local pakhawaj master.

Someone suddenly whispered in my ear that Pagal Das had not arrived. Some people had picked him up, but no one knew where they had taken him. The first opening performance, set to integrate the northern and southern traditions of classical music in the country, had been sabotaged. It was decided that Umayalpuram would perform solo. As I went to make the announcement, my bodyguard stopped me and instructed me to duck if I heard a sound or noise. I looked at him and at Vivaan, who sat near the stage watching me. He asked, 'What is this?' I quietly signalled to him and said, 'There may be something happening. Just be careful.' Vivaan also said, 'Be careful.' Suddenly a thought crossed my mind—what if someone tried to take a shot at me? Then what? I brushed this thought aside and made the announcement. Sivaraman came on stage with his *mridangam* in front of the huge gathering.

This SAHMAT concert had become politically charged. Everyone in the political world had taken a position—for or against it. From the day of the demolition of the Babri Masjid until that day, I do not think there had been any function or any event in response to it there as all the politicians had remained out of bounds and avoided the place.

As the programme progressed through concert after concert, a noise arose from among the audience and built up into a commotion. Suddenly, some sadhus and locals stood up in the audience and shouted, '*Jai Shri Ram*'. This continued for

about five minutes, during which the concerts had to be paused.
So, we turned up the volume on our loudspeakers, amplifying
our Anhad Garje recorded music to the full volume of 400
kilowatts. The sheer volume of the music drowned out the
slogans. Soon the police removed them from the venue and our
programme resumed.

As people settled down, I noticed Arjun Singh sitting in a
chair with one of his political colleagues, member of Parliament
Pawan Diwan, in the last row of the audience. It dawned on
me that the slogans may have been raised against the presence
of Arjun Singh, who had displayed public support for the
SAHMAT programme in Parliament and was now here among
the people of Ayodhya. He had strong objections to Narasimha
Rao's handling of the Babri Masjid affair. He stayed for half an
hour and then left in the night.

One young man followed me wherever I went. He wanted
to interview me. When I asked him what organization he
belonged to, he very matter-of-factly said he was from the RSS.
I said, 'Okay, but give me your questions written, and I will give
you written answers.' He refused to do that and kept pestering
me for an interview, but I did not oblige him. At one point
late in the night, I was thirsty and wanted to drink some water.
There was no water anywhere because we ourselves had pushed
all the hawkers far away in view of Magistrate Abdi's warning.
This lad said he would bring some water for me, but he came
back without any.

After some time, he asked me, 'Why do you want all the
questions written?'

I said, 'Knowing your organization, which is very upset with
and against this event, you people will misrepresent my answers
and put wrong words into my mouth, and I do not want to give
you any chance to do that.'

In the early hours of the morning, as the great Kathak
dancer Sitara Devi performed, sounds of *aarti* and *shankhs*

came from the temples across the river. At that moment, Sitara Devi and all present stopped the performance until the puja was over. This young lad was surprised and asked, 'How come you stopped your programme till the puja was over?' I laughed at his innocence and explained, 'This is how you show respect for other people's beliefs.' By now we had actually grown quite friendly with each other.

Girija Devi was singing a Ram Bhajan at sunrise. It was a moving moment and marked the close of the all-night Mukta Naad concert.

By now I was quite tired and very hungry, and I wanted to have some tea. This young lad came with tea in an earthen *kullad* along with some samosas for me and said, 'I hope you will not refuse this. I know you have not eaten anything all night.' So, I asked him, 'Do you know why? Because you people would have manipulated these samosas into chicken tikkas, and we did not want to give you any chance or excuse to start a controversy.'

I had his tea, and on his own, he confessed, 'I did not expect this kind of programme. We had been told something else. I may be from the RSS, but I liked the programme.'

At that point, I told him, 'Why don't you visit our Delhi office, and after observing what kind of work we do, then if you feel you can interview me, you're welcome.'

Once all was over at Ayodhya, most of us left for Lucknow with large numbers of the performers. Before I headed for Lucknow, I wanted to go to Mankapur, very close to Ayodhya, to see my younger sister. She had to migrate out of Kashmir with her family during the exodus of Kashmiri Pandits from the Valley in 1990, at the height of the militancy and terrorism there. She and her husband, along with her two sons, aged seven and nine, had come to Mankapur with one steel glass and one suitcase containing a few clothes. We had not met for two years, and I wanted to see how they were coping with their lives. Since my brother-in-law was telecommunications engineer with the

P&T department, he had received a transfer from Srinagar
to the backward town of Mankapur, a town with very limited
facilities. After visiting my sister's family for a couple of hours,
I left for the Lucknow airport.

Once I reached the airport, I checked in, but I did not
see the others who were to take the same flight. I panicked; if
they missed their flight, SAHMAT had no funds to purchase
fresh tickets for such a large group. I inquired with friends in
Lucknow. It seemed that they were travelling by bus and the
driver had lost his way to the airport. I tried to ask some officers
if they could delay the flight, but no one would give me any
definitive answer. I noticed Atal Bihari Vajpayee checking in
for the same flight. I had a bone to pick with him, because on
12 August, when Rajan and I had reached Lucknow, we had
picked up some newspapers before leaving for Ayodhya, and I
saw a full-page interview of Atalji's carrying the headline that
SAHMAT was an anti-national organization. I read the entire
interview. He had lied about SAHMAT and had accused us of
being anti-national. Seeing him at the airport, my blood boiled,
but I could not find the right opportunity to approach him. For
a moment I thought I would catch him when the aircraft was
in the air.

I boarded the plane and saw him sitting in the front row
with his attendant. I gave him a look, but he was looking out the
window. While I sat in my seat, an announcement was made
saying the flight would be delayed because some passengers had
yet to arrive from Ayodhya. I was relieved and waited for our
group to board the aircraft.

The first person to enter the aircraft was Girish Karnad,
followed by Shahji Karun, the Malayalam film-maker. Then
came Ram Rehman and Pablo Bartholomew, both well-known
photographers, and a large number of musicians with their
tanpuras and tablas. There was M.A. Baby, a member of
Parliament from Kerala. While all found their seats, I told Ram

Rehman that I wanted to have a chat with Atalji about his interview and his comments on SAHMAT. Ram and Pablo got excited and took out their cameras. They said, 'Once you go there, we are all going to click.' After a few minutes, and just before take-off, I took my chance. Atalji was sleeping, or pretending to be asleep, so I told his attendant with the big moustache that I wanted to talk to him. He said, 'Later. Let him rest.' So, we returned to our seats. After about forty minutes, I went again. This time I had taken out two cassettes of Anhad Garje, our music concert, which had proven a great success. These tapes contained Sufi and Bhakti music from all the Anhad concerts. Ram Rehman and Pablo again followed me with their cameras, but Atalji had not woken up. He continued to sleep.

Finally, when we landed and were loaded into buses to take us to the lounge, I saw Atalji sitting there with his assistant. In fact, M.A. Baby stood next to him on the bus, engaging in a light conversation with him. I finally approached Atalji, and M.A. Baby introduced me, 'This is Raina from SAHMAT, coming back from Ayodhya.' Vajpayee looked at me with a smile. I, without wasting any time, said, 'Sir, I have read your interview which you have given in Lucknow at your press conference against SAHMAT. Whatever you have said had errors and was filled with untruths about us. You have accused us of being anti-national. Do you really believe that? Anyway, I have a gift for you from SAHMAT. Here are these two cassettes of our anti-communal campaign concerts. Please listen to them, and then make up your mind about us.' With a smile on his face, he accepted the cassettes, and looking at me he gave a big laugh and promised to listen to them.

10

Kashmir Implodes

It was the winter of January 1990 when I suddenly received a call from Srinagar from my brother-in-law saying that my mother had a brain haemorrhage and had been admitted to the government hospital. In those days, terrorism in Kashmir was in full force. There were daily reports announcing killings and bomb blasts all over the Valley. With a curfew in place, I knew it would be difficult for me to move from home to the hospital. I rang my childhood friend, M.K. Razdan, now the CEO of PTI, and told him about my mother and that I needed to get home. Could he please help me to acquire a curfew pass? Razdan replied, 'When you land in Kashmir, go straight to Lambert Lane near Regal Chowk to our PTI office and meet Mr Sofi there. He will issue you two press curfew passes. Don't worry. I will phone him right away, and I hope all goes well with your mother.'

I bought my ticket, packed my few winter clothes and some cash, and left for Srinagar on a full flight. People on the plane talked about the state of affairs in the Valley, and somebody said that Jag Mohan had again been appointed as the governor of the state. Silence took over the passengers, and after some time the flight landed in Srinagar.

I did not know what to expect, but I was clear in my mind that I would take my mother and father to Delhi as soon as possible, where we could get my mother the best possible medical treatment. I left the airport by taxi, picked up my curfew passes from the PTI office and rushed home. My sister Girija was there; her children, aged six and eight years; my sister-in-law Shobha; and Babuji, my father. After dropping my bag there, I rushed to the hospital. It was a late afternoon; it was biting cold, and the streets were wet. There was a general air of gloom. There were hardly any people walking on the streets.

I was soon at my mother's bed. I saw that she was restless and wanted to use the washroom. The nurse and the doctor would not allow her to move, but she insisted on getting up. I don't know if she noticed or recognized me, because she was uncomfortable, disoriented and semi-conscious. The doctor finally gave her an injection, which immediately put her into a deep sleep. I asked the doctor in charge, 'What injection have you given her? Could you please let me know what the condition of the patient is?' All he said was that she had had a haemorrhage in the brain, and at this stage she needed to be placed under observation. And he abruptly moved on. My cousin tended to her that night. As it grew dark, I returned home, and in the night the family debated what was to be done. I suggested that the best option was to take her to Delhi, where we could all provide her with the best treatment. Under the prevailing circumstances in Srinagar, nothing much was possible there.

The next morning, I reached the hospital early, at around nine. I wished to meet the doctor. They had shifted my mother to a room with two beds. On the other bed lay a Muslim lady who had come from some far-off village. I went to meet the doctor in charge. He was a Kashmiri Pandit, also a Raina. I introduced myself, and he recognized me. I asked him about my mother's condition and expressed my intention to take her to Delhi for treatment. He explained that my mother had gone into a coma, and under such conditions, she could not be moved. And that would be so even if she were in New York. We would have to wait for at least two weeks to see if her condition stabilized, and then maybe fly her to Delhi. These two weeks were crucial as the bleeding in her brain had to stop. The treatment involved the prescribed injections. She could not eat in the regular way, and she was fed milk and orange juice through a tube. I thanked him and went to the ward to visit my mother lying there.

The atmosphere in the hospital didn't look normal; there seemed to linger some kind of tension. To spend two weeks in such a hospital with a patient in a coma was not a comforting thought. But with no other choice, we had to do it. The family decided that my elder brother and I would take turns staying at the hospital, while my sister and sister-in-law would take care of Babuji and my sister's two small children.

My first night at the hospital, sitting on a steel stool in the chilly winter, was tough. There was no canteen to buy food or some hot tea from. It was after many years that I was in my hometown in the winter. At around midnight, I heard loud screams followed by a general commotion just outside, in the main corridor. I grew tense but did not venture out to see what the noise was. I heard running footsteps and sometimes painful wails and cries of helplessness. I guessed something serious had happened, perhaps a terrorist attack on the hospital. I shrank on to my stool with fear, looking at my mother's gentle, calm face. For a moment I thought it may be the end for both of us. After some time, the noise subsided.

The gentleman attending to the other patient in the room also sat quietly, occasionally looking at me but not saying anything. The silence in the room was scary. A few hours later, this gentleman gathered some courage and quietly opened the door without making a sound to peep out. Then again, he quietly sat back on his stool. After a few seconds, we looked at each other, and he whispered, 'The wounded have come, and they're being operated upon now.' I did not say a word, but I wondered, 'Wounded? From where they have come?' He must have recognized my confused expression and explained, 'These are the wounded Mujahideen.' When his statement sank in for me, I passed out on the stool.

In the morning, all was normal, as if nothing had happened in the night. I walked through the corridor thinking I would see the wounded Mujahideen in the wards, but I did not see anyone. There was no trace of them. I grew curious and wanted to know where they had disappeared, but I did not have the courage to ask anyone. I went back to the room to make some orange juice for my mother and started feeding her through the tube. There was a knock on the door. Before either of us could open it, a young man entered and asked, 'What is wrong with your patient?' As I explained, he shot back. 'What do you do?' I thought, 'Oh my God, if I tell him I'm a theatre and film man from Delhi, he might misunderstand.' So, I lied, 'I teach English in a private college in Delhi and have just come to look after my mother.'

He took a long and penetrating look around the room, and then again said, 'What do you need?' I said, 'Not much. I need milk and oranges for my patient.' He explained, 'If you need milk for the patient, go to the duty room. They will give you cow's milk, but if you need milk for your tea, then they will give you powdered milk.' I thanked him, and he gave a last look around the room and left.

The duty room distributed free milk to all. It was a strange thing. I knew that duty rooms were meant for doctors to take breaks in between their duty rounds. Eventually, I did get milk from the duty room. Most of the day I spent just walking the corridors of this government hospital.

In the morning, the curfew would relax for two hours or so. I would leave for home and my brother would leave home for the hospital. We would both meet on the road for a few minutes, exchange notes quickly and plan on what was to be done. Then our paths would cross, I heading home and he to the hospital. While walking back home, I could sense the stress in the city. Groups of people, mainly men, talked in agitation to each other. I stopped near one of these groups and overheard them talking. They were annoyed because all night there had been a gunfight between the terrorists and the security forces. Soldiers had entered homes and roughed up people, broken the wooden platforms of shops. Someone had even provoked people, suggesting that they burn the Pandit shops to recover their losses. Fortunately, nobody paid any heed to that suggestion.

Looking at the anger that seethed among the people, I sensed that it was not going to be an easy road ahead. Upon reaching home I decided to stock up on provisions for our daily needs. Since all the main street shops were closed, one had to look for the tiny mohalla shops located in the narrow lanes and by lanes of the locality. Fortunately, some of these shops remained open. I found one and ordered dal, cooking oil, rice, soaps, and sugar in bulk quantities. Snow had started falling. No porters were out and around to hire to help me carry the provisions home. I asked the shopkeeper for a big gunny bag, and I carried the heavy load on my back like a coolie. I had no choice. The streets were wet and slippery from the thin film of snow beginning to collect on the ground. When my father and my sister saw me with this huge bag, they couldn't believe their eyes. My father was upset, but I made him laugh when I said, 'You made me quite strong in my growing-up days. So now let us have some tea together.'

The next morning, I had to rush back to the hospital so that my brother could come home. We crossed paths at the bridge, and I asked him how our mother was. After a long pause, he said she was the same. There had been no improvement. Once back at the hospital, I immediately went into action. I had bought oranges and milk on my way. After preparing the juice, I fed my mother through the tube. The hospital had been reduced to a skeletal staff of sweepers, a few nurses and some attendants. Looking at my mother, I couldn't tell what lay ahead for us. I had watched a doctor check the reflexes of my mother's feet, so that day I picked up a spoon, pressed it against the sole of her foot and slid it down. There was hardly any reflex motion in her feet. I started to worry, but then the eternal optimist in me hoped for the best. All I wanted was for her to be stable for two or three weeks, and then I would fly her to Delhi for proper treatment. The indifference of the hospital authorities in Srinagar was so apparent in their general neglect of patients that one did not know whom to speak to. All these days I had been there with my mother, I had only seen Dr Raina that first day, and that too for only a few minutes before he disappeared.

I went down onto the lawns of the hospital to a common tap, which somehow had not frozen in the winter cold. I needed to clean some utensils, even though my fingers would turn pink and partly freeze in the water. When I stood up from my work, a pale village woman came face to face with me with a child under her phiran, tucked in like a joey popping out his head from his mother's kangaroo pouch. When I looked at her, she broke down sobbing like a child. I asked her what had happened. She said she had come to this hospital with a sick child three days ago and had been without food the whole time. 'My child will die,' she sobbed. I asked her, 'How did you come?' She explained, 'First I took a lift in a truck and then on a tanga to reach this hospital. But there is no doctor here. I do not know what to do. I have come from the far-off village of Duru.' I asked her to follow me and took her into the so-called kitchen or canteen for the general public, which I had found a few days earlier. This poor woman had no idea what was happening in the world around her.

When I entered the canteen, it looked like a dark den with a couple of benches and tables and a kitchen with a burning timber stove. I told her to sit on one of the benches, and I asked the kitchen in-charge to give me two hot cups of tea and rice with a full plate of beans. I took the tea myself, and while instructing her to drink some, I put some tea in her baby's mouth with a spoon. The baby was really sick with a scary-sounding bronchial cough. Thick mucus dripped from his nose. Having had some tea and feeling a little more settled, the woman began to eat and feed her child, but tears continued to flow down her cheeks. It was an unbearable sight. I assured her not to worry and explained to her how to find my mother's room. I told her that after she had eaten and felt warmer by the kitchen's stove heat, she could come to where my mother was. There we would figure out what to do. 'But please do not cry,' I implored. 'All will be well.' I took out a few hundred-rupee notes from my pocket and gave them to her. A young fellow approached us. Standing in front of me, he asked, 'What is the matter with her?' I related the woman's story to him, and he said, 'Okay. You have given her money. All right.' Looking at the woman, he told her to not worry. 'You will get food here,' he assured her. I requested him to please help her. He smiled and replied, 'All right, you also don't worry.' He returned to sit with his other friends on a nearby bench. They all had been watching the woman and me since the time we entered the canteen. I was intrigued by this group of young men.

When I went back to my mother's room, my brother-in-law had come to visit. His coming had been very risky, and I wanted him to return home as soon as possible. He knew a shortcut from his house, which he assured me was not so dangerous. He would leave using the medical college exit, so I went along to see him off. When we reached the main gate, he pointed out a man with a long shawl wrapped around his body walking freely through the street, and he said, 'That is Javed Nalka.'

'Who is he?' I asked.

'He is one of the most wanted men and a leader of some terrorist organization,' my brother-in-law explained. 'And you see how he's moving around without any fear or apprehension?'

I saw my brother-in-law off and turned back to go to my mother's room. While passing through the lawns of the hospital, I saw a big hole in the boundary wall of the hospital that opened onto the embankment of a small river tributary below. Back in the room, the other patient's attendant asked me, 'Where are you coming from?' I told him I had come in from the rear end of the medical college.

He asked, 'You saw that big hole in the wall?'

I said yes.

He smiled and said, 'You know, all the wounded Mujahideen, after undergoing treatment or surgery, are taken out from the hospital through that hole and then into the boats, and they disappear, and nobody dares to touch them. Did you notice that the security people stay outside the hospital and will never come into the hospital? They have between them a kind of ceasefire. The security people will not enter the hospital, and no one from the hospital side will shoot at the security people. It's a good deal for both parties.'

The fog gradually lifted from my eyes. The large group of young men in the hospital canteen, the fellow who had told me to get milk from the duty room, the disappearance of the wounded from the hospital after the surgeries, the absence of doctors in the hospital during the day—it all started falling into place for me. It was all a meticulous arrangement of the separatist movement in the Valley.

That night at home we heard sounds of gunshots somewhere, not very far from us. Nobody could sleep, and nobody knew what it was all about. In the morning, while it was still dark, I went to buy milk from a nearby milkman. The milkman was listening to the BBC news bulletin and was quiet, not talking much. All of a sudden, he noticed me and wanted to know when I had come. When I told him about my mother, he started to pray for her. He knew my mother; she used to buy milk regularly for him. I asked him about the news on Kashmir on the BBC.

He looked at me, surprised, and said, 'Were you sleeping last night? Did you not hear the gunshots?'

I replied, 'Why, yes, but where was it happening?'

He said, 'Gaukadal. There was an all-night battle between the Mujahideen and the military. Now the army is searching for the houses of the area.'

While he was very kind to me, at the same time he displayed a sense of pride about the Mujahideen. I paid him for the milk and left. I had to reach the hospital within a few hours while curfew was relaxed.

My sister-in-law Shobha had packed a tiffin box full of food and asked me to take it back with me to the hospital. I asked her what it was for, and she explained that there was a possibility of a total curfew. She had heard some neighbours talking about it. 'If any of you get stuck in the hospital,' she said, 'at least you will have food to survive.'

I readied to leave and said goodbye to my father, who hardly talked these days; he was suffering everything in silence. When I reached the main gate, there was not a soul on the street except a truck transporting government official from their homes to their offices. I flagged the driver for a lift and asked him to drop me at the government hospital. He agreed since he was going in that direction anyway, and I boarded the truck. As it moved through different parts of Srinagar City, dropping people at their offices, we could see the devastation that had happened that night—burnt vehicles, still-smoking half-burnt tyres, and other things aflame. The city looked like the aftermath of a major riot. We saw the lonely wet winter roads with hardly anyone walking. The truck journey became quite long and heavy, and I wanted to reach the hospital and send my brother home. After almost two hours of travelling through the roads and lanes of the city, I finally reached the hospital.

The truck dropped me at the emergency gate. When I went through the gate, I saw that there was total confusion in the emergency ward. People ran in all directions. Someone offered meals to people from a plastic pocket, and everyone drank from a single glass, one by one. They were all young and seemed tired and breathless. I did not stop but kept moving towards my mother's ward. It was a long walk. At one point my eyes met with those of a young man who kept crossing my path. He gave me a curious look, which unnerved me a bit. I kept walking, and when I turned to climb the steps to the first floor, I saw the same lad pass me with the same fixed look. I grew a bit worried but didn't look back.

Once I reached the ward, my brother was nowhere to be found, so I left my tiffin box in the room and went out to look for him. I couldn't find him. I asked the other attendant in the room, 'Did you see my brother?' He replied, 'He has left for home because of the strict curfew,' Since curfew used to be relaxed only for two hours in the early hours in the morning, people used to rush to buy necessary things and run back to remain indoors before the curfew was reimposed. It was very necessary for people to reach on time to their places for safety. I realized why my brother had left the hospital. Relieved, I sat on the stool and tried to relax for a few moments. As things deteriorated in the city, further restricting the movement of people, it was hard to know how to cope with all this. Looking at my mother, serene in her sleep and unaware of the world, I again checked her reflexes with a spoon under her feet. They seemed all right, and again I counted the days for two weeks to end so I could take her to Delhi.

I was sitting in a hospital with no doctors, no nurses, only a few service staff members and patients, my mother in a coma, and no work to do. I could only sit and observe my mother and think about the many problems ahead, hearing the occasional distant sounds of fire tenders and gunshots. Stuck to glass panes in the corridor were stickers of the Jammu & Kashmir Liberation Front, carrying slogans of freedom and sacrifice. The azan resounded from many mosques simultaneously. The ambience was scary, frustrating, boring. Looking at my mother's face, calm as if she were in meditation, I wondered when all this would be over. The situation was turning worse. Anything could happen at any time. Every day in the morning I watched taxis carrying Kashmiri Pandits to Jammu. They were abandoning their own homes and their ancestral world for an unknown destination. A thought crossed my mind, sitting by my mother's bed. How do I cope with this? Is it the end for my family here? My mind went blank, and I quietly waited for nothing.

My thought process was broken by someone tapping me on my shoulder. I opened my eyes. There stood the same young man who had passed me in the corridor with that curious look. My heart beat faster as I rose. He said, 'I need a donation.' I immediately took out a small bundle of currency notes that I kept in my pocket for an emergency and set out all the notes in front of him. He looked at me and then at the notes. He picked up just a single ten-rupee note and left. I did not know what to make of it. I sat back on my stool, wondering what was going on. Was he trying to make sure that I'm really with the patient and not some kind of informer (*mukhbir*)?

While I was pondering the situation, an elderly gentleman entered, reciting Quranic verses and blessing the patients. He carried a basket of fresh local bread and was offering it to the people at the hospital. When he offered it to me, at first, I hesitated and did not accept the bread, but he insisted that I have one and put a piece of bread into my hands as he said, 'Allah will bless your patient.' He left reciting the sacred verses. With the bread in my hand, I looked at my mother. Strangely, I felt a little better, and I started eating the bread.

I remembered an incident in this very hospital, many years back, when I was in school. My mother had been admitted here for some surgery. My aunt always took care of my mother whenever she was unwell. Both my elder aunts were like mothers to my mother. They pampered her, feeding her all kinds of good Kashmiri cuisine. One day, some person came into the ward with a basket of local breads, offering them to the patients. Normally, my mother would politely excuse herself and thank him, telling the person that she had enough bread of her own and to please give it to someone who needed it. That day, on seeing the bread, she had insisted, almost begged with both her hands, for one. My aunt and I were surprised. My mother looked at both of us and said, 'I have been refusing the bread of charity. I had better accept it and eat it. Otherwise, I will be coming again and again to the hospital. I must eat my share of charity.'

Back home from the hospital on the night 19 January 1990, all of a sudden, we heard the blaring of loudspeakers blasting Islamic slogans: *Nara-i-takbeer, Allah-hu-Akbar, Nara-e-risala Yo, Muhammad Rasoollkah, Yeh Mulk Hamara Hai, Iska Faisla Hum Karenge* and many more separatist slogans. When I woke up to this, it was not clear whether thousands of people had come out onto the streets or whether I dreamed all this. These slogans came from all directions and reverberated from the nearby hills, creating a war-like commotion. It also sounded like a riot against, or perhaps an attack on, the minorities.

My entire clan was awake, quietly listening to these slogans and vigilant against possible attacks. In the narrow lanes of the mohalla, a group attempted to set a wooden boundary wall on fire, but some elders intervened and stopped them. If they had succeeded in lighting the wooden wall, the fire would have engulfed the entire neighbourhood.

After almost two hours, I quietly opened my window and looked around. I soon realized that there were no people on the roads. We had been hearing pre-recorded cassette tapes playing from loudspeakers from mosques all over the Valley. The noise lasted until the early hours of the morning namaz. Nobody from the minority community slept that night, all expecting some kind of attack. The comic part of this scary night came once all the Islamic slogans were exhausted. Suddenly there arose the sound of a man singing a devotional Hindi film song, 'Kamli wale ke sadqe mein ya rab'. This song made me smile, and I could not help laughing. First, all night it was anti-Indian, pan-Islamic slogans, and now a popular Hindi film song!

The all-night hungama had created fear and suspicion among the minority Kashmiri Pandit community, and within a few days, the select killing of well-known Kashmiri Pandits began. I remember buying vegetables at the Habba Kadal market. News came that a young Kashmiri Pandit, Satish Kumar, had been shot dead. Someone had arrived at his house asking for him, and when he came out to meet them, they shot him dead at point-blank range. This incident created tremendous insecurity and panic among the Pandits, and quite a few of them began to leave the Valley. The murder confirmed the fear in the minds of the Pandits that it was now dangerous for them to stay here.

In the mornings when I returned from the hospital, I would pass caravans of taxis carrying Pandit families to Jammu. One day, in the late afternoon, I met my childhood friend who lived in front of my house. After inquiring about my mother's condition and commenting on how things had become tough for Pandits, he went inside his house. The next morning, as I left for the hospital, I noticed a big lock on the main door of his house. He had left Kashmir without telling anyone out of fear and for the safety of his loved ones. Fear was pushing the Pandits out of the Valley.

After a few days, while brushing my teeth early in the morning at the common tap in the garden, I saw my elder uncle and his son locking their home. I asked my uncle, 'What is the matter? Where are you going this early in the morning?' He very matter-of-factly said, 'We are leaving, tell Jana [my father] that I have left and moved on.' I was dumbfounded. I could not believe that an elder brother would leave without telling his younger brother. I carry that shock to this day. Knowing well that his younger brother's wife was in a coma struggling for life in the hospital, he escaped quietly. This uncle and my father had been buddies. My father had been a big support for this elder brother during many a crisis in his life, and here, while my father slept hardly ten feet away, this elder brother did not even think it fit to say goodbye to him or to give him a few words of sympathy for what his younger brother was going through.

Fear of death had reached such a level that people had become indifferent to others and relationships were turning absurd. Being alive became paramount . . . the reason for one's existence! The centuries-old links of interdependence that existed among neighbours were washed away. No one talked to each other. Nobody looked at each other. The majority, in their helplessness, just kept quiet and let all this happen to the minorities. And the minorities left . . . for where they themselves did not know.

Strict, indefinite curfew had been imposed for days now, relaxed for just two hours in the morning. On 25 January 1990,

I was at home and my brother was at the hospital. My mother had spent fourteen days in a coma. I discussed the various possible modalities for our travel to Delhi. It was a cold and dark night. Around 8.30 p.m., a knock came on the ground-floor window. The entire family fell silent; a knock in the night was dangerous, the sound of terrorists when they came and demanded anything they wanted or killed a person whom they suspected was against what they stood for. The knock could be for a Pandit or Muslim. For some time, we did not know what to do. Then I heard the voice of my brother asking us to open the window. When I opened the window, there he stood, exhausted and with tears in his eyes saying, 'The story is over, come out and take her in. She's outside in the ambulance.'

I understood that my mother was no more. In the pitch dark of the winter night, we brought my mother's body in from the vehicle. There was no electricity in the city, but some cops with their torches lit the lane so we could carry the body home without any problem. As per custom, the body was placed on the floor and an earthen lamp was lit. We all sat around the body for quite some time in silence. My two little nephews didn't understand much, both looking at us and then at their grandmother, but not uttering a word. My three cousins offered great help and support.

The next day was 26 January 1990, a Friday and Republic Day of India. In Srinagar, the government had ordered a complete shutdown and shoot-at-sight orders, which meant no movement on the roads. Everybody had to stay indoors. My brother told me that he had had a tough day at the hospital. My mother had passed away during the day, but there was no way to bring her body home. Nobody from the hospital helped to give him a vehicle to take my mother's body home. As the orders for a shutdown had been announced, nobody in the hospital wanted to take any initiative.

It was that boy whom I had met in the corridor that day and who had taken the ten-rupee donation from me who had helped. He had swung into action, yelling at the medical officer to provide a vehicle for the person who had died. My mother's body was lifted into the vehicle by a Bakarwal, a fellow attendant with the other patient in the room. My brother told me that the young man said he would have accompanied the body but, 'You know, times being bad, I cannot. Give my condolences to your brother.'

Through those pitch-dark roads without headlights and with no streetlights, my brother had brought the remains of my mother home. It had taken the driver more than an hour to travel a distance that would usually take only fifteen minutes.

A funeral seemed impossible. My father had advised us not to worry; we could postpone it and see how things would unfold the next day. All night I did not rest. My mind was stuck on how my mother's cremation could take place and on time. I felt it was her right to a funeral, and it had to happen on time. Things were so bad that even our next-door neighbour did not know there had been a death in our house. The roads were sealed, and telephones lines cut. My uncle had a telephone, which he had voluntarily disconnected by cutting off the cable lines from the lamppost, in case he was suspected of being an informer to the security forces. The distrust among people had reached such a level that there was suspicion between father and son, brother and brother, and Pandit and Muslim. The best way to be safe was to disconnect phone lines publicly.

There was one phone in the neighbourhood, owned by a telecommunications officer. My cousin and I crawled through our lane to his house, and through whispers, we woke him up and made a call to the operator at the post and telegraph exchange office. Those were the days when one could not dial long-distance numbers directly, one had to book a call through a P and T operator. I begged the operator to call just one number in Delhi to inform my wife about the passing away of her mother-in-law, and that she should inform our relatives about this and that they in turn should inform every relative they knew. But no one should think of coming to Srinagar.

I did not sleep all night. I waited for the morning, and finally, at daybreak, I zipped up my jacket and left our lane to speak to the cops who had watched us last night bring the body home, hoping that as they knew about the tragedy, they would be sympathetic and listen to my request. When I came out, I noticed a machine gun aimed directly at our lane with its belt of bullets flowing down the sides, like the ones seen in Hollywood films. Behind the gun was a soldier positioned to shoot. The image was very frightening. Watching me walking towards him with my hands up in the air, the soldier behind the machine gun screamed, 'E behenchod! Marne nikla hai? Wapas ja nahin to goli lagegi [Have you come out to be shot? Do you have a death wish? Go back, otherwise, you will get hit by a bullet].'

From his accent, I realized that this soldier was from Haryana. Last night the cops were from the North-east; they had changed guard overnight. I realized that this person had no idea about the death in our family. As I kept moving towards him, he spat out all kinds of curse words, not listening to what I was trying to explain to him. Finally, when I was face to face with him, I explained to him in pure Hindi why I was out on the road risking my life. I presumed that the reason he did not shoot me was because I kept my hands up all the time. My friend Amitabh Shrivastav had told me when he was in Poland with a National School of Drama performance during the anti-communist rule of General Gernosky, he had been caught in a similar situation. A cop had shouted at him in Polish, a language he could not understand of course. Some cautionary passing pedestrian grabbed his arms, pulling them out from his pockets, and sent them into the air. He was saved from being shot.

Standing before the cop with a machine gun, I said, '*Meri ma ka dehant hua hai. Smashan jaana hai. Unka daah sanskar karna hai. Permission chahiye* [I needed permission to take my mother's body to the cremation ground, I pleaded].'

He was in a foul mood and said, '*Aaj na koi aayega, na koi jaayega. Bhago saale* [Nobody was going to venture out, and fuck off].'

I persisted, explaining to him that we could not keep a dead body at home: '*Hum ghar mein shav ko nahin rakh sakte.*'

Now another cop appeared, with a stun gun on his shoulder. He asked me, '*E, kya baat hai? Saale, kya karne nikla hai? Ghar mein pani hai* [What is the matter? What have you ventured out for? Is there water at your home]?'

I replied, 'Yes.'

He ordered me to go and fetch him a jug of water, '*Daud jaldi kar* [Run, hurry up].'

I ran back. My sister-in-law had been watching this all from the glass window, shivering with fear. I asked her to get some water. She did but kept begging me not to go back. I took the jug of water from her and ran back to give it to the cop. Taking that, the cop disappeared into another lane. I think he wanted to clean his arse, having shat somewhere in the lane. After some minutes he came back. All the while I kept my hands in the air.

Now the machine gun cop asked this one to take me to the Sahab. With a stun gun aimed at my back, I moved towards the police station, which was about half a mile away. While I walked, Hassan, my childhood friend, saw me from his window. He was very surprised to see me with a cop and called out to me in Kashmiri, 'What happened? When did you arrive? Where are they taking you?' I only told him, 'My mother is no more, and I'm going to the police station for permission to cremate her.' I kept moving.

At the police station, a big, grey police truck sat outside the station with a unit of Central Reserve Police Force jawans with their weapons, stun guns and light machine guns on duty. Seeing me with the cop pointing his gun at my back, one jawan shouted. 'Where did you get him from?' Most of the jawans laughed. They presumed that some bearded terrorist had been caught. I don't blame them. With my Kashmiri looks, jacket and unclean appearance, I looked like one of them.

When the door of the police station opened, I saw a Sikh commander sitting next to a *bukhari*, keeping himself warm at the local timber heater. He gave me a look and said, 'Yes?' in English. I was relieved, realizing that he was an educated English-speaking officer, probably of a senior rank. I explained everything to him and asked for help so I could cremate my mother. He paused for a moment, gave me a look and said, 'I know you people have many difficulties. I can give you a truck for this purpose. Is the body ready?'

By this time my cousin had arrived, and he answered, 'No, sir, we have to get the shroud and other religious articles.'

I said, 'We cannot get all that since everything is shut.'

My cousin replied, 'We can get them if the Ganpatyaar temple is open. They keep everything there.'

This meant rushing to the temple of Ganesh and acquiring all the things that were needed, including the *arthi*, the wooden plank to carry the body. The police officer allowed us to go to the temple, but as we rushed to the Ganesh temple on the main road, there was another machine gun positioned on the street there. The jawan in charge of that gun screamed and ordered us to go back. Finally, a local J&K policeman rushed to him from the police station and informed him that their Sahab had permitted us to go. He let us go, giving us a stern warning that we should return within fifteen minutes or not come back at all. We ran through the narrow lanes, and to our good luck we found all that was needed for a Kashmiri Pandit funeral.

Our funerals have very elaborate rituals at every step, but in those circumstances, where could we get a proper priest to perform all the necessary customs and rituals? So, though we returned home with all the things, we still had no priest and no idea how the rites would be performed. All night my only obsession had been a timely cremation for my mother. The rest was, to me, unnecessary. To our relief, the pujari of our mohalla temple of Sheetal Nath volunteered to conduct all the customary rituals, right up to the cremation. Finally, my mother was given a proper bath, according to our ritual and custom. She was now ready to leave for her final journey. There were a few people with us to share our grief. We carried her arthi to the Sheetal Nath Temple and rested her there for a few minutes as this temple was where she used to go every morning.

From there we reached the police station where the commander had kindly kept a truck ready for us. When we were about to leave, Ghulam Rasool, my father's childhood friend, came running, wanting to accompany us. I requested him to stay with his friend, my father, who sat alone at home and would feel better to have him for company.

The truck started winding its way through the main roads of the city. That day we must have been the rare lot of people driving through the city with a dead body. There was not a soul on the roads except the soldiers and their weapons. The truck did not dare pick up speed. That would have been an offence in the eyes of the soldiers. Every 200 feet, the soldiers had blocked the roads with big coils of barbed wires. At each point, we had to stop. The soldiers would order all of us to get out of the vehicle and then conduct a thorough search of everyone. They would order us to show them the face of the dead body by lifting the shroud from the face to make sure that we were not carrying

someone else instead of a dead body. The soldiers would take
a look at the lifeless body, fold their hands in a namaskar, drop
their heads—in reverence or from fear of seeing a dead face—
and then order us to move forward. These checkpoints took a
lot of time, as we were stopping every 200 or 300 feet.

It became suffocating. How many times did we have to
remove the shroud from my mother's face? It angered me. At
one checkpoint, a soldier asked me, 'How did she die? What
was her disease?' At another, they asked us our names, and
once they confirmed that we were all Hindus, they allowed us
to move on. However, we had a Muslim friend with us, so we
asked him to change his name to Suresh but were quite afraid
that this could land us in deep trouble. For him that would have
been particularly horrible.

When we crossed one of the bridges near Chhota Bazar,
near the second bridge of Habba Kadal, there was a loud blast
nearby. We stopped our vehicle and froze. We heard the sounds
of guns being loaded, and within a few seconds, hundreds of
soldiers ran in all directions, some of them taking positions near
us. Most of us panicked. I got the fright of my life and went to
the driver, who was shaking, scared to death. I asked my brother
to go to the back of the truck and I sat next to the driver. I
asked my brother to light a cigarette for the driver. The driver
puffed on the cigarette as if he was eating it up. After a few
moments, he recovered from his panic. I kept talking to him to
make him relax. I noticed a young army officer rushing towards
us, shouting, 'Move out. Fast! And clear the place.' Our driver
had by now recovered and pressed the accelerator to rush out of
that place. From that point on we didn't face much tension, and
soon we reached the cremation ground.

Someone wondered what we would do if there was no
cremation man there. I said, 'We will do it ourselves.' Once
we brought the body down from the truck, I found a graceful,

pious-looking white-bearded man emerging from behind the chinar trees. He called and gestured to us to come that way. He was our cremation man, a Muslim. In Kashmir, it is a centuries-old tradition that Muslims perform the cremation ceremony for Kashmiri Hindus. There is a saying that the bond between the Kashmiri Hindus and Muslims stretches from birth to death. My mother's cremation happened with all the customs and details taken care of by the Guruji of Sheetal Nath and this pious cremation man. When, finally, we prepared to leave the place, I was heavy-hearted, yet felt as if a weight had lifted off my chest. A sense of peace descended upon me. All I had wanted was a timely funeral for my mother, and that had been achieved despite the horrible situation, all with the support of my three cousins, Jawahar, Manohar, Tej, a Muslim friend and the Guruji of Sheetal Nath Temple.

Returning home was another battle. Due to the previous bomb blast, none of us wanted to take the same route back, so we decided to follow another road through the Batamaloo area. To be safe, we kept with us the arthi, the wooden plank used for carrying a dead body to the cremation ground, as proof of where we were coming from. Again, we were stopped at many intersections, checked, frisked and interrogated. Even though we displayed the arthi everywhere, our return home was growing time-consuming. Someone suggested that we go to the police headquarters in Batamaloo and ask the authorities there to help us.

We drove straight into the campus of the Srinagar police headquarters. Once there we saw a flurry of activity of uniformed men. It looked like a scene from a war movie, with the camera lifting on a crane to reveal the entire location in a long shot. There was a fleet of armoured vehicles, and army Jeeps and uniformed soldiers were moving around in their battle gear. There were CRPF men, regular army soldiers, and Jammu and

Kashmir police personnel. This campus looked as if it was in preparation for some big battle. Light tanks stood parked and ready for any eventuality. Military transport vehicles zipped in and out. Everybody was busy; nobody was interested in us. I thought to myself, 'What is this? What is going on?'

I went into a room where the local police officers sat and explained my problem to them. They heard me but were of no help. One senior officer among them said, 'You know, you have to go first to the first floor. There is an army major, and he should be able to help you.' I left the room. One superintendent from the Jammu and Kashmir Police recognized me and asked why I was at the police headquarters. When I explained to him why we were there, he replied, 'Don't worry, just wait. My driver's having his lunch. Once he comes back, you follow my Jeep, and I will make sure you reach your home.' We waited, but the driver never came. Soon this police superintendent disappeared too.

Finally, I went to the first floor, where I met a young Indian Army officer of the Dogra regiment. He was examining a big, detailed map of Srinagar City and was giving instructions over his wireless sets. Seeing me enter the room, he stopped, 'Yes?' I repeated my story to him and requested that he let us reach our home. 'My people at home will be worried, as it is quite late, and we had left for the cremation ground very early.'

He asked me the name of the location of my area, and I said, 'Sheetal Nath.' He said, 'Show me the area on this map.' I asked him, 'Can you tell me where I am on this map?' With his pencil, he pointed out the spot. Once I traced where my mohalla was, he said, 'Okay, now tell me the names of each one of you and also the vehicle numbers.' I immediately borrowed his pen and paper and wrote down all our details. Then he explained, 'I cannot give you any written permission, but what I will do is to inform the first check-post on your way home, and then they will pass on your details to the next post and so on till you reach home.' I thanked him and rushed out of the room. That is how we reached home. When Babuji, my sister and all the other members of the family saw us safely back, they were greatly relieved.

All through the day I was in a strange state of mind. I felt like a zombie. I was concentrating on my duties as a son, but many a time I felt as if I was watching some tragicomedy. In this atmosphere of chaos, rituals and customs, everything became meaningless when thousands of people were migrating every day to some unknown future. There were funerals, protests, gun battles and killings happening. The basic fibre of a centuries-old world was being ripped.

For the next thirteen days, there were some daily ceremonies that had to be performed by my elder brother Ashok Kumar at home for the departed soul. The poor fellow—he had to get up early in the winter chill to do these religious functions every day while outside our house in the city, it was like a war zone. Every day there were sounds of gunfire, bomb blasts, killings and major confrontations between the militants and the security forces. Rumours spread that many Afghan and other terrorists had infiltrated the Valley to carry out terror attacks.

After a few days, one evening my cousin called from his house and said his father was calling everyone to his room. Hearing this, we prayed that it was not something too serious; he was eighty-five years old, the senior-most in the family, the head of the clan, now suffering from leukaemia. We hoped nothing was wrong with him. When we all gathered in his room, we saw him restless and agitated. He looked at his younger brother, my father, and told him, 'No, no, Jana, we cannot leave her there. Anything is possible here now. You need to pick her up as soon as possible.'

The first thought that occurred to everyone was that he was hallucinating. We were all trying to figure out the meaning of what he said when finally, it dawned on my father, who responded immediately. 'Oh yes, yes, we will do that. But the question is, where will we go and immerse her ashes?'

Everyone then understood the reason our uncle had called the whole family. He was concerned about the ashes of my mother, still at the cremation site. As conditions were worsening every day and most of the Pandits were quietly migrating out, we could not leave her ashes unclaimed. We promised him we would do this the next day, early morning when the curfew was relaxed for two hours. It was not possible to go to Shadipur Sangam in Kashmir, where the Jhelum and the river Indus meet, for immersion. That was too far away. He said it did not matter where we immersed the ashes, but they had to be immersed. It could be in the River Jhelum nearby or even in Dal Lake. That would be beautiful.

All the cousins decided to leave early in the morning, at around 5 a.m., in a hired Matador van. When we left it was dark. Before picking up the ashes, we had to buy an earthen pot from the potters. We woke him up. At first, he was frightened, thinking some cops had come to search his house . . . a regular thing. We had to shout for him to open the door and then explain to him the reason for our visit. He opened his door and soon brought out a big earthen pot, and then we hurried to a dried-fruits shop. Early morning and under curfew, naturally the shop was closed, but fortunately, it was a shop-cum-residence and the shopkeeper's wife told me that he had gone to the masjid in the next lane for early morning namaz. We rushed to the masjid and found him there. He was taken aback when he saw us all there. He knew our family very well. When I told him that my mother had passed away and we had to pick up her ashes, he immediately replied, 'Come, come. I know what you need.' We followed him back to his shop, and on his own he packed all that was required for the ceremony, all the while blessing my mother's soul and praying to Allah to send her to *swarg*.

Once we collected everything, we rushed straight to the cremation ground. By this time daylight had broken. Upon reaching there, the last remains of my mother were on the ground, now turned into white-and-grey ash. The same old cremation man came, took all the articles we had brought and directed us, according to the customs, telling us how to pick up the ashes and explaining the significance of each action. He asked us first to sprinkle water and milk all over the place so that the ashes became visible. Then he asked us to light *agarbattis* and sprinkle flower petals and dried fruit all over. He then told us to pick up the ashes according to our custom. While we did this, he asked my elder brother to pick up the ashes from a particular spot. He then directed my brother to drop it into the milk-water pot. Like the Hindu Pandits, he explained, 'Look at it. This is called *paurush*. You can see the form it takes; it looks as if somebody is in deep meditation in a lotus posture. Put this separately with other essential ashes and immerse them all in the Ganga at Haridwar.'

Watching him and listening to his instructions and knowledge about my religion, was like listening to some rishi. The soothing words and his blessings were superior to those of any learned Pandit I knew. He blessed us and we took leave of him, thanking him for everything he had done.

From there we had to rush to the river Jhelum, to a point where it leaves the city of Srinagar and flows towards Baramullah. When we got there, a large number of people were exiting the masjid after namaz. One gentleman saw the earthen pot on my lap and understood immediately the purpose of our visit to the river. He rushed to the bank of the river and shouted out to a fisherman who was fishing in the early morning and asked him to come to the bank as a sacred deed had to be performed. The fisherman, my elder brother and I, with the earthen pot in hand, got on to the boat. The boatman pulled us into the middle of the river, where the currents of the water ran faster. Here my brother and I, not knowing any mantra or sacred verses, picked up the pot and poured all the ashes into the water of the Vitasta, or Jhelum. While pouring the ashes into the water, I mentally recited the Gayatri Mantra, which my mother had taught me as a child. What these words meant exactly I had no idea, but quietly I said goodbye to my mother. As the earthen pot flowed down the river, my eyes teared up as they followed it. For the first time, I felt that I had truly lost my mother as she moved with the currents of the Vitasta on her eternal journey.

We returned to the riverbank. My cousins, who waited at the ghats, shouted, 'Give some money to the fishermen.' I took out my purse and offered a couple of 100-rupee notes to the boatman. He gave me a long look and said, 'For this pious service, you do not transact in cash.'

I woke up from some slumber with his profound statement, but as he was a really poor fisherman, I insisted he accept some money. He refused again. As we jumped out of the boat, my cousins again shouted out to us, insisting that we give him money, as part of our religious custom. I appealed to the boatman to accept money from us, but the boatman was firm, 'For such a sacred service, money is not exchanged. Go, your mother will go to swarg *ya Peer Dastagir*.' He pulled his boat back into the river. I watched as he floated away. He was obviously not well-off, otherwise, why would he be catching fish this early in the morning on such a chilly winter's day and during curfew hours?

Unfortunately, my cousins did not understand the depth of the fisherman's sentiment and kept explaining to me the scriptures and the importance of paying for my mother's after-life journey. I realized that we had different levels of understanding. They worried about life after death, while I looked at life in the present.

To encounter so many experiences in a single day—with the potter in the morning, the dried-fruit seller, the cremation man and, finally, this fisherman—it seemed a complete journey, unfolding the warp and weft of the socio-cultural mosaic that made up by Valley, woven over centuries and now in so much danger.

Even after a few weeks of my mother's passing, we could not leave my father alone in the house, and he was not ready to move out. Our mohallah was almost empty of Pandit families, and the situation had not improved. On the contrary, it had deteriorated. The curfew was still in place, except for those two hours in the morning. There was an army presence all over the place. It had become suffocating for me to stay indoors all day at home. One day, the curfew was relaxed during the day. I decided to take a long walk along Residency Road and up to Zero Bridge to see if I could meet someone I knew. There was hardly a soul on the road, except for policemen and army jawans with weapons zipping by every few minutes. It was a solitary walk, and after some time I reached Doordarshan Kendra, next to Zero Bridge. I felt tempted to find out if there was anyone there I knew.

The security at the main gate of Srinagar Doordarshan stopped me to find the name of the person I wanted to meet. As I had no idea as to whom I could meet there, I just asked, 'Who is the station director?' They told me, 'Lassa Kaul.' I requested the security to kindly call him on their local system and give him my name. Within no time a window on the first floor opened and Lassa Kaul was peeping out, looking at me in surprise. He ordered the security staff to let me come up to his room. After the routine checks, they gave me an entry pass and let me in. I was meeting him after many years. After the usual handshakes, hugs and greetings, we sat, and he ordered kahwa. Thus began our chatting session. I let him know the reason I had come to Srinagar in this winter and in such turbulent times.

We talked about the present situation in the Valley. He seemed worried and tense. He had not returned to his residence because of the fast-changing action in the Valley. It was V.P. Singh's government and Jagmohan was the governor of the state. The Governor had been tough from the day he had landed.

Kaul told me all kinds of stories from those uncertain days. The Central government had instructed him to report on TV as he saw the situation, and accordingly, he had reported in his news broadcast the last night that there was a shutdown in the Valley and all shops were closed. For this, he was pulled up by the local authorities and the governor had wanted him not to report any negative stories. Kaul was in a dilemma and concerned about how to bring any credibility to the news and to Doordarshan Srinagar. The migration of the Pandits disturbed him, and he said, 'In the morning, when I go sometimes for a small walk from my station up to the tourist reception centre, I see these Kashmiri Pandit families from the villages leaving in buses without any kind of belongings with them, just wearing a phiran and carrying a small bag. It breaks my heart. Looking at them, I asked myself, "What will they do and where will they go?"'

The happenings inside the administration troubled him, too. He revealed another unknown story about the revolvers issued to the local MLAs for self-defence. Now, with the change to the Governor's rule and with no elected representatives in the government in place, there was no trace of those revolvers or the names of the MLAs who had been issued them. Nobody had a clue. We had many cups of tea, and at about 2 p.m. he called two of his producers and asked them to interview me. This interview was purely a formality because the interviewer didn't have the courage to ask me any questions about the present state of affairs. It remained, bizarrely, all about my work, given the circumstances. At around 5 p.m., Kaul and I said goodbye to each other, and I headed home. After a week or so, Lassa Kaul, director, Srinagar Doordarshan, was shot dead while on his way home to pay his ailing old parents a short visit. This news shook the Pandit community even more.

At home, we decided that it was no longer possible for any of us to stay in the Valley. We worked out how and when the family members would move out. My father finally agreed to leave, but before that, he wanted to meet all his Muslim neighbours who had been his friends throughout his life. From his childhood, he had shared many ups and downs with them. He said their connections went back to his great-grandfather's time, so he could not just leave and disappear. He asked me to proceed to Delhi, assuring me that he would leave with my elder brother's family for Jammu, where he needed to meet my mother's brother and his family. They had come to know about her death only after nearly ten days.

So, this was the condition in the Valley. Communication lines were cut, citizens were stressed, and if anyone in the family did not return home by their scheduled time, panic and commotion would overtake the house. A sense of insecurity was prevalent everywhere.

When I left alone for Delhi, I begged all my family members and uncles not to delay their departure from the Valley. It was not safe anymore to stay back. At that time, no one could imagine that a return to Kashmir would be an impossibility. Many Kashmiri Pandits, in their innocence, believed that things would improve soon, within two or three months; that when spring returned and the educational institutions opened after the winter break, they would be able to come back. Many, including my cousins, believed that Governor Jagmohan would sort things out soon and all would be well and back to normal.

When I reached Delhi, my two friends Rajan and Sohail Hashmi were waiting for me. After a few minutes of our meeting, Sohail asked me, 'Raina, have you seen your face in the mirror?' I realized that I had not looked in a mirror for over four weeks. I said, 'Why did you ask me?' He replied, 'Because your face looks like you have been in jail.' I responded, 'Sohail, Kashmir is a jail with acts of violence happening every minute.' I immediately went to look at my face in the mirror, and I really could not believe that stress could change one's face to such an extent.

After four days, I received a call from my brothers saying they had all locked their houses and left Srinagar. My father preferred to stay in Jammu, as many of his friends, acquaintances and relatives were now in the city. At that moment I felt that my Kashmir, my home, where I was born, brought up, educated and nurtured, was now a closed chapter for me. But my mind was not ready to accept this fact.

11

Delhi—The Dilemma

In Delhi, I began to pick up the threads of my work after those dreadful weeks. I tried to return to my daily routine, but every day disturbing news came from the Valley. Reports of the burning of Kashmiri Pandit mohallahs poured in regularly. My other sister with her husband and two little sons had managed to get a transfer posting to Mankapur in eastern Uttar Pradesh, a backward area. Since it was not a developed region, things were difficult for her family in the beginning. They tried to put their lives together in this alien place where they knew nobody. Every now and then we talked on the phone and tried to keep their morale high. It was a strange new world, a new beginning with an unknown future. But over two-and-a-half decades, until their retirement, they managed their lives fairly well there. The resilience of the Kashmiri Pandit community is amazing. Despite the pain of leaving their home where they had lived for centuries, they rebuilt their lives as a community, brick by brick, tears upon tears, with courage, dignity and determination.

Many years passed. Kashmir grew entangled in more complex terror-related operations. The plight of the Kashmiri Pandits was not a priority for India to tackle, and the Kashmir issue became more and more politically complex, with international ramifications. India's mainstream political parties

paid only lip service to the migration of lakhs of people out of
the state. They did not pick up their cause either at the national
or international level, except for the BJP, which identified itself
with the tragedy of the Pandits, which it used too. Coinciding
with the peak of the BJP's Ram Rath Yatra and Ram Temple
agitation, the Kashmiri Pandit migration came as a blessing to
them, a gift which they diligently exploited for decades and still
milk today.

I was appalled and shocked to see the leading secular parties
of India hardly bothering to foreground the plight of these
homeless people. At many conferences and seminars, I heard
intellectuals suddenly justifying the migration, putting forth the
argument that Kashmiri Pandits were a landed and privileged
community who had always backed the Maharajah's feudal
rule. These arguments, based on half-truths, showed that these
intellectuals lacked knowledge of the anti-Maharaja struggle in
which Pandits played a leading role against the oppression of
the feudal government. None of these secular opinion makers
could see the undercurrents of the pan-Islamic movement in
the uprising of Kashmir. Being secular does not mean that
one cannot see sectarian poison. None of them could see that
Pakistan was the main player in the jihad in Afghanistan and
had the full support of the US imperialist parties.[7] It saddened
me that those who believed in a syncretic India failed to see
the writing on the wall. Gradually, the secular space began to
shrink, and a new, loud, violent and intolerant ethos expanded
and claimed more and more space.

It was strange. During all this upheaval, no one within the
secular space had even the curiosity to at least ask me what
happened of my family in Kashmir. It pained me to hear my
Kashmiri Pandit friends pose questions to me such as, 'Why are

[7] Memood Mumdani, *Good Muslim Bad Muslim*, Harmony, 2005.

your left and secular parties not supporting us?' Frankly, I had no reply. There were those Kashmiri Pandits who had been part of many non-political progressive democratic organizations in the Valley. All they expected was at least recognition of their plight from their counterparts in the rest of India. There was a strong left and progressive movement in the Valley, mostly in the educational institutions. The anger towards and disillusionment with the secular leadership of India pushed the Pandits into the lap of the political right, with some exceptions.

I must confess that for fear of being labelled as communal, I used to keep quiet and suffer our tragedy in silence. In fact, in Mumbai, when one of my old friends once said, 'You have started behaving like a communal-minded person, Raina,' it hurt me deeply, because all these years, all I had owned was my belief in a multicultural, multi-religious India for which I had joined all the movements and struggles that were in support of communal harmony. I still believe in the idea of India, a legacy of the Independence movement, led by all sections of society. The only person who did ask me about the plight of my family was my teacher, my guru, E. Alkazi. He wanted to know the details of the migration of my family out of Kashmir. He even shared with me the story of his own family. When Iraq attacked Kuwait, he lost all contact with his family. Finally, he was airlifted home by an Indian airplane.

Kashmir continued to explode because of terrorist violence, and killings became regular, a new phenomenon that Kashmir did not know. My community had to leave their homes to head to an unknown future. The clans separated and scattered to different parts of India. Kashmiri Pandits became refugees in their own country. Most of them took shelter in refugee camps where the conditions were inhumane and unhygienic.

Life became meaningless and absurd, but the human psyche kept holding on to some unknown hope, continuing to try to heal his own wounds. That is what Kashmiri Pandits did, and still do.

The shock of leaving the land of their ancestors, condemned to live as migrant refugees, was a difficult reality to accept. So, to breathe and feel normal, Kashmiri Pandits sought some calm, or pockets of it, where they could feel a part of their own community. In Delhi, the Pandit men, in small numbers, started visiting Coffee Home on Baba Kharak Singh Marg near Connaught Place. Soon this place became a small meeting space away from the suffocating small places where they had to spend most of their lives with their families. The coffee was cheap, and the migrants could afford it and spent some hours of the day there. Here at Coffee Home, they met with their friends and relatives. Often, one would see there a group of Kashmiris huddled together around a big table, having coffee and discussing Kashmir and their personal problems of survival. These meetings gradually became a daily feature, so much so that their Kashmiri Muslim friends too would drop in to locate their old Pandit friends. Generally, this place allowed them to take out their frustrations. It was a place of solace where they could guide each other, not a venue for hot, angry arguments. If you looked at this gathering from a distance you would be reminded of Kashmiri Coffee House at Regal Chowk in Srinagar, where all the artists, intellectuals and politicians of the Valley would meet for coffee and conversation.

Sometimes, people would meet after a long interval. Coffee Home became a place for them to seek the whereabouts of lost contacts. The migration had separated friends and relatives, and the Coffee Home gatherings helped some to unite again. The Kashmiri Table became something of a permanent feature for the people from the Valley.

Similarly, the Press Club of India in New Delhi had a dedicated table where, in the evenings, a big group of Kashmiri

Pandits would gather. Most of them were reliving their nights at Lubb Kaul's bar in Srinagar. After a couple of drinks, they would leave in the darkness of the night and back to their migrant nests. Every evening the Kashmiri Table was full of life. All kinds of journalists and social and political activists would sit together to discuss the various problems in Kashmir. Many friends from the Valley would join for a drink to debate the betrayal of the Indian state vis-a-vis Kashmir Valley. This table always looked like a non-stop party, with guests continually dropping in and out, and it still does.

Most evenings I'm rehearsing, so the Press Club isn't a place for me to spend my nights. When I could go, it was always a pleasure to meet people and receive their affection, and often a lot of leg-pulling. One day I had to meet someone there. This time during the winter of 2005, I was introduced to a young man, Liyaqat, then the current big boss of the Anantnag area. He had shining pink cheeks and beautiful blue eyes. When I sat at the table, a server came carrying a tray with five glasses of rum and placed them in front of Liyaqat. While smoking his cigarette, he picked up one glass of rum and gulped it in one go. After a few minutes, he gulped another glass. I was taken aback watching this young man consuming liquor at such speed. Then someone revealed to me that he was an Ikwaan Party leader, a very powerful man of his area. They told Liyaqat that I was working in the village of Akingam with the Kashmiri Bhand Pather folk performers. Interested, he told me, 'If you have any problem just inform me. I will sort it out immediately.'

I grew very curious about him and wanted to know more, so I asked him if he had been across the border, and had he been trained there. He started to laugh, 'Well, that is a long story.' I probed again, 'How was it there, on the other side of the border?' By this time, he had picked up his third glass of rum. He seemed well-satiated, enjoying his evening. His three quick drinks had their impact as he lost his inhibitions. I kept pestering him, asking him what kind of training he had received there. Now he was in his element and began unfolding his story.

'I did a lot of weapons training because I was good. I was sent up for further training at the Hikmatyar camp. I've seen it all, you know,' he said. 'When I crossed the Kashmir border into Pak-Occupied Kashmir, we were seven boys from my village. I was wearing my Nike shoes, Hara jeans and a warm jacket. The moment we reached our camp, we were immediately ordered not to be seen in our jeans, and one dirty-looking Afghan terrorist gave me a shalwar and kurta. I looked at the shalwar, its bottom opening was about twenty-four inches wide and was very loose for me. I did not like this outfit at all. I loved wearing my fashionable dresses. So, the next thing I did was to narrow the width of my shalwar bottom to fourteen inches. It now looked quite smart. I showed it to my friends, and we were joking in our Kashmiri language. Suddenly somebody yelled at us and ordered us not to speak in Kashmiri in this camp. I looked at this man. Again, it was another shabby-looking Afghan. His teeth were stinking of *naswar* (snuff). I almost vomited. All the time there were only harsh orders to be obeyed. Whenever we Kashmiri friends spotted these filthy-looking Afghan instructors, we used to signal to each other suggesting the nicknames we had coined for them—'Naswari Shalwari'. This made me laugh.

He continued, 'You know, many well-to-do and good-looking women used to come and visit our camps as social workers and give us lectures on our tasks and often appreciate our bravery. Sometimes they would invite some of us to their homes for a good meal, where they would make us feel very inferior with their behaviour and with their comments. Really. They believed that the Kashmir we lived in was very backward, without any progress or development. One day, a very attractive and well-placed lady displayed her refrigerator and said, "See, we keep many things in it, and you can see they remain very fresh." She opened the door of the fridge and showed me her vegetables and said, "I know you people have not seen such things. Now, inshallah, when Kashmir is liberated, you people will also have all these kinds of things." I just could not suffer this insensitivity anymore and replied, "No, we do have refrigerators in our homes, but we keep our shoes in them so that they remain fresh and cold." Everyone at the table burst out laughing.'

Liyaqat gulped his fourth drink. I asked him, 'Why did you leave terrorism and what were the reasons you changed your mind?' He did not like my question. He gave me a penetrating look, took some drags from his cigarette and remained silent for some moments until he said, 'One day in the camp, you know, there was a morning assembly, and some six boys were made to stand before the entire assembly. It was announced by an Afghani instructor that these six Mujahideen would cross the border that day and fight the kafir Indian military. Everyone prayed for their long life, and all offered namaz. Some of these boys were friends from our village. I bade farewell to them, and they left. After just about three days there was an unscheduled announcement for an emergency assembly. When all of us in the camp gathered, the officer in charge announced that our brother *mujahids* who had left three days back to fight for jihad had attained *shahadat*. There was unease and dead silence. Then *fatiha* was offered in their honour, and immediately all of us were ordered to go back to our usual training. I just could not believe that I had lost two of my friends from my own village. I had crossed the border with them. I was lost and started crying quietly, mourning their death. I thought of their families. Their parents did not even know that their children were dead and gone, who buried them, whether they were even buried, or their bodies were lying under the open sky for vultures to eat? I realized that we Kashmiris are like sacrificial goats for them. There were no feelings, no remorse for the loss of our boys. All in the camp went back to their routine jobs. No funeral, no *janazah*.

'It changed my thinking and my resolve. I decided that day that when I was sent to cross the border back into Kashmir, I would leave all this and surrender to the Indian security forces. I was completely disillusioned. They had no value for human life. It could have been me instead of them. I decided that I had to leave all this. And that is what I did.'

He now picked up his fifth drink and drank it quickly, took out a fresh cigarette, lit it and took a long drag. After a long silence, a mischievous smile appeared on his face. It looked cynical. He started to laugh. 'What is it now?'

He replied, 'You know, Kashmiri boys are very good-looking and attractive.' Then he looked at everyone around the table and said, 'We enjoyed a lot of women and sex. They wanted us. They would keep some of us for days. We really enjoyed fucking them.'

Personal Dilemma

The intolerance we witness in the country today . . . its seeds were sown many decades back when our myopic political vision made all kinds of compromises and gave all kinds of concessions to the mischief-makers. Trouble brewed surreptitiously in Kashmir and other parts of the country. Communalism and terrorism have nothing to do with religion, but religion is used as a mask and exploited for a dangerous idea of India.

I did not allow my personal tragedy to overcome my beliefs. I continued doing everything possible in my professional capacity and as a cultural activist. In fact, the Kashmir tragedy led me to merge my beliefs and my creativity. I kept working, travelling and performing in various parts of India and abroad. The formation of SAHMAT was a great boon. Here at least, we did not sink our heads into the sand. The constant challenges taken up at SAHMAT and its constant involvement in issues of the day helped me heal and also keep my objectivity rooted in my belief in a syncretic world. My travels and meetings with all kinds of people across India affirmed my belief in the strength of Indian diversity. My journey in theatre, working in many vernacular languages, opened new frontiers of theatre for me. I was humbled by many experiences during these years of travel.

I felt blessed and at peace from these experiences. I started making documentaries and television programmes that took me to remote corners of India. Many of my experiences during this phase changed my understanding of the people, mostly the poorest of the poor, and their struggles. Their humanity was as great, heroic and historic as that of any learned person.

When I was making a series of films on the literacy movement in India, especially focused on women who had emerged as the leaders of the movement, I travelled in Jharkhand to the deep tribal forests of Tundi, a Naxalite-prone area. There I met a young Adivasi woman named Sheila Mani Tudu, young and still unmarried, and the leader of the literacy movement, educated and experienced in working in her tribal villages. She travelled at least fifty kilometres every day on her bicycle to teach and educate her people. She lived in a tribal hut with her father and mother. Her family could feed themselves for eight months of the year from their own produce. For the rest of the months, they either starved or had one meal a day by borrowing from the local Bania, and somehow they managed to survive. For her literacy work, she received very little salary, insufficient for the family. Because she was a well-educated young woman, it was difficult for her to find a husband as most of the young men in her community had much less education than she did. She had received many honours and awards for her work, but no young man looked eligible to marry her. In her own words, she said, 'Now all this education and recognition has become a curse for me.' She was a pretty young lady, but her commitment to literacy work among the people of the community, despite her own poverty, was complete.

This area being Naxal-prone, she was aware of the dangers to her life. Her parents always feared she would be caught between the crossfire of the Naxalites and the security men. She understood the undercurrents of RSS activities and influence and knew about their involvement in this area, but she also believed in the power of education and knowledge and did not worry about the possible dangers to herself.

Similarly, meeting Titri Devi in the midst of the burning coal fields of Jharia, near Dhanbad in the state of Jharkhand, was another eye-opener. Jharia is a huge area, almost fifty kilometres in diameter, where coal has been burning underground for years. The area looks like an abandoned landscape . . . evoking images of the Chernobyl nuclear disaster site of the 1980s in Russia. The only difference was that here thousands of human beings lived with their families on the same land, while in Chernobyl an area within a radius of 100 square kilometres had been evacuated.

On this land of flames and gas fumes lives Titri Devi, a strong and committed lady who worked as a coal loader, which meant picking up and carrying black coal in big baskets and loading them onto trucks. She had been involved here in Jharia on two fronts: learning how to read and write in adult literacy classes and fighting with the authorities to give contracts to the women's collective for loading the coal trucks. This meant gaining an education and fighting with the Rangdars, the local coal mafia who controlled the area. She had learned the basics of reading and writing and understood what wages were to be given to women. She used to say, 'Baba, no more teepa now.'

Teepa referred to the thumb impression on paper they would give to receive their wages. 'Now I can read before I sign,' she stated. 'The other day I learned how to sign my name. I decided to fight the old Rangdari system. We women will fight till the end to get our loading rights, no middlemen now.'

In her speech at her women's group meeting, she said, '*Marna hoga or maarna hoga* [We will have to die or we will have to hit]. Then only we will be free and become masters of our own destiny.' I asked her, 'How can you live on this gas-filled and smelly land?' She laughed and said, '*Babu, main yahan badi hui, yahin beti ki shaadi karaungi aur yahin maroongi* [Babu, I was born here, I will get my daughter married here and I will die here].' I admire her and the many women like her raised through the literacy movement. I started calling these women 'Black Diamond Women'.

12

Working in the North-east

When I emerged from the Imphal airport, I was struck by the large number of armoured vehicles with mounted machine guns on top. There were many soldiers on duty. The airport looked like a military garrison camp, and I commented, 'This looks like Kashmir.' I had come to direct a big theatre workshop for the local talent for a period of forty-five days. The state of Manipur had been on the boil for many years now. Violence was part of their daily routine. There was strong political activity, but along with that, there were underground terrorist groups too.

As we started working, the local senior theatre people warned us not to work or stay in the area, which was a little outside the main city of Imphal. For the first few days, anyone whom I told about my theatre workshop in that particular locality in Imphal would say, 'Immediately get out of that area. It is not safe.' None of us could understand why they were so insistent about this, until one night when I woke up to loud noises and shouting from the main road. Our boys, who were sleeping on the top floor, had come down, angry, shouting at and abusing the people outside. Luckily, our building was locked so our students couldn't go out. They demanded that we open the gate, which I did not allow. Nobody would tell me what was happening. I was frightened when I saw two of my students brandishing *khukris*, almost looking ready to kill. Alarmed, I tried to calm them down. I succeeded after an hour and a half to bring them back to their dormitories.

I called one of my local coordinators and asked him to explain what had happened. He said, 'The area you are in is a Naga-dominated area, but all the boys in your workshop are Meitei. Since there is not a single Naga student in your workshop, the Nagas are very angry and want to attack your workshop and shut it down.'

I now understood that relations between the Nagas and the Meiteis were not good, just like the Hindu–Muslim tension in certain areas of India, and that anything could happen. The tension between the two communities stemmed from a larger political issue between Nagaland and Manipur. The young men I had met outside the workshop area were sweet, gentle and soft-spoken, but it was they who had instigated the showdown, in a complete reversal of what they had appeared to be, but our boys from the workshop area had equally responded. It was unnerving, I now understood the warnings of my friends, but with a dearth of good venues in Imphal, we could not change the site of our workshop. So, we continued there. Gradually, things settled, and we started to make progress.

However, the absence of Naga students at my workshop bothered me. 'Why were they ignored by the local Sangeet Natak Academy?' I wondered. During breakfast one day, I encountered a young man who asked me the reason and purpose of my work. I responded as I would to anybody else and explained what it was. He asked me why there weren't any Naga students in my camp. I explained to him, helplessly, 'That part had to be looked after by the local people. For me, all are welcome. I cannot distinguish between Naga and Meitei boys. You are all the same to me.'

He said, 'No, there is not a single Naga student in your workshop.'

I said, 'I can only apologize, but I would love to work with all and why should I make a differentiation? It is not good for us. The showdown that happened should not have happened.'

Then I asked him, 'Are you a Naga?'

He replied, 'Yes.'

I shook hands with him and said, 'I understand your anger but trust me, I have nothing to do with it. All are my friends.'

He shook my hand, said bye and left. I wondered what this meant and what would happen now, but nothing untoward happened afterwards. After that encounter, I presumed that this young man must have been a leader of the Naga boys and wanted to meet me. For whatever reason, things improved after that.

One day, our young men and women were not concentrating on our play work. Irritated, I said, 'I'm fed up with you. Do what you want. I'm leaving.' And I did. The next day, when I came in the morning to my small office, one student, who was very bright and sweet, ordered me to come down to the rehearsal space. I told him to proceed and that I would come a little later, but he stood his ground and insisted that I go with him right then. Frustrated, I shouted back at him, 'I will come a little later. Leave me alone.' As he left he said, 'I'm waiting.' After a few minutes, when I came down to the rehearsal hall, this boy accompanied me.

When I opened the door of the hall, it was a different sight from the day before. All fifty of the workshop students, boys and girls, sat in a big circle with their eyes closed, meditating. At the centre of the circle stood a kind of altar with burning incense, flowers, fruits and candles, and the script of the play at the centre of this altar. No one spoke. The entire space in the hall seemed charged with some unknown energy. The silence was overwhelming, and I too joined the circle. After five minutes of pure silence, one by one, each participant got up quietly and walked to the altar with folded hands, prostrated before the flames of the altar, and then quietly went back to his or her place in the circle, sat down and continued with the meditation. Once all the participants had bowed at the altar, they opened their eyes and turned their gaze towards me without uttering a single word. By this time something had happened inside of me. I also stood, bowed before the altar and sat back in silence. Still, nobody said anything. They continued to look at me. I was moved and touched by this silent ritual. This message of silence humbled me and brought tears to my eyes. I could not find any words.

Finally, I said, 'Shall we start our work?' They all responded softly, almost in a whisper, 'Yes.' Then one girl got up and gave the fruits as prashad to all. It was such a feeling of relief and peace that I felt that day. I tried to make sense of all this but could not come up with any sensible explanation until the boy who had insisted, I come to the hall conveyed it to me later, 'We were not respecting our script. That is why things were getting messy.'

There are many incidents that have helped me understand human nature with all its complexities. Sometimes I feel blessed that I have gone through the experiences I did; they have shaped my deep belief in the spirit of human capacity, which is not limited to one's caste or race, but which has led one to see beyond boundaries and limitations.

13

A Desire to Return, Fulfilled

Between 1990 and 1999, Kashmir was all over the newspapers and television. The feeling that I had lost my Kashmir, my city, my permanent address, forever, depressed me. The fact that I would never be able to go back haunted me. Every evening, Kashmir would appear within me quietly and leave me quietly. The stories of the killings, violence and horror that came in every day saddened me. The letters my father sent from Jammu unfolded his loneliness and sense of loss. My brother put it like this one day, 'This man has lost his house, his home, his independent life, his friends, his work and his world, just in five minutes.' He never had any serious ailments and used to go for his morning walk of five kilometres in Srinagar, but now in Jammu, his blood pressure was wreaking havoc on his body. I brought him to Delhi, thinking I would take care of him and make him relax and try to give him a good time.

On the very first day, the doctor checked him and said his blood pressure was running very high and that he had to get an injection to settle it. My father did not recover. His condition deteriorated fast, and within six months we lost him. At his funeral in Delhi, there were a few relatives who were themselves refugees now. Some of my friends came, even though they had never known him. He could never go back to Kashmir after he had to migrate out of the state, but surprisingly, until his end he had firm faith in the principles of secularism for the Kashmiri people with whom he had worked from the time he was a young political activist of the National Conference. He had participated in the people's struggles against the feudal rule of the Maharaja of Kashmir. As a young man, he had had his share of batten beating by the Maharaja's security guards during the Quit Kashmir Movement and was very active during the Kabali attack by Pakistan in 1947.

After many years of his leaving the party, I asked him, 'Why are you not going to the meetings of your party which you used to attend for years regularly?' His reply came after a long pause. He said, 'Now the party has been taken over by the lumpen elements, who have no clue about the constitution of the party, the history of its struggles and sacrifices.' When he left this world, I thought my connection to Kashmir was over and I would never go back. What would I go back to? I re-read his many letters, which I still keep with me. They reveal the tragedy of a man who did not know any other place on this planet other than Kashmir and who felt his life had been snatched away from him when he had to leave it. For him, there appeared no purpose in living. In fact, one day he said to me, 'You know, I am lost.' He didn't speak after that.

After my father's death, Kashmir has always faded in and out of my consciousness. Often, I used to suffer, like a fish washed onto the shores and thrashing about on the beach. It was that kind of suffering that used to visit me regularly, but I never articulated it to anyone. Sometimes it was like hearing a call from the very soul of the wounded Valley, making me restless and plunging me in pain.

Return or Not to Return

After my entire clan left Kashmir in 1990, never to return, I believed my relationship with my home state where I was born and nursed was over. But being a known cultural activist and a person who had been part of many campaigns in defence of cultural diversity or freedom of expression and so on, one question used to often plague my mind—why was I not in Kashmir, when it is in pain and suffering? I could not explain my absence from there, but this question used to haunt me every day.

I would often hear the news of some folk theatre performer, or the other being killed. It would send shivers down my spine. No one in the media reported on the attacks on the basic cultural fabric of the Valley, and how for years the cultural space had been taken over by religious diktats and militant organizations. For more than ten years, no cultural performances had taken place in Kashmir. The folk-song parties and the folk theatre performances of the Bhand Pather had been told that performing plays and singing folk songs was un-Islamic and hence banned. Musical instruments were broken, in broad daylight and publicly, and the artistes were beaten up.

The famous Muhammad Subhan Bhagat, a playwright and a winner of the Sangeet Natak Academy award was tried by the gun-wielding militants in his own home. He was about to be shot when his fellow Bhands begged for his life and he was saved, but he had to pay a hefty fine for pursuing his art. He was put under house arrest and warned that if he came out of his house he would be shot immediately.

Many eminent poets were forced to pay huge sums of money at gunpoint to terror groups as part of their contribution to the cause. Some folk actors in the countryside told me they were forced to become carriers of ammunition bags, and if they refused, they had to face harsh consequences. Many academics who did not believe in the politics of the terror group or had a different point of view from theirs were forced to sign letters of apology. The rich, progressive culture of the Kashmir Valley was erased. The centuries-old syncretic culture of Kashmir was silenced. Hearing all these stories and incidents, I waited for an opportunity that would let me enter the burning space of Kashmir to see if I could help douse some of the flames in my own little way. For that, I had to wait many years.

*

One day, by chance, I met Siddharth Kak, a fellow Kashmiri who had lived most of his life outside the Valley. he wanted me to join his team as one of the directors of a culture series programme for Doordarshan called *Surabhi*. This series made history for its powerful content and images of the diverse cultures of India. I worked with a team of four directors put in charge of North India.

This project was a God-sent opportunity for me. In charge of north India, I got to travel to some of the most unknown places in the country, allowing me to experience India at its best. I became quite greedy in recording stories from places that people in general hardly visited or even knew about. I filmed stories from the heights of the Himalayas to the deep and remote forests of Chhattisgarh. The programme enriched my life and my knowledge of our country with its intricate and complex cultural mosaic. It was unknown India that *Surabhi* brought to the drawing rooms of the urban Indian masses as well as to its rural heart. The amount of feedback that arrived at the *Surabhi* office was amazing—not only letters of appreciation but actual samples of art and craft from distant parts of India. *Surabhi* integrated India by showcasing the country's cultural manifestation.

I brought stories from the Changthang area of the high Himalayas of Ladakh, located at a height of 17,000 feet, and from the megalithic excavation sites in the Adivasi forests of Bastar. I was the first person to shoot the prehistoric rock paintings in the caves of Bhimbhetka in Madhya Pradesh.

This project also let me enter my Kashmir in 1992 June after a gap of two years, but only for twenty-four hours only. It was the period of tough militancy days. I got a call from Siddharth in Mumbai saying that had spoken to the governor of J&K, Girish Saxena, and he wanted us in Srinagar. I would accompany him. The next day, Siddharth arrived with his wife Geeta, who was unhappy about us going to Srinagar because of the situation in the Valley. During this time, some foreign tourists had been kidnapped and nothing was known about them. And a Polish tourist had been beheaded. This was the period when terrorism had the upper hand. Geeta tried to dissuade us from going to Srinagar. Siddharth, however, was cool and persuasive and finally somehow convinced her about our trip.

The next morning, both of us took a flight to Srinagar. To our surprise, we were received by an army officer with a car carrying the governor's flag. I looked around out of curiosity and saw two military jeeps with machine guns mounted on them, a part of the security cover for us as, it seemed, state guests of the governor. We moved out of the airport with one jeep in front of us and the other behind. This arrangement gave Siddharth the scare of his life. His face was tense. And I was upset because the arrangement made us stand out as targets. When I expressed my displeasure to Siddharth, he understood and also seemed concerned about it. All along the route, the roads were empty, and the shops closed. There were only security personnel posted all along the road. Some security units patrolled the lanes of the city.

It was a surreal sight to suddenly see a bridegroom emerge from a tiny lane, dressed in his green suit and a yellow turban, with a garland of currency notes around his neck, walking with just two men, perhaps headed to his wedding ceremony. Normally, he would have been on horseback with a long procession of relatives and friends, with women singing Wanvun, the wedding song.

We reached the government guest house where we would stay. Our meeting with the governor was scheduled to take place at 3 p.m., so there was time before that meeting. I came out onto the lawns of the guesthouse. In front of me stood Amar Singh Club. I remember my early days when I played cricket on the lawns of this club. My home was just a fifteen-minute walk from here, but due to the prevailing situation, I could not leave the guest house. Instead, I spoke to the gardener tending to some rose shrubs. I looked at him and addressed him in Kashmiri. At first, he could not believe that I was a Kashmiri. I asked him how the situation was, and he was lost for words, until finally, he said, 'What should I say, look at these beautiful roses. They look grand, but where are the people to appreciate the beauty? The story is over.' He went back to work.

Before leaving Delhi, I had asked Siddharth to carry two videotapes with him, hoping we might be able to shoot a story for *Surabhi* in Srinagar. The governor was waiting for us on the beautiful lawns of the Raj Bhavan overlooking the famous Dal Lake. When Siddharth explained to the governor our intention and what we wanted to do, the Governor heard us patiently for some time and said, 'I think you can come in September when the situation will show some improvement. At present, things are quite tough and uncertain. We are facing a lot of challenges from the terrorists. They have been kidnapping foreigners, and many more attacks are happening, so you will have to wait till then.'

I asked him, 'What are the chances of rescuing the foreign tourists?'

He replied, 'Well, you think we do not know where they have kept them? But at this point in time, we cannot do a clean job. On the contrary, we will be putting their lives in danger. So, we are waiting for the right moment, and we do not want to give the militants undue publicity.'

When we left, Siddharth Kak wanted to visit Chashma Shahi and Pari Mahal. These areas were clear of trouble for the simple reason that these locales fell under the governor's estate. We drove to Pari Mahal and spent time at the monument of Dara Shikoh's observatory and library. Dara was the eldest son of Emperor Shah Jahan and a great connoisseur of Sanskrit and Persian literature. Dara wanted to understand the cultures of Persia and India, and he authored an important book, *Majmai-Baharin*, about understanding these two rivers of civilization. From the monument, you could see the hills of Hari Parbat and Shankaracharya. For both Kashmiri Pandits and Muslims, these are sacred sites. In the foothills of Hari Parbat stand the monuments of the *khankah* of Mullah Akhun, the spiritual ustad of Dara's, and a masjid.

After some time, we descended to Chashma Shahi. While driving, I heard the sound of the swarnai, a Kashmiri folk instrument that plays an integral part in the folk theatre of Kashmir, the Bhand Pather. I could not believe that during these difficult times, someone would perform Bhand Pather in these secluded places. I asked the driver to stop. When I stepped out of the car, I saw a traditional Bhand Pather theatre group performing their folk music in the courtyard of a CRPF camp. Many CRPF officers and jawans were enjoying the performance, and Siddharth and I joined in the concert. There I met an old acquaintance, Mushtaq Ali, with a camera unit. The moment he saw me he begged for help to get him out of the situation he was in. Actually, he was caught filming without any official permission in this high-security area. As a mild punishment, the officer had asked his folk musicians to play some music as proof that they were really musicians.

I understood the problem. I introduced myself as a guest of the governor sahab and requested the officer to let them go because these swarnai musicians should not play for longer periods of time less their throats should bleed. The officer understood, smiled and let them go. I thanked the officer, and all of us left together.

In some time, we reached the Dal Lake Boulevard Road and stopped. There I requested Mushtaq Ali to lend me his camera in the morning for two hours for a short shoot at Chashma Shahi for *Surabhi*. He more than willingly offered me the camera unit, along with his cameraman. That was how we made our first two stories in the Valley of Kashmir for *Surabhi* and left for Delhi immediately.

Frankly, I did not want to stay any longer. I felt suffocated, surrounded all the time by security. I did not want to go and meet any mohallah elders or my Muslim friends under the cover of these soldiers with their guns. How would they have felt meeting me? I thought it would look vulgar and uncivil to meet them under the present circumstances. After so many years since the passing of my mother, I wanted to find out about their welfare, what they had gone through and what they had to say about the present conditions. I needed more time with them, but then it was not possible. So, we departed from the Dal Lake straight to Srinagar airport with a few bottles of Chashma Shahi water to carry to Delhi as a gift for Siddharth's wife Geeta.

This visit to Kashmir sparked my desire to return. But I had no plan in place to do so. I kept working in films, making television serials and directing plays with my group Prayog and with different organizations all over India. Many years passed. Every day some story or other about the happenings in the Valley would appear in the media. The possibility of working in Kashmir diminished day by day until one day I received an offer from the North Zone Cultural Centre in Patiala to conduct a major theatre workshop in Ladakh. I grabbed the opportunity and started planning the project. I contacted my colleagues to join my resource team and work with me in Ladakh, in the state of J&K, quite close to the Kashmir Valley. It would feel good, closer to home.

In June, we started our work in Leh with about fifty participants, half of them girls. In Ladakh, where society adheres to a matriarchal system, female participation in the workshop was far better in comparison to other places. Even so, working there at the height of 12,000 feet above sea level was not simple—the altitude meant we breathed thin air, which we weren't used to, and the food took adjusting to as well.

On the work front, however, we achieved more than we expected. Apart from the regular training that we did, the most fascinating part of working here was that everything was developed or fabricated locally by our own participants. For the final performance, we transformed a local folk tale into a major open-air performance on the front side of Leh Palace. Thousands of local residents and tourists came to watch the performances. Seeing the eagerness of the audiences, the local administration—which had refused any support in the initial stages of our production—suddenly opened its doors for any help we may need. The divisional commissioner of Leh, after watching the performance, promised to develop the local theatre building and make it an updated performance space. He ordered the staff to begin work on this by equipping the building with proper lights and seats.

While the theatre project achieved more than we had expected, something happened for me too, personally. I spent hours interacting with the many small Kashmiri traders in Leh; we would sit and talk about the conditions and plight of the people in the Valley. Every evening, we met in some restaurant, the traders bringing me updates about the latest in Kashmir Valley, and our sessions would continue late into the evenings.

In my hotel sat an annexe where a large group of Kashmiri traders stayed. Some of them would travel back to Kashmir and return to Leh after a few days. This group of Kashmiris kept mostly to themselves, rarely mixing with the other residents of the hotel. Among them was one who chain-smoked while drinking tea. Every morning, I would wake up to see him sitting on the lawns with a full glass of tea, sipping out of it and smoking cigarette after cigarette. He intrigued me very much, but I never had the chance to join him in the early hours on the lawn.

We used to leave for work in the morning and return only after dark. One day, when we returned to the hotel, a large group of residents, including local Ladakhis, sat in the hotel lobby watching the film *Ben Hur* on television. Out of curiosity, I joined them to catch a few moments of the film. I noticed the tea drinker appear next to me. We exchanged some pleasantries in English, and I asked him his name. He replied, 'My name is Aslam.'

After a few moments, I asked him, 'Are you a Kashmiri?' 'Yes,' he replied. 'Then why are you not speaking to me in Kashmiri?' I asked. We switched to our mother tongue. He couldn't believe that I was Kashmiri-speaking. Full of excitement and shock, he rushed into the courtyard and shouted in the direction of the annexe, 'Haji sahab! He is a Kashmiri.' Haji sahab's head popped out of the window, and he shouted back, 'Who?' 'The man with the beard,' Aslam answered. Haji shouted back in our direction, 'Arre, we have been discussing you for many days and trying to figure out your nationality. And here you turn out to be one of us.'

Haji invited me into the annexe area, and all the Kashmiris came down from their rooms in the courtyard to meet me. One of them said, 'Would you like to have some salt tea?' When

I said yes, the atmosphere changed into a complete Kashmiri gathering. Aslam said, 'For all of us you were a foreigner, either from Germany or from Russia.' I could not help laughing, 'For God's sake, how could you come to the conclusion that I am a foreigner?' 'Because of your dress,' one of them replied. 'You wear these multi-pocket shorts, and jackets, and because of your caps.' I could not stop laughing through this entire session of our salt tea party, complete with Kashmiri bakery items they had brought from the Valley.

I wanted to know what each of them was doing here in Leh. After a long silence, Haji, with a certain amount of humour, explained, 'Since you people left the Valley, we keep receiving orders from our well-wishers. This time, we have been ordered not to drive Maruti Gypsy jeeps. Since we cannot question and dare not disobey, I have come to dispose of my Gypsy.' Then he offered to let me buy it. 'At least I would have the satisfaction that my Kashmiri brother was driving my jeep,' he sighed. 'Honestly, if you ask me, I have come here to breathe.'

I responded, 'Haji sahab, I am a man of limited means. I have no money for this kind of luxury.' Haji, in his own style, said, 'Then take it for free. I swear I will be happy.' I thanked him for the offer. Then, with an air of frustration, he continued, 'I am fed up there in the Valley. I have come here to breathe some free air. It is suffocating there.'

Nobody spoke for some minutes until Aslam lit his cigarette and asked me, 'Where do you eat?' I answered, 'At any dhaba here. They serve their local food, and some even serve Punjabi food.' I asked, 'Where do you people eat?' Aslam replied, 'We have created our own Kashmiri community kitchen in the annexe. It is not great food, but we manage somehow. We cannot expect fine cuisine here in this God-forsaken place.'

I said, 'Why, there is a fine Kashmiri restaurant in the main market. The food there is very tasty. I liked it and whenever I have a chance to go there, I enjoy their food.' Haji sahab grew very excited and declared that we would get some dishes from there and all have a grand dinner that night. We went together in his jeep and bought some tasty ristas and goshtabas and all enjoyed the Kashmiri feast at the height of 12,000 feet above sea level.

The next morning, Aslam as usual had his tea and cigarettes. I joined him with my morning tea. We learned which places we had both come from in Srinagar and discovered that both of us had studied at SP College there. Over the next few days, we grew closer, and we would spend more time in the morning talking and discussing the Valley. Agreements and disagreements arose between us, but we grew to like each other's company.

After a few days, I asked him, 'Why do you drink so much tea and smoke so many cigarettes? It's not good for your health and also not good for your family.' Taking a deep puff of his cigarette, he said, 'You don't know my tragedy. I cannot trust anyone. Now, what I feel, what I want to express, I cannot. Every day I go to the masjid. I perform my namaz quietly without exchanging a word with anyone. I return quietly home. I have a younger brother whom I love, and I'm sure he loves me too. But believe me, I cannot express to him what I think or feel because I don't know what he is thinking. The lack of trust has gone very deep. Brothers have become strangers. So, when I talk to you here, a heavy weight is lifted off my chest. I can breathe without fear with you.'

I had no response for him. We continued having our tea. Later I asked him, 'When are you going back to Srinagar?' He replied, 'Inshallah, when you complete your project and leave for Delhi, that very day we will also leave for Srinagar.'

I met another Kashmiri a few days later at the main entrance of the hotel. He introduced himself to me as a driver in the government transport department who made frequent trips between Srinagar and Leh. I had not met him before. But obviously, he participated in the Kashmiri hotel dinner group. He wanted to confirm something with me. He asked, 'Are you a Kashmiri Pandit?' When I said yes, he continued, 'Look, I am going to Srinagar. What can I bring for you from there?' I was surprised and told him, 'Nothing, only offer my respects at the Dastgir Saheb shrine and come back safely.'

He responded, 'Just lift both your hands and pray for my demise to the Almighty, I cannot see all this happening.'

I thought he was a crazy Kashmiri who needed someone to talk to, so I said, 'Please don't speak like that. May Allah grant you a long life.'

I wanted to move on, but he stopped me and explained, 'Do not think I'm a madman. I mean it. I'm well off. My children are educated and doing very well. But do you know Kanhaiya Lal? He was my neighbour, and he used to teach my children for free, all through their graduation and then guided them in their professional careers. And today, I don't know where he is or in which city. He must be suffering in this summer heat. He left his home without even letting me know. How must he have felt at the time of leaving his ancestral home? I really do not want to see all this, so please pray for me, please.' With tears in his eyes, he muttered to himself as he walked away, 'Where will I find Kanhaiya Lal?'

We performed our play, *Chakhung*, based on a Ladhaki folk tale, with a contemporary interpretation of 'in unity there is strength', in the open air, between Leh Palace and the adjacent mountains. The performance was considered a major cultural happening in Ladakh, but on the final rehearsal day before the performance, a very ugly incident occurred. A little Muslim girl was watching our rehearsals when, suddenly, one of my favourite actors lost his cool and started shouting at her. He threatened her, saying that if she stayed, he would behead her.

This was a shocking moment, and it dawned on us that there was huge tension between the Ladakhi Buddhists and the Ladakhi Muslims. There was a social boycott of the Muslims by the Buddhists. We had not given it a thought, but it could lead to a violent and vicious showdown. To avoid any violence during the performance, we wanted to go before a Buddhist religious outfit called the Ladakh Buddhist Association, which exercised much political and muscle power in the city. We went to their office in the town, where only Buddhist monks were present. I presumed it would be easy to get the association's nod for the show. I was wrong.

They behaved like serious judges, asking all kinds of questions. I explained to them that the play was based on a Ladakhi folk tale and adapted by a Ladakhi monk. The language of the play was Ladakhi, and it was all about Ladakhis and their culture. I asked their association to support us so that the play could happen peacefully, and no violence would take place. That was all the help and support I wanted from them. They listened to me patiently, and then one of the monks responded, 'We will first see the play rehearsals, and then we will decide whether to allow the performance or not.' Since there was nothing objectionable in the play, I accepted this condition and asked them to come the next day to watch the rehearsals.

The next day, the monks arrived to see the performance. For some time, they watched with poker-faced expressions. As the play progressed and unfolded, my eyes were trained not on the performance but on these young Buddhist judges. I observed their body language, watching as they gradually relaxed and little smiles spread across their faces. After some time, these innocent monks were giggling and jumping in their seats, tapping each other with their hands, making comments among themselves. They were genuinely enjoying the performance. After the performance, they seemed excited and said that they planned to send the message around to the villages for the people to come and watch the play. To me, they said, 'Rainaji, do not worry, nothing will happen, and all people should come and watch the play.' I felt relief.

The next evening, the opening night of the play, people came from all directions, climbing the mountains and occupying their seats on time. Thousands attended, including my Kashmiri group from the hotel. They didn't understand the language but were overjoyed to see a spectacle of this kind.

The next morning, all of us with our bags packed soon left for the airport and flew in separate aircraft in different directions, some to Srinagar and others to Delhi. As we waited for the flight at the airport, Haji sahab and Aslam gave me their addresses, and I gave them mine, with a promise that our next meeting would happen in the Valley of Kashmir. But it never did. I lost their addresses somewhere. And although I have gone to Kashmir now regularly for years, I never met Haji sahab or Aslam again.

Taking off from Leh airport, crossing those snow-covered Himalayan peaks, I looked at the Khangri peaks through my window and imagined the day when I would travel beyond them into the Valley to the place where I had a home and where my family and my ancestors had lived for centuries. But no one from my clan lived there anymore. Then why this urge within me, continuously knocking at my head, to revive the memories of my home? Why did I want to work in Leh, a part of my home state and yet not my place anymore? When would I cross the Peer Panjal mountains and land in my city, where I was born and grew up living the life of any average Kashmiri boy?

When my flight landed in Delhi, I thought of Aslam and Haji Sahab. They must have reached home to live in the city of stress. While in the taxi, I decided that I had to go back to Srinagar and see what could be done. How, and when, I had no clue.

Sometime later, I received a call from my friend M.K. Razdan, CEO of PTI, asking me to think of a television programme for Doordarshan. I responded immediately, 'Sorry, I cannot do a propaganda programme on Kashmir.' He said, 'All right, but let us meet soon. And in the meantime, think up some ideas that you feel we can pursue.' I said I would get back to him soon. We left it at that. Inside, I grew quite excited at the idea of returning to Kashmir and started brainstorming. I did not want to do a fiction piece; many people had already made those. While some ideas brewed in me, I was reminded of an incident that took place some time back in Goa.

We were there for our annual family holiday. One of my friends, Orojit, a very fine designer, had shifted to Goa and ran a shop selling all kinds of handmade items like T-shirts, handbags and costume jewellery. One evening he suggested that I visit a Sunday village market to find many rare things made by local people who come from far-off villages. Plus, there would be very good Goan food.

The next Sunday, we all went to this village market. It was quite large, with lots of local people bringing and selling local and non-local goods that you do not always see in the typical markets. It had a Konkani ambience, and some people sang Goan folk songs. Our group had spread in all directions to look at the richness and variety of crafts and food. At one point I heard my daughter Aditi's voice pipe up. She was around seven years old at the time. She was asking a fellow selling silver jewellery about the price of some earrings. The fellow replied that they were for Rs 450. My daughter refused to buy them, deeming them too costly. The shopkeeper asked her how much she would pay. My daughter simply replied, 'No thanks. I do not want it.'

While they haggled over the price, I realized that the shopkeeper was a Kashmiri handicraft seller. I shouted at him in Kashmiri, 'Why are you selling them to her for such an expensive amount?' The shopkeeper gave me a surprised look. I continued, 'She is my daughter.' He smiled and looked at both of us to confirm this. Looking back at me and laughing, he said, 'You are a Kashmiri.' I said, 'Of course!' He picked up the silver earrings, packed them in soft tissue paper and handed them to my daughter. 'Then this is my gift to your child,' he said. He became sentimental, and when my daughter refused to accept them, he insisted that she did. Finally, I intervened and paid him, giving the earrings to my daughter.

I kept talking to him, and he revealed that his family had come here to Goa. Many Kashmiri people lived there. The government had issued them identity cards so they could avoid any kind of harassment. He gave me his local address and insisted that I visit him. He called over more small shopkeepers and introduced me to them. They too invited me to join them in the evening for the *Iftar*, and I promised them that I would attend.

In the evening, I went alone to meet those Kashmiris for Iftar in one of their big shops. There were at least twelve presents there. All the dishes they had prepared were Kashmiri, and the salt tea too. We had a very good time, talking about everything from Kashmiri politics, economy, families and terrorism. At one point, I asked them if they felt comfortable and happy in Goa. Did they face any discrimination for being Kashmiri Muslims? With all very positive responses, they said that there was no kind of discrimination there against them for being Kashmiri Muslims and revealed that there were, in fact, friendly relations between the local community and them: 'The locals visit Kashmir, and we look after them once they are there. These relationships have grown over the years into very strong family friendships. We invite each other for weddings, and for that, they come to the Valley to be part of our celebrations. And we, on our part, join their celebrations. They are Hindus and Christians, and we are Muslims. But it does not matter.

This bonding has grown over decades since when our grandfathers used to come here for work. There is another truth and reality. We are all young here. Our families do not want us to get involved in any trouble in Kashmir. So, they prefer to send us here to remain safe and out of danger. Here in every market, you will notice that at least 25 per cent of the shops sell Kashmiri art and craft. We have our businesses even in Kerala, Madras, Orissa and Bengal.'

It was already dark when I returned home in the evening. I realized that thousands of Kashmiris had been trading all over the Indian states for years without any problems, yet this fact was generally unknown. I called M.K. Razdan from Goa and explained my idea for the proposed series: 'Kashmir anywhere and everywhere'. I explained to him a travel shows on Kashmir, showing both Kashmir and Kashmiri integration with the rest of India through our artisans and their crafts. He did not fully understand what I was saying and asked me over to his PTI office. When I returned to Delhi, I met Razdan in his office. He gave me blank sheets of paper and a pen and said, 'Write down everything that you want to tell me.' I started writing, and within a few hours, the complete project was written and ready for submission to the Doordarshan authorities.

I considered it a socio–cultural travel show, and fortunately, it did not turn into a Doordarshan propaganda series. When I landed at Srinagar airport for the first shoot, my excitement disappeared, and for quite some time I was lost in thought. As I picked up my bag, it struck me, 'Where am I supposed to go? And where will I stay? There is no home, no friends.' A strange fear gripped me, and I started cursing myself. Finally, I left the airport. There I saw one of my junior colleagues, Arshad Mushtaq. I had just informed him of my arrival, but since he hadn't responded I did not expect him at the airport. When I saw a bright smile on his face, my confidence returned a bit. After short pleasantries, Arshad asked me, 'Where are you going from here?' A very difficult question. I thought for a moment and directed him, 'Let us go to Regal Chowk. There is a Lambert Lane, and on that lane, there used to be a tiny little hotel of one Haji sahab.' During my college days, my friends and I used to eat kebabs and have tea there regularly–this was not the same Haji sahab from Leh.

We boarded a taxi and headed out. It wasn't a hotel in the real sense but rather a tiny joint with a few rooms; mostly people coming from Kargil would stay there. It was a very inexpensive accommodation. The best part about its location was the memories it sparked from my teenage days spent in this area. I felt safe here because of the familiarity. My home lay just ten minutes away by foot. It was an area had grown up in and I knew every lane. Psychologically, it helped me become part of the city.

After checking in, I met Haji sahab after decades and had to remind him who I was. He finally dug up old memories and said, 'Yes, there used to be three of you sitting in that corner of the lawn and laughing. Yes, now I remember you.' After some tea and refreshments, I got working on our schedule as my technical team would arrive in two days to shoot the series.

Between fear and apprehension, we started filming our stories to capture all aspects of culture and heritage in Kashmir. We set out around 10 a.m. and returned at around 7 p.m. every day. In the beginning, I held a lot of fear in my mind about working there, given the tense situation around me, but gradually, wherever I went to film, I met with complete support and encouragement. Soon I conquered my fear and moved to locations out of the city limits of Srinagar. Thus far I have not contacted any official authority. I was on my own, and the pace of our work accelerated. Every day we could record at least two stories. During the day, disturbing events kept happening—

whether killings or confrontations between police and security forces. Anything could happen at any time, which unnerved us, but we kept working.

One day we took boats down the river Jhelum, recording the city of Srinagar standing tall with its centuries-old wooden houses, mosques and temples on both sides of the historical river. Our boat crossed the second bridge, Habba Kadal, and we neared the third bridge, Fatha Kadal. On the left side of the bank, there stood the Raghunath temple. I had never visited before, so I asked my boatman to anchor us at the ghat to take a few shots of the Shah Hamdan Shrine from across the river. We got off the boat, climbed the steps leading to the temple, and before setting up a camera for the shoot, we ventured inside. We were shocked to find that the temple had only empty walls and not a single statue of any deity. There was pin-drop silence— none of us could utter a word. The empty site was scary; there was just black graffiti with all kinds of political slogans painted on the walls and some anti-India slogans painted by the Islamic separatists. This graffiti spoke volumes about the Kashmiri conflict. Some local boys played in the compound. We asked them about the condition of the temple, and they simply said that people had come with guns. They shot the huge chain that had supported the metal bell of the temple. As we looked around, we noticed that all the houses of the Pandits were burnt. All around were mostly ruins, including the houses. Old windows hung, making visible the interiors of some of the remaining rooms, but everything was a complete rubble, a gloomy and pathetic sight to see.

When we set up a camera overlooking the opposite bank of the River Jhelum facing the Shah Hamdan shrine, my cameraman felt something under his feet. We all looked and found a well-polished, smooth, rounded stone. He and I tried to turn the stone over to take it out of the soil, where it was stuck in some wild grass. When we moved it a bit and turned it upside down, my cameraman exclaimed in his Tamil accent, 'Sir, it is Ganesha.' Being a very religious person, he cleaned it a bit with his hands and the disfigured image of Ganesha emerged. Upset, he said, 'Sir, I'm taking it home.' I reminded him that we could not take anything from here, even a disfigured deity. We could all land in big trouble, so we decided to just take our shots and leave quickly.

Suddenly, an army unit with all kinds of guns appeared. The soldiers started interrogating us, demanding our identity cards. After explaining everything and satisfying them, they ordered us to clear the area immediately. Before leaving, out of curiosity I asked the senior officer, 'How did you know we were here? Nobody saw us.' The officer laughed, 'We got a wireless message about you people.' We must have been followed from one area to the next, and so the message was passed on to another security group in another area. They must have kept a close eye on us. After we packed up and got back into our boats, nobody wanted to talk. Only the sound of the oars was heard, pulling the boat downstream.

Another day, I planned to shoot a story about copperware-making, and how the local artisans made beautiful pots and pans and very decorative objects with delicate designs out of copper. In this special craft, the master craftsmen made world-famous objects. My taxi driver grew interested in the kind of work we wanted to film and volunteered to take us to the copperware workshop. The next day, we ventured into downtown Srinagar where the copper handicraft makers' workshops were spread in abundance. Our driver took us through narrow lanes and by-lanes of the Old City until finally, we entered a big Kashmiri house.

The owner of the workshop welcomed us, happy to receive us. He addressed me as his brother, a kind gesture from him.

He had tea ready for all of us. While we were enjoying the tea, he explained all the details of his craft, from taking a flat copper sheet all the way to making beautiful articles out of it. He made us shoot every stage of the process in detail as he explained the intricacies of this art. We took almost one full day to shoot all the elements of this old, traditional craft, revealing all the techniques and the various chemicals needed to make it aesthetically rich. Having covered the whole process, we started packing our equipment. The owner again insisted that we have tea. To me, he said, 'You are going to have a special salt tea with me, while the rest of them will have the Lipton tea.'

In fact, it turned out to be a big tea party, not a simple one but an elaborate one consisting of cakes and special Kashmiri bakery items of different kinds. I told him that he need not have bothered with this elaborate arrangement. He replied, 'Since my brother has come for the first time to my house, that too from so far, this much is mandatory. And all these people with you must know what Kashmiri hospitality is.' He expressed his unhappiness about the Kashmiri Pandits leaving their homes. He was a very warm-hearted person. As we left, he again invited me to spend the night at his home. From this warmth and love, I said to myself: the Kashmir that I grew up in, isn't it still alive?

When we sat in our taxis, my driver, without whose help we could not have done this, asked me, 'So, are you happy with your work today?'

I replied, 'Of course, and only because of you.'

He gave me a smile and said, 'Do you know in whose house you were working?'

I said, 'How would I know?'

He smiled again, 'This is Latrum's house.'

I asked, 'Which Latrum?'

A bit surprised, he said, 'Don't tell me you don't know Latrum?'

I replied, 'I swear I have no idea.'

He laughed, 'Mushtaq Latrum.'

Suddenly I woke up, 'That Mushtaq Latrum? Who was exchanged at the Kandahar airport when the Indian Airplane was hijacked by terrorists from Amritsar?'

The taxi driver said, 'Yes, this is the same Latrum. He is this man's brother.'

We were scheduled to go to Hajan to record a famous folk musician, Ali Muhammad Shaikh. When I phoned him to request the recording, he insisted that the recording happen at his house in Hajan, a hot spot of terror in those days. Almost every day news came of killings by some unknown people. We embarked a little early in the morning for Hajan. After travelling by the highway for an hour or so, we turned off to take a small link road between green paddy fields. At one point, as we turned left to cross a culvert, we saw many buses and vans parked at a checkpoint. I got out of my vehicle and saw a group of local young men with AK-47 guns checking every vehicle and frisking people. My heart stopped, thinking this would probably be our end. I looked at their faces—the images of ruthless killers, eyes without any expression, like fisheyes. They looked filthy, perhaps having not bathed for weeks. I told my non-Kashmiri crew members not to exit the vehicles until I told them to. I feared for their lives.

One of the gunmen approached me and asked in Hindi, '*Kahan ja rahe ho* [Where are you going]?' I replied in Kashmiri and explained to him our task of recording the famous singer of Hajan, Ali Muhammad Sheikh. Right then, an Indian Army jeep passed, with some senior officers sitting inside. The jeep didn't stop, but the group of gunmen saluted the officers, shouting 'Jai Hind, sir!' I was confused. Someone whispered to me that they were Kuka Parey's men working for the Indian

Army. I realized that they were renegade terrorists working for the Indian security forces.

I relaxed a bit. Soon one fellow among them began asking questions and wanted to check our equipment, particularly the camera. I told him it was an empty camera that we would load with film at the time of shooting. He smiled and demanded, 'No, show me your equipment. You know that Ahmad Shah Massoud, the commander of the anti-Taliban forces in Afghanistan, was killed by a bomb placed in a camera which was brought for an interview. The bomb exploded and he was killed.' We quietly opened our bags to let him check everything. Afterwards, he allowed us to go on our way to the town of Hajan. We did not know whether to laugh or cry as we drove away. It was a bizarre check-point experience.

We entered the main bazaar of the town of Hajan, where most of the shops stood open. The shopkeepers all looked at us strangely, and we noticed one young man in a shop with the barrel of a gun showing from inside his phiran and another man displaying his gun openly. They kept a vigil over everything and everyone crossing the roads. It reminded me of the Turkish film *YOL*, by Gune. In one of the sequences, the political thugs and goons position themselves inside the shops of butchers, blacksmiths and carpenters to keep the city under strict control. If any protest or resistance took place on the streets, these thugs would jump into action and quell the protest, killing and maiming the protesters. This film had been banned and the maker of the film was imprisoned for anti-state activity. The Hajan street looked like a real version of a scene from Gune's film.

Upon reaching the house of Ali Mohammed Sheikh, he first asked me, 'Did you meet our *rehnumas* (caretakers)? They are taking good care of us in this town.'

After a break with some tea, we started recording. He sang some very popular, heart-rending songs. We talked to him about his life and about the present state of affairs, and he intelligently avoided commenting on the situation in the state lest he should pay for it with his life. As we left his house, we did not want to take the same route back, so Sheikh himself suggested an alternative road to return us to Srinagar safely.

This series allowed me to travel into the interior of the state and to many other parts of India. It was fascinating to meet Kashmiris everywhere and to see their talent and their contribution to nation-building after 1947. We discovered amazing stories no one knew about. It was eye-opening for the entire unit to realize that the Kashmiri people had worked quietly for decades in the fields of art, craft, education, folklore, oceanography, linguistics and many others without any public attention. While making this series, titled *Ghaas* (Vision), I met many people who helped connect me to others, giving me an opportunity to discuss the various issues pertaining to culture with academicians and civil society members. We looked into the conditions of the various cultural institutions of the state, like the Cultural Academy.

What unfolded was upsetting. Within a period of eleven years of terrorism, the Kashmiri cultural landscape had been rendered barren. One section of artisans had stayed back in the Valley, creating quietly without any exposure or exhibition of their work for fear of being singled out as traitors to the cause of the terrorists. Fear gripped the creative community so tight that most of them had withdrawn into their own shells, creating in silence. Another large section of artistes simply left the Valley. In fact, the creative community of Kashmir was partitioned the day the mass migration of Kashmiri Pandits from the Valley began. Whenever I met any of the artists who remained or who had left, they expressed anger, helplessness and sadness at their sense of loss.

I remember during one seminar at the University of Kashmir that I happened to attend by chance one day, I had met Ghulam Nabi Khyal, an eminent poet and fiction writer, after a session. He asked me, 'What did you think of the seminar?' Out of politeness and a little curiosity, I didn't want to offer my critique. I simply said, 'It was good.' His immediate response was, 'What are you saying? It is an incomplete seminar, you people (Kashmiri Pandits) used to contribute the other point of view. It was one-sided.' I did not say anything to him but recognized the truth in what Khayal sahab had said. The Pandit community had no political significance, but their interventions in the realm of academia and culture had widened the scope of debate and discussion, lifting the entire discourse.

14

Exploring Diverse Cultural Spaces

One day I went to meet the Bhand Pather community at Akingam in South Kashmir, near Anantnag. I had a longstanding relationship with the Bhand Pather community, having worked with them off and on, but with the rise of militancy in the days before mobile phones it was difficult to keep in touch with them. They lived in villages quite far from Srinagar. The day I arrived the Bhands had all gathered at one house. I entered the house to warm hugs, but quickly the mood shifted to one of mourning. Most of them sobbed quietly, including the ustads of the form, men very senior in age to me. One of the senior Bhands, the late Ali Mohammed Bhagat, related the story of what they had been through over the decade. Since the violence began, they had not performed even once in ten years. They hid their swarnai, which were long, thin flutes, fearing that militants would destroy them, as they had their costumes, properties, masks and drums. They had been directly ordered to cease their performances as they were considered unIslamic and against the instructions given in the holy Quran. Their young children had left their ancestral art and preferred to earn their living through manual labour or other small jobs. The younger generation looked down on their own art, feeling that it had not given them any respectability in society or a decent living. They did not want to continue the tradition.

The Bhands had already lost a leader in Mohammed Subhan Bhagat as a result of the dictates of the local terrorist groups. The militants considered him pro-India and put him on a 'trial' presided over by five militants in his own house. I have already described earlier how they spared his life, but on condition that he would remain under house arrest and pay a fine. This humiliation in front of his family and the villagers affected him badly. He lost his voice and passed away sometime later from an unknown illness, probably more a psychological ailment than any disease.

I listened to the Bhands for a while. At some point, I asked them if they felt an urge to perform. They unanimously replied, 'Yes! Of course! But how?' I did not have an answer at the time, so I told them that I would return and that hopefully, we would work together. Since they had lost all their properties, drums and costumes to the destructive militants, I gave them some money to buy new ones. We left with a promise to remain in touch with each other.

The National School of Drama has an extension programme through which it conducts all kinds of activities in various parts of the country. They organize different festivals for arts like folk dance, music and theatre, mostly for regional artistes, especially from the North-east. They have national festivals that encompass multiple art forms in various states in the North-east. The cultural groups from the Northeastern states also perform in different parts of the country so those states have a year-round cultural calendar. This is done in the hope of exposing the rest of the country to the vibrant cultures of that region and also to integrate the cultures from the region into the rest of the country's cultural map. Unfortunately, no schemes like these existed for the state of Jammu and Kashmir.

While the ground realities in certain states in the North-east of India were similar to those in Kashmir, I could not understand this hypocrisy on the part of the Government of India.

We all realized that in the state of Jammu and Kashmir, due to various circumstances and major breakdowns everywhere, a certain kind of vacuum had formed, which needed to be addressed. Because of the regular closing down of institutions, universities, colleges and schools, hopelessness had crept into the psyche of the people, who were exhausted by the constant presence of violence and death and the oppressive gaze of the security personnel. For years the younger generation had not experienced what one could call a 'normal' day. People preferred to remain indoors for weeks. All this created many psychological illnesses. The task of helping them seemed enormous and impossible, but one had to start somewhere.

So when the National School of Drama extension wing asked me to direct a four-week theatre workshop in Chhattisgarh, I said to the director of NSD at the time, Devendra Raj Ankur, that I had conducted theatre workshops in Chhattisgarh for many years, since 1976 onwards, and that the prospect did not excite me anymore. I proposed that we showed some courage and conducted a theatre workshop in Kashmir. Ankur immediately responded, giving me a few days to come back to him with a plan. I had finally found an opening to resume work in Kashmir.

I could not believe that the NSD committed funds for the first workshop in Kashmir. When I started planning in the summer of 2000, the situation in the Valley was horrible. This workshop had to be an in-residency programme, so I had to find a place where we could all live and work on the project. I rushed to Srinagar to find a venue available free of cost for four weeks. I met some of my friends and some fellow travellers, not theatre people but part of the society of Kashmir—academicians, civil servants and social workers. Initially, they did not understand what this kind of project would involve. I explained that when this kind of project is offered to any state, the local people have to join as partners and contribute at least a free venue, local stay, food and other basic logistics. Fortunately, none of them carried any political baggage. They simply felt concerned for the citizens of the state. My civil servant friend Shafi Pandit, who understood my requirements, served as a great help.

He called the Sher-i-Kashmir Agriculture University registrar, Gora, and explained to him our project and its requirements. The registrar of the university wanted to meet me to understand exactly what we needed. I rushed to Shalimar Garden, where the university is located. From the main gate, the campus looked fabulous, located amid huge orchards and surrounded on three sides by the mountain ranges of Zabarwan. Nature dominates the university campus; it is green and peaceful as if representing Kashmir in all its old grace and beauty.

The registrar, Gora, was warm and welcoming. He took me to tour the campus. We drove through the hilly roads of the campus and stopped in front of a bungalow in the middle of a forest. The registrar showed us where we would stay. It was an empty hostel building with a big hall and a kitchen. It worked for us, but I had already decided to stay in a small hotel in the town with the other faculty members.

When we had looked for our faculty accommodation, we had zeroed in on a hotel, but it was quite out of our budget. Surprisingly, the hotel owner insisted that we stay anyway. When I explained to him that it was beyond our means, he looked at me and said, 'You all are staying in my hotel, and you will pay the government rate of rupees five hundred for each room per day.' I could not believe that we would live in Hotel Welcome on the Boulevard, a prime location in Srinagar. Terrorism had reduced the demand for hotels to such a level that owners readily accepted any amount just to maintain their places. We paid practically nothing for our stay.

We were advised to run an ad in the local newspaper announcing an educational theatre workshop to be conducted by the National School of Drama, emphasizing 'education' to avoid any separatist opposition to our project. On the day of the opening of the workshop, we had asked the participants to meet us at Press Colony on Residency Road at 11 a.m. From there we would transport them to the university campus. That morning it started to rain. My colleagues Lokendra Trivedi and Souti Chakravarthy, both NSD graduates, and I waited for the participants to arrive. We waited for hours on the road, but no one came. It was getting cold, and the three of us kept looking at each other wondering if anyone would show up for the workshop. At about 2.30 p.m., Souti asked me, 'Sir, if there are very few participants, are we going to continue our workshop?' I replied, 'Souti, even if there is only one person, we will continue our workshop.' He and Lokendra gave me rather curious looks but asked no further questions. We did not have our lunch as we waited but drank copious amounts of tea at a tiny shop nearby to keep warm on the roadside.

Finally, at about 4 p.m., one young man arrived from Baramulla. Relieved to have at least one student, we entertained him with some tea and biscuits. Within fifteen minutes another participant arrived. We continued to wait until around 5 p.m., but no one else came. That time in the evening in Srinagar was considered quite late in those days. We all got into our jeep and proceeded towards the university with our two precious participants. At the campus, Ali Mohammed waited with his hot salt tea and local bread for all of us.

Since these were not normal times, one had to keep in mind the rules of working under such tough circumstances. After settling the two participants in the hostel, as it was getting late, we left quickly to avoid the security people who gave us lots of trouble. At the hotel, we expressed concern about people not enrolling for our workshop. I made a few calls to my friends to spread the message about the project.

The next day, we started with our classes in total seriousness even though we had just two participants. My two colleagues had understood the intent and purpose of this kind of work. To pep them up I recited a verse by Bertolt Brecht:

In the dark times
Will there also be singing?
Yes, there will also be singing.
About the dark times

It was the secret theme of our workshop. To our surprise, more people arrived on the first day of the workshop. We continued our classes, and by the evening another four arrived from far-off towns. Talking to them, we learned that it was not easy to travel within the Valley. At all kinds of security posts, people were questioned, and their bodies and bags searched, adding significant travel time. Security suspected that youngsters may join the ranks of terrorists, so they interrogated them more thoroughly.

As word-of-mouth works better, within another three days we had about thirty participants. Among them, there was just one girl. Twenty-nine of them stayed in residence with us, but the lone girl had to return home every day. To make her feel comfortable, I decided that our transport would drop her at home, otherwise, she might discontinue the workshop, an unacceptable cost for me.

Since we did not have big funds, we adopted a Gandhian style of working, which meant that part of the training was to take care of arrangements ourselves. The entire class was divided into six groups of five participants each. Each group had the responsibility of tasks such as maintenance of our workspace, food arrangements, supplies and stock-taking. The intention of the workshop was not just to teach the right kind of theatre but also to inculcate values in the participants, to teach them to become responsible, rational human beings who could work in a group and care for others' welfare. The purpose was not only to teach them the world of theatre but also through theatre to get them to know the world.

Our approach was to make the students understand Indian theatre and culture and its links to other cultures. We wanted to expose them to new theories and practices in the performing arts, with special emphasis on Kashmiri theatre, literature and other performing arts of the state.

The average Kashmiri knows very little about his past because most of the preserved knowledge is unavailable in the language of the masses. Most of our textual records are either in Sanskrit or in Persian, both languages of the rulers and not of the common man. For some reason, Kashmiri has never been the language of the courts and or even of education. Through the sheer determination of a small number of intellectuals who wrote fiction, poetry and drama in the Kashmiri language, there exists an original body of work in Kashmiri. Unfortunately, there is still a colonial hangover and hypocrisy attached to our mother tongue, a misplaced belief that the Kashmiri language does not have the capacity to communicate complex ideas and concepts. Thus, an inferiority complex about our own mother tongue has damaged the growth of Kashmiri as a language.

Hence, my team and I consciously started our workshop by familiarizing the participants with Kashmiri culture, Kashmiri folklore, Kashmiri writing, Kashmiri folk theatre and Kashmiri music. From there we would expand the area of study into the larger space of Indian theatre and then move out into the theatre of the world.

There is a saying in Kashmiri: 'One should have the capacity to enter through the needle's hole and then exit through the elephant gate: *Achun gachi sichine gadi ken nayrun gachi hasteni darvaz.*'

All the activities of the workshop happened at the rear end of the university campus, in an empty hostel, quietly, without bringing any attention to what was going on inside the building. Luckily, tall poplar trees blocked views of the hostel building. The registrar had told me that recently eleven dead bodies were brought down from the mountains by security forces. The area was not quite free from militancy, so we had to be extra careful about the people who ventured into the campus. Since the university was closed and had no students, all the beautiful gardens were free for us to do our work in.

When we started working on body and mind exercises to teach body control and concentration, we confronted very different responses among the participants from what we normally did. For example, in one exercise they had to share their inner thoughts with someone in the group or with the whole group—the students could choose. This exercise unfolded before us as a sense of surrender on the part of most of the participants, who displayed their broken bodies and minds, their lack of self-esteem and their sense of hopelessness. The exercise continued for a couple of hours. Individual after individual gradually opened up, telling us stories that had impacted them in the last ten years of militancy. Each story held a history of the circumstances they lived in. These histories were not *about* the politics of the times but were *because* of the politics of the times. Often during these sessions, we had tears in our eyes.

Late in the night, we faculty members met and discussed the day. We concluded that we were not dealing with normal theatre participants to teach them the regular theatre theories and practices. We were dealing with injured minds. We realized that the teaching plan had to be repositioned for a while. For that, we had to innovate different exercises that would work as a balm to their hidden wounds. We changed our strategy. We had to help them reach a state of relaxation. We need not emphasize the performance part of the workshop. In theatre, it is necessary first to have a team of people who can express their ideas without fear. We had to turn our programme upside down. We had planned to undertake rigorous psychotherapeutic exercises, truth games, improvisation and story-building sessions, but we recognized that these participants were not ready for that yet.

One afternoon, we did an out-of-the-box session where we invited my friend Yaqub Sheikh, a great santoor player and singer—an ustad of the Kashmiri Sufiyana tradition. He explained the background and history of this musical form, then gave a small demonstration about the technique of santoor playing and its application. He started singing one of the famous old Sufi poems about love:

Harmuk ber tel zaga y madano, ye dapa ham te lagayo.
[Waiting at the gates of Harmukh, whatever you will ask me, I will follow.]

Soon all the participants started joining in. Even the teaching faculty joined in. The singing continued until it was dark. One could sense a strange kind of ecstasy on the faces of all singers. They kept repeating the lines. Yaqub stopped singing and let the participants, who did not want to stop singing, carry on. The atmosphere was charged with the sound of bliss. The words of the poem lifted themselves to some sort of '*sam*'. There were smiles and tears all around as if some hidden pain was healing itself. The students would have continued, but our man Friday Ali Mohammed, so moved by this long musical session, entered with a big *samawar* of Kashmiri salt tea and local bread and announced that it was his contribution from his peer, Merak Shah Patshah, a local *fakir* whose dargah was located close to the university. Everyone went for tea with a very different energy. Looking at the relaxed participants relishing the tea and talking to each other with smiles on their faces, I whispered to my two colleagues, 'I think the key has turned, and it has unlocked the lock.'

Since it was already dark and too late to go back, I asked Yaqub the ustad to spend the night with us. Yaqub said, 'No way, my wife will die if I do not reach home. You know things are not normal. My family will be already worried as it is quite late.' So, Lokendra and I accompanied him to his house, an hour's drive from the university.

While we drove, I thanked Yaqub for such a special session that everyone had enjoyed. Yaqub said, 'If the times had been normal I would have stayed back with you all, and we would have sung all through the night. That is the tradition of *Shub* in Kashmir.' He volunteered to do more sessions with the students. On reaching Natipura, his home, we immediately turned back, worried because of the various security barricades on the roads now.

Since it was quite late by Kashmir standards, our driver Hussain accelerated the vehicle. Suddenly we saw a cop with his SLR rifle aimed at us standing at the centre of the road. Hussain stopped the vehicle immediately with a screech. I heard foul curses hurled at us from the soldier. He walked to the driver's side of our car and slapped Hussain a couple of times. He yelled at Hussain, 'Why were you not driving on a low beam? You are lucky. I was about to open the fire on you, but luckily I saw Baba [me] with his white beard, and I stopped pulling my trigger. You idiot, you are lucky because you had kept the inside light on, and I could see Baba's white beard.' After a pause, the cop said, 'God saved me also from killing you guys.' I could see that he was frightened too because he said that he thought it was a fidayeen attack on the check-point. I again properly apologized for our mistake. He asked me where I was from, and I replied that I was from Delhi and had come here to teach. He looked at

Hussain and advised him, 'They are your guests and make sure that they are safe.' He then ordered him to leave.

For some time, none of us talked, silence filling the jeep. After a while, Hussain broke the silence and said, 'Actually it was my mistake. I forgot to drive on a low beam since we were in a hurry to return.' I said, 'Relax now, Hussain, we are safe.'

But when we were hardly half a kilometre away from our hotel, around 9:30 p.m. when cops again stopped us at another check post. Many manned this post. One of them came up to Hussain's window and started asking him the usual questions: 'Your name? Where are you from? Who are these people with you?' Then the cop turned to me and asked me: 'Where are you from?' When I said Delhi, his next question was, 'Which part of Delhi? I am also from Delhi.' I asked back, 'Which part of Delhi are you from, Major sahab?' I was told that addressing these cops as Major sahab made them less hostile, bloating their egos and making them deal with you more leniently. He gave me a look, and I realized he was drunk. He said, 'I am from Garhi village.' I replied, 'I know, it is near Lajpat Nagar and Moolchand Hospital.' He replied, 'Yes, yes, now I can confirm that you belong to Delhi.' Then, looking at Lokendra, who sat in the back, he asked about him. I replied, 'He is from Lakshmi Nagar, Delhi.'

Now I thought he would let us go, but no. Now he wanted to know my profession, and what I was doing in Kashmir. At that point, I politely requested him to let us go. We had worked all day and the other people at the hotel would worry for us. But no, he would not let us go. I realized that he was enjoying harassing us and that none of us could do anything about it since he had a loaded gun on his shoulder. We had to handle this drunk cop carefully because he should not lose his cool and do something silly that could harm us. I had to lie to him that our project of education and theatre was for the local people, and I had to convince him that I was a teacher. If I had told him that I acted in movies and directed plays, I would have had to stay there all night and answer his questions.

He got some idea of my work here in the Valley, but what exactly we did was beyond his comprehension. I again requested him to let us go. He laughed at me and then looked at the moon, saying, 'It must be full-moon night today, see how beautiful it looks.' He started singing some filmy song. After he finished his song, he turned towards us and asked, 'Is it getting late for you? It was nice meeting you and talking to you. Normally nobody talks to us here, but I enjoyed my conversation with you. Ok, thank you. You can go now, but remember do not travel during the night, it is dangerous.'

It was funny but revealing. I could sense his loneliness and desire to communicate with someone in the darkness of the night.

The workshop started picking up pace and we started bringing in other ideas for our classes. Since our workspace was small and could no longer accommodate all our practical work, we quickly took to the lawns of the hostel to test public reaction. We were apprehensive about people knowing about our work. There could be all kinds of local interpretations of our project, and all our work would go to waste. If this information reached any militant organization, there was a possibility of trouble. We had to be careful and always look over our shoulders in case someone was watching us. There was always this feeling that anything could happen at any time.

As we started working on the lawns where we could do our body movement exercises easily, villagers started coming and watching our work. We did not want them to, but we could not stop them from watching us either. When we started working on proper improvisation around certain themes, the audience increased. Initially, only women and children came, but later men joined in too. We could not hide anything now, but even so, the presence of the people during our exercises had an advantage for us. With the immediate feedback from the people, we felt as if we were performing on the street, enjoying live responses from the audience.

Our workshop had many components, such as bodywork for the actors. It involved taking up huge physical space. Then we had design classes for making sets and costumes.

Another aspect of the workshop involved acting, speech and story-making. Because of the constant presence of the villagers, we changed our schedule. Before noon, we did the exercises for body training work and design. The afternoon and evening sessions were for story-making and play-making preparations. This change of schedule helped us have our village visitors come in the latter part of the day only.

Initially, we had no plan to perform our work before the public because of obvious security reasons. But week after week, our students' progress compelled us to reconsider showcasing our work. Finally, I zeroed in on some important short stories from Kashmiri contemporary writing. We decided not to do a proper play because the plays available were already done and could not include all the participants. We wanted all the students to come on stage to perform and to do backstage work too.

The stories finally chosen were the path-breaking stories from Kashmiri literature, like Amin Kamil's *Kafanchoor*, Hari Krishan Koul's *Shamshan Viaraag* and Aslam Jehangeer's *Goburchuchoor*.

The purpose of public performance was not to give a grand show. We aimed to use every individual's talent to the maximum so he or she could become a creative being and contribute with mind and intellect to build a performance with an ensemble of human beings as a team. We wanted to show how, through the process of hit and trial, addition or rejection, a democratic consciousness can be built. And the process of creating a dramatic performance, the joy of learning from each other in a team, liberates each participant's hidden talents. This process builds self-confidence among the participants. This kind of approach to work was badly needed in the Valley. We saw ourselves not just as teachers but also as participants and, at some point as catalysts, imparting our knowledge to provoke the students to convey their own knowledge and experiences through theatre. During times of crisis and oppression, when ordinary, powerless people cannot take responsibility for their condition into their own hands, it is important and necessary to inject in them the faith that they can tackle the situation and contribute to bringing about new change.

The purpose of NSD training is to impart the basic principles of theatre—a composite art with elements of painting, sculpture, design, acting, music, speech and more. All these forms come together to create a theatre performance. The other aspects of theatre are the society, stories, and the people's struggles and dreams. No theatre can happen in a vacuum. Its main partners are the audiences, and the general public for whom the theatre is put on. Hence, knowledge of the people for whom one is performing is very important and necessary.

Here in Kashmir, the very lives of the people were entangled in many realities, like state confrontation, gun-wielding militants (local as well as foreign), and hidden foreign agencies. This was not a society at peace with itself. The social fabric of the local people was being ripped every day. It often led to some major tragedy, usually a killing. Death is Kashmir's constant companion.

Conducting a normal academic training programme would have been unproductive here. Theatre deals with the human condition through human materials. The students were socially and politically conscious. They had experienced the turmoil that had ravaged their state, and each had his or her understanding of and conclusion about the situation they were in.

Hence, at every stage, we had to reinvent new approaches to pedagogy to impart the essence of theatre to them, not just as entertainment but also as a tool and device for organic change in society. We had to show that theatre people are not mere entertaining actors, singers, and performers but protagonists of change who believe in the discipline of democracy and equality.

With this new approach to equality among a group of creative people, where anyone could openly express their ideas before everyone else through debate, discussion, try-outs and improvisation, they could realize and conclude that there can be many truths possible to the same issue. Gradually, the students started enjoying this process and saw in this kind of work the principle of creativity. This kind of creative process starts inculcating in you an attitude of how to work together in a larger group where you respect each other's point of view. This approach to work gave a big push to whatever was happening in the workshop. Often, we reached a stage where the students asked me to go away until they could sort out their problems and come up with the best possible solution. I could see elements of leadership developing within the groups as they accepted each other's ideas.

The group of participants emerged from their previous amateur experiences in theatre, where the director is the last word who can never be questioned, but here, students learned how to be creative contributors themselves. They now wanted an experience of performing before the public in a proper hall. Tagore Hall was the only performance space in the Kashmiri Valley, which was open to the general public, that too after ten years. Militants had burnt this hall twice, so it was hardly used for any performances. Our show had to start at 2 p.m. and end by 4.30 p.m. so that everybody could return home before it was dark.

The students invited their friends, neighbours and relatives to the show. One bus filled with people arrived from some rural area with women, children and many elders. I thought there would be a select number of people, but it was a surprise to see a packed auditorium. The management of the performance was entirely under the control of the students. Many academics, writers and poets arrived at the auditorium for the play. It appeared like a celebration of some event after many years, and a certain amount of optimism spread among both the audience and the participants. Before the show, I went up into the lighting control room, where I met Mehraj-u-Din, the senior in charge of lights. Excitedly, he congratulated me, saying, 'Ba Khuda, I am going to Dastagir Sahib's *ziyarat* to thank him. It is after years that my auditorium is packed with people and not by government officials. These days only fifty or sixty people come if Chief Minister Farooq Abdullah has any function. Raina sahib Mubarak.'

The performances went very well. I loved my actors, who were at their best improvising during the performance. They came up with remarkable lines, tongue-in-cheek remarks, on-the-spot puns and jokes. There were many funny comments about me. The audience was delighted. Rehman Rahi (great poet) hugged me and said just 'Thank you for coming'. Naseem Shafia, an eminent poet, said in Kashmiri, '*Luss, Baya,*' meaning 'Bless you, brother.' Their reactions mattered so much to me because they had themselves gone through torturous times and yet were still creating wonderful poetry.

During the four weeks, from morning to late evening, that this workshop progressed, every day we made calls to our families in Delhi. It became a routine that followed all these weeks as we knew our families back home would worry because there was no peace in the Valley yet. Mobile phones had not arrived yet, so we used a PCO booth just outside the main gate of the university to make our calls. One day, I went to make a call but had to wait behind four people in line waiting for their turn to call. After the person already on a call left, it was the turn of a CRPF jawan to make his call. He picked up the receiver and started talking to someone. We could hear what this jawan said but could only imagine what the person on the other side must have been saying.

This jawan's conversation went like this:

Ja
kaise ho
yeha tu theek hai hai
Amma ko bolne do
Are tum fikar mat karo
Tum apane amma ke paas ja
Mai abhi mel nahe sakta
Tum rona mat
Sun, apne ko sambhalo
Mai hu na
Tum bache ko lekar apne ma ki paas ja
Mai hu na
Mai hu na
Mai hu na
. . . it went on for a long period.

We watched the meter, already showing more than Rs 200. It soon crossed Rs 250. His repeated refrain of *'Mai hu na'* started haunting me. After a few seconds, he paid up for his call, which was more than Rs 250, very quietly picked up his gun, put his purse in his pocket, walked out of the booth, crossed the road and stood there on duty for the rest of the day.

All present at the booth fell silent. We all understood the jawan's story and his helplessness. Those three words *'Mai hu na'* hit me so hard I didn't feel I could call my wife to tell her 'All is well here, and I am fine, and I am there for you.' The situation here looked normal, but anything could happen in a matter of seconds. Many years have passed since this telephone incident, and who knows what happened to the CRPF jawan. But those three words still haunt me.

My first theatre workshop in Srinagar opened a little space, like a ventilator. Many individuals who had felt suffocated for years wanted to breathe together. These people understood the damage that this new violent phenomenon had inflicted on the state. They felt that somehow the situation needed saving from further erosion. Most of the concerned people felt we needed to come together and take a look at what was at stake in the larger context.

One day, a meeting was organized to form a cultural organization by the name of CHECK—Centre for Heritage, Environment and Culture of Kashmir. The core body of CHECK had academicians, civil society members, some civil servants and me. During the first meeting, the discussion centred on the activities that this body could take up. Under the present conditions, it turned out to be an interesting and important meeting to take stock of the present situation in all aspects of Kashmiri life. Our botanist friend made a disturbing presentation about the flora and fauna of the Valley. He said the great *Ambri* apple of Kashmir was nowhere to be found. One of the rare varieties of rice, known as *mushk budej*, with a fragrance one could smell from almost two hundred metres away, had disappeared. Many varieties of wild fruits seemed to have gone forever. The Kashmiri language, which has a textual record from the fourteenth century onwards, was unfortunately not taught in educational institutions. It was felt that a large city population in Kashmir had adopted half-baked Urdu as their language, resulting in a tongue that was neither Urdu nor Kashmiri. What they spoke was composed of three words of Kashmiri, a few words of Urdu . . . making for a hybrid cocktail conversation. You laughed at the incongruity of it all.

We decided to work out a comprehensive plan of action. Our state being in a most complex and vulnerable position, it was not advisable to pile up any project that would meet major objections. Because the space for cultural activity had shrunk, we decided to pick an apolitical project to begin with, one culturally important but which would fetch no opposition from any side.

Documenting all the heritage buildings of Srinagar City, with its ancient temples, mosques, *khankhas*, wooden buildings, havelis and Mughal gardens, seemed the right kind of project to begin with. No separatist or unionist would have any problem with that. It would be meaningful work to create a permanent document for prosperity. Four young and dedicated architects, Sameer Haamdani (heritage architect), Saima (conservation architect specialist), Abid Khan (architect) and Jabeen Manzoior (architect) from the Valley itself took on this task, and within two years completed their project, which is now available in four volumes. CHECK curated an elaborate exhibition-cum-presentation function, presided over by Chief Minister Mufti Mohammed Sayeed, with some of cabinet ministers attending, at the Shari Kashmir Convention Centre, the first high point CHECK achieved in a very short time. The exhibition was received by the general public and appreciated by everyone who attended.

When I returned to Delhi for a whole year, I did not receive any meaningful information from CHECK on any project, but when I returned for my next trip for another theatre project, a meeting of CHECK was called by its chairman, Shafi Pandit. On the day of the meeting, Shafi Pandit, Saleem Beg and I were present, but no other member attended. Since the required number for making decisions was not met, nothing was taken up; in fact, there was no meeting at all. I grew concerned with this kind of response, especially when compared with our last meeting. After some days, I learned of some differences between the CHECK members and about some high-handed behaviour by some of the members. Nobody felt it necessary to attend the meeting. It surprised me to find that after the last grand public meeting, they had never met. I could sense the death of CHECK before it could attain solid prestige in the state.

All the members were and still are my friends; all of them were fond of me and still are. I was proud of their involvement in a voluntary organization like CHECK, committed to rescuing the cultural disintegration of Kashmir. They had supported me individually and helped in all of my endeavours after they saw the results of my first workshop. But as a collective, they found it difficult to work together. The work I do in my individual capacity uses the art of theatre in various training programmes in the Valley. Most of my CHECK friends, in some way or the other, are involved with me. I had dreamed that CHECK would achieve much more than what the Kashmir Cultural Front and Progressive movement had in Kashmir from 1947 to 1967 in the areas of art, theatre and literature. But even before it took its first baby steps, CHECK had stumbled and disappeared from the landscape of Kashmiri culture.

However, I continued my *ekla chalo* journey as a foot soldier of Kashmiri culture in the Valley, and that was possible because the people understood the need to fill the cultural vacuum that had set in. I collaborated with many well-meaning organizations, which were not related to the activity of CHECK but were concerned about the social educational impact of terror and violence on ordinary people and particularly the young and vulnerable. My work expanded from showcasing just the narrow meaning of theatre as solely an instrument of entertainment. We applied the magic of theatre among children, women, students, teachers and even office-going people. I wanted to push the boundaries of theatre as a form and use it to bring about basic social change in that environment of violence and uncertainty in the state.

I worked with Help Foundation, led by a dynamic lady, Nigat Pandit, a compassionate and concerned human being who never believed in saying no. She was always ready to lead from the front, despite her delicate health. I got involved with their orphan children, who today have achieved good positions. This foundation is a rare example in Kashmir of a group working on education, culture and many poverty-related programmes. I have seen how it began for small children and grew into a major centre for the helpless people of Kashmir. During the Muzaffarabad earthquake, the Help Foundation galvanized into action in time to work in the forward areas of the Uri sector in Baramulla District, where the earthquake had a major impact.

Working with the students from Kashmir University entailed a different energy and was difficult. Full of questions and arguments and filled with pent-up anger, these youngsters were warm at heart and caring. If they accepted you, it was with an open mind and love.

Working with the Bhand Pather, the traditional folk theatre community of Kashmir, was like doing deep digging for archaeological work, and from the excavation pits gradually rebuilding the lost form of theatre. Then we started to document, revitalize, reinterpret and create a training methodology for positivity in the community. This was a tough challenge, and the work still continues. If a genuine contemporary theatre ever emerges in Kashmir, it will grow from here. Bhand Pather has its repertoire of plays, its pedagogical training, its old knowledge pool of music and its well-preserved audiences in the rural areas of the Valley.

Some of the most interesting work that happened in these years came from the most difficult projects in which, as a team, we completed them between the shut doors, stone-pelting, cordoning-and-search operations, cross-firing and lathi charges. Living in the middle of death, threat and danger meant there was never a normal working atmosphere. Many a time, one or the other of us would withdraw into a shell because we could not take the stress of the situation continuously for weeks, 24/7. Any time in the dark of the night, we might awaken to loud bangs on our doors. Out of fright, we would open the door to a large group of soldiers fully armed, who would barge into the room and start interrogating us then and there. We worried about our junior colleagues, among whom were some young ladies, in their rooms nearby. What would be their condition? Would they endure late-night harassment and continue working? Working in conflict areas is tough because you can always be caught in the crossfire. You cannot afford to take sides. Most people look at you with suspicion. You're always vulnerable. You wonder, if this is what is happening to you, what will be the fate of ordinary people?

While working in Srinagar, one evening I got a call from Aditi, my daughter. She asked me to arrange with some ordinary schools in the Valley that she could visit for her undergraduate thesis on 'Impact of Violence on School Children'. I was not comfortable with her decision to come and work in Kashmir. She had never been here in her life, and at that point in time nothing was okay in the Valley. She would have to contend with regular militant terror attacks, cordoning-and-search operations by the security forces, and random checks at any time by paramilitary men. As a daily practice, one had to carry one's identity card on one's person all the time. I knew people who carried multiple identity cards—like an employment ID card, voter ID card, police ID card and so on—to be safe when security people demanded ID proof. If often made for a humiliating experience if you were caught without an ID card.

When I tried to explain to Aditi that it would be difficult and that it was not a safe situation in Kashmir, she shot back some very uncomfortable questions at me, like, 'How do you know? You work there for months. You always say that the situation is fine, and your work is going on as per your plan. If you can work, so can I. What is your problem? I will not disturb you; you keep doing your work, and you only have to arrange for me to visit some simple and ordinary schools, the rest I will manage

myself. You do not have to worry about me.' Knowing Aditi and
her resolve well, she would not budge from her decision. My
wife Anjali always says, 'That is how we have made them grow.
Never a straight road, always against the flow of the current.'
Finally, I assented, 'All right, but please give me a few days, and
I will see if I can arrange your visit to these schools.'

I talked to some of my friends and my colleagues about
what Aditi wanted to do. After initial surprise, and then after
giving some thought to the idea, they said they would find out
which schools she could do her work in. 'Since Aditi did not
want to visit any elite school for her work, it was difficult to find
some safe schools that were not in dangerous areas. Most of the
schools with limited means, where parents with modest means
sent their children to school, were located in the downtown
areas of Srinagar. Finally, Nigat Pandit told me not to worry;
she would find the schools that Aditi needed. Pandit's Help
Foundation was dedicated to orphan children and the widows
of Kashmir and was a home for children from class one to
class twelve.

When, finally, Aditi arrived in Kashmir, my taxi driver
Hussain took it upon himself to watch over Aditi throughout
her stay. Nigat Pandit took her under her wing and arranged for
her to visit schools in the downtown area and also took good
care of her throughout her stay in Srinagar. In fact, while Aditi
stayed at my hotel, Nigat Pandit, Hussain and my theatre friend
Javed Hakim were really the ones who guided her. She would
leave at 9.30 a.m. for her work and return at around 5.30 p.m.,
when I would also return from my work. All day she worked
in three or four schools and in the evening made her notes.
Before going to bed, I would ask her about her work and her
impressions of the place and the people. She developed a close
bond with the Hussains and was now calling our driver Hussain
Chacha. She developed her own relationship with his family,

particularly with Hussain's daughter Shabnam. Both loved coffee and would meet to have it whenever possible. Nigat Pandit and her husband, Shafi Pandit, grew quite fond of her, and on one weekend they took her along to spend a few days at Pahalgam.

Aditi's work was going fine, but soon she too realized that what appeared normal was in fact quite the reverse. She sensed that all was not well in the Valley of Kashmir. The presence of cops everywhere gave her a feeling of constant unease. In the evening, whenever I asked her about her work with the children, she gave me an upsetting and grim picture of the state of education and the low level of children's education. In her observation, the children showed very low levels of self-esteem. What they felt and suffered, their anguish or their fears, they did not express in language. Most of the time they remained silent.

Before she left for Delhi, I asked Javed Hakim to show her at least the Chasma Shahi spring and the Mughal gardens. She was always hard-pressed for time, and she could not visit any of the places of importance in the Valley. On the last day of her stay, Javed took her to Chasma Shahi before going to the main garden. There was a security check-post where you had to show an identity card, and then, and only if the cops allowed you to proceed, could you go up to the garden. Javed asked Aditi to stay in the taxi until he got clearance from the security cops. When Javed showed his identity card to the cop, he was told to show some other proof of identity. Javed had carried his voter's card and showed it to the cop. Still not satisfied with these two cards, the security man asked him to prove his identity with something else. Javed then displayed his police ID card. All this happened with Aditi sitting in the vehicle, watching the cop roughing up Javed. At one point, the security cop threw all the cards on the road and started shouting all kinds of foul words at Javed. Aditi could not watch this humiliation of Javed.

She started to cry and in frustration shouted to Javed to come back so they could return to our hotel. At that point, the other cops realized that something had gone wrong, and finally, they allowed both to go ahead. By that time Aditi had no inclination to enjoy the world-famous royal spring.

Aditi was upset and very hurt. In the evening, I met her at the hotel, and she confronted me, saying, 'Nothing is right here.' She told me the entire story of Javed's humiliation. She said that if cops behaved like this—throwing away voter cards on the road—then what kind of proof was there for anyone to prove his identity? How could anyone insult a normal citizen and not expect any retaliation? The standard of children's education in the schools was so pathetic and bad, how would they cope in the future? No one in the establishment bothered about these innocent children, who watched all the violence and killings quietly. Most of these schoolchildren were terrified and psychologically disturbed. Someone had to address the problems of these children.

While listening to her anger and worry, I realized that my daughter had grown up though she was still an undergraduate. Her compassion for the situation came as a sort of wake-up call for me. I questioned myself—I had been working here through theatre and I had never thought of the children? What these little children must have been going through, without being able to articulate their inner, hidden fears. Nobody asked these little souls what they were going through.

Aditi's observations opened my eyes to one of the major areas of neglect. Her confrontation with me made me think and ponder over the issues of children in Kashmir. What could a person like me with limited resources contribute to this highly forgotten aspect of the Valley's future? This awareness made me collaborate with Nigath Pandit's Help Foundation, the INTACH Kashmir chapter, the Rajiv Gandhi Foundation

(RGF) and many small but meaningful organizations to develop ideas and concepts by using theatre, films, plastic arts and various therapies to help the children of Kashmir heal their wounds and suffering.

From here, we took up some major programmes for children and with children. Many conclusions in Aditi's undergraduate study became my guiding paths, and we developed them further by working with children and teachers and sharing our experiences with the school education departments. Unfortunately, the officialdom of the state education department stayed stone-deaf while school and school administrations were ready for the challenge.

15

Children without Fathers—Search for Pedagogy

I received a call in Delhi one day from Ratna Mathur of the Rajiv Gandhi Foundation. Somebody had told her about my work in Kashmir and wanted to meet me. When we met she told me that they had a very strong children's programme in the Valley, but I had never heard of it. Nobody in the Valley had ever mentioned it to me. She revealed to me that RGF children's programmes had supported many orphan children through scholarships for their education in the Valley. They also ran other programmes in the schools for children. Ratna Mathur wondered how they could expand their involvement with the children of the Valley. Out of curiosity, I asked how they selected children for the scholarships. She explained that the main emphasis for receiving a scholarship was that the child's father or mother had been killed by terrorists. The logic of RGF was simple, since Rajeev Gandhi had been killed by terrorists, a child who had lost his or her parent to terrorism qualified for the scholarship. I wanted to know if RGF representatives had ever met some of those children, the victims of terrorism, and talked to them. Ratna did not think they had.

I explained, 'Do you know the impact of terrorist violence on children during all these years of militancy? It has created major psychological problems for the kids. Unfortunately, it has not been addressed enough nor given any priority. A whole generation of these growing children is going to face major mental health problems in the future, which will ruin their personal lives and the lives of their relatives and of the community in general.'

I suggested to her a pilot project with these children to see what could be achieved. At least we could begin to recognize the problem and the tragedy of their lives. We agreed in principle on this, and she said she would get back to me after discussing it with her seniors at the foundation.

After many meetings with Ratna Mathur, my mind started ticking on the issues that should be dealt with and the kind of people who should join me if the project came through. It would not be a typical children's theatre workshop but a project to help children change their state of mind from one of delusion into one of positivity and hope. While waiting for the green signal from RGF, I kept planning the kind of workshop and the pedagogies that would be needed for such a project. I restlessly waited for a positive response from the foundation because it would mark my chance to work with children after a long period of time. After all, I had begun my career working in children's theatre.

After leaving drama school, I had worked as a senior drama instructor at Bal Bhavan and the Central Children's Museum, New Delhi. I had supervised hundreds of children from various age groups for months without any break. I had made small children's plays, performed by children for the children audiences. We used to have free-flowing sessions, and as an experiment, all responsibility and management of performance was given to the youngsters, who after some time managed magnificently well. We did many major and some small plays for child audiences. Here, ideas were thrown open before the kids, and then in a group, the children would develop them into performances. Often, a small idea was discussed and improvised until it was shaped into a public performance.

I must thank Shanta Gandhi, then the director of Bal Bhavan, who was also my Sanskrit drama teacher when I was studying at the National School of India who gave me full cooperation and the freedom to develop different modules, using theatre techniques, for all kinds of themes relevant and necessary for the development of children's minds and personalities to lead them to the path of inquiry and questioning.

Shanta Gandhi, herself an accomplished dancer, theatre director and Sanskrit drama teacher, had been at Rabindranath Tagore's Shantiniketan during Gurudev's time. She used to join many of our sessions with the children. She had a childlike aspect to her, which came out during the sessions.

With me, she would share many of her experiences during her stay at Shantiniketan, about Tagore ideas for and insights into children's education and the role of education in the development of a holistic personality. I was fortunate to hear first-hand accounts of her days with the Indian People's Theatre Association (IPTA), which had created one of the major progressive cultural mobilizations in India. She had worked at the legendary Uday Shankar's Almora Dance Centre. She would narrate memorable stories of Uday Shankar's genius work there.

Working at Bal Bhavan with children in the drama section along with other creative instructors in other disciplines of art like painting, sculpture, crafts and science, made for a unique experience. Giving children multi-disciplinary experiences developed in one unique way of looking at things. These experiments at Bal Bhavan were responsible for all the creative instructors opening up to new possibilities. Since Bal Bhavan was solely dedicated to the creative development of children, quite often there were new experiments undertaken to unlock their creative imagination.

When India's ambitious project of Saksharta Abhiyan was flagged off in all the states, millions of educated volunteers joined the literacy mission in its campaign to make India 100 per cent literate. Many NGOs fully dedicated themselves to this movement. I had done a play called *Mother* by Bertold Brecht in Hindi, based on Maxim Gorky's novel *The Mother*, the story of an illiterate factory worker's mother.

In September 1993, the joint secretary of education in the government of India approached me to perform the sequence of the play on International Literacy Day on September 7.

Later I got a call from the new secretary of education in the Government of India, Sudeep Bannerjee, asking me to meet him at his office. Sudeep was a calm, quiet revolutionary civil servant, a poet and a playwright, a very determined human being with a compassionate mind. When we met, he started making fun of me, saying, 'Why are you wasting your time by doing all these theatre productions?' Quite surprised, I replied, 'If you believe that is a waste of time, then why do you come and watch all of them?' He laughed and said, 'Why can't you help us in our literacy movement?'

'What will I do there? I cannot teach A B C D, which is not what I am trained for,' I countered. He again gave a big laugh and explained, 'Do you have any idea what is being done in the country? We are creating a second war of independence, and that cannot come without the participation of poets, writers, scientists, musicians, theatre people, academicians and social workers. And in many states, they have already joined and are working in the field.' He meant every word he uttered. After a long pause, I asked, 'Can you give me some material on their project? I am sorry I do not know much about this movement. All I know is that Ernakulam District in Kerala has become the

first 100 per cent literate district of India.' He picked up some
publications from his side table and gave them to me. I looked
at the material and told him, 'I will get back to you once I read
all this material and will come up with some ideas.' He smiled
and said, 'I will be waiting for your response.'

From this meeting came two important, intensive, in-
residence workshops, one in Lucknow and another in Indore.
The participants were young volunteers already working in the
literacy movement, making some street theatre plays around the
theme of literacy. Most of the volunteers had come from rural
backgrounds. Some of them were school or college teachers, and
others social workers. They realized that their understanding of
the literacy movement was limited to a call to the people to
come and learn from them so they could create a revolution
to usher in a new sunrise of educated people in India. They
had been given a very superficial and limited propagandist
way of presenting new ideas, with insensitive and not-at-all-
subtle aesthetic dimensions with any depth. Further, there was
a simplistic attitude behind their work—that they as literacy
volunteers knew the whole truth of education. After watching
their work, I realized that their attitude of superiority and
the readymade easy solutions they offered would be counter-
productive and would not make people think or reflect about
the complexities of life. There was no room or space to ask
questions or to go beyond the obvious narratives.

When we finally started our intervention at the workshops,
I addressed all the participants. The first thing I told them
was that they had to change their attitude. I explained that
we did not know all the answers to all the issues. I had to
let them know that the word 'saksharata' would be banned
at our training workshop. 'Do not use this word because it
limits the imagination, and we start taking refuge under this
word to simplify our explanations. You have to be original
in your ideas,' I explained. 'You want your mother and your

grandmother to join in your literacy classes, so you start with the assumption that she is uneducated and that you will teach her all about education. Because you have really decided that you know everything. This notion is not correct. Just think for a moment about when you were little in front of your mother or your grandmother who took good care of you. She, who taught you with all her love and affection how to speak your first few words; then she sang lullabies to you in the evening so that you could sleep comfortably. As you grew up, she recited folk songs and narrated to you many folk and epic stories. She kept giving you lessons on moral behaviour, on what is good and what is evil. To protect you from any illness, she displayed her knowledge of herbs which grew in your surroundings. She knew a lot about her fields and crops. Now ask yourself a question: is she an uneducated person? What you are offering her are just a few shapes and forms, which we call letters of the alphabet, which she cannot decode. This is all you offer her at this stage. However, she knows the meaning of these words formed by these letters, perhaps more than you do, through her experience of life. Hence, your attitude of being a literacy volunteer needs a course correction and change so that she accepts you to lead her and teach her the joy of learning.'

This changed the course of the workshops. The poems and the stories for the literacy training developed later, after this talk, and their imagery had a very human touch and the smell of earth. The metaphors and references used now had a certain element of humanity and a lot of genuineness. Finally, the plays made by the participants were down to earth, filled with warmth and had great success when performed before rural audiences.

It is not knowledge of theatre acquired at the drama departments and schools of drama alone that is important. Theatre people in particular need to understand the difference between educational theatre and theatre that is done purely for entertainment or for the box office.

It was after these years of experience with literacy movements that I finally got a chance to work with the children of Kashmir during time of conflict and very trying conditions where anything could happen.

The RGF Workshop

Finally, after many weeks, I got a call from Ratna Mathur to prepare a detailed proposal for the children's workshop with the orphans of Kashmir. Once I gave her a general approach and the aims and objectives of the workshop, I held many meetings and discussions with her. She wanted the exact details of each session—impossible in a situation dealing with something through a creative process. One did not know how the sessions would unfold and where they would lead us. I tried to explain to her that she had to give my team complete freedom to explore the methodology without a fixed syllabus of any kind. It was not a regular school activity. We did not know how children would react and how they would respond to what we asked them to do. One has to have the freedom to do the work. After many disagreements and discussions, she understood my predicament. We developed a loose schedule, alterable if the need arose.

The workshop lasted twelve days in a residence with fifty children. When it came to taking a decision on the venue, I suggested the city of Jammu for practical reasons. For years these children of the Valley had not experienced or enjoyed a completely normal day. For most of the year, schools had remained closed. These children had remained indoors under the strict control of their elders, most of the time because of disturbances, violence and agitations near their homes. I wanted them to have a free and peaceful atmosphere where they could breathe without any fear, where suddenly things would not come to a halt because of some law-and-order disturbance.

When the question of the final participating children came up, I threw in an idea. We would have children from both the Kashmiri communities at the workshop, meaning Muslim kids from various parts of the Valley and Kashmiri Pandit children from the Jammu camps. There was a long silence, and nobody responded. After some time, objections from all our well-wishers came up, mostly from Kashmiri friends. Someone said it was a counterproductive idea. One did not know how the children would behave and react when they met each other. Who knew what kind of poison had been fed on both sides into these young minds in their homes? If something even remotely like a disturbance took place, it would be a major scandal and would be reported in the media. In fact, one of my dear Muslim friends insisted, 'You are mad. Do not do this. You will unnecessarily land in trouble and will be accused by both communities.'

I heard all the objections and arguments, but they did not convince me enough to change my mind. I had worked with children in India, and somehow my sixth sense said that all these fears were based on the adult understanding of the situation and not from the perspective of a child living in an atmosphere of fear in which he/she has no say or space to express his/her anger, pain or even happiness.

This child lives in an oppressed home where there are hardly any conscious attempts to reach out to him. What is he thinking? What does he want? How does he feel in this atmosphere? Unfortunately, there were many other priorities his elders had to deal with in the rotten situation they were caught in.

For quite some time I did not say anything. I needed more time to ponder on the matter before I took a final call. In the meantime, I decided that the resource persons for this kind of workshop need not only be theatre people but others too, like educationalists, child education experts, craft teachers and musicians. I thought that in the early days of the workshop, we would have all the resource persons gathering in joint sessions to make all of them familiar with all the kids. After some time, each resource person would take her special session separately.

The date of opening of the workshop approached, and the idea of conducting the first workshop at Jammu in February 2004 was finally accepted. It was heartening that one dharamshala offered to host the children without any payment. Jammu University gave their huge gymnasium for our workshop. The big space had tremendous potential for what we wanted to do with the children.

My friend Saleem Beg, who had who had expressed his worry about bringing Pandit and Muslim children together at this workshop, met me again and repeated his concerns about the possible consequences of such an experiment. As the date drew nearer, my anxiety too grew. All of a sudden, an idea struck me—to ask the mothers of some of the children to join us during the workshop. If anything happened during the workshop, these mothers would act as a soft cushion between us and the children, as our interface between the children and the resource persons. Further, these mothers were themselves widows who had gone through tough times. It may be a nice idea to let them come out of their surroundings to be with us. Their presence in a way would make the workshop like a large family. Ratna of RGF readily accepted this idea, as did my other colleagues.

Finally, on the day we met in the gymnasium of Jammu University for the first time, we had fifty children, aged between twelve to fifteen years, five resource persons, Ratna and the mothers. Thirty-five of the children were from the Valley and fifteen from the migrant camps. I asked everyone to form a circle so that we could all see each other. I remember looking at the faces of these children. They looked either serious, poker-faced, nervous or tense. Some looked frightened. They were also clinging to their mothers. I asked the mothers too to join our circle. Next, I wanted everyone to introduce themselves one by one. Nobody wanted to start. There was silence. So, I introduced myself first, then came Rakesh Kumar Singh, Kanaya and all the theatre people, and after us Asha Sharma, the child educationist, and Anita Rampal, professor of education at Delhi University. Again, a long pause followed. Finally, one girl volunteered to introduce herself. Hardly audible, she just mumbled something in Kashmiri, which nobody could hear, but we moved on to the next kid, who spoke a little louder, saying her name was Noor. After this, each kid followed, mumbling something unheard, making sounds from which we couldn't understand a single word. I could hardly remember their names, but even so, we completed the exercise, letting each person complete his or her introduction.

I remember telling them, 'This is your workshop, and here you have every right to say what you feel or what you like to do. We are not your schoolteachers here, but your friends and we will be playing games and having fun and doing other activities also.' They hardly responded to this, so we broke for tea.

We had planned to begin with some ice-breaking exercises. We soon changed to some psychotherapy games to see what happened. The tea breaks were not only to have tea—all the resource people fanned out and mixed with the children to engage them in general conversation. During these thirty-minute breaks, we actually planned an exercise to get the kids familiar with us. We kept rotating the resource people from one group to another so that we all got an informal introduction to all the kids and gathered as much information about each as possible. In the evenings, the team would share and discuss the information we got during the tea break to help us plan our sessions.

When the ice-breaking session games started, led by Rakesh Kumar Singh, the children started running in all directions.

In these exercises, we mostly worked on reflexes, responses and trust-building. We had plenty of space to work in the big indoor stadium. It was the size of a hockey field and offered immense space for the children to move, run, leap and jump. Elements of body control, concentration, observation and such were woven into these playful exercises. As Rakesh pushed the children to do unusual motions that they would not normally do, I observed the movements of each child, concentrating on the tension points in each specific body.

Here in my workshop, we had to unlock these stiff tension areas, achievable not by pointing them out but by subtle exercises to relieve the mind space. For that, we had to find new ways to exercise to address the problem.

The group still did not communicate much with each other, though they remained polite. The Pandit group remained separate, as did the Valley group. After one break I displayed a white sheet of paper, on which was printed the outline of a tree, in front of the kids. I simply asked them, 'What is it?' They softly replied, 'A tree.' I again asked, 'What kind of tree?' A few of them smiled at my question, but some said, 'It is the chinar tree.' But one Pandit boy hesitantly answered, 'No, it is an apple tree.' Thus began a game in which the kids gave all kinds of names to this outlined sketch of a tree.

I then gave each child a box of acrylic colours and asked them to fill in the outline of the tree with the colours and the details to depict the tree they believed it was. Within forty-five they had finished the colouring and handed the sheets back to us.

We set all the sheets on the floor of the gymnasium so that the children could see each other's work. The kids from the Valley had all coloured the trees entirely green, except for one girl who had used dark purple with zigzag strokes.

The Pandit kids had mostly painted green trees with coloured fruits, all alike and with no variation at all. This surprised us all, but it seemed like a problem too.

Asha Sharma, one of our resource people, pointed out why this might have happened. One was that they had not experienced any painting session like this in all their years. The other was perhaps that they only really knew the colour green, the colour of the green valley they live in, which might be at the back of their minds. All these years, and since the day they were born, they had rarely been exposed to any pleasant experiences. I observed another strange thing: the Pandit children had painted trees with fruits. This seemed quite baffling because these Pandit kids had only heard of fruit trees growing in their gardens from their parents or grandparents. One girl had coloured her tree in dark purple with very expressive strokes.

As we know, young children cannot express in words what they feel or have gone through. This kind of exercise provides a statement of their minds, which needs to be understood and addressed carefully. To try to take them away from a monochromatic state of mind, we tried another exercise using another image—a black outline of a house. We again distributed sheets to each student. We did not make any comments to them about their previous drawings. Now I asked them to colour this house, a little quicker than they had their previous sheet. After they finished, we laid the sheets out on the floor again so all could have a look. The Valley children had mostly repeated the same green colour to fill in the houses with. The Pandits had painted theirs in brown or black colours.

During these colouring exercises, something interesting did happen—the children started exchanging a few words among themselves. At one point, one Pandit girl changed her place to sit next to a Muslim girl. They started conversing with each other and working on their sheets.

When all were done painting, we sat together, and I invited an informal discussion. I asked, 'How come you forgot to pick up any other colour from your colour boxes, except mostly green, when there were many other colours looking at you and telling you please pick me up also? But you did not hear them. Now, tell me, is green the only colour in a tree? You used only green, but there are other colours there in a tree too. Just think for a minute.' The children were all quiet. Then I asked them to come out with me to the playground, and there we sat under the shade of many trees. I asked them to look carefully with their eyes open and to count in their head the various colours in the trees and to observe what else they saw in them. I gave them ten minutes for this. But before this time ended, they started telling me the number of colours they had observed. They reported nests in the trees, worms and birds. One kid came running and said he could hear the sound of some bird but couldn't see it; it turned out to be a cricket. This exercise soon turned into a game, and they ran around and climbed the trees. All of a sudden we saw thousands of birds descend from the sky onto these trees, making a lot of noise, and after a minute they all flew off, making a circle in the sky and gliding back to the trees. It looked like a game of gliding played by hundreds of birds. While all of us enjoyed watching this game of the birds, I asked the kids to notice the different colours all around the lawns of the university. Sunset had approached and the colours in the winter sky were changing. These innocent kids were so very engrossed in this game of changing colours. I requested the mother's group to sing a Kashmiri song that we too could join in. At first, the mothers hesitated, but then they did sing. The mood changed as the kids joined in, forming a large chorus. We sang until almost dark. One could see joy on the children's faces, and they now started talking to each other. Our group of mothers also started talking to each other, and they began to contribute in their own way.

I am not an expert social scientist and have not trained as a psychologist. But we did catch an impulse of the moment and turned it into some positive energy.

We started learning about the children's backgrounds. We only knew that back home they had witnessed their fathers killed by terrorists in front of them. One child had held her father's legs while he was being dragged out of the house. When the attackers could not drag her father further, a terrorist had pointed his gun at him and shot him, with this poor kid still holding on to his legs. She had seen her father's blood all over herself. After this horrible and traumatizing experience, this little girl had developed a distorted, stiff expression on her face. She never looked straight into anyone's eyes and remained alone most of the time. Another girl would faint at least two or three times a day and then withdraw into her shell, weeping for her father. She had three sister and no male in her house. Relatives had abandoned them. Another girl had studied in an elite school, but when she lost her father she was enrolled in an ordinary school, shattering her dream of becoming a doctor. She would suddenly break down and start howling.

All of us felt that most of the girls needed a father figure. On the contrary, most of the boys behaved like grown, mature men. They would never express themselves openly, except if someone chatted with them in private. Some of them had shut themselves up and would never open up.

One day we decided to take them on a picnic to a zoo; it would be a free day without any proper sessions. The zoo in Jammu was small, with a limited number of animals. Surprisingly, they had many varieties of birds. The children loved these birds with their colourful feathers. I noticed some children making notes of whatever they saw from the information about these birds put up on each cage. It took us a couple of hours to go around the entire zoo. During lunch break, Kanaya asked the children to recall the shapes and colours of the birds they had seen. We took a long walk within the zoo, which had a forest within its premises. I asked some of the kids, 'Where you stay, trees are green in colour; did you notice how many kinds of greens there are in each tree?' This was just an off-the-cuff remark, to make them aware of the various shades of greens, opening their sense of sight. The best takeaway from the day, though, was that the children were talking to each other without any hesitation or awkwardness.

The next day, back at the gymnasium, Rakesh led a fun-filled exercise in which the children had to use their entire body, from head to toe, to make images, using their bodies as vehicles of expression. The previous day's visit to the zoo helped them imagine birds and animals. The image-making led them further to images from nature, or whatever else arose in their mind. Rakesh used different kinds of music to stimulate their minds. From making images together, slowly the session turned into making individual images. Here, each child now worked on his or her own, using body and mind to create different forms without anyone interfering, instructing or correcting them. What was important to all of us was the children's involvement and concentration on themselves. Music played throughout their work process, indirectly helping and inspiring them. It was a delight to watch them continuously make new forms. We watched their bodies transform into many objects and shapes, many incomprehensible to most of us, but that was not important. What was necessary was to get them into the act of a creative process where their personal, emotional memories could pour out and lead them to experience their own selves.

After this session concluded, they were told to relax. Relax? This was new to them; they couldn't do that at all. Finally, we had to instruct them to concentrate on their breath while lying on their backs. Gradually, if done properly, they could reach a point of complete body relaxation, a yogic exercise that works wonders to take away all stress and tension.

When this session ended, I very softly called for a break, but there was a strange silence. I saw little Noor collapsing, cold and lifeless. Sultana cried out aloud, and one boy quietly sobbed in a corner. Soon the other boys and girls were rushing to help them all, bringing water and expressing words of sympathy. It was a type of bonding among the children. We consciously did not interfere with them; we let them handle the situation themselves. They sat in groups of ten to twelve, talking and helping each other. Boys took the lead at this point. Any schisms between the groups of migrant children and Valley children melted away completely. Our mothers' group joined in and gave their motherly warmth and advice. It felt as if a large family had gathered.

My mind asked, 'What next?' At every stage in such a situation, a certain amount of redesigning of the sessions has to be done in order to move on.

Soon after the tea break, when we reassembled, some boys said they did not want to do any class now. When I asked what had happened, their reply was, 'We are tired with these exercises. We want to do something different.' I asked them, 'What would you like to do?' Their demand was to play some sports, so we got some footballs and a cricket set from the university sports section. Immediately, some of the children started to play cricket and others football on the sports field.

I went to make some phone calls from a public PCO booth. When I returned after nearly forty-five minutes, I saw my resource people watching the children happily at play, but the moment the children saw me, they stopped and rushed towards me. 'What happened?' I asked. 'Why have you stopped playing?'

They replied, 'Sorry, sorry, sorry, sir, let us go back to our class.' I was intrigued, so I told them, 'No, now I also want to play.' I joined the game of cricket and started to bowl, but within minutes of my playing, they again stopped and asked me to start the class. I asked them, 'Are you sure? There is no problem; we can keep playing. We have lots of time.' But they insisted on the class being resumed.

We went back into the gymnasium. I made them sit and spoke to them. I could sense that they were not happy about what they had done and were feeling a bit of guilt. I said to them all, 'You know, I am very happy today. You said what you wanted to say. Remember what I had said to you on the very first day when we met? I had said you have every right to say what you want to say, and today I am proud of you that you spoke your mind. This is what you have to inculcate in *yourself*, the spirit of asking and not keeping it pent up inside you.' Since, thankfully, I had the advantage of being able to say all this in their mother tongue, they received it well. 'You are always welcome to accept or reject what we offer to you,' I continued. 'We need your feedback regularly. That is how we also learn.' We felt confident about the workshop when we saw the new dynamics within the group. Looking at their courage today, it belied all those fears and warnings that I was given by our friends about problems arising between Pandit and Muslim kids.

A new session started, again with a sheet of white paper, this time with an outline of a bird only. After distributing the copies along with colour boxes, I asked them to fill in the outline the way they had done before. This time we saw a dramatic change. Using the outline of a simple bird that we had provided, the children made colourful birds of all kinds, filling their entire sheets with bright colours.

Next, we started the game of story-making. As usual, we always started by sitting in a circle, followed by some games and concentration exercises. Before we began, I saw one girl from the Valley, Zoya, cross the circle and join Sunita on the opposite side, both holding hands. It was not a simple crossing, for they were exchanging smiles. I whispered into Rakesh's ear, 'The key to the lock has turned and lock is perhaps now unlocked.' We both laughed. We were quite happy with this development.

The game of story-making or story-building had all children add only one sentence to the previous one to make a story. Each child adds a single sentence, and the story keeps building itself, moving forward from one child to the next. It is like building a wall, brick by brick. This way the story continues as long as each person contributes and adds new dimensions, doing the rounds of the participants again and again. It can lead to a very small story, but if you keep applying your imagination, this game can weave a long dastaan too.

In the beginning, the children could not add much substance to the story, which hardly made a single round. We tried many times, but not much progress could be made. Finally, Rakesh and I joined in the game. When a story collapsed, the room filled with laughter. Finally, Rakesh and I created a sort of demo for the kids, adding one line each to make and build a story, which went on for almost ten minutes. We included all kinds of characters—demons, magic carpets, kings and animals. Every time a major moment developed, the children would laugh and clap. They saw through our example the possibilities of improvisation techniques. The emergence of a major story that did not fall into any typical category of stereotyped plots allowed for an open-ended journey into other worlds of the imagination.

After this, it was the children's turn to make a big story. This time it was different, and a story grew, full of adventures, wars, underwater creatures, fairies and dacoits. They created a strange serial story.

We broke them into three groups and asked them to make new stories. This time all three groups had fun, doing all kinds of exaggerations on their improvised stories. Once they completed their stories, we asked each group to narrate their stories to all the rest. They took some time to put the sequences of their stories in order and then started presenting them. Each story was a great effort by the children.

The next step was to ask them to enact their stories, which meant they had to embody the characters, improvise dialogues, create movements and arrange spaces. At this time a couple of these children came to me and said, 'You are very clever; you are making us do all the work.' It was a sweet protest, which I loved. Even Rakesh laughed at their comment.

At that point, I told them the story of a fish and a fishing rod. Then I asked them, 'Would you like to have a fishing rod with which you can catch fish yourself any time you want, or you would like to be served fish?' There was silence for a few moments. I said, 'We are here to let you know and realize how much talent you have. In this workshop, you have to learn to take decisions and make mistakes so that you learn from your mistakes your hidden potential. Remember, no one is judging you. We are all learning from each other by actually working and exploring. So, you can go now, and within one hour make a proper presentation of your story for all of us here.'

After one hour, all three groups made their presentations of about five minutes each. It was a delight to see them using space and creating characters. On top of this, one group sang a song, written and composed by Noor!

After the presentations were over, we discussed the themes of the plays. They liked our comments and were happy about their achievements. At the end of the day, I said to them, 'Did you realize that you did all this by yourself?' Big smiles crossed each face as they realized what they had achieved.

Asha Singh, our expert in children's education, wanted a full-day session with the children to get them to 'share some of their hidden secrets'. It was supposed to be just a talking session. Asha asked the children to talk about the happiest day or incident in their lives and the saddest. She explained to them that if they wished to, they could share their stories with the group or choose any participant to share their secret stories with, quietly in some corner.

This exercise left the children disturbed for some time, as they would have to come out of their shells and find the courage to speak in front of everyone. The exercise was meant to unburden them, to release some feelings that might have been repressed in them for years. There was silence and more silence. The children did not know what to do, and some grew very tense.

We all expected that this would be the time they would talk about the violence and terror they had witnessed, that the Pandit children would talk about the stories of their exodus and humiliation. We expected things to explode that day, but to our surprise, none of the kids said anything that reflected the situation in the Valley or about the impact of violence on them personally. They had their own stories of domestic difficulties, accidents, or deaths of grandparents or relatives. Strangely, none of them touched on terrorism. Their narratives were about day-to-day humanness, about loneliness, about poverty, about education and their future. What was most moving as they narrated their stories were the responses that came from the other children as gestures of support and solidarity. For example, one girl's saddest story was of an accident in which she was injured, and her brother had died in the hospital from his injuries. At the end of the story, she broke down and cried, 'I do not have a brother now.' One boy sitting behind her spontaneously lifted his hand, touched her on the shoulder and said to her, 'No, you have a brother here in me; you are not without a brother.' Like this, many stories with sad endings brought very moving responses from the kids. Noor talked about her mother's lone struggle with her three sisters. The entire class quietly wiped their tears when she told us about her mother's difficulties. Even the mothers' group (the widows) joined in with their stories, some funny and some tragic.

The widows lifted the curtains over their lives. They told us how, as women without a bread earner in the family, every day became a struggle, without any support coming from any quarter. Surprisingly, they never blamed the political situation for their plight, or perhaps they could not articulate or understand that aspect. It became clear that their relatives and extended families were not in any position to support them either, or that society at large was helpless to do anything for them. The entire class was in tears; it was like a scene of a funeral or of mourning.

The children narrated the stories of their happiest days of joy and laughter, but it was the tears that brought all of us closer to each other. The moments of catharsis untied the knots of hidden pains quietly suppressed deep inside each child. These kinds of experiences bring on tension points in one's body because they have never been addressed or resolved. Nobody said anything to anyone; there were just gentle hugs in silence as we all came out of the gym for a cup of tea. Pain was shared without words, and all had become one.

In the evening, before the workshop closed for the day, two mothers met me separately, requesting help to get themselves medically examined. One mother was experiencing pain all over her body all the time, and the other complained that for months she had not been able to sleep and remained awake most of the night. She had never gone to a doctor for a check-up because of lack of support and the prevailing condition in the Valley. I promised them help, possibly the next day.

Aneeta Rampal, an educationalist, initiated a new session with the children. Naturally, her discussions brought in the role of teachers and the condition of schools. The children harshly criticized their teachers, who were not well trained and could not impart their teaching well. In conclusion, the children were not happy with their school environment or the way of teaching in their schools.

It was Zoya who had studied in a good city school until her father was shot dead by militants. After that, she had to join an average school. She insisted that she still wanted to be a doctor and wanted to know why it was not possible to study in an ordinary school. She pointed out, 'After all, our books are the same. Why is the government supporting bad schools and bad education through bad teachers?' The discussion became very animated, almost explosive.

All of us enjoyed the level of discussion and the questions raised by the children. Now I felt I had the confidence to push these children into some major areas of creativity and planning. At this stage, while the kids were out on a short break, I unrolled two long white paper rolls on the floor. When they walked in, they looked at the sheets as if some feast was about to be served. People had to sit on either side of these white paper rolls.

I asked them to split themselves into two groups and to pick up their watercolour boxes and brushes and take places on any side of the paper roll. I asked them to do a group painting on the theme of an ideal school, whatever they thought a school should have. The children were surprised but glad and excited to plan a project of that kind. I instructed them, 'You must first discuss among your group members, agree, disagree, convince each other and then make a joint painting, where every one of you is participating and contributing.' I had to explain to them how to carefully use the watercolours. They could also use their fingers and even pieces of foam to paint with. 'Just enjoy your ideal school painting project,' I said. 'You need not worry about not being a painter; your idea of the school is more important.'

It was very interesting to watch these children planning use of the paper space, which was around thirty feet in length and four feet wide. Both groups engaged in animated discussions, agreeing and disagreeing. Some children emerged as the leaders of the groups with many ideas, while others listened to them. Before executing the final painting, the children took the serious responsibility of deciding who would paint which area of the space. We adults only listened to their interesting conversations. After so many days, the children were now an organic group, relaxed and concentrated on the job.

Some important lessons were built in this kind of big exercise, such as the sharing of materials, the art of joint discussion, persuading each other and respecting each other's points of view. The purpose was simply for each team to learn how to work in a democratic way for a common goal. It took them a couple of hours to complete the paintings, done in near-pin-drop silence. Working in a joint group with complete concentration was a new concept for all of these children and worked like group therapy for them.

Once they completed the paintings, we all had a look at their work. It was revealing as to what these children could achieve. Their paintings had a sense of space, colour and planning. There were school buildings, playgrounds, water streams for swimming in, complete with boats, fish and swans, sports fields, a lovely green forest and wild animals. In the distance, they drew a long line of mountain ranges and forests.

The imagination of both groups was amazing and original. Whatever they had thought an ideal school should have been all placed in proper spaces. The displays were colourful, and we loved both paintings. It was not easy to do thirty-foot-long paintings. We raised questions about the necessary things, from a utility point of view, that the kids had not thought about. What about electricity for the schools? Where would it come from? Where were the streetlights? Where would all the waste and garbage go? Where was the canteen space? When they realized that their planning was incomplete, they were disappointed with us for raising all these issues. I insisted that they give thought to all these issues and come up with solutions by the next day. Without solving those problems, we could not think of this work as a proper, functional project. Still, we praised their ideas and layouts.

It was heartening to see these children, who would not talk to each other just a few days back, achieve so much within a week of the workshop.

Another question we wanted them to address about their schools, apart from the technical points, was what kind of children could join them. We decided that their big paintings would be put up jointly for proper execution on the ground. A big space was allocated, with an improvised module of the structure made with the help of Kanaya, who was an accomplished craftsman and theatre director. With the help of all the children, we built a large model of a school from the paintings they had created. Within three days, we had a functional model built, with new details incorporated into the model as we worked on it.

From the exercise of painting in watercolours to converting their long paintings into a three-dimensional model, the children had taken a journey through craft, engineering, hygiene, pollution control, landscaping, distribution of spaces and more. While reviewing the project details and solving the emergency problems, it was interesting to watch how last-minute changes were incorporated into the paintings. As the model developed, these changes kept in mind the practicality of the project and the applicability of the suggestions. The final three-dimensional model was never completed, but the children would come again and again to keep adding some detail and decoration to it until the very end of the workshop.

Finally, we undertook another play-making session around the theme of education and learning, asking about the difficulties faced by village children in getting to their schools, which were far away in some mountains. They set out to create a kind of day in the life of a child in rural Kashmir. Soon the children developed two different narratives around this theme. They painted these narratives on paper rolls and made presentations of their improvised stories. The narratives of both groups remained roughly the same, but the treatments in terms of the use of space, locales and colours were very different. Both groups had different interpretations of the theme, which itself was unchanged. This was the most interesting element of their creativity.

From here, they had to make a performance of their narratives. At this stage of the workshop, I made a small intervention by explaining to them the concept of structure and the unfolding of a plot. I told them how to depict the unfolding of events in an interesting way. I told them about the idea of space and time through the concept of a seed, which they must have seen at their homes. I explained that in a seed is hidden a plant, and through germination, it flowers, and finally through its fruits come more seeds. But to go through these stages requires time; the seed is like a capsule in which time and space are enclosed.

I explained all of this, and I wanted them to unfold their stories keeping in mind the journey of a plant from a seed to a plant and back to a seed. During the preparations, they could freely ask me for help. We had given them two hours to develop their stories and then perform them for us all. I made use of this time to arrange for their mothers to be seen by doctors. Ratna had arranged appointments for them with the doctors.

After checking them, the doctors talked to them about their problems. The doctors had given them some medicines and instructions and asked the mothers to see them again before they returned to Srinagar. Later, one of the doctors conveyed to us that these poor ladies had no actual physical or clinical ailments. They were mentally under stress and needed psychological treatment. Hearing about their need for mental health treatment, we took this up with Ratna of IGNCA. They promised to look into the matter soon and find capable doctors to help them locally in Srinagar.

As the kids worked on their own, they went through long discussions among themselves, with Kanaya and Rakesh helping. They rehearsed as I, along with the other faculty, watched them from a distance. The children seemed in full command, developing sequences and then discarding them to start once again. At one point I approached a group to see what was going on. To my surprise, Zoya saw me and pushed me away, saying, 'No, you are not allowed to see or interfere in our play, please go away.' I was delighted by her confidence. The kids could now confidently make their own decisions.

After two-and-a-half hours, the kids said they were ready for us to watch their performance. The performances turned out to be very serious. They created a village ambience through folk songs composed and sung by Noor, the girl who used to faint. Many of the scenes came from their personal experiences. Both groups performed seriously as if they were professionals. I could see their attempts to use the seed-plant-seed principle to create structure and space.

On the final day of the workshop, we had invited some friends to watch some of the performances and to see the paintings and the school-project paintings and models. The children performed their plays, and the guests present were so moved by their talent that many of the guests wanted to know how to support more projects like this one. I took them on their word and promised them that when I needed their help I would definitely contact them for our next workshop at Srinagar, for which there had been a lot of demand.

Finally, when the bus for the children who had to travel back to Srinagar arrived, there was a lot of restlessness, and no one was going into the bus. The children wanted to be together. They were quickly taking down each other's addresses and phone numbers, and when they were told to go into the bus, the scene changed. There were tears and the children were crying and holding each other's hands. Some of them broke down completely. It was a scene I could not handle. It was too painful for me to see these young children from both communities wanting to be together. After some time and with a lot of effort and difficulty, the children got onto the bus and the driver was signalled to move on. Even the driver was hesitating to start his bus. At last, in the midst of tears and sobbing, the bus moved. The children who had to go back to their migrant camps ran after the bus to some distance and then stopped and stood there till the bus disappeared.

With their moist eyes, the migrant children were now looking at us. After some time in silence, they were put on their bus, and with a heavy heart, they left for their refugee camps. A question came up in my mind: when will these beautiful children also go back to their homes in their Valley.

We soon received a lot of encouraging feedback from people and also a demand for another workshop from our well-wishers. But this time in the valley itself which was tough. But me and Ratna Mathur started talking about the next workshop. For this kind of work, where local governments do not offer any kind of support, it becomes quite tough to set up infrastructure of any kind. Based on our Jammu experience we seemed confident to venture into a workshop in the Kashmir Valley, where we will have now migrant children coming into their ancestral land for the first time. About which they have only heard of and where they actually belonged. This is going to be very challenging.

In Kashmir, it is always said, 'One does not know which agency is operating where and how.' Working in Kashmir is full of surprises. Being a conflict area, you have to be very vigilant and careful, otherwise you can land in trouble. One night during this new workshop which had started in May 2004 in Srinagar, in the dead of the night at around 2 a.m. at the hotel, I heard a knock at my door. I woke up to hear another knock, this time a little louder. I switched on the light, and there was a group of army jawans at my door with their AK-47 rifles aimed at my door. I was unnerved for a while. I could not believe it to be real. Then their commander walked into the room, followed by the armed jawans. They checked out my room. And after they were satisfied their Sikh commander said, 'Oh, you are here.' It seemed he recognized me. He then explained to me that they had got some incorrect information, and left saying he was sorry for the intrusion.

During one of the workshops, which was part of the work undertaken for children without fathers at the Srinagar workshop, I was in Srinagar with some migrant minority children from the Jammu camps. I had planned an outing to the heritage sites for them, with a picnic added. The fear among these migrant children and some of the mothers who had come with the children was phenomenal. They were scared and would not venture out of the workshop premises. As usual, a bus was arranged, and it was decided we would go to Pahalgam and on our way there would visit some of the important heritage sites. When we were about to leave I asked the migrant mothers to join us. But they were not very enthusiastic and avoided coming with us. They wanted to go to the Kheer Bhawani and other temples. Since Pahalgam was in a different direction, it was not possible to do both as that would have taken a lot of time. I assured these women that we would arrange a temple tour for their puja some other day. There was one lady named Usha who belonged to Bhavan Town, which fell on our route to Pahalgam, whom I asked why she did not want to go and see her home in Bhavan, which she had left many years back. She did not utter a word, but her eyes were moist, and she avoided any eye contact with me.

I invited her again, saying, 'You will feel better if you go with the group.'

She replied, 'No, I am scared to go.'

'Scared of what,' I asked.

She said, 'You do not know, please leave me here.' I tried to reassure her that nothing would happen to her.

Finally, when the bus was about to leave and all the children and faculty were in their seats, Usha stood looking at the bus from a distance, a little bit restless. I told her again, 'Usha, do not miss this opportunity to visit your home, just get onto the bus. All of us will be back by evening.' When the driver pressed the accelerator with his foot and the bus moved just a bit, Usha ran to the bus and got in. It would take them around four hours to reach Pahalgam. Ratna and Aneeta from the resources team went with them. I did not go as I wanted to attend to some work in Srinagar.

Before planning this heritage visit-cum-picnic, I had a long chat with the kids about our heritage. The migrant children had never been told about their heritage except about a few temples. So, I talked to them about what they would see on this tour. I told them that before reaching Pahalgam they would visit two ancient monuments at Avantipura. These were the ruins of two stone temples constructed during the reign of King Avantivarman in AD 700. To our surprise, even our local children had never visited any of these heritage sites, because the schools had been closed for months due to the militancy and it was not safe to take them anywhere except maybe to the Mughal gardens on school picnics. It was also revealed that these local children had never visited the great famous Jama Masjid of Srinagar or even the Shah Hamadan shrine. Both are great medieval architectural sites apart from being sacred places. On being asked if they had seen ever the inside of a houseboat, the answer was 'never'. I was not surprised. It is a fact that Kashmiris as a community only visited religious places on auspicious days, and now, with the advent of violence and terror, people prefer to remain safe indoors at home.

Aneeta Rampal and Ratna Mathur, who were with the kids going to Pahalgam, returned from the trip to report to me that when the bus crossed Anantnag and was heading towards the town of Bhavan, Usha started to get restless and was looking out from the windows at the shops. As the bus crossed the Bhavan Temple and the gurudwara on the way to Pahalgam, Usha screamed, 'There, there, that is my home.' The bus had already crossed her home, but Aneeta told the driver to stop the bus, which was brought to a grinding halt. Usha became very tense and did not know what to do or say. She was looking out of the window but strangely avoiding getting out. All the children were looking at her, wondering whether she would step out of the bus or not. Finally, it was Aneeta who went to her and asked her not to worry, that everything would be all right. Usha took some minutes to think, and finally alighted from the bus, looking in only one direction as she walked slowly towards her home. Aneeta said there was a young local boy, aged about ten, who was watching all this. Next, he was guiding Usha.

All followed Usha, and at one spot she stopped and looked at her house and broke down completely. Her crying could be heard all over the place. Many neighbours rushed out and recognized Usha. They hugged her, welcomed her and started to ask her about her family members. Strangely, Usha's family had left their house keys with some Muslim neighbour, who now brought the keys, and Usha opened the main door of her home after almost fifteen years. She looked at the walls of her room. Everything in the house was there the way she had left it in January 1990. Nothing was touched, Usha's sobs and tears mingled with her monosyllabic replies. Aneeta said her aimless look was heartbreaking. I remember when my elder brother Ashok Kumar had gone to our home in Srinagar during the height of militancy to have a look at our home at Sheetal Nath and check its condition, he returned with a small polythene packet containing some pictures from our teenage days. I had asked my brother 'Bhaijaan, what is it?' He had replied, 'This was all that was left in our house, as our inheritance. These black-and-white pictures were scattered on the ground floor, and I thought at least let me pick them up.'

But today, after many years, Usha's visit to her house had become a welcoming occasion with a tinge of sadness. No one knew what the future was. Usha was asked by the young schoolboy to have some tea, but she declined, telling her mohallawalas that it was getting late for the children to reach Pahalgam. She thanked everybody, locked her home, handed back the keys to her neighbour and very quietly moved out of the mohalla, along with her old friends who were reassuring her and wishing her well. All got back into the bus. Aneeta was looking at this young boy who seemed to have understood everything. Aneeta invited him to join them for the picnic; he thanked her and said, 'Inshallah, maybe next time.' And the bus moved forward. For quite some time nobody had talked. There was silence in the bus. All were lost in their own worlds. The silence was broken by the feeble voice of Usha, who almost in a whisper told Aneeta Rampal, 'Thank you, I feel better.'

One day during this workshop, I was walking on Residency Road, and somebody said there had been heavy firing in the downtown area and many young boys had been killed. I was unnerved because again there would be agitations, shutdowns and God knows what. The chain of violence had not ceased for years now; there had only been some pauses. Terrorists, the security forces and the separatists were entangled in a very complex, violent game with no exit in sight. Every day, stories of killing or stone-pelting would reach us regularly, and before we could think of any new activity these incidents used to weaken our resolve. Saleem Beg and I would often discuss our limitations in the battle of culture in the prevailing circumstances. I would often ask myself if there was any point in the kind of work we were doing. Saleem would often say, 'If we do not then who else will?' Our major worry was the depigmentation of our cultural life—how rapidly things had changed and how Kashmiris as a people had got divided into 'us' and 'them'; how opportunist sharks had taken over the social life of the people; how the element of suspicion had grown so much between people. The principle of trusting each other had become a thing of the past. The value of a human being had become so cheap. For hours we would talk and feel lost. A question that crossed my mind during one such discussion was 'What am I doing here? What is the meaning of all this?' When my work was so limited and humble, as against the big powerful game being played with guns and with lives? How relevant was our work? I had no easy answers. But we kept holding each other's hands between the cross-firing and continued our journey. It seemed our work was like that of a darner, who with needle and thread was quietly trying to repair the torn fabric of our Valley.

I went to a PCO booth to call home early in the morning. There were many people waiting for their turn, and so was I. Soon a security truck of the CRPF stopped by the roadside and two jawans came, waiting for their turn at the booth. While waiting, I could overhear their conversation. They had come after their night duty. The gist of their conversation was about when their posting in the conflict zone would end and when the conflict would be over. The senior cop was explaining to his junior that after three months he would retire and be happy to go home, and hopefully, nothing should happen to him before that. But if one had more time in service then one had better be careful; after all, they were ordinary people with family responsibilities and with no back-up support.

As they talked, I stood up. Even these guys with their guns and commanding authority worried about their families and about their future. For them, their posting here in this conflict zone of Kashmir did not seem like a happy one. After all, violence is violence.

After the successful theatre workshops, I went to Jammu to see my elder brother who had retired from his Central government job. After staying with him for couple of days I took an overnight train to Delhi. When I woke up in the morning there were still a couple of hours to go before the train reached Delhi. I was having my morning cup of tea. The passengers travelling next to me had also come from Srinagar and were going on their annual leave. We got talking and one of them asked me if I was from Kashmir. I said yes and no, because I had a home there till 1990, before our clan had to leave forever. This man's surname was Tyagi. He said, 'I know sir, I have seen you people leaving the Valley to save your lives before my eyes. I am an officer in the Central Reserve Force and have been in the Valley on duty for years. I still remember January 1990, when my regiment was pressed into action.'

I got quite curious and also intrigued by his comments and wanted to know more from him.

He said he still remembered that late afternoon in January 1990 when his regiment had just arrived in the Valley, and they were immediately put on duty. Before going for their first operation, they were addressed by their commander. He had said, 'Remember, today we have been called to save our motherland. Remember, if you win this battle for your country nobody is going to talk about you—but we will be victorious. But if we lose this battle you will be known by your names, who lost and who could not save their motherland from the enemy. Remember this, Bharat Mata has to be saved from the enemies.'

'This was our first battle at Gawkadal,' said Tyagi. 'All night we were fighting without any knowledge of the landscape. People at Lal Chowk dread my name. Ask any shopkeeper at Laal Chowk about Tyagi and he will tell you about me and my deeds.' Then, after a pause, he continued, 'I had really become like a dog who could smell trouble. Now, with God's grace, the situation is different, things have improved. We had to practically retrieve Kashmir back from the enemy's jaws at any cost.'

I again asked him why he had said he had become like a dog and that he could smell suspicious people. He smiled and said, 'One day in winter, it was a holiday, Sunday or something, I felt quite bored. I told my boys, let us go for a drive. The boys said, "In uniform?" I replied, "Are you crazy, we are just going for a simple drive to just relax." The boys asked whether we should carry our weapons. I told them all right, just keep a few weapons under your seats because we are not on official duty. When we were driving on the Srinagar highway towards Pampore—it was a very beautiful day in winter—there was hardly anyone walking on the highway, and we were chatting and cracking jokes.

'After about ten kilometres we saw a young man walking on the road. We soon overtook him, and after a kilometre of driving I said to my driver, just reverse. All the boys were surprised and said, "Why, sir?" I said I suspected that fellow who was walking on the road. I found his body language suspicious. And soon we met him. When he saw us, his body language again made me suspect him. I asked him some questions, and he searched for words. He started vomiting some useful information. When we pressed hard, he mentioned a name of a man whom we had been looking for months. When we pressed him further to reveal something about this man, he said that man was going to get married on such-and-such date, in such-and-such village.

'We started our inquiries, and it was confirmed that there was a wedding taking place. On the day of the wedding, we laid an ambush in the late night, at about midnight, and went into action. We caught him in his bed with his newlywed wife, both naked. When I saw this young nude girl and my boys started staring at her, I said to myself, Tyagi, this may be your end. We started investigating the man. He was a confirmed terrorist who had committed a bank robbery with some of his fellow militants. He was a prize catch. We had to extract as much as we could. "Whatever I have is hidden here underground," he said. We made him and some of his male family members dig open the ground. We found three AK-47 rifles, lots of ammunition, a few grenades and cash amounting to more than Rs 2 lakh. I asked him where the rest of the money was. He said it had been distributed among the group members. Here, again, while I had caught a wanted, dreaded terrorist, I was again worried about my life and the risk to it from my own boys. My boys were already looking at the cash and then looking at me. I could see the greed in their eyes for the cash. After all, nobody would know about the recovery of big cash. To save myself, I again started shouting and ordering for all the recovered articles to be packed and for us to leave as quickly as possible along with our prize catch for further interrogation.'

Last Journey, Last Post

After a gap of six months and winter, my next workshop in Srinagar was being conducted in the building of a local passport office near Bakshi Stadium. This place is in the centre of the city which has no proper infrastructure for cultural activity, except for some spaces which are under the J&K Cultural Academy. But to get them on board to become partners in our kind of exercise would call for a complex, time-consuming, bureaucratic discussion based on many factors, and was beyond our reach. So, I always depend on my friends for help. This passport-building space was again obtained using the good offices of my fellow travellers.

This time we had planned to present two new theatre productions, apart from usual training classes in various aspects of theatre, like set design, costume design, actor preparation, make-up, etc. This time we had a very large number of participants, and we became a little ambitious. We decided to produce Samuel Beckett's *Waiting for Godot* and Bhisham Sahni's *Hanush*. The idea behind choosing these plays was to present the absurdity of the situation in Kashmir. The plays were adapted into Kashmiri, and both were very fine pieces of Kashmiri writing. *Godot* was a European contemporary classic and *Hanush* is the most significant play by the writer of *Tamas* who is also called the Bhishmapitamah of Hindi short-story writing.

We thought of introducing a new young local director from the Valley itself, who had been part of the early training programmes. This was also part of passing on the mantle of Kashmiri theatre to the younger generation. The new director we chose was Warshad Mushtaq. He would direct *Waiting for Godot*. I decided to direct *Hanush* myself. In the beginning, all was going fine. The *Godot* adaptation became a group written by the actors and the director himself. *Hanush* was adapted by Manzoor Meer, again our old workshop student. As I had mentioned earlier, we had developed a kind of core team from among the students of our precious training programmes, who would often come and assist in our new programmes.

The working space at our new venue was located near the main road where Bakshi Stadium stood. After the main entry gate, there was a big ground on whose left was located the indoor stadium and on whose right stood our workshop building. Quite often we used the indoor stadium for our major exercise classes. The whole campus was very inspiring and big enough for our work.

One day, when all the participants were arriving in the morning for our work, we noticed some unusual movement of CRPF jawans. They were erecting a tent and a big platform on the open ground. We could not understand what was going on. Soon, about thirty minutes into our class, we heard the slogan 'Bharat Mata ki jai' being shouted many times. We stopped the class and rushed out to see what was going on. To our shock it was the wreath-laying ceremony for four soldiers, whose bodies were in boxes covered in the national tricolour. Many were watching all this from a distance. One senior officer placed a wreath on each box. The other jawans gave them the last-gun salute, lowering their guns as a mark of respect for their fallen comrades, and the bugles played the last post. After this ceremony, the boxes were carried by the jawans in a ceremonial march and placed on waiting vehicles. The vehicles drove away to the slogans of *Amar rahai, amar rahai* [They are immortal]. An elderly-looking old man said 'Ye bhi *kisi maa ki bete the—ya Allha reham kar* [They are some mother's children. Ya Allah! Have mercy!].'

All of us standing there did not know what to do next. A strange feeling of unease took over all of us. We quietly went back to our workshop. We carried on with our work. We had now reached a stage when all our energies were geared to the production for which we had to fabricate costumes, sets, etc. We had opted for local materials and local tailors, carpenters and painters to help us create the stage, the sets and other related things for the final show.

After a few days, again in the morning, we noticed the same kind of activity on the part of the CRPF jawans that we had witnessed before. This time there were two boxes wrapped in the Indian national flag, and again it was a repeat of the ceremony we had watched before. It was not at all comfortable for us to witness all this, but it could not be helped. It used to leave its after-effects on all of us, which was very hard to explain. No one used to be in a position to carry on work. So, we used to close for the day.

Unfortunately, this wreath-laying ceremony was happening every now and then. Now we began to take a look at the ground first thing in the morning, to see if there was any activity by the jawans. Since we had been working for four weeks regularly, from morning to evening, our response too was getting gradually dehumanized. It started becoming a sort of routine affair for us as we had got used to it, and a certain degree of strange cynicism started creeping into our minds, making us quite bitter and emotionless. Nobody liked to see this happening, but the participants started asking, humorously, '*Aaj kaarikram hain kai* [Is there a programme anywhere today]?' It almost became a stupid and sick joke. And finally, one day I had to reprimand the students and bring some sense into them.

In the hotel where we stayed with my teammates, we used to eat our dinner together, and that was also the time when we used to discuss and plan for the next day. After dinner, discussions would continue quite late into the night, and then I would make some tea for all the teammates in my room. During one of these post-dinner meetings, all of us heard a big blast, which shook our hotel building. Then a heavy exchange of fire went on for almost forty-five minutes. We had to switch off our room lights. It sounded like it was happening in our neighbourhood. When, finally, the firing stopped, one could hear the sounds of fire engines and the sirens of ambulances. We opened the windows of our room and saw huge flames of a fire just about three blocks away. After some time, all melted away into their respective rooms.

In the morning, when we all went for our workshop we knew for sure we were going to see some hectic preparations. Someone said eleven CRPF jawans had been killed the previous night and four terrorists. It was a major fidayeen attack on the CRPF camp in the night. Within no time eleven boxes came with the Tricolour on each. The same ceremony as earlier began again. Looking at those eleven boxes, I felt numbed. The other participants of the workshop were blank. Some CRPF men had come towards us before the boxes arrived. They were checking everything around for security reasons. They even questioned us, asking, 'Who are you', etc. When I satisfied them with my answers and they were about to leave, my eyes caught the cop's name on his nameplate— Bijoy Ganguly.

I just asked him in my broken Bengali '*Ay ki holo*', to know what had happened. He gave me a surprised look and asked me if I was a Bengali. I said no but I understood a bit of Bangla. We stood there till the vehicles drove away with the bodies wrapped in the Indian national flag.

I used to go back to Delhi to be with my family from time to time during these times away because I could not stay longer in the Valley as it used to cost quite a lot during the summer tourist season. Hotel rents would skyrocket beyond our budget, so there was no question of staying longer or beyond our work schedules. Another important reason was that staying for longer periods of time and working under constant stress used to be tough on one's nerves. These breaks at home used to repair our nerves and give us enough time to assess our work.

16

Bandh Pather—People's Theatre of the Kashmiris

My relationship with the Bhand Pather community of Kashmir goes back many years, to my college days, and has endured till the present times. When I was working in Kashmir with the urban theatre people, with children or youth, I would often involve the Bhands as guests to demonstrate their art to the participants. These demonstrations used to be followed by question-answer sessions with the students. Generally, the reactions to the Bhand demonstrations were mixed.

Having been brought up in an urban milieu many youngsters looked down on these rural performers as unsophisticated. But it was also equally true that these urban youngsters had never been exposed to the traditional performing arts. Unfortunately, in India, the impact of colonialism and the culture of Bollywood cinema have influenced contemporary performances so much that you can easily see in them the elements of the popular. Most young urban performers in India lack the necessary understanding and appreciation of the traditional performance arts.

But once the Bhands occupy the performance space and start displaying their skills and talent, the attitude of the urban people towards them often changes. The change is even more drastic after the question–answer session takes place, when it becomes a different story altogether.

During these sessions, I used to deliberately act as a catalyst, as a bridge between the folk and urban performers, and help the Bhands communicate their beliefs, art and intellectual capacities to the urban lot. My work in Kashmir centred on the application of theatre and other art forms for the healing and physiological rehabilitation of children, youth, teachers, etc. I have considered this work as pushing the envelope of theatre beyond the boundaries of just drama as entertainment, to lift it to another level where culture becomes an agent of change.

Now my desire to work on Bhand Pather as a form of pure theatre was to investigate the many aspects of the form—like the use of space, acting styles, musical elements, costumes and crafts, purely as an academic and aesthetic project. Unfortunately, the poverty of the Bhands over the years has reduced them to the level of mere survival. None of the Bhands in Akingam owned any land. They mostly survived on the meagre incomes they earned from weaving baskets, making *kangaris* (fire pots) or performing manual labour for the landlords. Socially they are lower in the pecking order, and they live on the periphery of villages, separately from the other communities, like lower-caste people in the village hierarchy.

The last time I had met them in their villages their economic condition had not been good. They had not performed for years and had had to hide their instruments. It was as if the community had melted away into oblivion. For more than a decade they had not performed as a result of the regular violence and threat to their lives. All had lost their self-confidence as performers. As I have mentioned earlier, it was as if they were in mourning over some death. For all these years no one had visited them to find out about their plight. They had taught me about the strengths and weaknesses of Bhand Pather. When I had travelled with them to the interiors of rural Kashmir I witnessed the popularity of their performances. Thousands of people from the villages would come to watch their performances and shower them with cash and in kind. Villagers would invite them to their homes for feasts. Their visiting a home is considered very auspicious and a good omen for their guests.

Bhands by faith are Muslims who believe in the tradition of Rishut (the Rishi tradition of Kashmir) the indigenous Sufism of Kashmir. It is a must for all Bhands to perform at the Rishi shrines on the annual *urs* of the saints. Bhands have the traditional belief that in performing at the Rishi shrines, they are blessed with good luck, prosperity and happiness around the year. In fact, they are the star performers at all the *urs* in the Kashmir Valley, and the general public waits for hours to watch them perform.

In 1992, I was directing a new play, *Bhand Duhaye,* by a Kashmiri playwright, Moti Lal Kemmu, for the National School of Drama repertory company in New Delhi. The play was set against the backdrop of Kashmir militancy and its impact on the Bhand community, who had been ordered by the local militants not to perform, as the act of performance is *kufur* in Islam. This play has a complex structure and demanded the Bhand Pather style of acting and many other elements of the form, which urban-trained actors could not deliver unless they had the experience of Bhand Pather performances or had at least studied the form.

I had heard that the Bhands were in a lot of trouble in their villages and almost starving as they got no opportunity to perform. They were surviving but rusting, what with all the humiliations they were suffering at the hands of orthodox Islamists and their diktats. Those were the times, in 1998, when it was impossible to communicate with them in the Valley, where they were caught between the guns of the terrorists and the guns of the security forces.

For my production of *Bhand Duhaye*, in 1998, I wanted to get them to Delhi and help my production by teaching the National School of Drama repertory actors the subtleties of Bhand Pather. It would be good for some of them to get out of the hell their villages had become too. Through a friend, I wanted to send them a message to talk to me on the phone from some PCO booth. But that friend of mine passed on my message to his friend who was a Border Security Force commandant in the Achabal area. This commandant in turn ordered a group of his jawans to locate the Bhands of Akingam and convey to them my message to call me on my Delhi number. But when these BSF cops arrived in their jeeps with their loaded guns searching for Gul Mohammed Bhagat, there was panic in the villages. Everyone thought they had come to arrest him. His sister Saja told the cops that her brother had gone to Anantnag and would be back after a couple of hours. A BSF officer left him my message and left the village. The villagers could not make any sense of it all. Gul Mohammed's sister walked about a kilometre on the main road and waited there for a couple of hours for her brother. When he returned, he saw his sister waiting on the road and wanted to know what she was doing there. She told him not to go back home and that the military had come to arrest him. Fortunately, Gul Mohammed had already received my message through another source. He smiled and explained to Saja not to worry, that the cops had come with Raina Sahab's message inviting some of the Bhands to Delhi for a play. The next day I received a call from Gul Mohammed. I explained to him that I wanted two swarnai players, Ama Kak, Rasool Chacha, and Gulam Mohammed Bhagat himself to soon come over as work on the production had already begun. We both laughed at the confusion that had been caused by the arrival of the soldiers.

Finally, when the Bhands arrived for their first rehearsals at the Rabindra Bhavan studio theatre, they looked as if they had been released from jail. All looked weak and tired, having travelled from their village to Delhi by bus.

On the very first day, I asked the Bhands to just watch the rehearsals of the play by the NSD actors. While they were glued to the play, suddenly Gulam Mohammed Bhagat, one of the most versatile Bhand Pather actors, ran out of the rehearsal studio screaming and crying. All ran after him, just to see him huddled in a corner of the foyer, sobbing loudly. We tried to console him. He said he could not 'bear to see the rehearsal of that death scene. All these years we have seen only death all around us'. For my NSD actors, it was all strange and different, real but unbelievable. It impacted them in an altogether different way. Rehearsals had to stop, and we broke for tea. Our repertory actors took great care of the Bhands. They were very sympathetic to the Bhand performers and were already receiving and imbibing the thematic undercurrents of the play through this very incident of Mohammed's breakdown.

Later, after tea, we all sat together. Our music composer Kishenji Langoo, a very eminent Kashmiri music composer from Kashmir, said, 'Let us sing the songs of the play.' These were based on Kashmiri folk melodies and also on the pattern of the Bhand Pather musical compositions. We all sang song after song and the Bhands were listening. It was as if their veins had been hooked up to some IV bottles. As they listened, subtle smiles gradually appeared on their faces and their eyes went moist. I asked the senior *surnai* player (a wind instrument, like the nadaswaram) Ghulam Rasool Bhagat (fondly called Rasool Chacha) to play a *mukam* (raga) on his instrument. He took out his instrument and started to play, but he could not produce any sound on it. He tried many times, but every time he failed to produce any note. He put his surnai aside and in a choked voice said to me, 'I have lost my breath, I have lost it, I cannot create any sound, I am done.' I just could not believe it, having heard him play for years some of the most complex mukams and folk songs. How could this happen to a master musician like him? I just could not believe it. I did not know what to do . . . I began to wonder, could stress reduce an individual to this condition?

It was strange and ironic that the characters which repertory actors had to play where actually sitting in front of them. They were real and our play was about their reality. Here the line between the real character that was depicted and the actor playing his role blurred. So, the enactment of the Bhands' reality became the final goal for the repertory actors. The actors realized this challenge, and gradually the relationship between the Bhands and the repertory actors grew, achieving the real.

All night at home I was thinking about Rasool Chacha. How would we heal him? I felt I had to somehow break the walls for Rasool Chacha and free him from the fear that he seemed to have internalized. Kashmiris Bhands are religious but not fanatics, and Rishiism for them is like a ventilator, helping them breathe out negativity and inhale positivity. It is a kind of meditation.

The next day luckily turned out to be Thursday. I told my company that we would all be going to the Nizamuddin Aulia dargah in the evening. I announced that Rasool Chacha would play the swarnai there at the Mazar of Hazrat Nizamuddin. A sort of therapy, it may work on him, considering his belief in the power of sufi saam where they sing and dance all night in Kashmiri shub, mostly done in the presence of Peer and his mureeds. It is believed to take away the negative spirits.

In the evening, we all entered the Nizamuddin complex. I had already bought the offerings to make there from the lanes around the complex. First, we all visited the mazar of Hazrat Amir Khusro, the great poet, musician, composer and scholar of Persian and Hindavi. I explained to Rasool Chacha the significance of Amir Khusro, and he immediately replied, 'Ah, a great Sufi ustad.' He lifted his hands and prayed at the Khusro mazar, and so did others. After this, we all moved to the dargah of Nizamuddin Aulia. There was a large gathering there and a music party was already singing in the courtyard of the dargah.

In the morning at the rehearsals, Gul Mohammed came and whispered in my ear. He said the old man (Rashool Chacha) had got up at four in the morning, and after his morning ablutions had taken out his swarnai and started playing, which had woken them all up. The rest asked him what was happening, and he had replied, 'I am fine now.' At that very point, Rasool Chacha walked in for the rehearsals. He walked straight towards me and said, 'I am fine, something happened in the night, and see!' He took out his swarnai and very dramatically blew the opening notes, and that was it. He continued to play for some time and the entire repertory company listened in rapt attention. All were surprised to see what a fine artist he was.

The Bhands of Akingam in South Kashmir are like my adopted family; or rather, they have adopted me. I have lived in their homes, worked with them and travelled across the interiors of the Valley watching them perform at various religious *ziyarats*. I have spent large chunks of my time working with the Bhands of Akingam. Being located in the interiors of the Valley, they have been able to retain most of the original form, without any outside influences. I find them very skilled and their music unadulterated, very close to the age-old original form. Interestingly, the villages in and around the Akingam consist entirely of Bhand Pather performers, swarnai and percussion players and dhamal dancers. This area has a unique combination of actors, musicians and dancers whose talents are greatly interdependent. Along with the performing talents here, the villagers are fine craftsmen, being potters, weavers, etc. These additional skills make for their back-up support, bringing the performing artists with some additional income.

Since my area of work is not limited to theatre alone, I can see the interconnectivity of the arts serving as the spinal cord of any culture. One cannot be isolated from the other. I was very concerned about the survival of the ancient performance of art of Kashmir, Bhand Pather, and I had to find ways and means to initiate a major project for it so that the significance of performing art is seen and felt through the lens of contemporary times and not left to perish, like many other precious things in Kashmir.

Finally, in 2004 summer I wrote an elaborate proposal for reviving Bhand Pather, which had many chapters, such as for workshops, training, documentation, rejuvenation and performances. It was like a blueprint for the rebuilding of Bhand Pather from its present state to lift it, so it finds its own place in contemporary Indian theatre. I submitted this proposal to the India Foundation for the Arts, Bengaluru (IFA), and also to the National School of Drama. I knew these two organizations supported theatre projects from all over India, and who knows I may fetch a response from one of them. For months there was no response from either, but later I received an email from IFA saying that it was a big project, and they did not have the kind of resources it would require—which meant a very polite 'no'. From the National School of Drama, there was no response at all.

After a month or so in April 2005, I received another email from IFA, and this time it was a little positive. They were only interested in the workshop chapter of the long proposal I had submitted. The duration of the workshop would be four weeks, and they could support. I was delighted and immediately wrote back thanking them and offering to work out the details. They made me answer more queries about the people who would be involved, and so on, and soon a grant was mentioned by the IAF for a workshop. In my excitement, I started planning the workshop in detail. I rushed to Kashmir and met the senior Bhand masters of Akingam for their advice. They too were very excited about the project. After taking stock of the present condition of Bhand Pather, it was unanimously decided to invite two youngsters from each Bhand village across the Valley and ask them to join the workshop for a training period of one month. This workshop was to be in residence. Since the Bhands are spread all over Kashmiri Valley in its remote corners, it was decided that Ali Mohammed Bhagat, the senior-most ustad among them, would visit the Bhand communities and personally invite the youngsters to avail of the training. The responsibility of hosting the workshop was given to Kashmiri Bhagat Theatre, the oldest Bhand Pather organization comprising the most talented artists in the state, some of whom had won national and state honours for their work and their contribution to Bhand Pather.

The next problem that needed to be sorted out was the venue for the training. So far, whenever we had worked together, it was under some apple or walnut trees in their village itself. But since a large group of youngsters would be coming we needed a closed place for our exercises, etc. After pondering on the issue, someone from the group said there was an upcoming village medical hospital with large halls, which would be good for our kind of work. Since the hospital opening was going to take a lot of time, we could easily do our workshop there, provided the authorities granted us permission to work in the empty building. Some of them went to see the hospital building. It was still incomplete and there were no shutters on the doors and windows. It was just a skeleton structure and nothing else. Even the floors were not tiled. But, honestly, beggars could not be choosers, and we decided to make use of the building in whatever condition it was in. But we needed to acquire permission from the chief medical officer of the area. I personally went to meet him and requested him for permission to use the building. He did not appreciate our request and asked us to leave his office. On my persuading him further, he got

quite annoyed and asked me to leave his office or he would have
to ask his staff to take me away. At that point I could not resist
telling him, 'Is it necessary to get orders sent to you from your
superiors, and then only you will let me work?' He, naturally, did
not expect that kind of statement from me.

We started working in the open air, in the shade of some
trees, which had been our usual working space for quite some
time. Soon our workshop participants started arriving from
distant villages and were soon accommodated in the village
homes. For this kind of project, it is necessary to involve the
local community. They become partners in the endeavour and
work becomes smooth. We also decided to involve the women
of the Bhand community to take charge of the kitchen, which
they readily agreed to do.

Finally, we started our all-day classes in the open air.
But within three days of this we received a letter from the
same chief medical officer granting us permission to use the
hospital building. Who ordered whom for this permission is
not necessary to dwell on here, but the most important thing
was that we would now be working from the premises of the
upcoming hospital where we had at least a roof over our heads
so the rains would not disrupt our work. Every day the first thing
we did in the morning was to wash the floors of the building
and then mop them before we began the training routine. All
the participants and faculty members used to join us in cleaning
the place.

Most of the participants were born during the period
of militancy in the state from 1990 onwards and had never
experienced a normal day. The world they had grown up in was
very different from the world we had grown up in. For example,
they had never seen or met a Kashmiri Pandit. They had no idea
what a syncretic culture meant. All they had seen or experienced
was the violence of the militants and the security forces. Since

all these participants had had some schooling, it was a little easy to explain to them some aspects of Bhand Pather, but as they lacked experience our general pedagogy had to change. One could see the pent-up energy in their bodies. Our every session had to be practice-oriented, and it was through the practices that the theatrical parts had to be explained.

Since there were no textual references for the study of Bhand Pather, one had to depend on the performances that are still preserved by the Bhands. Thus, teaching through practical work and by means of oral transfer of knowledge was the only way for us to train young people. Along with the tenets of Bharata's Natyashastra, there have been influences on Bhand Pather that came from political trade and cultural contacts with the cultures of Central Asia and Persia. By just looking at the geographical location of the Valley, one realizes that many cultures must have crisscrossed through this beautiful Valley, which must have brought new cultural elements that influenced the native Kashmiri culture here.

2005 Summer—First Bhand Pather Workshop

The day was divided into two sessions. The morning was used for body training, which meant exercises for body control and exploration of the physical limits of the actor's body. Here we preferred to start with the experiences of the participants themselves, taking off from their use of their bodies in their daily village routines in their natural surroundings. Their activities such as ploughing the land, preparing the soil, sowing seeds, harvesting, and so on, were imitated, as all of them came from rural backgrounds. This opened the path of our participants to an understanding of their own physical selves, and they created for themselves many exercises and body movements based on their routine activities. Finally, content-based movement pieces were created by the participants. In this way, the process of exploring body movement and its application was pushed further, using their personal experience of, say, visiting the jungle for various activities. Their experience of dealing with animals in the forest, or of tending to the cattle in their village, were depicted in movement. From here they moved to the next stage of becoming animals themselves, imitating their movements.

Once the concept of body movement has been understood, then one could prepare the content; now a real or imagined story or incident could be conveyed through movement to make for a small performance. Their rural life itself was an ocean of stories and incidents for the training of the body and for body movement. We did not need theoretical books here to make the actors conscious of their bodies and its possibilities. The study of nature itself offered infinite lessons. One only needed an eye to recognize them. Since these participants lived in the lap of nature, it was easy for them to learn by taking off from various aspects of the natural world and then incorporating them into body movements to improvise on various themes and ideas.

For aesthetic movement and rhythm, we simply employed the traditional dhamal dance form. This is a form of dance which is ritualistic, robust and consisted of acrobatic movements involving leaps and jumps. This dance gradually builds in tempo, the rhythm becoming faster and faster until it reaches a crescendo, at which point many dancers get into a trance. Performed by very select families as a ritual at many dargahs, it has great possibilities of incorporating into itself the main structure of Bhand Pather, which we were already training in.

Since the use of masks is an integral part of Bhand performances, our next step was to train the participants in mask-making and teach them to apply suitable body movements that would match the masks. For this, the village potters were brought in to teach participants the skill and method of making the masks. The participants were also sent to the village of potters, both for training in techniques of mask making and to understand the community that lived quite close to the village we were training in. The youngsters learned to create earthen moulds and use papier-mache techniques for the production of the mask. This way the partnering of the community in our project became very vital and strengthened the endeavour of sharing between the two communities of artists. Soon participants started creating small performances featuring different characters, first individually and then as a group.

This training in the first half of the day went on for almost three weeks, using the traditional method of working purely on the body of the actor. Soon, many contemporary games and more exercises were incorporated in this model for the holistic training of the body. Now there were both traditional and urban contemporary theatre exercises and games at the workshop.

The second half of the day was set aside for understanding Bhand Pather itself, like the making of a pather, understanding the structure of the art, the various characters of the form, the various rituals and songs . . . Here again, our approach was to take the path of practice and experience, which meant understanding the essence of Bhand Pather as a performance art, its sociological setting, and so on. Since the participants had seen many pathers performed by their respective families, it was necessary to study those old pathers to unravel the various elements of the form.

Every day, we picked one pather to discuss it in all its aspects. In the beginning it was easy for the participants to understand the narrative part, but our senior ustads explained to them the hidden sub-texts by revealing to them the references in a particular play, which could not be decoded or explained otherwise. The Bhand ustads and I spent a lot of time on these discussions, providing the trainees the historical and political background to locate Bhand Pather in the various historical time periods when, and spaces where, the changes, exchanges and influences might have occurred to shape the form into what it currently is.

Bhand Pather is a traditional folk drama of Kashmir. In fact, I call it Kashmir's traditional school of drama. It had its own method of training and knowledge of the stage, and the music and the unfolding of the narrative were passed on from father to son. When Bhand Pather is examined closely, it reveals many elements that are considered avant-garde today, which gives it a strong edge over many other art forms for adaption for contemporary theatre.

While Bhand Pather is an outcome of the confluences of many cultures, it is secular in its perspective and is layered with strong social and political insights. 'Bhand' means actor or a performer, and 'pather' means to play. A Bhand Pather performance takes place in the open air, during the day, and also on special occasions, as for instance during the *urs* of a Sufi dargah. It incorporates dance, music, acting, mime and masks. The language used in the performance is predominantly Kashmiri, but Gujjar, Punjabi, Dogri and Persian are also used, and sometimes some words or phrases from English too.

The *maskhara*, or jester, is one of the most important characters in Bhand Pather. He is a constant factor, serving as a link between the sequences. He uses various kinds of humour, such as *hazal* (mockery), *mazak* (jokes) or *tanz* (sarcasm). Using these the maskhara would often poke fun at the kings and the upper classes, exposing their corruption and greed. The maskhara is the rebel who defies the oppressor.

Bhands dance to the tune of specific *mukams,* and their musical accompaniments include the swarnai, dhol, nagara and *thalej*. The swarnai is longer in size than the shehnai and is the soul of Bhand Pather. Each pather has its own thematic musical score. It is a highly developed system of music based on the principles of the Kashmiri Sufiyana Kalam (classical music of Kashmir) heavily influenced by the Mukams of Central Asian Sufiyana music traditions and, also the Indian classical music traditions, with intricate and codified patterns. The dhol is a percussion membranophone and is central to the Bhand orchestra. Many rhythms in various permutations and combinations are played on this instrument, and often the nagara accompanies the dhol, enhancing the rhythm as the performance proceeds.

Two props integral to every performance are the *kodar*, a long whip, and the *baens*, a short length of bamboo. The kodar when used creates a pistol-like sound and may be used to whip a character a hundred times without of course actually hurting him. The split bamboo stick is used by the maskhara to make sharp sounds, evoking great laughter.

Animal masks such as those depicting the hangul (Kashmiri deer), lion and horse, are often used in the main action of the pather. The mask of a dayan, or slut, as an evil spirit appears in certain plays. The style of acting swings from realistic to highly exaggerated. In some Bhand Pather performances, there are many sequences which are very close to many elements of contemporary theatre practices, which gives this form an edge over other traditional forms. There is enough freedom and scope to explore the space of the play physically as well as in abstract terms. For example, performance can spread all over the village area, actors can get onto rooftops or climb nearby trees and can convert the entire village landscape into a total performance space; thus, breaking the imagined wall between the actor and the spectators. Actors can use a small earthen pot as a dark well and talk into it as if talking to a ghost hiding inside the well. This kind of treatment gives many times Bhand Pather a certain kind of abstract quality thus making it a mosaic of diverse elements functioning together.

This form and its actors fall in the category of the typical definition of an Asian actor. The Asian actor is a total actor—he is a dancer, acrobat, singer, musician, craftsman, pantomime artiste . . . all rolled into one. This is quite in contrast to what one sees in Western training schools, where there are separate categories of actors, like the singing actor, the movement actor, the dance actor and so on. In all Asian traditional theatre, whether Indonesian, Chinese, Japanese, Malaysian or Indian, the performance styles call for multi-skilled and multi-disciplinary performers. A performer may have to sing and dance in one scene, and display strong histrionics in another, and do acrobatics in still another.

In his chapter on acting in the Natyashastra, Bharata divides the entire art into four segments: Aangikam (body movements), *Vaachikam* (sound and words) Aaharyam (adornment, meaning costume, properties, sets, etc.), *satvik satvikam* (confluence of the first three). All forms of traditional Indian theatre have trained their performers on these lines. While the first three segments are visible and physically concrete, the last section, satvik is something abstract. If the first three elements of *aangik*, *vaachik* and *aaharya* are tuned correctly, the fourth, which is like the fragrance of a flower that cannot be seen, will result, conveying a nice sensation or feeling to the audience. It is this feeling that is transmitted by evolved actors to the audiences and creates in them various emotions *(Rasa),* which can be happiness, pathos, romance, etc.

The actor's body is therefore like the four strings of the tanpura, and when each string is correctly tuned and they are played together, their vibration creates a drone in which the musicians hear all the notes of the musical composition they sing or play. It is riding on this chariot of notes that the musician effortlessly plays his. Raga to evoke the rasa of that particular emotion.

At one stage of the workshop, we invited the various Bhand Pather companies in the Valley to come to Akingam and perform one of their pathers. All these performances had to be done in the open air, where villagers, along with our participants and faculty, came in large numbers to watch. After the performance, the visiting party, the participants, the ustads and I would sit together and initiate a major discussion and debate on the pather that had been performed. Many questions would be raised by our young Bhand trainees, which would first be answered by the leader of the visiting group and then by their actors. Later, our ustads would join in to share their own experiences of the performance and their own interpretations of it. These talks by the seniors made for a very lively and enjoyable experience for everyone. Working in a village, there is the added advantage of audience participation without any hesitation. Many a time, a very elderly spectator who had been watching Bhand performances from his childhood would give his response to the performance. It was really a boon to listen to what these spectators had to say. Sometimes they would share their memories of old performances or talk about some very popular actors of the past and recall their qualities. These debates and discussions opened up new horizons for our youngsters, who were inspired to ask some very pertinent questions. Gradually, some of these young men started opening up and inquiring about the very relevance of Bhand Pather. This process of learning through observation, listening and experiencing was a very meaningful process of learning for them. This pedagogy started opening up their bodies and minds much faster than one would have imagined. The young men started participating unhesitantly in the training without traces of self-consciousness.

This training, consisting of performance-cum-seminars, continued for many days, creating an atmosphere of festivity in the village. These performances had the additional dividend of the Bhands from very far-off areas getting to meet each other after a long gap and a new network of Bhands getting established. Because of militancy, these contacts had been broken and they hadn't been able to meet for years.

One day, around noon, a big pot of hot, sweet halwa arrived at our hospital campus. And Basheer Bhagat, one of the persons in charge of the arrangements, brought out plates and started distributing the halwa to everyone. I asked Basheer how his kitchen could make halwa when we had limited funds. He burst into loud laughter and said, 'Sir, this is not from our kitchen but from the nearby army camp. They have sent it for us.' I asked, 'But why, what is being celebrated today?' It appeared that they had not shot at anyone nor fired for the last eighteen months, and they wanted the villagers and the shopkeepers to join in their celebrations.

This baffled me. I had no idea where this camp was, and frankly, none of us ever wanted to have any connection with them, lest we should be misunderstood as being part of the security set-up. Since the time I had started working in the Valley, my decision had been to only concentrate on my work and keep everything else about myself and my colleagues as transparent as possible. That way, the hidden gun-wielding man does not suspect you. Many of my friends used to advise me to take the help of the security people. But I was never comfortable with the idea. Imagine being guarded by cops for all twenty-four hours of the day. All your freedom of being with the people is gone, and you can possibly become a sitting duck, inviting attention to yourself, and who knows someone may take a potshot at you one day. I believed in the village people, and the people I was working with had been my best security cover for years now. That was why I could move around anywhere or visit and meet anybody without any fear. I had always believed that I was working there with my people, the way I had with the people in Manipur, Kerala, Dhaka or Lahore.

I had no idea about the political orientation of the people in the Valley around Akingam. Since we were located at the foothills of the Peer Panjal range, we had to be careful about people whom we did not know or recognize. Terrorists always descended from these Peer Panjal mountains and then mingled with the general public.

For our new workshop when I arrived now in 2006 summer and met my seniors bhands and enquired about the local political situation Only a few days before our workshop, Gul Mohammed Bhagat told me, that a group of Afghan and Arab terrorists had appeared in the evening at his house. He had no choice but to let them in. They were heavily armed with guns, wireless sets, hand grenades, dried fruit and a large quantity of ammunition. While Gul Mohammed welcomed them to station themselves on the top floor of his house, he had already signalled to his womenfolk to slip out of the house using the ground-floor window at the back to stay in his elder brother's house. He himself was scared, and even he did not want to stay in his own home. He requested the senior-most member of the Bhands, Ghulam Rasool Bhagat (Rasool Chacha) to take care of the strangers. They had stayed for four days. All night they were on their wireless sets talking to someone in their own language. All the days they stayed they had to be fed good Kashmiri cuisine. Rasool Chacha, in his true Bhand cunning, had told them about his poverty and how he would not be able to offer them good food, especially meat. He made them cough up a good amount of money so he could buy mutton and chicken for them, and of course for himself. Rasool Chacha said that he had a great time and a good feast with them at their expense, like the good maskhara of *Darza Pather*. Who through his wit, humour and cunning first gets whipped up by this oppressive king, suffers his violence, gradually exploits him to win his trust and finally elopes with his concubines. Finally, they left after four days in the late hours of the dark night and disappeared into the fields. I asked Ghulam Rasool Chacha what his situation was now—did he think we could work here

without any problems? He smiled and said 'Inshallah, things are
better now and most of the local boys have been neutralized.'
I asked him how. He gave me his mischievous smile and said,
'Since the mobel (mobile) has come, people quietly report the
location details to the nearby army camp, and then you relax,
and they do the rest of the work. By using the mobel this
way nobody can accuse or even suspect anyone for of being a
mukhbir (informer). Before this you had to get to know who
the informer was, get hold of him and shoot him publicly for
his betrayal. But now with these mobel phones nobody knows
who has betrayed them and informed the security people. It is
safe now and there is some peace here in the countryside. So
hopefully nothing should happen, but then who knows?' I got
concerned about our safety listening to these stories of his.

But these days it appeared that there were no untoward
incidents in the Valley, and we could work peacefully. But
nothing could be predicted, and things could change within
minutes for the worse. I had invited the India Foundation
for the Arts, our funding organization representative, to see
for themselves what work was going on. A lady officer came
and stayed with us for three days. She witnessed our morning
sessions and also the performances of the various parties that
had been invited from different parts of the Valley. At the time
of her departure, she said, 'We at the foundation had never
believed that it is possible to work in Kashmir. We had very
serious apprehensions about the possibility of undertaking any
serious activity here in the state. In fact, we did not believe in
you and in your project. But thank you, it is unbelievable, what
is happening here in this remote area.'

It is true when the media is filled with the stories of violence
and killings, nobody is going to trust you with your ideas for
projects during these dark times. I was a little happy to hear
comments, and relieved as well.

Our work continued, and our next stage was what I call making stories, but here in this project we were leapfrogging, so to speak, and getting straight into making plays. We had time constraints, and we were ambitious to achieve something concrete—and hence the leapfrogging. Since most of the Bhand repertoire of plays had been performed already at the workshop by various Bhand companies, I needed to take my students into the depths of the themes of each play, and I also wanted to be sure that they had understood the subtext of each pather. Students articulating in words what they had imbibed and understood was not sufficient. They could not express in words their entire experience because they were too self-conscious to speak out before an audience on the themes and the acting in the plays they had watched.

So, I tried another way, asking them to paint the narrative of the plays as they saw them. They had never painted or used colours in their lives. But I insisted that they did, even if they had never picked up a brush or even used colouring crayons. We gave them each a set of water colours and sheets of white paper Each participant painted the play of his choice. The style of their painting consisted of impressions of the sequences of the pather they each chose. Each student painted many sheets to complete the whole narrative of the play. It was interesting to see that they had unconsciously and instinctively applied in their paintings the concepts of space and composition. Thus, the images they had painted on their sheets of paper, were articulating the sterilized traits of each character of the pather through lines and colours. None of the paintings were to scale, but that did not matter. This exercise gave us a good idea about their understanding of the pathers they had watched. We felt that they were not able to understand the depth and the subtitles of the sequences at certain points in the plays, and those needed further discussion. These were the areas where the action of the play they had painted the narrative became abstract, and their decoding needed more explanation on our part.

Once we were over with this exercise, we decided to pick up three sequences from three different pathers and create three separate performance modules for the participants. The sequences we picked up were from Darza Pather, (this pather is about a king who is an outsider in the Valley, enjoying the pleasure of drinking and dancing with his concubines, and he meets a local maskhara, who with his typical maskhari elopes with his concubines. This pather has a lot of political undertones but is performed with lot of dances and singing), *Watal Pather* (this pather is about the lower cast subaltern community their typical ways of daily lives, their weddings songs, fights, rituals and struggles of their existence, performed with slapstick black humour. The performance is filled with spactle of songs, music dancing) and *Shikarghaa* (this is a performance of the animal kingdom of the Pashupatinath the shiva. Here you see the inhabitants of shivas forests. The deer, bears, lions, birds, etc. All done using masks of all the forest characters. The play is about their coexistence with the man. Apart from the movement and dances of these animals with the humans, it raises major questions about the environment and ecology). The participants were divided into three separate groups, and each group had to develop one pather sequence as their final performance module. It was very interesting to watch these young participants struggling with themselves, as we faculty members had asked them to think for themselves and execute their own ideas. This was to inculcate in them the confidence to make their own decisions for the final performance through team consultation. Each bit of their work would be discussed every day with all of us and with the participant teams. The points of discussion would then be further worked upon.

To become the author of their own creation, they started working themselves up to improvise. The typical use of space in

Bhand Pather was quite difficult for them to execute. The ustads would have loved to teach them to imitate the performance of the seniors or by mugging up the lines. That would have been an easy way for them to learn to create their own space. But once their worries and fears had been overcome, their own interpretations began to flower. These were original, and it was an exciting process for them to command a sequence and explore the space they had through improvisation. By creating their own dialogues using their own words, puns and colloquialisms, it became fun for them, sending their confidence soaring. They came into their own and were creating new, fresh and original sequences. Ali Mohammed Bhagat, the old master performer, was laughing and enjoying every bit of these new and upcoming performances. He said to me, 'These kids are terrific. Now I understand why you are not directing them but only explaining to them the sub-text of every sequence. These boys are doing everything differently from what I would have been doing.'

For some time, all the boys were running through the sequences, and every time they did something new would be added to a scene spontaneously, at the spur of the moment. They did finally understand the power of being creative, and day after day they brought in new ideas and elements to their performances. Every passing run-through would look fresh and original.

Rejuvenation of a traditional form of art does not mean photocopying the past. But by creating fresh, new contemporary moments within the boundaries of the traditional form, and if the need arose even breaking the boundaries of the form to give birth to new interpretation, new life is given to the form. This way the form will be saved from becoming a stagnant cesspool of the past. This consciousness of change and continuity enriches the traditional form in content and style. Let us remember that there is nothing in tradition that remains stagnant. Folk art always responds to time and space and keeps grappling with the present. It is a grave misunderstanding to believe that the traditional should not be touched but kept as it is. This understanding as a contemporary theatre person is harmful for the growth of the form. Hence, when the owners of the traditional forms lock out understanding and knowledge of the changing world, the form starts losing its power and relevance, and with the decline of skills and talents too it just withers away.

My intervention in Bhand Pather is to regain for it its lost glory but not to recreate or remake it as it was, but to allow it to grow into what it should become in the contemporary times. Hence the workshop that I and the Bhand masters at Akingam were engaged in was to revive, rejuvenate, document and revitalize the art, finally taking new works and also its good masters to the larger world of theatre. It is also for challenging the strength of the form by working with new texts and new narratives, which the Bhands had never imagined or confronted before. I see Bhand Pather growing into a modern theatrical form with infinite possibilities for experimentation.

Bhand Pather has in it all the elements of past traditions mingled with streaks of avant-garde contemporary art practices. I also see the abstract and the absurd elements in this form. When you closely examine any pather, whether it is religious, feudal, anti-establishment, etc., there is always the presence of the sacred. The sacred in it is woven on the strings of a secular outlook and values, and therein lies its contemporariness. The workshop that we were working on had twin purposes. One was for the knowledge that the ustads carried to be shared with the participants, and the other was for people like me from contemporary theatre to share their knowledge with the participants. The aim was to sow the seeds to create thinking theatre persons sensitive to the times they were living in but also able to reflect the intricacies of Bhand Pather and its interlinkages with other art forms in the Valley.

The last few days of the workshop we had been hearing disturbing reports of stone-pelting and police firing in many parts of the Valley. Only twenty kilometres from our workplace in Anantnag, there had been a huge confrontation between the public and the security forces. Many young boys were shot and killed, which had worsened the situation, and there was tension and uncertainty in the areas nearby too. Luckily, at Akingam there were no disturbances, but the general ambience was not good. One could sense a certain restlessness among the people. At the workshop, we gave the participants a day's break and did not play any instrument, lest the people should misunderstand us. We did our classes quietly. We even stopped working in the open air and remained indoors, within the hospital premises. The reports coming from all parts of the Valley were bad, as young boys had been shot and killed. A boy of around eighteen years of age, who was going for his morning tuition classes, had been shot dead in Anantnag. This was followed by a hartal by the shops and transport services. However, we kept working quietly with our village tailors, blacksmiths and other skilled people.

We faculty members were four and were staying about five kilometres away from Akingam, at a place called Achabal, in a tiny government tourist guest house with common toilets and bathrooms. This place was next to the beautiful Achabal Mughal Garden. The mineral water of this area which ran in the water fountains was oozing out from under the foothills, which had dense pine forests. We used to leave for work at 9 a.m. and return in the evenings, so we hardly got to enjoy this pretty location. Our work used to take up most of our time. The person in charge, a cook-cum-manager of the tourist place, was a nice man but very *chalu*, unofficially running a kitchen-cum-drinking joint for the local people. In fact, he did not like to have us staying there because our presence was interfering with his clandestine business. We had to be careful, given the kind of characters that were coming into and disappearing from one of the rooms up to late evening. But we could not say anything because this was the only place in the entire area where one could stay. There was a small market near the bus stand of Achabal with a few tea shops. We used to often sit there to have tea and chat with the locals there. They were curious to know who we were and what we were doing in the area. After over two or three visits they got some idea of the work we were doing, and they became quite friendly with us.

Right in front of this tea stall was an area with many deserted houses, most of them in bad condition. On their doors were traces of floral paintings in multiple colours, reminding me of the wedding days in the houses of Kashmiri Pandits. The entire neighbourhood looked like a ghost mohalla, with broken windows and run-down walls, all looking like the ruins of some past structures. Next to these houses was a small temple, looking very lonely without its worshippers. There was a house standing on the beautiful running freshwater stream, almost hollow, with a very sad appearance. This was the house I had visited a couple of times when I was a school kid and my cousin used to live there. She was now living in a refugee camp somewhere in Jammu.

The situation had not improved, and the killing of a large number of young boys had angered the entire population. There continued to be pitched stone-pelting battles with the security forces.

I received a phone call from the vice-chancellor of Banaras Hindu University to be a member of the selection committee to interview some faculty for the appointment of some professors and assistant professors. I explained to the VC that it was not possible for me to come. He requested, rather insisted, that I did. His problem was that without my presence he could not conduct the interviews as I was President of India's nominee as a visitor at the university and my presence was mandatory.

The VC told me that without me those appointments could not happen, and the deserving candidates would retire soon, missing their chance to be appointed as professors at the University. I replied that I could not promise but would try to come.

I had discussed my Banaras visit with my team and the consensus was that I could go. The trip would be a matter of three days only. I rang up Manzoor Meer in Srinagar and asked him to purchase a return ticket to Banaras for me. But a curfew was imposed in the Valley, and I lived seventy kilometres from the airport.

How would I reach the airport during curfew hours? I was told that if I was travelling on the main highway I would encounter no problems in reaching Srinagar airport. But before hitting the highway I had to travel around twenty kilometres to cross the town of Anantnag, and that area was under a strict curfew and there had been pitched battles between the local stone-pelters and the security forces. My taxi driver suggested that if we left at around 4.30 a.m., when there would be no trouble, we could reach the airport faster and without any problems.

The next day, I left alone with my taxi driver at 4.30 a.m. I had asked Manzoor to meet me at a certain point in the city with my air ticket when I reached Srinagar. It was pleasant when I left early in the morning. We wanted to get on the highway as soon as possible so that my driver could return home by around 9 a.m. There was not a soul on the roads. We reached the narrow road, Lakad Mandi, which connects Anantnag with the highway. At the exit point was a large picket of security people. Unfortunately, the night curfew was still on, and we had broken it, which was not at all right. The moment they saw our vehicle approaching they signalled us to stop. I was quite alarmed. Without asking any questions one group of cops pulled me out of the vehicle and the other dragged my driver out and started beating us very badly. Both of us were on the ground, screaming in pain, when I suddenly raised my voice in protest. Hearing my protests, one of their seniors appeared from somewhere and signalled to us to go back. Limping in pain, we boarded our vehicle, and the driver reversed our taxi to go back. I thanked my stars that we were not arrested for breaking the law; that would have been very bad. I noticed that my driver was in severe pain, but he drove for about five kilometres, after which we stopped the car, and both went down to a stream. We pulled up our trousers and saw that we were bleeding. What would we do now? Two elderly villagers were watching us from a distance. They asked the driver what had happened. Once the driver explained the situation to them, they first sympathized with us and then came up with the suggestion that we take an alternative road through the network of small village roads that led to the highway. The detour would be a little time-consuming, but we were sure to reach the highway. None of us had ever taken this route, which went through narrow village roads and lanes, crossing shallow riverbeds. We had to keep asking people in every village the right route to take to make sure we had not lost our way. Since it was early morning, around 6 a.m., people were quite surprised to see two strangers trying to find their way to the highway. But every village we passed, the people were warm hospitable and would often ask us to have a cup of tea before we proceeded further.

At one village we noticed a large gathering on the road. There were maybe 500 people, mostly elderly men. They all turned to look at us; they looked both surprised and curious. The driver slowed down the vehicle and he looked to his left, and I too turned in that direction. There was a village graveyard there and these elderly men were lost staring at a fresh grave. My driver in a choked voice said, 'They have just buried the boy who was killed yesterday in the Anantnag firing.' Then, with a heavy heart, he said, 'A conflict created by the city folks, and country folks have to sacrifice their loved ones.' This statement by the driver bothers me to this day. We moved forward, and within one and a half hours he got me to the airport. It was just 7.30 a.m., and the gates of the airport were still closed. I treated my driver to a quick cup of tea and a hot omelette and asked him to rush back home safe. I had to wait until 10 a.m. when the airport gates opened. Before they did, I received a call from my driver saying that he had reached home safely.

We were now in the final stages of the 2005 summer workshop. The final rehearsals were happening, along with all the properties, costumes and musical instruments. Every day there were at least two run-throughs, and after every run-through there would be discussions where more inputs would be given to improve the performance and to hear the problems of performers and find solutions to them. As the date of performance was getting closer there was more excitement among the participants.

The performance venue was a hilly area in the village. The high slopes were for the spectators and at the foothills was our performance area. This kind of site reminded me of early Greek theatre performances, which used to take place at the base of a hill. But here we had improved the space for the plays. The characters would use a larger area for acting by also performing in the midst of the spectators. This multiple entry and exit points charged the entire performance space, and the actors, by being close to the audience, would find a new, dynamic relationship developed between themselves and the spectators. Here the illusion of theatre was broken completely. The formal and informal illusions and the reality would be in interplay throughout the performance.

The entire hill was occupied by the villagers. Men, women, children, the elderly . . . all were present. They had come from five different villages. There was no invitation, or any message sent to the public to come for the performance. It was simply by word of mouth that people had got to know about the timing of the show.

The participants developed an exhibition of their drawings, paintings, clay work, etc., by mounting their personal work on the poplar trees next to the performance venue so that the general public could see their work. On the final day, the parents of the participants also came from the far-off villages in the Valley.

This exhibition and the performance demo gave some idea of the training being imparted at the workshop to the general public, and the Bhand parents in particular understood the seriousness of the training, which if taken up by their Bhand groups would enrich them individually. The actual performance had a festive look to it and was watched by a couple of thousand spectators. There were some guests of ours who had come all the way from Srinagar. There were some journalist friends who had also come to witness the effort of the youngsters in the midst of the crisis all around. These media people lodged a friendly protest and registered a complaint with me for not informing them about the performance. I had to explain to them that our work here was not for any publicity. It was a serious cultural project, which was very important given the times we were in. We were all involved here in creating the seeds of culture. And in fact, we did not want any of this publicized, as that would be counter-productive to our work.

While the performance was at its peak. I noticed dark clouds in the sky. I realized that it is going to rain. Just when the performance was about to get over, a strong breeze started, and soon it turned into a storm and then a downpour. All the people ran for shelter. Our participants were still performing the last bit till it became impossible to carry on. Within minutes the entire hill was empty of people. Costumes were soaked in the rain and the exhibition was completely torn into pieces by the rain and wind.

I asked all the participants to change into their personal clothes and gather at the house of Gulam Hassan Bhagat, convenor of the Kashmir Bhagat Theatre. There we would conduct the concluding function of our workshop on a happy note.

I opened the harmonium and started playing, and soon everyone started singing the songs from our plays. For almost an hour or so, all the actors, ustads and guests joined in the singing, jamming and dancing. It was the best improvised finale that the first Bhand Pather workshop at Akingam could have.

17

Bus to Muzaffarabad

After a couple of wars between India and Pakistan and after the killing of thousands of people on both sides, there was a lot of bonhomie between both the nations. In 2004, many initiatives were being taken to normalize the relationship between the two countries. Mufti Mohammed Sayeed was the chief minister of Jammu and Kashmir State. He, along with the Central government, initiated the process of starting a bus service between the two parts of Kashmir—that is, between Srinagar and Muzaffarabad. The date of starting the bus services was fixed on 7 April 2005. I had heard about this development in Delhi, that finally the two parts of Jammu and Kashmir would be connected by a bus service after almost six decades. There would be trade activity between the two parts of the Valley. I felt good hearing this news because what one can achieve through peace cannot be achieved by war. If the South Asian nations joined hands together, it would bring huge prosperity to their poverty-ridden people.

My family had a very close connection with the city of Muzaffarabad. My grandfather had been posted there in the revenue department of the state for years. One of my granduncles had an organization in Muzaffarabad dedicated to the cause of the widows, and it had been in operation till

1947. My grandmother used to narrate non-stop stories from her long stay in Muzaffarabad with my grandfather. From the time of my childhood, an image of that place was etched in my mind from the joyful stories I had heard.

The date of the April 2005 was finally announced as the day when the bus service would start. Out of blue, I received a call from Saleem Beg, saying that the Kashmir government had decided to celebrate this moment in a big way and that he, as the director general of tourism, has been roped into the celebration committee along with some other government officials. He has been put in charge of the cultural component of the celebrations. He asked me to think about some cultural events that could be part of this mega-celebration. I asked him to give me some time to think about it. He shot back saying there was hardly any time and we had to make our presentation in two days, so I had to please start thinking right away. I laughed and said, 'Saleem, good ideas need time. Anyway, let me put my head together and see what can be done in this short time.'

I started pondering over the possibilities for the cultural event. In the morning, I again got a call from Saleem saying, 'Mufti sahab, the chief minister, has instructed us to create a memento or a badge for the occasion which can be distributed to the people.' I wanted to know whether they had any particular design in mind. Saleem replied, 'No, you develop some designs and then send them to us, and we will get one of the designs approved by the chief minister.' I told Saleem I would have to ask a designer to create a design. Saleem, in his style, said, 'Come on, you have so many friends you just request them to help.' I again laughed and said, 'All right, sir, I will try.'

By evening my friend Rajendra Arora, designer, publisher, poet and printer, sent me three designs: one had a blue colour scheme, another yellow and the third green. Each design carried the images of a bus, a boat and a blossom in a circular composition, and on the outer circle was written a verse by Nund Rishi, a fourteenth-century Kashmiri poet, the flag-bearer of Kashmiriyat: 'I broke the sword and forged sickles out of it.' This was written in Kashmiri, and there was also an English translation of it in the design. I mailed all three designs to Saleem for approval. After a couple of hours, I got a call from him asking me to go to the house of Mehbooba Mufti at Shahjahan Road in New Delhi and show the three designs for the badges. She would make the decision.

When I reached Mehbooba Mufti's house, I asked her security guard to let her know that I had arrived. Within a few minutes, he came back to tell me, 'Madam has said to come in the evening.' I did not like this at all. I told the guard to tell her that I could not come in the evening as I lived far away. I could leave the designs there and she could choose anyone she liked and let Saleem Beg know of her decision. When the guard came back, he said, 'Please come in.' When I entered the drawing room, there was nobody there. After around ten minutes, Mehbooba Mufti entered, and I showed her the three designs. She looked at them, and within a few minutes, she decided on one. She looked at me and asked, 'What do you think?'

I said, 'Mehboobaji, you know better, but I think you should not decide on the green design.'

She was surprised and said, 'Why, what is wrong with it?'

I replied that the green, unfortunately, was associated with Pakistan. 'Your critics will sharpen their attack on you and your efforts. I suppose you do not want to give them a chance to attack you and your father.'

She did not utter a word for quite some time but kept concentrating on the designs. Then she turned to me and asked me 'Which design do you like?'

I replied, 'I prefer the blue one.'

She again wanted to know why. I replied to say that blue is considered the colour of peace, the colour of the United Nations flag: 'And your government is initiating a process of peace after about fifty-eight years. The entire world is going to watch, and I am sure there will be international media channels recording the happenings on both sides of the border. This is a great moment for your government. That is why blue will be the appropriate colour for such a historic event. She kept looking at the designs, gave me a faint smile and said, 'Okay, then we decide on blue.'

I left her place and immediately phoned Saleem Beg to narrate to him the details of my meeting and told him, 'I hope I did not cross the line.' He laughed and said, 'What you could tell her none of us could have gathered the courage to, thank you.'

But it did not end there. The next day early morning I got a frantic call from Mehbooba Mufti, asking me to stop the order for the badges. 'We have the verse of the Quran which needs to be printed on the badge instead of Nund Rishi's verse.'

She recited the verse:

God! Bless our land with grace
With refreshing greenery and with peace

I loved the verse. It was indeed a great sacred prayer. Then I suggested to her that we have both verses on the hoardings. That would be a complete statement of peace. She agreed, and finally, both verses were displayed on all the publicity materials.

In the meantime, I developed some possible ideas that could be taken up to celebrate the occasion. One performance would be at the time of departure of the bus from Srinagar, at the place where the VVIPs would be making their brief statements before the prime minister of India flagged off the bus in the presence of the general public and the world media. And the second performance would happen on the arrival of the bus from Muzaffarabad. The third event would consist of the people of the city welcoming this new beginning of peace, harmony and friendship.

For the departure of the bus from Srinagar, one could not suggest much, as there were overwhelming security concerns. It had to be simple and brief. There would be indigenous melodies played before the function started and when the bus departed.

The next morning, the secretary of culture, government of Jammu and Kashmir, Nayeem Akther, and Saleem Beg arrived in Delhi without any prior information. I was told that all my ideas had been liked and accepted, but I would have to execute them myself. This was a bit different from what I had expected as I had my work in Delhi to complete. We had frantic meetings. The badges and floating candles were ordered in Delhi. When the next morning the organizing party was going back to Srinagar, they put it straight to me that they needed my help and wanted me soon in Srinagar. They were not confident that things would work out there if I continued to stay in Delhi. 'We will be waiting for you,' said one of them. Both being more than friends to me, I could not refuse their help. And I too felt that I should be part of this historic event.

I agreed on one condition—that this would be my small contribution to my Valley which had given me so much and I did not want any professional remuneration. They smiled and got into the car taking them to the airport. While leaving, Nayeem Sahab again said, 'We are waiting.'

I arrived on 2 April 2005. The office of the director general of tourism at the historic tourist reception centre was the organizing centre for this event. Everything was done out of that room. It was also my restroom. I was given a room on the premises of the tourist reception centre for my stay.

The next day the preparations were in full swing. A local band from Jammu and Kashmir Police was brought in to rehearse with me to perform at the time of departure and arrival of the bus. The band worked with me for a couple of hours. These band members were quite lazy and very limited in their training. They just could not pick up simple folk melodies. So, after the rehearsals I rejected them and asked for a better band. Frankly, if I had my way I would have loved to have a large number of traditional swarnai players with twenty dhols and twenty nagaras. It would have created a magnetic impact of the auspiciousness of the occasion, that too in pure Kashmiri sounds. But it was conveyed to me very quietly that the chief minister and the others did not like the Bhand and their music. I wanted to open the event with the blessings of burning *isband* (also known as harmal seeds), which is always used at auspicious functions by Kashmiris (both Hindu and Muslim). But again, due to security reasons, that could not be done. I do not understand why politicians shun traditional cultural elements.

I recall an event that was organized by a Kashmiri Pandit organization in Delhi in the late 1970s where Prime Minister Indira Gandhi was the chief guest. At the time of the opening, Kishori Kaul, an eminent Indian painter, appeared on stage wearing a beautiful Kashmiri dress and carrying a well-decorated *kangari* (fire pot) in her hands with *isband*. She requested Indira Gandhi to come on stage, and in typical traditional Kashmiri style, welcomed her by burning the isband. There was an uproar of applause in the auditorium. There were Muslims, Pandits, Dogras and Punjabis in the auditorium. For almost five minutes there was joyous cheering and clapping. Indira Gandhi was so moved she stayed for the entire programme though she had come for only twenty minutes. That was a rare example of emotional sentiment connecting one to one's land and culture.

The next day, the 6 April 2005, another police band arrived from Jammu for rehearsals. Their leader was a Kashmiri and I explained to him that we were not going to play any marching band compositions. We would learn and practise only our folk compositions. I hummed some of the old tunes which were very popular among the masses. The leader of the band would first play them on his clarinet, and then they would be picked by the group of bagpipers, then gradually by the bugle players, who would finally be joined by drummers. Within two hours we lined up about ninety minutes of folk melodies on the instruments of the police band after conducting full run-through rehearsals. Their leader, fondly called 'Masterji', had done a remarkable arrangement using all the instruments of the band. All the songs sounded wonderful, with the various instruments of the band joining in and fading out. All the officials of the tourist reception centre came out of their offices to see the band practice, enjoying the music with smiles on their faces.

Finally, Masterji and I worked out the order of the tunes according to the sequence of the ceremonies that would go on till the departure of the bus. We were supposed to meet the next morning at the Amar Singh Club lawns, the venue of the function. It was decided that we would arrive half an hour before the event, at around 9.30 a.m. The function was to start at 10 a.m. I thanked the band players for their efforts, and they left.

I went to the room of the director of general tourism to get some water. A young daily wager was inside, helping me with my glass of water. There I heard the sound of a gunshot as if it came from next door. It was followed by the sound of rapid firing, which seemed to come from every direction. One shot hit the French window of our room and glass shattered all across the floor. Another shot came from the back window, followed by loud explosions. The firing did not stop. Rather, it accelerated, and within minutes I heard loud explosions, which shook the window of the room. It sounded like a battle scene. The young workman and I both lay prostrate, flat on the ground under a big table.

I had learned to do this during my college NCC training days. The sound of firing from the AK-47 or stun gun did not stop. More shots came from the direction of the bathroom now, and the window was smashed. One did not know what to do. If one attempted to go out of the room one was sure to get shot. Our twenty minutes of lying on the floor felt like ages. There was a clock on the wall of the office, and I was looking at the time. This poor boy with me was shaking with fear. I was trying to reassure him and keep his morale high. Fortunately, I did not lose my cool. All I was thinking was about when we would get out of this mess. We had no idea what was happening outside. All we could do was to wait and only wait. Then there was a sudden silence and a lull. No sound was heard whether of a gun or any movement. After a pause, I gathered some courage. I crawled to the window and peeped out through the broken window. There was not a soul. A big, armoured vehicle stood there, and in its pill box, I could see a soldier with a mounted machine gun. When he noticed me, he shouted, 'Put your hands up and come down.' The boy and I opened the door of the room. I held the boy's hand, and we rushed out. In the corridor, many office people were hiding under their tables. When they saw us they too started to crawl out and we all started to come down the wooden staircase. I saw Hakim Javed (my theatre colleague) crouched under the staircase. He was so shaken that he had to be supported to walk. When all of us came out of the building and crossed the courtyard, I looked back. My heart nearly stopped. I saw black smoke coming out from the floor of the room where the boy and I had been lying down. When the boy looked at the smoke he said, '*Es dazhan dunvay* [We both would have burnt alive].'

The scene outside was one of utter confusion. Most of the office people were in groups talking to each other, some shouting in anger and some asking others to calm down. Someone in the crowd was saying loudly, '*Hata massage to diya tha lunch se pahaly nikal* [I had told you to remove before lunch].' By now the tourist reception building was in flames and there were huge blasts still going on. These blasts were from the bursting of the gas cylinders which are used in Kashmir as fuel for a device that heats up rooms. The entire tourist complex here had a large number of these heaters in its offices. And now they were bursting, creating big flames. The fire had started to spread through the other wings of the heritage building. I wanted to get out of the area and asked my driver Majeed to get the jeep to leave the place. But strangely, the security cops did not allow him to drive out of the premises. Finally, when people started to move out of the complex, a lady employee in a yellow shalwar-kameez, who was consoling the crowd by saying 'Do not worry,' suddenly collapsed. She had received a stray bullet from the direction of the burning buildings. There was commotion and soon she was rushed to hospital. It was now dangerous to stay there, as more contingents of army men were arriving, led by the director general of police, Makdumi. We knew each other quite well, but at that time he was marching in the building. We only exchanged looks as I rushed out of the burning tourist reception building. The office of the DG of tourism, Saleem Beg, was already in ashes. There were thousands of floating candles, digitized copies of Mani Kaul's film on Kashmir *Before my Eyes* and many more articles that were to be used for the opening ceremony of the bus service in that building. Saleem Beg was out somewhere for some official meeting and it was difficult to reach him.

When I came out of the gate of the burning building out to the main road, it was a sight to see: hundreds of television teams from all over the world had arrived with their cameras and there were long boom rods as the reporters made their live presentations with the burning flames of the tourist reception centre as their backdrop. The moment I came out, I saw at least twenty-five if not more cameras and boom rods rushing towards me. I knew some of the anchors personally. All of them surrounded me, the way they do people at public events, and started asking me questions. They were pushing each other to get a byte from me. But at that moment, when you have just escaped from the jaws of death, you are not in a state of mind to give any interview. I just hid my face and wanted to get out of the circle of these television crews. But I was not able to move, and finally, I had to shout at them. I even used some four-letter words as I somehow pushed my way out of the ring they had created. I started walking towards Residency Road. The camera crew was disappointed and angry with me. Even now some of them do not talk to me. They were interested in getting their bytes, but I had to think of many issues before I could open my mouth. For example, I work in the Valley with many kinds of people—from theatre, film, literature, etc. It would not have been fair or right to become a public face of this event. It would have been counter-productive for my work in the Valley. Also, I needed to reach out to my family in Delhi before they got worried about me, but my mobile did not work, as if it was a dead phone.

When I neared the State Emporium lawns, there were Indian Army soldiers positioned on the main road with their weapons aimed in the direction of people coming out of the tourist reception centre. There were army trucks and armoured vehicles with mounted machine guns. It looked like the soldiers had taken positions to tackle any major eventuality. The sight unnerved me. I thought if any stray shot came our way from any side, all of us who were walking on the road would be killed like chickens. I put my hands up in the air and asked all the people walking along with me to put their hands up too. There were hundreds of us with hands up in the air, to make sure that we crossed this military contingent without any harm. It is always safe to lift your hands up so that the opponent knows that you do not have any weapons on you and that you do not mean any harm to them either.

When I reached Adhoos Hotel, I met a journalist friend, Shujaat Bhukhari. After we had greeted each other, he asked me where I was coming from, and when I told him the whole story he was very sympathetic and said, 'Thank God you are lucky.'

But a few years later on the same Residency Road, only 500 metres from where we stood talking that day, Shujaat Bukhari was attacked by terrorists and brutally killed, with at least sixty bullets in his body, just outside his *Rising Kashmir* office.

All telephone lines were cut. When I entered the Adhoos surprisingly hotel reception area, most of the staff were glued to the television and were watching reports of the attack on various news channels. I asked the receptionist to connect me to Delhi so that I could send a message to my family that I was safe. I could not get connected. But surprisingly Manzoor Meer, my local theatre colleague who was with me throughout this incident, had dialled my house number on his mobile phone. Luckily it worked. Mobile phones had started in the valley recently and I could talk to Anju to tell her I was all right. I did not tell her anything about the fire and the other happenings. Strangely my Delhi mobile number did not work but Manzoor's local mobile number did, I suspected perhaps inter—state telephone services had been cut off.

After this, I did not know what to do next. I had no information about Saleem Beg and his phone could not be reached. I started asking about my friend Vinod Raina, who had checked in at Adhoos Hotel. I had chatted with him on the phone just two hours before this fidayeen attack. At that time, he was around Lal Chowk, and I had advised him not to move around in that place as it was dangerous. And now, when I found him in his room, he kept laughing at me. 'What is wrong with you,' I asked him. 'I had a narrow escape, and here you are making fun of me.' He replied, 'You were advising me to be careful and see what happened.' Then, after a moment, he said, 'Jokes apart, thank God you are safe.' He ordered some tea and snacks for me since I had not been able to have my lunch. While enjoying the tea, it occurred to me that it would now be difficult to go to my room at the tourist reception centre as it was still burning. Fortunately, the building in which I had a room was saved. But entry into that building was impossible because the main entry gate was still on fire and huge beams of wood were falling to the ground. It was getting dark now, and with no personal transport, it was impossible to move anywhere in the city. I decided I would stay with Vinod Raina in his room for the night and see what was in store for the next day in the event the inaugural bus did leave for Muzaffarabad. For some time, I felt abandoned by my friends, whom I had travelled to Srinagar. None of them had called or inquired about me.

At about 8 p.m., I got a call on my mobile. I was surprised this time my phone started functioning. The call was from Saleem Beg, asking my whereabouts. When I said I was at Adhoos, he said he would send me transport to get me to the Sheri Kashmir International Convention Centre (SKICC) as the team were all there. I said to Vinod that I would go for some time and return.

At the SKICC, all the bureaucrats involved in the event were there. Some of them hugged me and prayed for a long life for me. I gave them the entire low-down on the fire. I told Saleem Beg that all the articles for the next day's celebrations had been swallowed by the fire. It appeared to me that his office room had been one of the main targets of the attack. A senior bureaucrat came in and disclosed that some passengers who were supposed to go to Muzaffarabad on the bus were now too scared to make the journey. I said in a lighter tone, 'No they will have to go, for them, I almost lost my life and now these fellows are saying they won't go. Hold a pistol to their temples and you will see they will go.'

This senior bureaucrat instructed all his colleagues to go into the rooms of the passengers and convince them to make this important journey. Someone reported that there was a passenger who had been provoking the other passengers not to do the journey. The senior bureaucrat, Saleem Beg and I went into a couple of rooms where the passengers were lodged. These were poor, ordinary folks from the Poonch and Rajouri districts of the state, and they were genuinely scared and worried about their families. They were made to talk to their family members on this senior bureaucrat's mobile phone and convince them that nothing was going to happen to them and not to worry. While we were still in their room, we heard some loud arguments going on in the corridor. All of us rushed out and saw one of the officers of the Tourism Corporation confronting a local Kashmiri passenger who too was an employee of the corporation. It was he who had been quietly provoking the other passengers to abandon their journey to Muzaffarabad the next day. When the concerned officer confronted him, he first denied everything, but when one of the bearers who was serving these passengers confronted him about his conversation with the passengers, he could not defend himself. He was exposed completely. This fellow did not know that the bearers who were serving them were basically police intelligence men in disguise and also in charge of their security. He was asked to pack up immediately and sent back home. The officer also warned him, 'We will see to it that you are blacklisted, and you will never be able to take this bus journey ever.'

I suddenly woke up and started putting two and two together. I suddenly remembered the voice from the crowd that morning when I was running to save myself from the bullets and fire at the Tourist Reception Centre. It had said, '*Message diya tha lunch se pehley nikal jana* [Message had come to leave before lunch].' I connected the two—this person who was caught here persuading the bus passengers not to go and the person from the crowd who had mentioned the message. It seemed that the two were interconnected. Some people had perhaps been given the job of sabotaging the bus event, and all of them were undercover.

Even before this entire incident of the fidayeen attack on the tourist reception centre, the passengers of the bus were being hosted by the Government of Jammu and Kashmir. One day before the horrible incident happened, the passengers had asked to the authorities to allow them to offer their Friday namaz at the mosque located on the main road, just outside the tourist reception centre. The police had refused them permission. One of the policemen had said, 'I will accept all the curses of Allah for not permitting them. You have no idea; these rascals are waiting to create some mischief to get some publicity. You can curse me, but I will not permit them to go out of the tourist reception centre for Friday namaz.'

And within a day or so the fidayeen attack had happened, reducing the tourist reception centre to ashes. This building was made of beautiful walnut panels. It had wooden Khatamband ceilings with very fine murals made by Ghulam Rasool Santosh (an eminent Indian painter). It really was a heritage building.

I stayed at the Adhoos Hotel for that one night only. When I woke up, Vinod Raina asked me if I would go for the bus functionon. I replied, 'I do not know, I cannot change my clothes, I do not even have my entry pass, so I have no idea.' We had tea. I had a bath, wore the same clothes in which I had spent the night and left for the tourist reception centre, to check if I would be permitted to go to my room and change into some decent clothes. I stood at the main gate of the centre; many half-burnt beams were still falling. The fire service officers who were on duty did not allow me to go in. So, I was standing there, wondering how this function would commence as I had all the music cues and other instructions with me. The band could not play anything until I signalled to them to do so.

A white Ambassador car stopped in front of me and a police officer whom I had met during the security meetings for the event called out my name, 'Mr Raina, I have your entry card.' I decided to walk to the Amar Singh Club lawns along with hundreds of the general public who had been brought in buses from the countryside for the occasion. But I could not enter the main gate of the venue with the entry card I was given. I had come on foot, presuming that since my card was for a special category of persons I should be able to walk towards the VVIP gate. When I displayed my card to the officer there, he did not even look at me but ordered me very rudely to clear out of that space. I did not know what one did with a card on which was written 'CLOSE VICINITY', which possibly meant I could be present near the VVIP block. But nothing like that was allowed to me. I started walking back towards the exit road near the old church. All the enclosures were filled with village people, officials, army officers and police. There was very strict security in these enclosures. I kept standing on the road, looking for some face that would recognize me and take me into the main enclosure. The VVIPs had not yet arrived, but the bus was in position with passengers already sitting in it.

I located my band people, who were looking very smart in their ceremonial uniforms. Their master saw me standing outside on the road. When I told him I could not go in because the security was not honouring my entry pass, he asked how the band could get my instructions. I said I could stand on the road itself, where I already was, near the band contingent. The only thing was, we were separated by thick metal panels of wire net. Finally, it was me on the road, and the band inside the wire-net enclosures. When the function started, I started giving my instructions and the band started playing Kashmiri folk melodies. Luckily, this arrangement between the band and me worked out quite well till the bus departed. When the bus left, a very heavy downpour followed, and within minutes people ran away, as did the VVIPs. I saw Saleem and Nayeem Sahib (secretary culture, J&K government) running towards me. They hugged me for managing the event. They said they were watching me perform a faultless job. 'Unfortunately, the instructions given to us were not to move or even get up from our seats. We really were feeling sorry for you.' In the meantime, an Ambassador car stopped next to me. The man inside the car was the same officer who had not let me in at the VVIP gate. And he said, 'Mr Raina, I am sorry, I apologize, the security drill had changed at 4 a.m. in view of what happened yesterday, please do understand.'

We left for the SKIGC, where the evening function had to take place on the arrival of the bus from Muzaffarabad. It was quite cold and windy. We were all watching television. On a split screen, both buses were shown travelling in opposite directions. While watching television, the only thing I was being offered was Kashmiri kahwa. At one point I asked loudly, 'Can anyone here give me something to eat. I've had no dinner last night, no breakfast in the morning. Why are you all feeding me with this tea only?' One of the young tourist officers got up and said, 'Sir, give me just fifteen minutes, I will serve you the best Wazwan.' I did not believe him, but within minutes he came back with all the best and choicest dishes of Wazwan. I pounced on the food. I was really starving. Since there was so much food the other officers joined in too. I asked the young tourist officer how he had managed to get all that delicious food. He laughed and said, 'From the Congress party.' Ghulam Nabi Azad was

hosting a lunch for Congress party workers on the other side of
the building. All of us laughed and enjoyed our feast.

Looking at the television, I said, 'Thank God this has
finally happened, and it should bring good results.' To which
one of the senior officers responded, 'You seem to be very happy
today.' I replied 'Yes.' He asked, 'Who is there from your side
there?' I replied, 'Ok, I do not have any one on that side of
the border, but you have.' He laughed and said, 'Wait till this
bus crosses Baramulla, when all our passengers will hear the
sounds of *tusi-maynu-kithe*. I asked, 'What do you mean, there
are no Kashmiri-speaking people on that side?' He smiled and
said, 'Wait.'

In the evening when the bus from Muzaffarabad arrived, it
was raining heavily with very strong, cold winds. The passengers
were received by a senior officer of the J&K government. Many
gifts and mementos were given to the passengers. All of them
were ushered towards the ghats of Dal Lake. Eleven boats
decorated with spring flowers were waiting. Unfortunately, the
weather went from bad to worse. Rain and wind spoiled all
the ceremonies. The boats could not move beyond fifty feet;
strong winds were hitting them, not allowing them to move
forward. There was every possibility that the boats may capsize,
and that would be a major tragedy. The Kashmir temperatures
of Dal Lake did not allow everything to go smoothly. Finally,
somehow, the ceremony was imagined having been performed.
Since all the floating candles had been destroyed in the fire of
the previous day at the tourist reception centre, there was no
question of floating thousands of candles in the Jhelum. All
presents were soaked wet. The guests were ushered into the
auditorium for the final music concert. I quietly left with Vinod
to try my luck at getting out any bags from my room at the
tourist reception centre, so I did not have to spend another
night in Vinod's room at Adhoos Hotel in the same clothes I
was wearing the previous day.

18

Final Bhand Experiment

In 2006 November, I was asked by India Foundation for the Arts to attend their annual board meeting, where they invite some of their grantees to make a presentation of the work they have done with the support of their funds. At that time, I was in the midst of making a documentary on the women who had played a key role in the literacy movement in Bihar and Jharkhand. I had met these wonderful rural women before. Most of them were economically poor but with the determination of steel. They were volunteers of the literacy movement. They were literacy activists, street theatre actors, poets, agitationists and housewives from the most backward areas of Bihar and Jharkhand. Theirs was a story of struggle and success. Their stories were about how they had changed themselves and their families, and how they organized their kind of people to join in the literacy movement. For these women, this kind of movement meant freedom from exploitation by the labour mafia, labour contractors and the coal mafia of the Jharia Coal Fields.

I was going from village to village with my filming crew, working all day. This invitation from the India Foundation for the Arts was tempting, but the documentation I had to prepare for it demanded time, which I could not spare during this schedule. There were no photocopying shops and no fax machines in the area. We used to normally leave for filming around 10 a.m. and return by 7 p.m.

The only time available for any kind of other work was in the early hours of the morning. I started getting up at 4 a.m. and writing my presentation by hand. This I did for almost a week. I would again correct my writing. This I did several times till my presentation was finally ready. For the presentation, I had to travel by train from Dhanbad to Kolkata, and from there take a flight to Chennai.

When I made my presentation with very amature video footage and various photographs of the Akingam workshop, I was able to make my audience understand the conditions under which we had been working in Kashmir Valley and what was achieved. This presentation was followed by many questions on all sorts of issues about the Bhands, their problems and the present situation in Kashmir. How tough was it for me to work there when I had myself lost my home and everything there? Then questions on communalism, and so on. I replied to the best of my ability. I had to make it amply clear that I was not trying to become any kind of hero by doing this kind of work in Kashmir. I was aware of the risk of losing one's life doing these workshops. It was not that I was not scared of the dangers that were all around us, but I wanted to give the project an honest try, because I was genuinely concerned and worried about the melting away of traditional knowledge across India. Not much was being done to stop this cultural erosion and depigmentation of our heritage. But I was looking at it very rationally and not with any kind of nationalist sentiment.

The meeting was over, and it was now dinner time. I rushed to fetch a drink for myself. I was very tired and thirsty. I sat quietly at a separate table with my drink. All the other guests were busy. After about ten minutes, an elderly gentleman walked towards me with a drink in his hands.

'Mr Raina, you must be mad man to work in such terrible circumstances,' he said to me.

'But sir, somebody has to do this kind of work,' I very politely replied.

'What do you do next with these people?' he asked.

'I want to start a training programme for all the young fellows for at least two years,' I said.

'How much would that cost you?' he asked.

'I think it should cost me around Rs 12 lakh at the most,' I replied.

'I will give you that much money,' he said.

I could not believe him, but I politely thanked him for the offer. Later, people from the India Foundation for the Arts rushed towards me and the director of IFA, Anmol Velani said, 'MK, you have got the money, congratulations.' I said, 'Come on, Anmol, nobody gives grants just like that.' Anmol said the gentleman was a major pharmaceutical industrialist and the chairman of their trust. Plus, the estate on which we were in was his house. Then another officer from the Foundation asked me if I would like to take the money directly from him. I replied, 'No way—you are my representative here, and it should be given to me through you guys, like the previous grant.'

I just could not believe that I now had money for the training programme for the Bhands. In the morning, I had to rush back to Jharkhand Coal Fields to complete my filming of the *Black Diamond Women* series.

In the meantime, I informed my team members and also the ustads of Bhand Pather about this new development. We could train young youths from the Bhand community for a longer period of time. Soon, selection of students for the training took place and I explained to the ustads to design a concrete training programme. We now had four students who wanted to learn swarnai, four that wanted to learn acting and maskhari, and four the dhol and nagara. Classes would take place in the afternoon, from 4 p.m. to 7 p.m.

The story of setting up a training centre at Akingam for the Bhand pather was a very difficult task. It is easy to desire something one aspires for. But when you have to deliver and see that the aim is achieved, it is a different story altogether. The first requirement to start our classes to begin was to get our required instruments for the students, like swarnai, dhol, nagara and thalej. We had thought we would buy these instruments from the nearby villages. Some people do keep them in their houses as a memento of the departed swarnai player of their families. Our search did not yield any positive results because people did not want to part with their mementos and the associated memories they brought. They would not sell for very emotional and sentimental reasons. Those who were ready to sell to us asked for exorbitant prices, which we could not afford to pay. The most difficult to find were four swarnais, for other instruments we could go to the music shop and buy. But because of markets being shut down for months we had to wait. Swarnai being very much of a typical Kashmiri make we had to get them made by the master maker in the Valley. So, the next step was to go to Kulwama town, about forty kilometres away, and order four swarnais from a maker of the instrument. This maker was a well-known master at crafting this instrument and was about eighty years old at the time.

I went myself, with the two master players Ustad Ghulam Rasool Bhagat and Mohammed Ameen Bhagat, to meet him. When we reached his house in Kulwama, he immediately recognized both the players. He was now the only swarnai maker in this part of the Valley. After initial exchanges, our ustads asked him to make four swarnais for us. He replied that it had been years now since he had made one, and since the advent of militancy his work had stopped. No one was now asking to buy any musical instrument. He asked what we needed four for. I explained to him the purpose and the necessity of keeping the cultural heritage alive. He understood and said it would take him at least three months to make them. We agreed to wait. I paid him some advance money, and after being served traditional salt tea, we took his leave.

After only two months of this visit, I received a call from one of the ustads conveying me the sad news that the swarnai-maker had passed away. It was a shock to me and also a cause for worry. The tragedy was that with his death all knowledge of swarnai-making was gone. Unfortunately, he did not have any assistant whom he could have imparted his knowledge to. I told the swarnai master's to wait till I arrived in Kashmir, and we would think up some alternatives. When I returned to Akingam, we took stock of the situation and started discussing the arrangements for the classes and what we would do to acquire swarnais.

There was good news for all of us—construction of a building in the village on fourteen hectares of land had started, and it was coming up fast. The story of this building is very interesting. These friends of mine, Saleem Beg and Nayeem Akhtar, being senior bureaucrats in the state in charge of culture and tourism, used to feel quite helpless and guilty whenever they saw me working with the Bhands under the shade of an apple or walnut tree. They wanted to help me and my work in the village. It so happened that the Government of India had asked all the state governments at that point in time to develop the concept of village heritage tourism centres. These centres created in a rural setting would contain all the elements of the state's village traditions. To develop these centres, the government of India was going to provide funds.

Saleem Beg, as the director–general of tourism of Jammu and Kashmir, saw the possibilities of such a scheme and in his official capacity had set the ball rolling. He quietly acquired a piece of land in Akingam itself for the Rural Heritage Tourism Centre. I think he had started official work on it very quietly. After some time of getting to know about the centre, I was in his office one day. Saleem asked me to explain to him the reasons and justifications for locating this rural heritage tourism centre at Akingam. Off the cuff, I rattled off many reasons and justifications for it. He immediately said, 'No, no. Here are some sheets of paper, write for me a proper and genuine note giving me logical and convincing reasons for having this centre at Akingam. He also handed me a copy of the official scheme from the government of India. I asked him but why he wanted it all done so fast. He said many local politicians had come to know about the scheme and had objections to its location in Akingam and not any other village. Many politicians had their own vested interests and wanted it to be located in their own constituencies. The project had now got politicized.

I went through the Government of India document for the scheme. My very first reaction was that Akingam was indeed the best location for this kind of centre. I took my pen and started writing my note listing the justifications for having it in Akingam. There were four important reasons. The first was that all the villages in and around Akingam—Muhurpur, Aariham, Helad, Hangloo, Gund, etc., were places where the heritage of the performing arts was still alive and being practised. The village of Bidder had been famous for its swarnai players for centuries. There were several dhamal dance parties in some of the villages nearby. And Bhand Pather, the traditional theatre of the Kashmiris, was at Akingam.

The second reason, from the tourism point of view, was that there were numerous world-famous sites and locations near Akingam, which were visited by thousands of tourists every year. Some of them were the Achabal Mughal Gardens, Kukarnaag, Daksun and Pahalgam.

The third reason was that all along the route to Akingam there were some world-famous sacred sites, like the Shiva Bhagwati Temple at Akingam, the Zan Shah Saheb Dargah, the medieval *ziyarat* of Ash Mukan, the famous Amarnath cave, and the world-famous Martand Temple.

The fourth reason was that the area had some of the most beautiful and well-preserved forests in the state, and mineral and glacial streams. And it also had domestic Kashmir handicrafts-making households dotted all over the area.

Hence Akingam, a village enveloped by sacred, aesthetic and tourist-friendly sites, was therefore the best-suited location for developing a rural heritage tourist centre. When I finally finished writing this note, Saleem went through it and said, 'Now no one can stop us from developing the centre at Akingam.'

So, after many years of conducting our workshop in all sorts of places, now the Heritage Tourist Centre was going to be a sure worksite for us. The design and architecture were to be done by the INTACH Kashmir chapter. This building was going to have a big central hall, two rooms with attached washrooms and an open-air theatre for performances. The rehearsal space was big enough for any kind of performance. It was going to come up before we started our training classes. It would be the first home for the Bhands in the Valley.

But before the actual classes began we had to solve the problem of the swarnais. We went back to the house of the swarnai-maker in Kulwama, the three of us who had originally met him. As a custom, we offered our condolences to the wife of the old swarnai-maker. We three met his two sons who had a running business of furniture in the town. I asked these sons; had they ever watched their father making this instrument? They said yes. Then I gave them a little lecture about their father—how he had kept the heritage of Kashmir alive just by his making of this instrument. Would it be possible for the two brothers to try and take up the challenge of making it?

This way they would be paying a great tribute to their father's legacy. They agreed to try and make it, but it would take time, they said, because the wood used for the swarnai, called *tahal* in Kashmir, came from Jammu. Finally, they agreed to make the instrument. At this point our swarnai ustads told them to inform them when they made the holes in the instrument, they wanted to be called. They would make the holes together. So, the new swarnais were made with the makers and the players collaborating.

The building at Akingam was ready when we started our training programme. We had twelve students, and we soon received additional support from INTACH Kashmir, which donated many instruments for the learning of folk music and also awarded some scholarships.

We had new swarnais, dhols and other instruments for Bhand Pather training, and for the learning of folk music we had rababas, sarangis and harmoniums. We started imparting training in Bhand acting, like maskhari, dhamal dance and also scene work in various patterns. The swarnai being a very complex instrument, it was tough in the beginning for the students to learn to breathe in a cyclical pattern. It took them a lot of time. Once they had learned to play the basic notes, they started playing simple folk melodies. Later the various mukams would be introduced to them.

The teachers themselves had to learn how to teach. Since they had never been teachers, it was tough for them. These ustads or teachers had to develop a pedagogy of teaching, which they had never done before. In the beginning they were impatient and would lose their temper very quickly. They would even use violent methods of training. I had to intervene many a time to make the ustads learn the art of teaching. For that I had to give short workshops for the ustads myself. I had to explain and over-emphasize the method of teaching with

love and care. I had to teach them how to create a feeling of
love among their trainees for the learning of Bhand Pather. I
developed a session separately for the ustads to teach them to
narrate their own stories of learning the art of their theatre. I
had to tell them what it would mean for them to talk about
their journeys as performers, and about their struggles and
sorrows. These sessions with the ustads worked, and soon I saw
a good connection between the students and their ustads. Now
at least the ustads were not impatient and abusive towards the
students. The teachers were also learning as they imparted their
knowledge.

These classes went to the stage of preparation of an old
pather featuring the new students and the seniors. It was now
a collaborative project where experienced veterans and the
youngsters would create together. We decided on *Gosain Pather*,
old pather from the repertoire of the Bhands. This play, apart
from heavy demands of performance, also involved a lot of craft,
such as the making of masks, head gears and a large number of
properties.

The plot of Gosain Pather revolves round some sadhus who
come from all parts of India for a pilgrimage to Amarnath cave.
There they meet a greedy Kashmiri Brahmin Pandit family, who
take great care of these sadhus after their hard journey in the
mountains. In return, this Brahmin family expect some material
benefits. The play takes a dramatic turn when the character of
Aashik Gosain appears on the scene and wants to have darshan
of a mystic female, Gopali. During the conversation between
Aashik Gosain and a Brahmin from the greedy family, the latter
makes fun of and mocks Aashik. But Aashik, in response to the
Brahmins, reveals the reality and purpose of human existence
in the world. This is in contrast to the beliefs of the sadhus
who have arrived from the pilgrimage. The greedy family of
Brahmins also do not comprehend the depth of all these

contrasting statements till the end. They cannot even recognize the difference between the sadhus, who believe in practising tough and hard yoga, and Aashok Gosain, who speaks of the wider world beyond the narrow confines of material greed, caste and faiths. It is one of the best pathers of the Bhands, reflecting the Trika philosophy of Kashmir Shaivism through the verses of the fourteenth-century poctess Lal Ded, the great rebel mystic poetess of Kashmir. This philosophy is much closer to the Vedantic philosophy of formless energy. After revealing himself, Aashik Gosain disappears miraculously.

It was unfortunate again that the agitation started and continued for quite some time. We were not able to get our staff for the staging of the play and were stuck and did not know how to proceed. There were the usual shutdowns which went on for weeks. News filtered to us through the people. There were regular confrontations between the people and the security forces. All the rumours that one received were upsetting, and to top it all we had no electricity in our room. There was not a soul in the offices of the electricity department who could help us. We had to spend three weeks in darkness after sunset, with the help of some candles. It used to be very depressing. Since no supply of daily provisions was happening in the towns, more problems cropped up, such as no vegetables in the market. All we could get was the chana dal and rice for weeks.

One day I had a meeting with the students and explained to them the difficulties of acquiring things locally. A plan was put in place with the cooperation of everyone involved to get the required materials we needed—from the headgear for the sadhus to their *kashkol* (begging bowl) malas and trishuls.

The first step was made under the leadership of Ghulam Mohammed Bhagat (Mohammed) a versatile actor, a brilliant craftsman, a weaver and a fine singer. It was decided finally to fabricate everything from locally available materials and using local means. It was also an experiment in using indigenous methodologies for production of the articles we needed. We called it 'back to nature'.

There were too many properties and jewellery pieces to be made. First the detailed jewellery for the character of Gopali was necessary. This was a mystic female character whose darshan for Aashok Gosain was paramount. In the night under candlelight, I designed the traditional pieces of the character's jewellery, like the necklace, choker, bangles, big earrings, nose ring, etc. In the morning, I showed all these drawings to Ghulam Mohammad. He had an intense look at them with his good craftsman's eye and said, 'You have to give me five or six students who will go with me into the forest.'

The forest lay right in front of us. In the afternoon six boys from the workshop went with him and climbed the steep slopes of the hill, soon disappearing into the jungle. After three hours they came down carrying a huge quantity of slim and delicate shrubs on their backs. It was a sight to see this group of boys carrying huge loads on their shoulders and descending the hill. On the instructions of Ghulam Mohammed, the shrubs were put into a running stream of water to make them soft and moist for moulding. Then followed the sorting out of the twigs into small bunches. Ghulam Mohammed then asked the boys who had accompanied him into the forest to go with him to his house to work all night there.

In the morning a fine set of jewellery was ready. Mohammed had improved on my drawings and had made them more decorative and ornamental. He was so engrossed in the making that he soon made another set of jewellery, which was even more pretty, lighter in weight and more durable than what we might have picked up from the market.

The next step was the making of the malas for at least twenty-five sadhus. I thought of using the branches of Kashmiri willow trees, which has soft wood which we could cut into beads to string into malas. I must admit it that the genius of the rural talent was amazing. One of my actors, Sajjad, who was a part-time carpenter, took over this task and got all the boys to collect branches from the willow trees and put them in water to make them soft and supple and easy to cut and shape. He took another group of boys to his home, and using the small electric lathe, he cut the branches into all kinds of beads, and then all night the boys shaped them properly. In the morning, they arrived with a big bag of newly made beads, which the actors who were acting the part of sadhus strung into malas.

In this way the local talents made metal items, like the trishul, the *tabar* (axe) and the *kashkol*. Within three days we had got most of our needed articles ready for the play.

Similarly for costumes the village shopkeeper opened his shop in the night and gave us cloth, which was given to our village tailors to fabricate costumes out of.

This way, Gosain Pather—in a new avatar and a new interpretation and chronography and a different way of using space—was resurrected from the neglect it had suffered for decades. When it was finally performed before the village audiences, they were in raptures. The play was full of satire and fun, and the element of improvisation within the structure of the pather was in full display. I remember meeting a retired police officer after the show. After giving me a big hug he said, 'I have not laughed all these years of militancy. This play made me forget all the pain and suffering and made me laugh.'

Giving new life to an old play and putting it in a certain historical perspective had made it relevant in the present times. My work with the Bhands and Bhand Pather is not an attempt to just revive old stuff performed in new costumes, like filling old wine in new bottles. We are taking a deep dip into the waters of Bhand Pather. While we may revive a play, we are digging deep into the past by looking at the literature; history, sociology, anthropology, music and dance out of which the form has grown and shaped itself. We are also looking at the geography of the land and then exploring the interconnections between it and the neighbouring countries, then further looking at the cultural and political influences that might have enriched and shaped the growth of Bhand Pather. We are very aware of the fact that in culture there is nothing like pure. It is like the dispersal of seeds; seeds are carried in the air and travel across many countries, finally drop on some distant land. And if that land provides congenial conditions for the seeds, they will sprout and over the period of time become part of the heritage of the adopted land.

Recently, I had seen a photograph at the Tashkant Timur museum, of a group of musicians singing Sufiana Kalam. Their musical instruments were the santoor, the *saze* Kashmir (small in size) Setar (small version of Indian Sitar). I took a picture of this, and when I looked at each of the players faces, I discovered one musician with a tilak on his forehead. I was baffled. I wanted to know more about this person who featured in the picture. Unfortunately, no one at the museum could explain anything to me. I showed this picture to the Sufiyana musicians of Kashmir. At first they thought it was a picture of some well-known Kashmiri musician. They even gave me the name of some old musician who was no more. But on learning that the picture was from the Tashkant museum, they could not explain it.

So, my work with the Bhands is like that of an archaeologist who is studying and also digging for available teaching materials in the old pather as part of the module of training, since there is hardly any reliable textual matter on Bhand Pather that could help in our training programme. The pather that have survived and are performed currently are in fact like oral sketch books, passed on orally or by the watching of performances from one generation to the next. The genius of the Bhands lies in the ability of their performers to explore on the spot, and spontaneously improvise on these oral sketches; in how each Bhand play develops fully through its performers, who etch out a skeleton of a story into a detailed and complete pather performance. The available oral sketches contain within themselves all the major elements and the various stages of the pather structure. This is constructed on by the actors and brought to life through rituals, customs, dances, songs, mime and use of space, right from the opening of the play till the closing of the performance.

The greatness of the performers lies in their capacity to understand the available sketch of the pather, which is like a skeleton. The Bhand performer then fills it in, gradually growing its muscles and nervous system, and finally imbuing it with the soul of the performance. Since Bhand Pather performances take place during the day in the open air, the actor cannot take shelter under any artificial technology. He has to continuously keep improvising while the performance is on, simultaneously exploring the use of the space around him.

Once I witnessed a Bhand actor using all the available space in the village, climbing on trees and acting out an entire sequence from the tree itself or sometimes climbing on the rooftop of a village house. Thus, the entire village becomes the sceniographic background for the actors to play their parts. This way of executing space creates a very powerful dialectical relationship between the performer and the spectator.

The training of the younger generation of Bhands has brought in some awareness about the real condition of Bhand Pather. Many youngsters have started taking keen interest in our training programme. After every three months there is an assessment of each student. One could see the efforts of the ustads when each student presented his individual performance piece. One could notice subtle individual creativity gradually growing in them.

Soon we had with us around twenty students trained in acting, who were now ready to perform with the main masters of Bhand Pather. The following year, sessions started with crafts training, and for that an old pather, *Shikar Gha*, was taken up as a module. This pather has the maximum number of craft-related characters.

Once the final rehearsals of this pather were concluded it was decided to perform it near a forest where they were plenty of pine trees and shrubs so that the real feel of the pather could be experienced by the audiences. We had again a very big village audience and lots of children from the nearby schools. There was a great response, and after the performance, children came to have a closer look at the masks and the costumes. Some children wanted to put on these masks, which our young actors offered to them, and soon many children were seen wearing these masks and costumes and trying to enact the animal movements before other children. Ghulam Mohammed Bhagat, every imaginative Bhand actor, soon joined in with the kids and started improvising with them. In minutes a new impromptu play was created and performed. Our boys, along with some senior Bhands, also joined in and were having great fun. That Bhand Pather was an art of the ordinary people could be seen here in full display. While the process of developing and improvising on the narrative was going on, I was observing our students, who were taking the lead in this playmaking and improvisation without any of us interfering in the spontaneity of the experiment.

Ali Mohammed, the senior-most Bhand ustad, commented 'Now we have to accept that our boys have understood the essence of Bhand acting.'

19

Badshah Lear

From 2000 onwards, my return to my hometown had not been to reclaim my home but to reclaim my legacy and my heritage, which has now become for me a journey of rediscovering my Kashmir. When you are permanently living in a place for ages, you take everything for granted. You are in some kind of delusion—that you know everything about your place of birth and also believe that it is going to be safe and will never change or disappear.

But working in the Valley, I have been confronted by one problem after another, and like a foot soldier, I have been cooperating, assisting, advising or executing solutions to the distortions that have quietly crept into the cultural world of the Kashmir Valley.

All kinds of training programmes, workshops, lectures and film festivals that I have been able to organize in Kashmir or about Kashmir, for more than one and a half decades was possible only with the solid support of large number of concerned individuals, creative people, friends and my family. The endeavour of all these years has been to generate a new creative cultural energy which will focus on the contemporary changing world, and in that changing world how do we to hold our past and create our future cultural journeys. How do we define our identity in these contemporary times and how to preserve that, while not changing our indigenous and vernacular idiom of experimentation. When the final goal is to focus on inculcating the democratic thinking among the artists, as the vision for the future?

In 2008 summer during one of our past workshops with the Bhand youth, there was going to be a performance of Darza Pather, one of the most well-preserved and very popular pather among the people and which is often performed. For this performance I had asked most of the senior actors to perform the roles they have been known for. Among the Bhand it is a common practice to talk about the *laagun* ('donning', in their lingo) of a character. Any actor can laagun any character of any pather. It is an accepted norm for all actors know most of the situations, lines, moves and songs of the characters they are going to 'don'. The rest is left to the imagination and wit of the actors. How he will flower in his role and explore the character he is going to perform will depend on his talent and imagination. It is a fact that Bhands have fine memories and they can laagun any character if the need arises. The art of improvisation during a performance is the final parameter for judging a Bhand actor's excellence and his skills.

When the performance of Darza Pather started and King Darza made his first appearance along with the maskharas, I was struck by the characterization of King Darza by Gulam Mohammed Bhagat. His presence, his reflexes, his use of space, his dignity and his delivery of speech (which was made on the spot, all smartly improvised) were amazing. While watching him, I had a sudden flash—I said to myself 'King Lear'. I kept watching him till the play was over. I loved his performance. As an outstanding Bhand actor, he is most rewarding to watch as he goes about enacting various roles and interpreting each one of the characters he portrays.

After this performance I told Mohammed that he was soon going to perform the role of a very famous character called Lear. Mohammed could not make any sense of what I had said. Since the idea of getting him to play King Lear had come into my mind in a flash, I needed to think a bit before taking a final decision on it. So, the next day, when we met, I expressed my desire to take up Shakespeare's *King Lear* as the first major experiment in the Bhand Pather tradition as a challenge. Since my Bhand actors could not read or write, I told them the story of *King Lear*, giving them the background, telling them about Shakespeare the playwright, and other details. I explained to them that it was going to be a very tough project and we were going to begin preparations now so that the next summer we were ready with the production of Lear.

When I narrated the story of *King Lear* to them, it was like someone narrating any folk story. There was a king who had three daughters . . . After listening to the entire plot, the general comment of Bhands was that it was nice, but where was the pather in it? My reply to them was simple. What I had narrated to them was not the play. We would have to read a Kashmiri translation of the play. And I left it at that. The next day I was to go to Delhi. I instructed Gul Mohammed Bhagat to acquire the published book from Srinagar. It was a Sahitya Akademi publication from New Delhi.

After a few days I got a call from Gul Mohammed Bhagat. All the Bhands had attended the reading sessions of the play, but none had understood anything of it. This was a confusing book compared to what I had narrated to them, he said. I asked him to read the play again, but a little slowly. He could then call me back. After few days I again got a call. This time all the senior actors were at the other end, all complaining together about the non-accessibility of the text they had read. They requested me to change my mind and stressed that there were no well-known traditional characters in it, such as the maskhara, magun, etc. I started to laugh and asked them why, what were those countries and the king's clown, etc.? But the Ali Mohammed Bhagat (the senior-most Bhand and a veteran actor) started complaining, 'But where is the pather in it? It cannot work with our audiences. Think of some other script.' I said all right and asked them to please try to read it at least once again. When I came down, we could decide on it together.

Their protests about the script were genuine, because Bhand Pather is all about satire, humour, jokes and puns, and *King Lear* is a major tragedy of Shakespeare's. The Bhands had never ever done a tragedy, and I sensed their anxiety. On top of it they had never dealt with a written text. They could not lend themselves to this kind of an experiment, where there was a written script that they had to follow. It was going against the very grain of pather performances.

After few months, when I finally arrived in the month of June, to work on Lear, we had by now trained actors from our long training programme of over two years. These youngsters were very excited to join the senior group. We started reading the Kashmiri translation of *King Lear* before the entire group. After every ten or fifteen minutes they would stop the reading and start making fun of the text of the play. So, the day ended with no positive reactions from the Bhands to the play. They had practically rejected the script.

For two days I think the Bhands went through the torture of reading and re-reading the text and trying hard to understand it. On the afternoon of the third day, they literally gave up and did not want to read it any further. I knew what was going on. Still, I asked them why they had stopped the reading. Bashir Bhagat suddenly went into fits of laughter and told me, 'For God's sake, please sir, tell me who speaks Kashmiri like this translation? This is not our language.' I responded by saying that that meant this script would not work for us. All of them said in unison, 'Yes, it will not do.' So let us drop this translation and we will translate ourselves the text of the play, I said. They could not believe me.

Next day, our elder Bhands, Rakesh Kumar Singh, my colleague who has been with me as an associate all through the Kashmir projects and also on my other projects that I had been doing outside Kashmir in various parts of India, and I began work on the translation. For three weeks we all worked on the translation—or rather, on the adaptation of the text, from morning till evening. This translation team was a unique combination. Except for two Bhands, who could read and write Kashmiri, none of the other veterans could read or write. So, they were the draftsmen, apart from contributing their talents to the adaptation.

Once we started doing proper readings with all the actors —both the senior and younger ones—the fact that most of the seniors could not read or write created hurdles. All the actors used memory and improvisation as the main vehicle for their rehearsals, which meant I had to follow the traditional techniques to explain the skeleton of the sequences and then let the actors build on that. This was time-consuming in the beginning, but later the pace picked up. The genius of these Bhand actors lay in their imbibing the mood, the subtext and the action of the play very quickly. After that, one had to remain patient and give them their space and time to develop and script the body of the character. They employed their indigenous talent, their Bhand Pather skills and their personal experiences to create fully developed, three-dimensional characters of the play.

After some time, as a director I fixed the moves for the actors along with their movements for dance, acrobatics and other elements, the actors seemed to stop improving further in their performance. It was frustrating to see no progress for days. Soon I woke up to my own mistakes. Their actions looked stiff and crippled, and they appeared stressed and worried about their next moves. I really felt stupid. Without realizing it, they were acting as if in a procession theatre. It was my mistake that I had not pointed out this problem to them earlier. I stopped the rehearsals and asked them to act the way they felt comfortable to. I had to explain to them that though it was a new play, I wanted them to prepare for it as they would for the performance of any other pather. I placed many people on three sides of the auditorium as spectators and asked the actors to rehearse. Now the actors while being conscious of the fact that audiences will be watching their performance from all three sides, for that if they feel to change things they are free to do that.

This change immediately brought in a new energy to their characterizations, as if they were freed from jail. From now onwards, we started pooling in all the elements of the pather performance. For example, the opening of a pather is very elaborate and ritualistic, like the *purvaranga* of Sanskrit classical drama, with all the Kashmiri customs. The most important properties of the form became metaphors later, as action in the pather develops and builds itself. One of these properties was the *kodar*, the long whip, the soul of the pather, the use of which signified oppression. Thus, the kodar would only be used by the ruler and by people in power, like the ruler's entourage of knights. Similarly, other typical elements of the Bhand Pather form were gradually woven into the structure of the play as we kept moving from rehearsal to rehearsal.

We reached a stage where we got stuck again and could not move together. The Bhand raised a vital objection about the daughters of Lear. It was an important cultural issue. They argued that no daughter would treat her father the way Lear's daughters treated him. They said that even if a daughter was poor and begging she would never behave with her father in an inhuman way or even intrigue against him. It was possible among sons, who could give this kind of treatment to their father.

These discussions grew intense, involving almost all the actors, particularly the experienced ones. After hours of discussion, argument and counterargument, we decided to change the characters of the daughters into sons. This major shift added more of the texture of Bhand Pather to the entire body of the play. It was interesting that the Bhands used their intellect and their Kashmiri cultural anthropology to interpret the play.

As we know, the heartbeats of the pather performance consist of the kodar, maskhare and swarnai. The elements of Bhand maskhari were gradually woven into the characters of the fool, the king and his courtiers. It appeared as if the king was surrounded by his clowns, who always carried with them a koder.

This time I wanted to make *Badshah Lear* a grand professional production with no compromises. The designs developed by Aditee Biswas and Supriya Shukla, which were made keeping in mind the budget constraints and the prevailing political situation, looked regal. They were fabricated by teaching the local village tailors, the potter, the blacksmiths and the cobblers how they were made. As we progressed with our production every day, some nice sequences would take shape, but a constant worry bothered all of us throughout the rehearsals. We regularly heard news of disturbances. Most days, in almost all the towns of the Valley, the local people and the security people fought pitched battles. Young boys received bullets and security people too got injured from the stone-pelting. Again, an atmosphere of uncertainty prevailed. Still, we worked regularly, even under the shadow of doubt. No one was sure about the final performance. We could keep working as long as our remote villages were not affected, but we could not be sure how the local village population would react to the killing of young boys. The idea of one hundred boys dying gave us all the shivers.

We had exhausted the supplies at all the cloth shops in the village, and we needed more fabric. The nearest market for good fabric was in the town of Anantnag, about twenty kilometres away. It was impossible to go there and buy fabric and the other materials we needed because most of the shops remained shut during the disturbances. I worried about the women designers visiting the markets of Anantnag. They had no clue about the landscape as this was their first visit to the Valley of Kashmir. It came as a major surprise to me when I discovered that these two designers had already worked out an arrangement with the shopowners of Anantnag for delivery of fabric. Fortunately, this time cell phones, and mobile service technology helped them immensely. The arrangement was that the owners of the shops would ring them up and tell them what time they could visit to pick up the materials and leave.

One day, when they were in a shop looking at the fabric, suddenly there was firing in the market. All the shop owners immediately pulled down their shutters. Our designers were scared and did not know when the firing would end. The shop owner understood their anxiety, and the owner, like any elderly uncle, directed them to take the back door of the shop into his house where his entire family lived. The family welcomed them and helped them relax, offering them tea and local Kashmiri breads. They stayed there chatting with the family for almost two hours, growing into family friends as they came to know more about each other. It was getting late, and at the rehearsals we waited for them, getting worried. Soon I received a call from them, saying, 'Not to worry, we are safe at Uncle's house.' I asked them which uncle. At that point the shop owner came on the cell phone and reassured me. 'They are like my daughters, and they are with my children and with my wife. They are safe.' And when the situation had calmed down in the evening, they returned, relaxed and with most of the fabric they required.

Finally, after weeks of rigorous run-throughs, we were ready to give our opening performance at the same foothills where we had performed for our village audience earlier. Everyone was excited about the premiere. One day before the performance, Gulam Rasool (Junior) shared his worry with all of us about the performance the next day. He talked about his apprehensions. He suspected there may be some trouble at the performance. He explained, 'Tomorrow is Friday, and with so many deaths of young boys during the last week, we may be misunderstood by the people, and there is a possibility of some reaction against the performance.' There was a long silence for some time as everybody pondered the situation. A senior actor asked him, 'Did someone talk to you to convey the message to us?' He replied, 'No, but looking at the circumstances, I felt I should share my worry with you all. 'All the Bhands and the rest of the team wanted my opinion, so I said, 'It does not matter, if you do not perform tomorrow, you can go ahead and perform on Saturday. I am leaving on Saturday, but you go ahead and perform.' At that point, Gul Mohammed Bhagat said, 'No, we will perform tomorrow only. But first, before that, we will all go to masjid and offer our namaz, and after that, we will come back and perform. Nobody will say anything to us.' To that, I said, 'You people take a joint decision, and I will be fine with any decision you make.' All agreed with Gul Mohammed's idea.

The next morning, all of us arranged everything for the performance. There was hectic activity all around. We did not announce the performance, but word-of-mouth publicity had already happened on its own. At about noon, all the Bhands went for their Friday namaz while the remaining crew prepared for the performance. About an hour later, all the actors returned from the masjid and started getting into their costumes. I saw Ghulam Rasool (junior), who had warned us that some trouble that may happen during the performance.

He looked at me and smiled as if he wanted to share something. I went near him, and I inquired, 'What happened?' He replied, 'Nothing,' but kept smiling and trying to avoid me.

I insisted on knowing what had happened, but his reply was, 'This is not right. It should not have happened.' I asked him again, 'What is it, Gulam Rasool? Has someone sent some message or threat? You tell me.' He said, 'No, no, it is not that at all. I feel ashamed to tell you what happened at the Masjid.' I again asked him what had happened, and he said, 'When we were getting ready for the namaz, a whisper went around that the drama would be starting soon, and our molvi who was leading the namaz speeded it up so it could get over as quickly as possible. But he should not have done this. This is not done. Now, see, the public from all the masjids are coming to watch the play.' Although he smiled, he did not appreciate what had been done, that too by a molvi.

A couple of thousand people marched in from three or four masjids towards the venue of the performance, which was already occupied by women and children. There was a festive look all around. The villagers were excited and eager to watch the show. When all our actors dressed up, we all met for our *duwa,* our prayer before the performance, and then they marched towards the acting area. They all looked royal, carrying their costumes with great pride. They wore lovely brocade turbans, specially designed caps, and more. Our designers had done a remarkable job of fabricating these complicated medieval dresses with the village tailors. It was a big achievement for the village tailors, the bar of their talent having risen many notches higher.

For many years, our capacity-building processes with the local craftsman had become part of our training programme. Self-sufficiency in most of the areas of production of our plays was gradually being realized, and the results of that were seen in the preparations for the *Badshah Pather* performance. Our blacksmith in the village, who usually made tin trunks for a living, was now our trained metal-property maker. For this play, I had asked him to make swords, and within four days he had made a strong, impressive-looking metal sword.

When I asked him where he had got the metal sheets in the village from, he did not want to reveal his source, saying that it was not my business. 'But did you like this sample?' he asked. When I said it really was good but that I was still intrigued about the metal sheets he had used, he laughed and said, 'This sword is made from abandoned coal-tar drums, which you see all over the roads.' I could not believe him because he had polished it so well. In short, the villagers around were gifted and talented men of culture and crafts who became our source of support. There is story after story about the sourcing of the materials for most of our projects. It had been an ongoing mission for us to become completely self-sufficient in most areas of play production. The actors and the community were closely involved in this endeavour of interdependence. They took it as a matter of pride to see that we succeeded in our endeavours. The theme of 'back to nature' was working well.

The final performance of *Badshah Pather* went off without any hurdles. At every stage of the performance, and right to the end, the play met with a lively response from the public. In the last scene, when Lear looks at his dead son, Mohmood bursts into a Sufi song. The last lines of the King before he too dies also became very ironic in the context of Kashmiris losing their sons. 'You are responsible for his death, you killed my son.'

After the performance, amidst feelings of joy and fulfilment, we began packing up because the next day we had to reach Srinagar for another performance at the Dara Shikoh festival. This show was for the educated elite gentry of Srinagar City. So, my team and I had to leave as an advance party for Srinagar. As we packed our bags at the guest house where we stayed, we were warned not to leave early. The town of Anantnag was very tense, and it being a Friday there had been major clashes between the stone-pelters and the security forces. There was routine firing in which many young men were either injured or killed. Leaving for Srinagar was now a complicated exercise. We delayed our departure for hours. The tourist officer who belonged to Anantnag was now more worried about reaching home herself, so I offered her a lift with us since we had to cross the town of Anantnag before heading to the Srinagar highway.

At sunset, the tourist officer rang up her husband and enquired from him about the situation in the town. He told her that things had settled down and we could all start our journey. With our bags on the top of our Sumo Jeep, we started for Srinagar via Anantnag. After six weeks there, we were all looking forward to a change. We were tired working fifteen hours a day in a remote area under the constant fear of untoward incidents and really needed a break. Seven of us rode in the Sumo, three ladies and four men. When we left from the Achabal Tourist Home, it was late afternoon and very pleasant. The sky was a pinkish red and a cool breeze hit our faces as our Sumo headed in the direction of Anantnag town.

After about forty minutes, we took a left turn to enter the town of Anantnag. We had to cross a narrow road, a link road between the main town and the north side of the town from where we were coming. We saw a large number of young men standing on this narrow road, obstructing vehicular movement. All of them stared menacingly at us. Our driver slowed down and stopped. The young men surrounded us. We were stuck inside the Sumo, and stones smashed the glass windows and panes of the vehicle. We were in shock. We were covered with shards of glass and some of us had been scratched by them. We sat in stunned silence. Our rucksacks saved us because we had covered our heads with them as we crouched in the vehicle. It must have taken us four or five minutes to recover from our shock. Our poor driver said, 'My owner will make me pay for these damages.' Somehow, we moved on with the shattered glasses all over us. The only saving grace was that the metal grills on the windows had stopped the stones from hitting us directly.

Nobody talked for almost thirty minutes until we reached a petrol pump where the lady tourist officer got out and went home. We all came out of Sumo and cleaned the inside of the vehicle, removing the glass splinters from our seats and shaking our jackets to throw them off. We washed our faces at a public tap. Passers-by looked curiously at us. I asked the petrol pump-in-charge where we could get the glass of the vehicle replaced. He explained where to the driver. I assured the driver that I would foot the bill for replacement of the glass. We checked ourselves for injuries. We all had small cuts on our arms and knees but no serious injuries. From here, shell-shocked, we moved on in silence towards Srinagar.

The Dara Shikoh Show at Almond Villa

The Dara Shikoh cultural festival was the brainchild of Jotsna Singh, daughter of Dr Karan Singh. She had organized many workshops, lectures and performances by local as well as outside artistes and intellectuals for this festival. The intention of this festival was to bring together various streams of the arts, and through workshops expose local talents and traditions to contemporary concepts of art and aesthetics. This festival continued for only a few years before it quietly vanished. Most of the people who attended came from elite and well-off circles, mostly the businesspeople of Srinagar city. Some people from outside the state participated, really enjoying their visit to Kashmir whenever the festival was organized. It was a cute and modest attempt to promote the arts and was well meaning in its intent. The festival aimed to bring together some good creative minds who would exchange ideas with the local participants. At times, the festival would invite a very original mind. Once it had the grandson of Mahatma Gandhi over; he delivered an eye-opening, illuminating lecture and presentation on Dara Shikoh.

He had long before written a play on Dara and read out some scenes from it. There were memorable musical performances, like those of Neeta Mohindra, an eminent Punjabi actor who did her solo performance *Bhuhe Barian* in Punjabi, directed by me. This iconic performance of hers had travelled all over for south Asia over the last twelve years.

An audience of about three hundred filled the back lawns of the Almond Villa on the evening we performed our new production *Badshah Pather*. This rested at the foot of Shankaracharya Hill facing Dal Lake, perhaps the most beautiful site in all of Srinagar City. While we made our preparations for the evening show, workshops for young students happened during the day.

Before the performance that evening, when the cream of the city began to arrive, I mingled among them casually. Many asked me about the performance. When they heard our intention was to present a Kashmiri Bhand Pather adaptation of Shakespeare's *King Lear*, they would pause awkwardly and switch off the conversation without hesitation, only asking me if I really believed that village performers could deal with Shakespeare's *Lear* and what a rather ambitious idea it was. 'What will these rural actors do with the great speeches of *Lear*?' one woman condescendingly asked her words reeking of the stink of class and caste.

I couldn't bear her, but I politely replied, 'Well, ma'am, we have tried our best. Let us see how you people receive it.'

She continued, 'Mr Raina, do you have a background in literature?'

Now I was pissed off, 'No, ma'am, I am a pure science person.'

At that point, some other people joined in, and the conversation returned to the village Bhand actors and the great men of Shakespeare. Finally, I couldn't suffer their snobbery and I said, 'Don't you know Shakespeare was a Bhand, like our

Bhands, and not a professor of English? He purely wrote his plays for his company of actors and not for classroom studies.' I immediately walked away.

By now my actors were readying for the show. They seemed apprehensive about the audience and their performance, which was very different from their usual performances. I told them to just act the way they usually did enjoy the performance and not worry about anything.

I went out to have a look at the seating arrangements for the guests. I arranged for some chairs. I again met people I did not know, introducing themselves with curious questions about what it was like to work with illiterate actors and that, too, on Shakespeare. I replied to them, 'Well, we are doing a Kashmiri Shakespeare, not the Shakespearian English play. This *Badshah Pather* is our contribution to the centuries-old Shakespearian tradition.' Looking at their faces, I realized they did not understand me.

These kinds of comments continued until the performance started. Finally, I met my friend Indu Kilam, who taught English. She ran towards me and whispered, 'All well?' I simply said, 'Yes.' But she continued, 'Your face is little tense. What is the matter?' I smiled and replied, 'This city needs a wake-up call. It is lagging behind in all aspects of the arts and education.' She quickly said, 'I heard the comments of the people, but you don't worry and get going and wish you luck for the show.'

I ran backstage to meet all my actors before they went on stage. They had been waiting for me. I said to them, 'Let us get all together for our duwa.' We made a circle, and I addressed them. I meant every word of what I said. 'You know, the turban of the Bhands has been taken away long back, remember that. When you are performing, you are performing for your turban, your honour and your dignity. You have suffered humiliation for years. Today they will know what talent you are made of and what they have missed for decades.' I felt emotional because I had felt suffocated and humiliated by the ignorant audience. I realized that this was what the Bhands must have felt all through their lives.

As we finished, all Bhands uttered the word *ameen*, and they had tears coming down their cheeks and spoke in choked voices. In fact, my eyes had tears too. I hugged each one of them, took my blessings from Ali Mohammed Bhagat, the master actor and eldest ustad of their art, and went to the lighting booth to control the lights. All my team members—Rakesh, Aditi, Supriya, Manzoor—stood beside me. We wished each other good luck, and the performance started. While my teammates watched the performance, I watched the audience. Somehow, deep inside, I knew what would happen. The first half of the play went off smoothly, but the audience members stayed silent, not speaking to each other. They had tea quickly at intermission, and only Joyti approached me to warmly shake hands, with a smile.

We all went backstage to meet the actors to encourage them to keep up the pace, just as it was. We assured them all was going fine.

After the interval, I returned to the control room. Rakesh came up and said the actors were ready. I signalled them to start, and the second half began. Again, I watched the audience. Mahamood, who played Lear, was at his best, totally absorbed in the character. When the scene of storm and thunder came, I saw one person in the audience wiping his tears. As the performance progressed, Mahamood's and the other actors' intensity when the third son's dead body was seen, and Mahamood's rendering of the Sufi song '*Chununpoosh*' brought tears across the audience. I realized that Mahamood was suddenly improvising the lines in the last sequence. He brought in the language of the common man's lament, and of Kashmiris crying while burying their lost sons. He literally joined the two together in that wail—the pain of the people and the pathos of the play. It was a moving moment.

I again looked at the audience. I could sense in their faces the reflection of their common pain during the present troubled times. When the theatrical experience strikes at the strings of the common man's suffering in real life, I think theatre serves as a place of healing. That was exactly what Mahamood as Lear triggered and brought to the audiences with the support of all the other wonderful actors of the play.

When the play was over, there was not only overwhelming applause, but people also came and hugged the actors. The stink of caste and class had melted away for the moment. It took the actors a long time to change out of their costumes. I was relieved and thanked my team for what their hard work had achieved. After dinner, I saw off all my actors who had to rush back home to Akingam. And in the morning my team and I left for Delhi.

20

To Be or Not to Be in Kashmir

We had planned to perform *Badshah Pather* in more villages after a short break of two months. Meanwhile, I received an email from a professor of theatre at Stanford University in the US. She had heard about my work in Kashmir and wanted to see some of the performances and talk to the Bhands. It was a surprise that someone so far away was interested in my work. It turned out that she was writing a book and wanted to talk about my work in Kashmir. I realized that Kashmir had become a boiling subject internationally. I replied to her mail informing her that I would be going to Srinagar, and if she could come during that time she could join me. Otherwise, she could make a trip on her own. I would arrange everything from Delhi for her. She immediately let me know the dates of her arrival in Delhi and wanted to accompany me to Kashmir. So, I made the plans, accordingly, bringing along my son Anant, now a documentary filmmaker and photographer, with me.

Again, things were not normal in the Valley. The situation was deteriorating, and again one did not know how it would all happen. One morning, Jisha Menon arrived and the three of us left for Srinagar. I had never met Jisha before, but we got along very well instantly. Luckily, on our day of arrival Srinagar was not closed, so we immediately headed for Akingam in a taxi.

This time we stayed at the Kukarnaag Dak Bungalow, in one of the most beautiful locations in the Valley, surrounded by a dense, protected pine forest and fresh mineral water streams. This Dak Bungalow was a modest space, just functional with a single caretaker.

The next two days we had planned for Jisha to watch *Badshah Pather* and some other old pather. The rest of the time involved discussions with the Bhands and me. While she made her notes, Anant had grown intrigued with the performances and the Bhands. He spent many hours with the young Bhands. What they talked to each other about I have no idea, but he grew interested in the theatre form and the lives of these Bhand performers and was always clicking pictures of them with his camera. Before we left Akingam, he told me that he wanted to make a documentary on this whole project of *Badshah Pather*. He had formed his own relationship with the Bhands. Jisha had made detailed notes for her research work. After three days, we all left for Srinagar to take our flight to Delhi. In Srinagar, we checked into a hotel for the night in Raj Bagh.

That night the separatists gave a call for a complete shutdown. Jisha was horribly tense and worried and refused to come out of the hotel premises. She had left her small son in Bangalore with her parents and did not want to take any chances. I wanted her to visit at least Dal Lake and the Mughal Gardens, safe areas to move around in, but she refused to, even after my assurances that she would be safe. She was only waiting for the next morning to leave Kashmir and head for Bangalore to be with her son. It was a strange fear and panic that had gripped her.

We had our dinner at the hotel itself. I narrated many stories to her, which she enjoyed, laughing. She suddenly asked me, 'M.K., how can you keep your sense of humour so alive when there is so much suffering happening all around? This killing, shooting, violence . . .'

I paused for some seconds before replying, 'You know, Jisha, nobody has ever asked me this question. I am a Kashmiri. We have an in-built sense of humour even in the worst conditions, and that is the only thing that keeps me going here. Otherwise, it is always morbid, tension-filled with fear of death or violence.'

We boarded the morning flight, reached Delhi and saw her off on her flight to be with her son. Later, I received a book written by her, *The Performance of Nationalism*. And after two long years, Anant completed his documentary, *Badshah Lear*.

21

Badshah Pather Tours

The next season, which is 2010 August we planned to take *Badshah Pather* to more villages near Akingam, but the political situation was not good. Agitation by the separatists was happening in all the districts, followed by civil curfews and Article 144 implemented in the Valley. The shutdown calls brought fear and confusion as to what action might follow by the separatists or the security forces. No matter what, in these conditions there was no possibility of performing. We waited and hoped for some break in the shutdown so we could perform freely in the countryside without any tensions. It became a hide-and-seek situation for us. Future planning was not of any use.

After a month or so, there was a break in the protests and shutdowns. We started making programmes. I wanted to record a complete performance of the play with at least two cameras. When we fixed the dates, my son Anant and I decided to reach Akingam four days before the final performances. Anant came with his complete equipment. We decided that he would handle one camera, and the other we fixed with a Srinagar group of film-makers.

After reaching Akingam, we finalized the dates of the performance in consultation with the village heads. Gul Mohammed Bhagat, Anant and I decided to visit the performance sites to make sure that enough daylight hit for the filming of the live performance.

First we went to Mudgaej, adjacent to the Kukarnaag Hill area. Here we located a beautiful site just outside the village, near a forest. A large hill sloped down to meet a grand, majestic-looking chinar tree. All three of us loved the site. There was enough space for a backstage for the performance too, so it was decided that we would perform under this tree.

Another performance of the show was slated to happen in the village of Ariham. Here the village houses surrounded a large common courtyard, which we chose as our performance site. We realized that at each location we were choosing, the experience of the performance space would be different and challenging for the actors.

The next day, around 10 a.m., Anant, Gul Mohammed and I ventured out around the villages near Mudgaej in a Sumo vehicle fitted with loudspeakers announcing the details of the performance and the venue. After an hour, all the actors left with Manzoor and Anant for Mudgaej to prepare for the show. I would follow them once the delayed camera crew from Srinagar arrived. I sat waiting for about an hour on the main highway for them while tracking our main party to see if they had reached the venue or not. The Srinagar camera crew were still on their way, so I kept waiting for them since they had no idea where we were performing.

I made a call to Anant to ask him how far they were from the venue. Anant replied, 'We cannot move fast as there are thousands of people walking towards the venue. It will take us some time to reach, otherwise all is fine.'

I waited for the camera crew for another twenty minutes. They were delaying our programme. As I was waiting I received a call from a very agitated Anant, 'Baba, rush fast, there is chaos here. Someone came to the venue as we were opening our costume trunks. He started shouting Islamic slogans, and a large number of people who had come for the play have joined in with their slogans. He has threatened us all with bloody consequences if this un-Islamic performance takes place.'

I asked, 'Where is Manzoor?' Manzoor came on the phone, 'This man seems to be some connected person. He has announced before the entire public that if this performance does not stop, there will be dead bodies all around here. So, sir, rush fast.'

For a moment I did not know what to do. Readying to rush to the site, I saw a car carrying the camera crew. I immediately got into their car, and we all headed for the venue. When I reached the outskirts of the village, I saw people still walking to reach the performance site. Once I reached the venue, all I could see were thousands of people—women, the elderly, children, and a large number of young people in small groups—talking to each other with animated gestures. It looked like the site of some village mela, with people in colourful dresses, particularly the women.

The moment I approached the performance space, I saw this man with a beard and a white skull cap approach, screaming and shouting. The moment he saw me, he threatened me, 'If you do not stop this, there will be blood all over.' I did not respond to him, but I did not want any blood or violence. Manzoor came close to me and whispered that someone believed he was carrying a pistol. I was alarmed. I told Manzoor to pack up quietly. We would not perform. We could not take any risk of someone getting killed. While we talked, this man called someone on his phone. I suspected he was calling his group, and if they arrived it would be dangerous. People covered the entire landscape, discussing with each other what was happening, some in the manner of explanation, some in agitation. One had to shout to be heard over so much noise and confusion. I was concerned about Anant—he wasn't familiar with the landscape and did not know the local language. I wanted to tell him to be careful, but I saw him already filming all that was happening.

This man again screamed, 'Wait, my people are coming.' At that point, I inquired of Ghulam Rasool (junior), our percussionist, whether he had deposited our letter to the police station. The letter, just a formality, letting the police know that we would perform and giving them the specifics of the place as a precaution in case there was trouble, for our safety's sake. Ghulam Rasool replied, 'Yes I have deposited it, and I am also carrying the receipt copy with me.' But there was not a single policeman around. I was relieved, because with the Valley under tremendous tension, if something untoward happened it could become a legal problem.

I called Saleem Beg in Srinagar. I gave him the entire lowdown on the situation. He got worried and asked where exactly we were, but I could not explain to him the exact location. I asked a villager to explain to Beg where we were, but after that call I could not get Saleem back on the line. I had no idea what he could have done for us, but at least he had some idea where we were, in case something bad happened.

The moment our actors started packing away the costume trunks, a large group of people, mostly youth, rushed towards the actors, shouting, 'No, no!' They stopped us. This group did not want us to leave without performing. It was a strange situation. Our driver, turning around our minibus, was ambushed by another group of people, screaming, 'No, no, you are not leaving!' They surrounded the bus. A large group of women and elders surrounded me, all speaking simultaneously so I could not understand them. Generally, it was an atmosphere of confusion, everyone screaming and shouting at each other. No one could understand anyone.

One group of people had come from the other side of the mountain to watch the play. They started pressuring me, insisting we change the venue and cross the mountain to perform in their village area. 'We would love to have you there, and we will arrange a feast for all you people.' One Gujjar from this group picked up one of our trunks and started walking away. But the villagers protested his move, the two parties nearly coming to blows over very hot exchanges. Finally, I had to intervene and requested calm and an end to the fighting among them.

Amidst all this confusion, people stopped a bulldozer passing by on the village road and ordered the driver to block the road to prevent our exit. One could not make any sense of all this confusion. One young boy came to me with a sickle in his hands and very quietly whispered into my ear, 'You have to perform. This fellow will not be able to do anything. You do not worry.'

I said, 'Look, we will come some other time, I promise you. I do not want any violence or blood that will defeat the very purpose of my endeavour.'

In his anger, this boy said, 'You want me to split his stomach open? I will do that right away with this sickle.'

He proceeded towards the fellow, but I immediately caught hold of him and begged him not to create a violent situation. We had not come there to spread violence. 'For God's sake, stay calm,' I shouted, 'We have not come for this. I promise you within this very week we will come back and perform.'

He looked at me and emphatically said, 'If you do not perform today then we have been defeated and that should not happen. These bastards will not let us even laugh.'

When this young man said these words—'Today then we have been defeated.'—I tried to figure out what that meant, but I was not convinced enough to perform.

By this time our young actors had packed all the trunks and equipment in the minibus. They waited for a final signal from me to leave, but the villagers still wouldn't let us go. They were arguing among themselves about the centuries-old legacy of Bhand Pather, emphasizing that this was part of their culture. By this time my voice had become hoarse, and I was thirsty. There was no drinking water anywhere. I looked at Anant and asked him if he had been able to shoot any good footage. He just gestured in affirmation.

Suddenly I felt a hand on my shoulders. I turned to see an elderly man with a long white beard and a *tasbi* in his hands. He led me away a few steps from the crowd. In a very soft voice he said, 'Look, I am very old, and you are like my son. Listen to me. You do not worry. You perform. We will give our lives if anything untoward happens. You leave it to us, and then leave it on Allah Tala.'

For a moment I thought all these people were giving me some message, and I glimpsed some truth in their insistence. That boy was ready to split open a man's stomach, and now this fatherly old man was determined to have our performance. I felt I couldn't let this huge crowd down. They had walked many miles to watch us perform. I made up my mind to perform. I had these people with me.

I called that young boy and asked him if he could mobilize some young volunteers to help keep order while we performed. He said, 'Yes, there is no problem.' He shouted to his friends and asked them to climb the trees, cut some branches and make sticks out of them to stand guard with during the performance. The group of young boys ran away to do his bidding, as if they had to prepare for some war. I had to shout at them and bring them down. I explained to them that they had to be non-violent and peaceful volunteers. I asked them to surround the performance space, and if anyone created trouble, they would take that person away without disturbing the performance. 'And remember, you will not beat or shout at anyone,' I requested them. 'Just quietly take him out of the venue. Do you promise me this?' All the youngsters agreed, and I signalled to the actors to come back so we could perform.

When people saw the trunks unloaded again, they rushed forward in excitement, shrieking and taking their places. During all this confusion and uncertainty, more and more people had arrived and taken their places. Within minutes the entire hill slope was filled with people. Hardly any space remained except the space for the actors to perform.

Within half an hour the performance started in pin-drop silence. The entire location looked charged with the energy of the actors. I sat in the backstage area during the play, exhausted and very thirsty. I noticed a boy and a girl carrying a big *samawar* of salt tea and local bakery stuff, walking ahead of their father. I was offered tea and also water. The children's father thanked me for selecting this site for the performance even if it was quite far from their village. 'All we could bring for you here is only this tea,' he said. I thanked them for their hospitality.

After drinking the tea, I wanted to take a look at the performance that was well underway. What I saw was hilarious. The audience had gradually encroached on the acting space as more and more people still arrived to watch the performance. Finally, as the play came to an end, there was only a tiny space left for Badshah Lear to die.

What baffled me was how in this remote part of the Valley there were groups who opposed our performance, but then there was this big majority of the people who wanted us to perform too. This majority of the public would have done anything to make sure we performed. Most of the political class are unaware of this narrative—that people do prevail in the interiors of the Valley. It seemed the people longed to live normal lives. When I told the story of this show to my friends, many advised me to talk to the press about the incident, particularly about the fact that the general public stood by me and made it possible for us to perform. I thought it was silly advice to publicize myself as some kind of a hero who could motivate people to stand by me. That kind of self-promotion would be superficial, shallow and myopic.

The fact is fear had gone so deep into the psyche of the people that it was going to take a long period of time to clean up the mess that had buried the truth. I often tell my juniors in Kashmir that this land had nurtured for centuries the theme of *lool* (love), and that land could not become a barren land devoid of compassion. This incident demonstrated to me that possibility and hope still existed. One must keep the flame burning without any fanfare for a larger purpose.

Soon we started receiving invitations from cultural and theatre organizations asking us to perform *Badshah Pather*. The group was flown to the North-east to give around a dozen performances in various cities of the region. The National School of Drama invited our production for their annual Bharat Rang Mahotsav in Delhi. We performed in Chennai at the annual Shakespeare Theatre Festival, and then in Pune and in Goa for their yearly literary festivals.

These long tours helped the Bhands heal the wounds inflicted on them by the militants, who hadn't allowed them to perform for years. By quietly working, training and rejuvenating Bhand Pather, we had made a strong political point of cultural resistance. This was not appreciated by either the state or the terror outfits.

Soon the Indira Gandhi National Centre for the Arts in New Delhi celebrated a festival themed 'Revisiting Bhand Pather'. This was the first time for the first time in the history of Bhand Pather that any academic discussion on it was happening. Leading scholars from Benaras, Delhi and Kashmir participated in the major seminar, presenting their insights into the past and present significance of this form. It was an eye opener to understand Bhand Pather from the point of view of Sanskrit, Kashmiri and Central Asian traditions.

As we completed our last season of performances in the Valley, my son, filmmaker Anant Raina, had been shooting with his camera. He had captured most of the performances in the various villages, interviewing the Bhands in different locales, including in their homes and at the sacred dargahs. He had been talking to me throughout the period about making the film *Badshah Pather*. He started interviewing me at various intervals around the year about my old days in Kashmir, but the interview he took with me on a shikara while going down the river Jhelum from Zero Bridge and up to the Seventh Brigade was the most disturbing one for me.

He asked me personal questions about my growing-up years in the city. I was looking at the buildings on both sides of the river. These buildings were part and parcel of my growing up. I grew up around these banks. The houses of my aunts and uncles still stood there, but someone else lived in them now. Anant had made this particular interview even more special for me. He had called his wife Akila to fly in from Delhi and join us, and both of them asked me all kinds of questions. They made me relive my childhood, my school days, my college life. While I answered their curious questions, they did not realize that I had been transported deeply into my past. I started wondering about those people now, the ones who used to inhabit and contribute to the life of this Srinagar City. Looking at the closed temples and empty houses on the banks of the Jhelum gave me a feeling of emptiness about the futility of life.

In the evening, as we had our dinner at our hotel, Anant asked me, 'Baba, can I see Dadaji's house before we go back to Delhi?' I was a bit surprised because he had never asked me this during any of his previous visits. I replied, 'Yes, it is not very far away from here. We can go in the morning. It is hardly a twenty-minute walk from the hotel.' Next morning, Anant was ready with his camera, and we started walking towards my house. It was now not my home. When we entered our mohalla, Anant took pictures of the houses. I pointed at a house and told him, 'You know, this was the home of M.K. Razdan, CEO of PTI. We used to play cricket in the ground of the school where I studied.' I pointed to another house and told him, 'This is the house of Veer Munshi, eminent painter and your middle-school arts teacher at your St Columbus School.'

While Anant clicked, I heard a very loud voice ask me, 'Who are you, and why are you taking all these pictures?' Anant stopped. Strangely, I behaved as if I was still a resident of the mohalla, and with all the confidence at my command, I asked this man, 'Who are you? You are not from this mohalla of Sheetal Nath.'

He did not like that. He shot back, 'What kind of answer is that? And who are you?'

I started laughing, and from the opposite lane Rehman, my childhood friend, popped out and recognized me. He came out rushing, and we hugged. He asked me to come into his house and meet his family. I then asked Rehman who this man was in whose house he lived. Rehman said he lived in the Daftaries' house. I looked at the man who had questioned my presence there and told him, 'See, did not I tell you that you are not from the neighbourhood; otherwise, you would not have asked me who I am. 'The poor fellow was quite embarrassed, and gradually he went away. After spending some time with Rehman's family, I took Anant to see our house.

When we entered the main gate from the garden side, many flashbacks zipped across my mind. I looked at the two houses of my elder uncles. I was reminded of the noise made by our large clan. The owner of my home now was a young bank officer. He welcomed us and wanted us to come in to have some tea, but I did not want to stay longer. My last memory of this house was the funeral of my mother on 26 January 1990, Republic Day of India, a most dangerous and horrible day here in the Valley.

Anant kept taking pictures, and I looked up at the first-floor window, where I used to study at my Gandhi desk. When the owner of the house heard me say this, he said, 'I recite verses of the holy Quran at the same window.'

I replied, 'Oh good, stay well and stay blessed.'

I had no anger about anything. After all, what are houses and homes? You come on this planet earth, stay here seven or eight decades, and then leave it.

By now Anant had finished clicking and we took leave of the owner, but he extracted a promise from me, 'When you come next, you have to come again and have a meal with my family.'

I replied, 'Inshallah.'

From here I had to go to visit Ghulam Rasool Dar, my father's childhood friend. He lived in a big old-style Kashmiri house. When I entered he was in his garden making shami kababs. When he saw Anant and me, he gave me a big hug. When he met Anant, he was surprised and even warmer in welcoming him. He told Anant, 'You have come at the right time. You will taste my cooking now.' He asked about Babuji, my father, and was sad and subdued when I told him how he had passed away from hypertension and other ailments. For some moments he did not talk at all, leaving an awkward pause. Finally, I broke the silence and asked him, 'How are you and the family?' His face grew very grim and thoughtful. He gave me a look and very softly said, 'You know, Nika (my childhood name), we are also thinking of leaving this mohalla.' I asked him why.

He replied, 'You know, after you people left, this mohalla is not the same mohalla. The people who are living in your homes, we do not know them. There is no connection between them and us. They are strangers to us. When you all Pandits were living here in this mohalla, we had been here together for God knows how long. Our relationships were different. These new people do not understand that. We feel quite lost and many times lonely. In the older days if I pulled up your ear for some mistake, no one from your family would have ever asked me any question. Do you remember when you used to make Pupa (his youngest son) cry if he did not play hockey? Did any one of us ever tell you anything or rebuke you? This crowd in your homes cannot understand these age-old relations. So, we have seriously been contemplating leaving this mohalla and living somewhere else. Your faces I miss every day. My previous memories bother me all the time.'

He made Anant taste his shami kababs, and as we were leaving he said, 'Keep coming to see me, who knows when I will close my eyes. Allah bless both of you, always remain happy.'

I left very quietly, with a heavy heart. I looked back and waved my hand and he stood at his main door looking at us.

Scan QR code to access the
Penguin Random House India website